The Essential Guide to
Irish Flute and Tin Whistle
by Grey Larsen

2 3 4 5 6 7 8 9 0

Visit us on the Web at www.melbay.com — E-mail us at email@melbay.com

table of contents

This book is gratefully and lovingly dedicated to my father, Leonard H. Larsen (1924–2002), whose constant support and encouragement made its completion possible.

epigraph

Listen to the story told by the reed,
of being separated.

"Since I was cut from the reedbed,
I have made this crying sound.

Anyone apart from someone he loves
understands what I say.

Anyone pulled from a source
longs to go back.

At any gathering I am there,
mingling in the laughing and grieving,

A friend to each, but few
will hear the secrets hidden

Within the notes."

– Rumi, from *The Reed Flute's Song*

foreword

While harps and pipes have dominated the pantheon of Irish folk instruments, flutes and whistles appear to have enjoyed an equally long and enduring presence in Irish music history. From the ubiquitous *cuisleannaigh* of Early Christian Ireland to Land League and Orange Lodge fifers in more recent times, these wind instruments have played a conspicuous role in the shifting currents of Irish folklife. As a child growing up in County Clare, my first foray into the world of tin whistle music was with the plebeian Clarke's whistle. The first one I ever saw was played by Joe Cuneen sitting on the sea wall in Quilty with his back to the Atlantic. With its blackened conical anatomy and soggy wooden mouthpiece, it was as omnipresent as tea and pipe smoke in most country houses. More costly and challenging, the "timber flute" - as the simple-system flute was called by our elders - lay at the other end of the music map from the humble Clarke's. Ironically, its popularity in Ireland owes much to the inventive labors of Theobald Boehm whose key-system flute first appeared in 1847. According to popular thought, the simple-system instruments that Boehm's flute eclipsed found their way into the ranks of folk musicians throughout Western Europe. Like Victorian era concertinas that followed a similar "downward" dissemination from the drawing rooms of "high society," these simple flutes made by German and English artisans had found avid patrons among Irish musicians on both sides of the North Atlantic by the end of the 19th century.

As with Irish fiddle music, it is widely accepted that some of the most significant developments in the history of Irish flute playing took place in the United States. With the advent of recording technology in the 1890s and the popular espousal of Victrolas and 78 rpm discs in the 1920s, Irish flute players followed in the tracks of luminaries like Patsy Touhey and Michael Coleman. By the 1930s, Leitrim flute master, John McKenna, had set unprecedented standards for Irish flute playing in the US while, in Ireland, the milestone recordings of the Ballinakill Traditional Players focused public attention on the unique flute playing of Tommy Whelan and Stephen Moloney. In recent decades, North America has again emerged as a creative cornucopia of Irish flute playing. Home to masters like Jack Coen, Mike McHale, Joe Murtagh, Mike Rafferty and others, the extended community of Irish music makers has now reached out and embraced a myriad of non-Irish performers who have added prodigiously to the artistic diversity of Irish flute music. Grey Larsen is a rare beacon in this new cohort of Irish flute players in North America.

Having worked and performed with Grey at various summer schools and festivals since 1995, I have been aware of his opus as it went through various stages on the road to maturity. Now that it has reached fruition, it is my pleasure to recommend it to readers, musicians, historians and, above all, to flute enthusiasts. Thoroughly researched and comprehensive in scope, exploring the history of the instruments, as well as proffering a compelling analysis of ornamentation techniques, it is astutely aware of the pedagogical needs of the first-time learner and mature student alike. In its in-depth treatment of great performances in the period 1925-2001, it is marked by an abiding sense of humanism. This is as much an affirmation of Grey Larsen's reverence for the traditional storehouse as it is a testament of his deference for the tradition bearers themselves.

The Essential Guide to Irish Flute and Tin Whistle establishes an important benchmark for future generations of Irish music students, historians and music teachers. Above all, it fills a conspicuous void in the literature of Irish flute and tin whistle playing in America.

Mo Cheol Thú, Grey!

Dr. Gearóid Ó hAllmhuráin, MBA, Ph.D.
Jefferson Smurfit Corporation Professor of Irish Studies
Music Department, University of Missouri St. Louis

preface

Since the mid 1970s, I have been forming and developing many of the ideas contained in this book. I became an eager student of traditional Irish music in 1973, having been captivated by its profound beauty and energy upon first hearing it as a teenager.

I am an American and did not grow up in an Irish community. But to my good fortune, I have been able to spend a great deal of time with a number of Irish musicians who emigrated to my home region. Three friends in particular had a tremendous impact on my musical world: Michael J. Kennedy (1900–1978), a melodeon player from Flaskagh, near Dunmore in northeast Co. Galway; Tom Byrne (1920–2001), a flute and whistle player from the townland of Carrowmore, parish of Geevagh, Co. Sligo; and Tom McCaffrey (born 1916), a fiddler from near Mohill in Co. Leitrim.

Michael J. Kennedy with melodeon outside his home in Covington, Kentucky
(just across the Ohio River from Cincinnati, Ohio), 1975.

7

Tom McCaffrey and Tom Byrne in Cleveland, Ohio, 1975.

To these three, I feel tremendous gratitude for all the learning that their friendships made possible for me. They taught me many great tunes, and much more about how they played the music and what it meant to them, both in their adopted homeland and in their younger years in Ireland. With open arms, they welcomed me into their homes, their lives, and their families, and offered me their whole-hearted encouragement and approval. They also connected me with musicians back in Ireland, such as Tom Byrne's former neighbor, Josie McDermott.

Flute player, whistle player, singer, and composer Josie McDermott (1925–1992), playing a reel on the alto saxophone during my visit with him at his home near Ballyfarnan, Co. Roscommon, 1979.

Tom Byrne gave me my first flute. Years later, I passed it back to his youngest child, in better repair and in a case of my own making. In the same spirit of humility and gratitude, I hope to pass on to you the insight and experience I have gained over more than a quarter century—through playing the flute and tin whistle; through the hospitality and generosity of scores of Irish people; through seeking out, listening to, and learning from the older and younger living players; through visiting Irish communities in Ireland and elsewhere; through research and study of recordings and written materials; through the probing questions of my students. I hope you will use this work in the same spirit, that it will spur you on to continually deepen your knowledge, to look to the older musicians as well as the current state of Irish music, and to pass your own insights on to others.

I am still, and ever, a student of this music. Having grown up outside of the rich culture that gave it birth, I have sometimes felt reluctant to claim the right to produce a work such as this. The sincere and enthusiastic encouragement I have received from Irish musicians whom I hold in the highest regard, as well as the urging of many students and other fellow musicians, gave me the confidence to articulate what I know of this art and to present my ideas on how to better understand and notate the music.

Irish traditional music is a highly sophisticated art form, possessing much greater depth of possibility in personal expression than is generally acknowledged. *The American Heritage Dictionary* defines "fine art" as "art produced or intended primarily for beauty rather than utility," and as "something requiring highly developed techniques and skills."[i] Central to Irish music are its functions as accompaniment for dance and as a vehicle for social interactions of many kinds. However, this usefulness does not diminish it as a fine art. To fully pursue Irish music is to accept an invitation to a lifelong journey of discovery and personal expression, one that brings you into a joyful community of music makers and dancers and listeners, one that occurs within the context of a rich history and cultural heritage, which has its heart in past and present Ireland and which branches out to the rest of Europe, North America, Australia, and the other lands where Irish people have brought their music.

As time and technology march on, geographical considerations no longer restrict or define the spread of Irish traditional music. There are people all over the globe who hear it and are deeply touched by it. As those who live farther and farther away from Irish communities are moved to learn to play Irish music, it is more important than ever that resources become available that will not only give them good information, but will also steer their inquiry toward a deeper understanding of the cultural cradle of the music and the traditional modes of learning it, where so much of the soul of the music lies. As someone who has come to the music from the "outside," I feel I am in a particularly good position to point the way for others like myself, few of whom, however, have had my good fortune of learning directly from elders in the tradition.

It is also my hope that musicians who have grown up in the embrace of Irish culture will find useful insight and information in this book. It can be the gift of the immigrant to shed new and different light upon the natives' treasures. As an immigrant to Irish music, I have learned mostly in the traditional manner of aural immersion, but also in a more analytical fashion, mainly through reading, as a fledgling player, L. E. McCullough's fine book *The Complete Tin Whistle Tutor.*[ii]

Upon being invited to teach Irish flute and tin whistle for intensive music workshops in America, I began a process of analyzing what I had learned to do. I had to find ways to convey the inner workings of the music to others who had not had my opportunities of traditional learning. The analytical tools that I had gained through academic musical training served me well, and I began developing my understandings and techniques of notating ornamentation quite early on. My intellectual examination of the music has continued for many years, fueled mainly by my teaching, and more recently through the culminating process of writing this book. There are new ideas here, ones that I hope will advance the understanding of traditional Irish music everywhere and motivate newcomers and veterans alike to listen to the music closely and extensively, especially to the playing of the older masters of the art, whether in person or on recordings.

You can learn a great deal by listening deeply to recordings. For many people outside of Ireland, this has been their only contact with masterful players, and, for most of us, it has been our only contact with the great ones who have passed on. In Ireland, too, players learn a great deal this way, and have ever since the early days when American-made 78-rpm recordings of Irish music made their way back to Ireland, as well as circulating throughout Irish communities in the United States. This, too, is learning by ear, by immersion, though the audio-only glimpse of the musical experience is quite limited.

This book is an analytical tool and it is chock full of detail. Irish music is very intricate, and one must pay attention to the details and gain competence with them. But take care not to get lost in them. In order to play the music with understanding and maturity, you must stand back and take in the bigger aspects of the music. While you are working with the nuts and bolts, continue to let the music wash over you and through you.

If you have been seized by the beauty and energy of traditional Irish music, I invite you to join those of us who have taken on its learning as a "delightful challenge." I came across this phrase while reading an interview with famed Irish musician Donal Lunny in *The Irish Times*.[iii]

I thought I had invented the lefthanded guitar! I got the notion of reversing the strings spontaneously and worked away at it. I had to work out my own chords and found this a delightful challenge. I used to have a piece of wood under the desk with the strings and the frets on it and when I should have been listening to the history teacher I was researching chords under the desk!

Don't be daunted by the seeming enormity of the task of learning traditional Irish music, for it is not a task but a process, and an ongoing joy. It will bring you into contact with many fine people who share your passions. This may actually be the best part of all.

Take inspiration from young students who cannot be held back from working on what is truly important to them, laboring surreptitiously under their desks to expand the world's artistic delights.

Grey Larsen
Bloomington, Indiana, USA

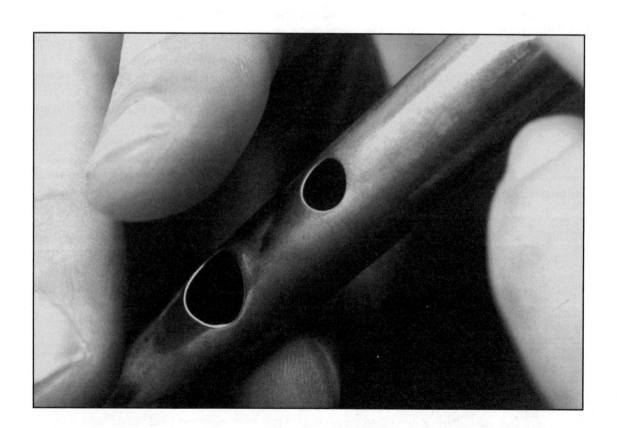

[i] *The American Heritage Dictionary of the English Language,* 3rd ed. (Boston: Houghton Mifflin, 1992).
[ii] L. E. McCullough, *The Complete Tin Whistle Tutor* (New York: Oak Publications, 1976).
[iii] John Kelly, "Following His Own Act," *The Irish Times,* September 5, 1998.

acknowledgments and credits

I consulted with many people while working on this book. Some read and commented on my work in progress, others helped me find information, recordings, and photographs. Their help was of great value, and our conversations sparked many fruitful ideas. In particular, I wish to thank Steve Cox for his unflagging support, enthusiasm, and indispensable assistance. I also gratefully acknowledge the contributions of the following:

Chris Abell, Artists Cooproductions, Kevin Atkins, Michael Anthony, Alain Barker, Robert Bigio, Ken Bloom, Tim Britton, Kevin Carr, Mike Casey, Deirdre Corrigan, Kathrina Cox, Kevin Crawford, Jo Cresswell, Rick Faris, Roland Gosda, Paul de Grae, Rob Greenway, S. C. Hamilton, Autumn Hills, Eleanor Hitchings, Linda Hitchings, John Hughes, Brad Hurley, Thomas Johnson, Sharon Kahan, Cindy Kallet, Diana Kay of Phillips International Auctioneers and Valuers, Niall Keegan, Becky Kleinmann, Robin Larsen, Siri Larsen, Teal Larsen, Kathy Lynn, Michael Lynn, Caoimhin Mac Aoidh, Joanie Madden, L. E. McCullough, Terry McGee, Bil McKenty, Paul G. Mulvaney, Andrew O'Brien, Bill Ochs, Patrick Olwell, Ken Perlman, Noel Rice, Dave Richardson, Paula Roche of Na Píobairí Uilleann, John Phillip Rush, Kevin Scott, Jeff Sherman, Chris Smith, Elizabeth Sweeney of the Irish Music Center at Boston College, Sura Gail Tala, Philippe Varlet, Mark Walstrom, and Lawrence Washington.

Scores of musicians have inspired me on my path. Chief among them are the elders and masters I have known well or even met briefly, for there is nothing as enlightening as sharing music, person to person, with one who has lived and breathed it for most of their life. These include Tom Byrne, Tom McCaffrey, Michael J. Kennedy, Phil McGing, Josie McDermott, Matt Molloy, Seamus Tansey, Cathal McConnell, Mary Bergin, Kevin Burke, Martin Hayes, Frankie Gavin, James Kelly, Liz Carroll, Seamus Connolly, Tommy Peoples, Paddy Keenan, Micheál Ó Domhnaill, Tríona Ni Dhomnaill, Paddy O'Brien, Noel Hill. . .the list could go on and on.

A special thank you to all of my students, who continually prompt me to think more deeply, examine more closely and stretch my understanding further.

Finally and foremost, my heartfelt thanks to my parents, my family, and my friends for seeing me through.

Photo Credits

Front cover:
  Photo by Rich Remsberg.
  (See Appendix D for a key to the instruments pictured on the cover photo.)

Back cover:
  Photo of Matt Molloy by Colm Henry.
  Photo of Grey Larsen by Irene Young.

Preface:
  Malcolm Dalglish: photo of Michael J. Kennedy.
  Richard Carlin: photo of Tom Byrne and Tom McCaffrey.
  Grey Larsen: photo of Josie McDermott.

Figures:
  Figure 1-16, photo © Peter Laban, Milltown Malbay, Co. Clare.
  Figure 1-17 and 1-18, John Hughes.
  Figure 1-19, photo by F.J. Biggar (died 1927). Photo reproduced with the kind permission of the Trustees of the Museum & Galleries of Northern Ireland.
  Figure 3-1, photo by M. Zaplatil, courtesy of Bonnie B. A. Blackwell, Ph. D. Director, RFK Research Institute, Williams College, Williamstown, Massachusetts. The flute is described and the dating given in the following two articles:
    Lau, B., B. A. Blackwell, H. P. Schwarcz, I. Turk, J. I. Blickstein, 1997. Dating a flautist? Using

ESR (electron spin resonance) in the Mousterian cave deposits at Divje Baba I, Slovenia. *Geoarchaeology* 12: 507-536.

        Turk, I., J. Dirjec, G. Bastiani, M. Pflaum, T. Lauko, F. Cimerman, F. Kosel, J. Grum, P. Devc, 2001. Nove analize "piscali" iz Divjih bab I (Slovenia) (New analyses of the "flute" from Divje babe I (Slovenia)). *Arkeoloski vestnik* **52**: 25-79.

Rich Remsberg: Figures 3-3 through 3-6, 3-10 through 3-14, 4-3 through 4-5, and 6-1.

Robert Bigio: Figures 3-7 through 3-9.

Figures 3-15 and 3-16, photo courtesy of Phillips International Auctioneers and Valuers, London, England.

Brad Jacobs: Figures 4-1, 5-1 through 5-8, 6-2 through 6-6, 8-9 through 8-11, 8-13, 9-2, 9-7, 10-12 through 10-15, and 18-3.

Figure 4-2 courtesy of the Dayton C. Miller Flute Collection, Library of Congress, Washington DC.

Section 8:

Tom Morrison photo courtesy of the Morrison family.

Photo of William Cummins' 78-rpm record label courtesy of the Irish Traditional Music Archive, Dublin.

Colm Henry: photos of Matt Molloy and Mary Bergin.

Kevin Taylor (son of Irish flute player Paddy Taylor): photo of Catherine McEvoy.

Christy Regan: photo of Josie McDermott. Also appeared in *Treoir*, Vol. 10, Number 6, 1978.

Tony Kearns: photo of Micho Russel.

Malcolm Dalglish: photo of Michael J. Kennedy and Grey Larsen.

Other:

Irene Young: photo of Grey Larsen in *About the Author*.

Rich Remsberg: instrument close-up photos throughout the book.

Illustration Credits

Lisa Nilsson: Flute and whistle drawings for the fingering charts, and the whistle drawing used in various diagrams in Chapters 7, 8, 10, 15, and 18.

Meghan Merker: Figures 6-7 through 6-11 and 6-14.

Bob Fink: Figure 3-2. From Fink, "The Neanderthal Flute," Crosscurrents #183, 1997, Greenwich Publishing, Canada. Also: <http://www.webster.sk.ca/greenwich/fl-compl.htm>.

Fingering charts conceived and designed by Grey Larsen, executed by Rich Remsberg and Lisa Nilsson.

Other Credits

Indexing by Nancy Ball.

Design consultation by Meghan Merker, Gambler Graphics.

Photo research by Rich Remsberg.

Copyediting by Jennifer Dotson and Gail Blake.

ıntroduction

What Is This Book?

First and foremost, this is a book on how to play traditional Irish music on the Irish flute and the tin whistle, and on how to adapt that knowledge to the modern, or Boehm-system flute. A great deal of the information I present applies to all three of these instruments. As far as I know this is the first book to address all three as a group, and the first to closely examine the similarities and differences in their techniques, capabilities, limitations, and their places in traditional Irish music. I also explore the history and development of these instruments in the Irish tradition, provide an orientation to traditional instrumental Irish music, and examine closely the personal styles of 22 masterful flute and whistle players who recorded between 1925 and 2001. This book does not cover the rudiments of music notation or ear training. There are many other good books that do.

This is the most comprehensive book yet written on Irish flute or tin whistle playing. Much of its information has not been explored in print before. It may be used as a thorough and systematic reference book. However, the material of later chapters is, to a great extent, built upon the foundation laid in earlier ones, so it is wise to progress through the book sequentially.

Section 1 features an orientation to traditional Irish music. Section 2 delves into the history and development of flutes and whistles in Ireland and the techniques of holding and sounding the instruments.

In Section 3, the largest section of the book, I share my thoughts on ornamentation. I have invented some new ways to notate ornamentation which I hope are much more simple and clear than the approaches I have seen in other publications. As of this writing, there is no consensus on how to notate or explain Irish flute and whistle ornamentation. I believe that no book before this one has examined the full range of sophistication that exists in the ornamentation of this music. My methods have made it possible for me to probe much deeper. In doing so, I have encountered and given names to a number of ornamentation techniques which, while being widely used by traditional musicians, to the best of my knowledge have not been clearly described or notated before.

My notation techniques can be applied, with some adaptation, to other Irish instrumental traditions, such as those of the uilleann pipes, fiddle, accordion, and concertina. Using my approach, very accurate and detailed transcriptions of Irish traditional tunes and performances are now possible. I hope that others will come to understand and use these new tools, and that this will help to create a deeper appreciation for this highly developed music.

Section 4 addresses phrasing, articulation, and breathing. In Section 5, I sum things up and delve into the areas of practicing and the playing of slow airs. Section 6 consists of 49 studies for practicing the physical skills needed in ornamentation.

The book contains numerous musical examples and exercises. Many of them are excerpts from traditional Irish tunes. Complete settings of these tunes are provided in Section 7.

In Section 8, I have transcribed, in great detail, 27 tunes as performed and recorded by 22 masters of the Irish flute and tin whistle. These performances are available on the artists' published recordings and I encourage you to seek them out. I hope to coordinate the issuing of a CD compilation of these performances in the future. You can check on the progress of this endeavor through Mel Bay Publications or my website, <www.greylarsen.com>.

The Companion CDs

The two companion CDs contain my renditions of the studies in Section 6, the tune settings in Section 7, and many of the figures and exercises that appear throughout the book. A CD symbol (note the number 1 or 2 in the center of the symbol) paired with a track number shows where to find the recording.

Track 88   *Track 88*

These recordings are provided for the benefit of every reader, not just those who do not read music. Even though the figures and exercises are notated in a detailed fashion, there are many elements of traditional Irish music that cannot be written down. Having both the notated and recorded representations will help all readers to better understand the music.

Those figures that have indications for phrasing tend to be notated in a phrasing style that is more typical of the tin whistle than the flute. Whistle players tend to use somewhat more tonguing and less slurring than flute players do. (If you are unsure of the meanings of *tonguing* and *slurring*, you will find these terms defined at the beginning of Chapter 20.) The CDs feature both tin whistle and flute performances. The phrasing in the recordings at times differs somewhat from what is notated.

These CDs also contain computer software. Access the software by placing either disc in your computer's CD-ROM drive.

COMPLEMENTARY TUNE COLLECTIONS

This book is complemented by my tunebook and CD packages, *Celtic Encyclopedia for Tin Whistle* and *Celtic Encyclopedia for Flute*, two volumes in Mel Bay's Celtic Encyclopedia series. These works, which present traditional tunes that are particularly well suited to the whistle and flute, respectively, contain the first large collections of transcriptions that make use of my notation techniques.

MORE TUNES AT <WWW.GREYLARSEN.COM>

There are more tunes, in both audio and transcription form, at my website, <www.greylarsen.com>. Please visit the site for more information on this and other items related to my Mel Bay books, as well as information on my recordings, workshops, and performances.

WHY IS THIS BOOK NEEDED?

There are numerous other books about Irish tin whistle playing, and fewer on Irish flute playing. While some are excellent in certain areas, none of them approach this book in depth and scope. Furthermore, many are at times superficial, confusing, and lacking in clear and complete explanation. Many musicians play both flute and whistle, yet as far as I know no previous book addresses in any depth the similarities and differences between them.

It is impossible to be good at playing Irish flute or tin whistle without basing one's learning on a groundwork of extensive and continual listening. This book is intended to encourage and be a companion to such listening. But it also provides a wealth of information that for many is very difficult to obtain through listening alone without regular, personal contact with experienced players.

This book provides teachers of Irish flute and tin whistle with a solid pedagogical basis for their work.

Furthermore, it presents the first deep, analytical, and comparative look into the playing styles of past and present masters of Irish flute and tin whistle.

WHO IS THIS BOOK FOR AND HOW SHOULD YOU USE IT?

This book is for flute and whistle players at all levels, from the novice to the highly advanced.

I delve most deeply into intermediate and advanced areas, but I also provide a solid foundation for beginners. For instance, I give detailed and thorough instruction on holding and blowing the flute and the whistle, starting with the first encounter with the instrument. The novice would be wise to take plenty of time to work on these and other rudiments of playing before venturing too deeply into the rest of the book.

Throughout the book I describe techniques and fingerings in terms of how they are played on the Irish, or simple-system, flute and the tin whistle, which share the same basic fingerings. Most of what I present can be applied directly to the modern flute, but some techniques require different fingerings or other special adaptations. As they work their way through the book, Boehm-system flute players may wish to refer to Appendix B, which gives information on such fingerings and adaptations. Whenever I use the word *flute* by itself, I am referring to the Irish or simple-system flute. (For clarification on these terms, see Chapter 3.)

Take your time with this book. It will serve as a thorough reference, regardless of your current level of playing ability.

CONCISE VERSION OF THIS BOOK FOR TIN WHISTLE ONLY: *THE ESSENTIAL TIN WHISTLE TOOLBOX*

I have written a shorter, more concise version of this book specifically for beginning and intermediate players of the tin whistle. It is entitled *The Essential Tin Whistle Toolbox* and it is also published by Mel Bay Publications.

READING MUSIC

There is a great deal of music notation in this book. As mentioned above, if you do not read music you can still use the book quite well, because I play most of the notated exercises and figures on the companion CDs.

I encourage everyone to learn to read music. It is an extremely useful skill, even for the traditional musician. However, it is very important to avoid becoming dependent upon written music. If you already are, then you need to begin to wean yourself from the notation. As you learn tunes, you should immediately start to internalize them. For much more on this subject, see Chapter 1.

The companion CDs can be very useful in that regard. You can learn to play a musical example or a complete tune solely by listening to it over and over on the CD. Once you have learned it, you may check yourself with the music notation in the book.

ANALYTICAL LEARNING AND IMMERSION LEARNING

You certainly do not need to use this or any book in order to learn to play Irish flute or tin whistle. These traditions have thrived and evolved for centuries with very little help from books. In Ireland, and in Irish communities outside Ireland, many musicians learn their music largely by immersion, the way that we all master our native languages. Most musicians who learn this way are not very self-examining about how they do what they do.

Analytical resources like this book can and should never supplant aural learning, but they can supplement it in important ways. This book supplies much-needed information for people who live far away from a thriving Irish music community. Even those who live in such communities will find plenty of new ideas, insights, and opinions here. I believe it is a very good thing for a musician to become aware of aspects of her playing that she may have been unconscious of for years. So I hope this will be a valuable reference book for all players, regardless of their background and learning experiences.

Although traditional musicians, on the whole, tend to learn intuitively, it is interesting to note that music reading is more prevalent in the Irish music tradition than it is in many others. Instruction books and tune collections have played a part in the propagation of traditional Irish music since the 18th century. The tune collections of Captain Francis O'Neill[i] and Breandán Breathnach[ii] can be found on the bookshelves of many traditional Irish musicians.

This book represents my own perceptions, opinions, and experience regarding traditional Irish music. As with any art form, there is room for a wide variety of viewpoints. Each one provides yet another way to illuminate a shared treasure, which, though firmly rooted in many generations of Irish culture, is alive and constantly evolving.

GENDER CONVENTION

In this book I have decided to avoid the cumbersome use of both genders for the personal pronoun. Instead of writing *he or she, his or her*, etc., I use the feminine gender. This way I can do my small part in helping to even out the imbalance caused by centuries of books that have used only masculine forms.

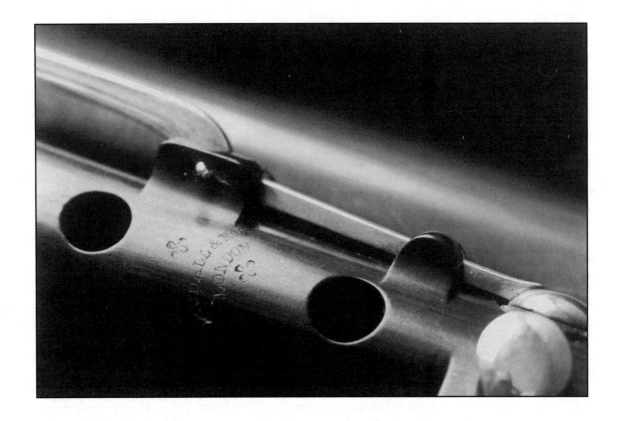

i Two of the tune collections of Capt. Francis O'Neill are particularly widespread. *O'Neill's Music of Ireland* was originally published in 1903 and contains 1850 tunes. *1001 Gems, The Dance Music of Ireland* followed in 1907. Both were published in Chicago where O'Neill served as Chief of Police. Both books have gone through several editions and are now published by Mel Bay Publications. See Bibliography.

ii Breandán Breathnach, *Ceol Rince na hÉireann*, 5 vols. (Dublin: An Gúm). Years of first publication: vol. 1: 1963, vol. 2: 1976, vol. 3: 1985, vol. 4: 1996, vol. 5: 1999.

❖ section 1 ❖

—

first matters

chapter 1: orientation to traditional irish music on the flute and tin whistle

SEEK OUT THE OLDER PLAYERS

As you embark upon the path of learning Irish music, you should realize that you are preparing to become a participant in a story that has been unfolding for centuries. In order to intelligently take part, you need to start developing a view of the big picture.

In this art, the key to all insight is listening. This is a theme that will surface again and again throughout these pages.

As you are learning your craft, it is inspiring to listen to the latest performers and their recordings. But it is even more important to seek out the older players who may not come into your view so readily. The soul of the tradition rests in them, the ones who have lived the music for 50, 60, 70 years. They may be highly accomplished or they may play roughly and slow, but they are the keepers of the deepest wisdom and eloquence that you can experience through the music.

In an interview in *Fiddler Magazine*[i], the great fiddler Martin Hayes tells about such a musician:

> One of my own favorites is a whistle player called Joe Bane. I have a tune on the album called "The Britches" [This refers to Martin Hayes' first album on Green Linnet Records, *"Martin Hayes"*. See Discography.] It's very simple. Anybody could play it. Any beginner could play every note I play. It's not technically difficult. And it wasn't technically difficult the way he played it. But when he played it, it would bring a tear to my eye. He'd look forward to playing the tune all night at a session, and when the opportunity would arise, he'd go, "Ah, sure, we'll play 'The Britches.'" He'd be waiting to do this. He loved it. It was like a lullaby——there was sweetness in it, there was humility in it, there was joy and love, everything in it, and it was the climax of his day, of his week, to do this tune. He had no chops, he had no knowledge, no theoretical anything, but his space was magic. He didn't need to know any more technical anything. The only thing that was amiss around him was a world that didn't understand what was going on.

If you do not live in Ireland, you may be able to seek out Irish communities or Irish people nearby, attend concerts, festivals, music camps, summer schools, take part in dances, workshops, sessions. Hopefully, you will be able to travel to Ireland. There are a great many resources for broadening your knowledge.

READING MUSIC, AND "WHAT IS A TUNE?"

If you do not read music, you are in good company. Many traditional Irish musicians don't. But a surprisingly large number do to some extent. I encourage everyone to learn this skill.

In Irish music, when we use music notation it should be only as a supplement and a convenience, a shorthand guide or reminder to memory. When used in these ways, it is very useful indeed. However, the most deeply vital aspects of this music cannot be written down and can only be learned through extensive, active listening.

If you have become dependent upon written music, the time has come to begin to wean yourself from it. Below I offer some insights that I hope will help you do this.

The full embodiment of a traditional Irish tune cannot be written down. One of the reasons for this is that improvisation and variation are intrinsic elements of Irish music. There is no such thing as the definitive version of a traditional Irish tune. Often a particular setting will become established among certain comrade players, among players of a certain instrument, or in a certain region, but even that setting is a vehicle for personal interpretation. In truth, a transcription of a tune is no more than a frozen skeleton of a snapshot of a setting of a tune.

A tune is something very expansive and alive. Infusing each tune is an essence that makes it immediately recognizable, beautiful, and whole. Each tune also carries rich personal associations for the player. With musical maturity and experience, one comes to intuitively grasp the spirit of a tune and shape it in one's own way.

THE HABIT OF INTERNALIZATION

When you begin learning a tune, with or without the aid of music notation, you should immediately begin to commit it to memory, to internalize it, as a part of the act of learning itself. If you are using music notation, immediately start to let go of it. This may not be so easy at first if you are used to hanging your musical awareness on a visual representation and storing it there.

A natural and effortless way to learn a tune is to simply hear it many times, over a long period of time. Without making a conscious effort to learn it, the tune seeps into you. One day you may find yourself lilting or humming it. By then, you know it. Now it is just a matter of transferring it onto your instrument. Attending a regular session is one good way to give yourself this opportunity.

For those times when you *are* actively learning a tune in a conscious way, here are some ideas that I hope will help you.

FINDING THE TONAL CENTER

A good first step to reclaiming, internalizing, and developing your musical awareness is to find and hold onto the *tonal center* of a tune. The tonal center is the "home pitch," what some people call the *key* of the tune. (Below I'll explain why *mode* is a more appropriate term than *key* for Irish music.) If you were going to add a drone to a tune, the pitch of the tonal center would be the most natural choice for the drone's pitch. Many tunes end on the pitch of the tonal center, or at least come to rest upon it at the ends of some important phrases. When you land on the pitch of the tonal center you feel more resolved, at rest, at home, than with any other pitch. If you have trouble recognizing this feeling, then you need to tune in more to how the different pitches of a tune make you feel inside your body.

Occasionally you will run across a tune for which a tonal center is not obvious, or seems to shift. In other tunes the tonal center is clear, but changes with different parts of the tune. An example of this is the polka *Maids of Ardagh*, which appears on p. 356. Its tonal center is D in the A part, but changes to A for the B part.

For the vast majority of tunes, the tonal center is clear and unchanging. After learning about modes later in this chapter you will have more information about finding the tonal center.

THE THREE DIMENSIONS OF MELODY

Here is a powerful and helpful insight from Robert Jourdain:

> . . . a melody's notes are largely perceived as offsets not from each other, but from an underlying tonal center. Melody is a harmonic phenomenon.[ii]

I would amend Jourdain's statement by substituting the word "pitches" for "notes." A *note* has pitch *and* duration. For the moment let's look at the pitch aspect alone.

The apparent contradiction of Jourdain's statement, that melody is a *harmonic* phenomenon, holds true because as we *retain* the pitch of the tonal center, we compare the pitch of the present melody note to it, and "hear" or sense the resulting internal harmony, or "vertical" interval, created by these two pitches. (An *interval* is simply the distance in pitch between two notes.) At the same time, we track the "horizontal" intervals that occur sequentially in time, that is the distance in pitch between one melody note and the one that precedes or follows it.

So, the process of memorizing melodies, which seems daunting to so many, begins with the simple task of internalizing and retaining only *one* pitch, that of the tonal center. From there, it becomes a two-dimensional process of hearing or sensing vertical and horizontal intervals, instead of a one-dimensional procedure of memorizing a long sequence of discrete, unrelated pitches. The two-dimensional picture reveals the connections and relationships between the pitches, and allows musical meaning to emerge.

Your ability to internalize melodies will improve even more as you learn to recognize the sound and "flavor" of each of the twelve musical intervals and learn their names. The smallest interval is known by several names: a semitone, a half-step, or a minor second. Each of the larger intervals can be measured by how many semitones it contains. The minor second of course contains only one semitone, the major second contains two semitones, the minor third contains three, the major third four, the perfect fourth five, the tritone six, the perfect fifth seven, the minor sixth eight, the major sixth nine, the minor seventh ten, the major seventh eleven, and the octave twelve. You can see and hear these intervals and their constituent semitones clearly by studying and experimenting with the fretboards of guitars or other fretted instruments, all of which have twelve frets to the octave.

It's not necessary that you mentally count the number of semitones in each interval you hear. But just as it is a carpenter's business to be able to look at a board and know whether it is two inches wide, or four, or eight, it is your business as a musician to gradually gain the ability to hear an interval and know whether it is a minor second, a major third, or a perfect fifth, etc., in other words to mentally "measure" it, to and know or feel what the distance is between the two pitches. Knowing what intervals are, knowing their sizes and names, and knowing that there is a sensible and proportional system to their relationships will enhance your ability to learn by ear, an ability that everyone has.

Enter now the third dimension: pulse and rhythm.

Aside from some slow airs, all Irish tunes have a *pulse*, a steady recurrent beat. When we tap our feet we tap out the pulse. The pulse is subdivided into either two, three, or four units of duration which most transcribers of Irish music represent as eighth notes, sometimes as sixteenth notes.

As stated above, a note has both pitch and duration. A melody then, or a tune, is formed by a succession of notes (pitches and durations).

Rhythm is hard to define succinctly. In *The Harvard Dictionary of Music*, Willi Apel attempts this by stating that "rhythm is everything pertaining to the temporal quality (duration) of the musical sound."[iii]

This broad definition will work for our present purpose, which is to integrate the *rhythms* of the notes with the two-dimensional *interval* "map" of the melody. This sounds complex, but it needn't be experienced that way. What we are doing is stretching our powers of attention so that as we learn a tune, we create an on-going, three-dimensional melody in our mind's ear.

Music is a profoundly physical experience. It is made up of air compression waves that affect our bodies and make them vibrate. Over-dependence upon music notation dulls our perceptions of the physical sensations of music and causes us to externalize and conceptualize music, to remove ourselves from it in a very real sense. Learning to learn by ear again, for we all did so as children, brings us back into full contact with music.

So, as you are learning a tune, immediately bring your focus to the physical nature of the sound: the relationship of each note to the tonal center; the sizes and feelings of these vertical intervals, as well as those of the horizontal intervals between the successive notes of the tune; the shapes and phrases in the melody; the pulse of the tune and the rhythms that overlay it; the patterns of your finger movements; and your own physical experience of the music. Store this awareness *inside* of yourself instead of externalizing it, relegating it to written music. If you enjoy computer metaphors, store the tune on your huge internal hard drive, not on a removable disk that you put away in some desk drawer. The more you cultivate this internalizing mode of learning, the more natural and sophisticated it will become.

OTHER AIDS TO MEMORY

Each tune has a name, or several names, which belongs with the tune for a reason. Often the reason is unknown or obscure to us, and many people seem to have trouble maintaining the connections between tunes and their names. Make an effort to establish this connection early on, even if its meaning is mysterious to you. You may remember the tune better by connecting it to an image, a person, even to an uncertainty or a curiosity; and to the larger world of the tradition. Connect the tune also to the time, place, people, and circumstances that surrounded you as you first heard it or began to learn it.

Notice these things about the tune: its tonal center, its mode, its first few notes, its meter, its dance tune type. Link all of these things to the name of the tune. Later, remembering or hearing the first few notes will bring the entire tune back to you in a flash.

Luckily, the structural aspects of Irish tunes, compared with those of classical music, are quite simple and even formulaic in some respects, and therefore easy to remember. Understanding these structures will aid your learning a great deal. It's what happens within and through these simple structures that is so endlessly various and beautiful.

Despite my observations and caveats about music notation, I make very extensive use of it in this book. The combination of music notation, the audio CDs, and these words on paper are the next best thing to personal contact. Thankfully, these three modes of demonstration, when used together, actually do convey a great deal of useful information.

SOME NOTATION CONVENTIONS

There are many good books that teach the rudiments of reading music. I am not going to duplicate their content here. However, I would like to explore a few aspects of music notation that are particularly relevant to this book.

THE MODAL NATURE OF IRISH MUSIC

In today's common practice of western classical and popular music, almost all tonal music is considered to be in either a major or minor *key*; that is, based upon the central use of certain major or minor scales. The major and natural minor scales have early historical roots and are only two of seven *modes* that came to form the tonal basis for Gregorian chant and the rest of western medieval and renaissance music. These modes, and others, are also found in many ethnic musical traditions.

The word *mode* has a number of meanings, but in this case we use it to refer to "the selection of tones, arranged in a scale, which form the basic tonal substance of a composition."[iv] There are many more than seven modes in world musical traditions, but for the moment we need only be concerned with the seven so-called *church modes* of western European music.

The vast majority of traditional Irish music makes use of only four of these modes: the Ionian (which we commonly call the *major* scale), the Dorian, the Mixolydian, and the Aeolian (which we commonly call the *natural minor* scale). In fact, the first three of these account for most of traditional Irish melody.

Each of the seven modes, shown on the next page, contains a unique sequence of five whole steps (major seconds) and two half steps (minor seconds) that occur as you ascend through its scale. The half steps in the following figures are indicated by slurs.

The simplest way to listen to and get to know these modes is to play ascending scales on only the white keys of a piano. Starting on C and playing in this manner, you hear the notes of the Ionian mode. Starting on D, you hear the Dorian mode, and so on. Note well the locations of the half steps in each mode.

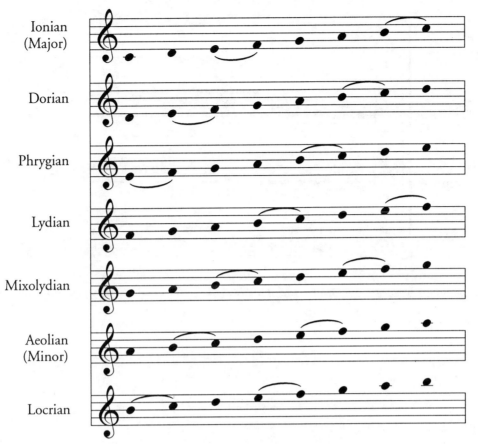

Figure 1-1. The seven so-called church modes, as played on the white keys of the piano.

Track 1

THE TONAL CENTER OF THE MODE

Each mode has a tonal center, which is the first, lowest, note of its scale. In Irish music this tonal center can reside on any one of various pitches, most commonly D, E, G, A, or B. We often say that a tune in the Mixolydian mode with a tonal center of D is "in D Mixolydian." Similarly, a tune in the Dorian mode that has a tonal center of E is "in E Dorian." The tune will usually come to rest on that pitch at various points, especially at the ends of some of its important phrases.

As mentioned above, it is very important to sense, identify, and retain this tonal center. The notes of the tune gain "meaning" in their relation to it. Keeping track of the tonal center and each note's intervallic relationship to it will greatly enhance your ability to learn, internalize, and remember tunes.

Those who are familiar with the major and minor modes (i.e. the Ionian and Aeolian), many find it helpful to understand the Dorian and Mixolydian modes in terms of how they differ from the Ionian and Aeolian. The Mixolydian mode is like the Ionian (major) with a flatted or lowered seventh note. The Dorian mode is like the Aeolian (natural minor) with a raised sixth note.

These comparisons are shown on the next page. Play through them on an instrument or sing them. Note how only the position of the second half step differs in each comparison.

G Ionian
(Major)

G Mixolydian

E Aeolian
(natural minor)

E Dorian

Figure 1-2. Comparisons between the Ionian and Mixolydian modes, and the Aeolian and Dorian modes.

Track 2

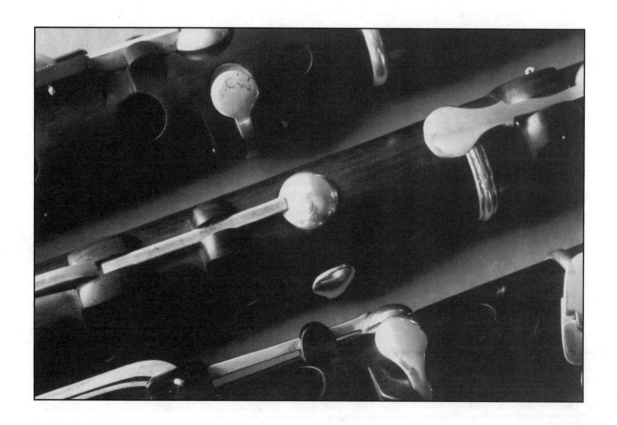

The combinations of mode and tonal center most commonly encountered in Irish flute, tin whistle, and uilleann pipe music are shown below in Figure 1-3. The ones containing G-sharps (i.e. A Ionian and B Dorian) are encountered less often than the others.

Figure 1-3. The modes most commonly encountered in Irish flute, tin whistle, and uilleann pipe music. Note well the mode signatures.

"MODE SIGNATURES" INSTEAD OF KEY SIGNATURES

Note that in Figure 1-3, I have used the appropriate "mode signature" for each mode, instead of using accidentals. *Take special note of these mode signatures.* Musicians who are used to operating on the assumption that every signature indicates a major key or its relative minor key will have to expand their thinking somewhat.

25

You may have noticed that there are no flats in these mode signatures. Modal scales that include flats, such as G Dorian, D Aeolian, and F Ionian are encountered in the special repertoires of the fiddle, banjo, and accordion. Players of keyed flutes and pipes can play in these modes as well, but traditionally they rarely do.

Throughout this book I will be using such mode signatures. Therefore, when you see a signature of two sharps, for example, don't assume that the tune is in D major (Ionian) or B minor (Aeolian). It could just as easily be in E Dorian or A Mixolydian. There is a growing trend toward using these mode signatures, as they result in fewer accidentals and they reflect the true modal nature of Irish music.

PENTATONIC MODES

Some tunes use fewer than seven notes, such as tunes that are in a five-note, or *pentatonic* mode. There are two such pentatonic modes common in Irish music. The first is formed by omitting the fourth and seventh notes of the Ionian mode. In the tonality of D this yields a scale of D, E, F-sharp, A, and B. We could call this the "Ionian Pentatonic" mode. The second is formed by omitting the third and sixth notes of the Dorian mode. In the tonality of E this yields a scale of E, F-sharp, A, B, and D. We could call this the "Dorian Pentatonic" mode. Note that these two examples, which are shown below, contain the same pitches and therefore share the same mode signature, though they have different tonal centers.

Even though neither of these pentatonic modes contains a C-sharp, the C-sharp is included in their mode signatures. If a player were to use a C as either a passing tone or as a variation of a tune in one of these modes, it would properly be a C-sharp, not a C-natural.

In practice there are few Irish tunes that adhere strictly and totally to either of these pentatonic modes. Most of them include at least one instance of one or both of the missing scale degrees. Many tunes have one part that is in a pentatonic mode while its other parts are not.

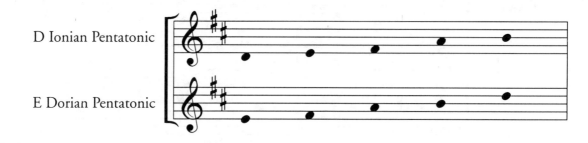

Track 3

Figure 1-4. Examples of the two pentatonic modes found in Irish music,
the Ionian Pentatonic and the Dorian Pentatonic.

The Ionian Pentatonic mode is commonly encountered with a tonal center of either D or G. An example of a tune in this mode is the three-part reel, *Christmas Eve*. The second and third parts of the tune contain a few passing notes that fall outside the pentatonic mode. The first part of the reel *The Banshee* is also in this mode.

The Dorian Pentatonic mode can be found with a tonal center of D, E, G, A, or B. An example of a tune in this mode is *Tom Billy's Jig*. (Complete versions of these three tunes appear in Section 7 on p. 347, 348, and 338, respectively.) The reel *Peter Flanagan's* is also in the Dorian Pentatonic mode. A transcription of flutist Cathal McConnell's recording of this tune appears in Section 8, p. 402.

OUTSIDE THE MODAL BOUNDARIES

There are many Irish tunes that don't fit neatly into the profile of any of these modes. Some use both major and minor thirds and/or sixths. Some employ notes that fall in between the half steps. This happens in particular in the area of C-natural to C-sharp and F-natural to F-sharp on the flute, whistle, and uilleann pipes.

C-natural is an especially variable note on the uilleann pipes which, according to Breandán Breathnach, possesses ". . . several colors . . . which are exploited to the full by the skillful performer. It lies approximately halfway between B and D. . ."[v], in other words, approximately halfway between the equal tempered C-natural and C-sharp. In fact, at least half the time C-natural is played according to our modern intonation expectations, but often, especially in tunes with a tonal center of G or D, the sharper "piping C" is used by traditional flute and whistle players. The pitch of C-natural can change even during the course of a single note.

On the flute and whistle, you can finger C-natural by using a cross fingering[vi] or by half-holing.[vii] On a keyed flute you may also have the option of using a C-natural key. You can also play this "piping C" by using special fingerings that we will explore later. All of these fingering options produce Cs with differing tone and pitch colors, and these relate quite directly to the tradition of uilleann piping. All of this will become more clear as you work your way through the book.

One more observation about C-natural and C-sharp: When playing C as a quick passing note between B and D, Irish flute and whistle players will almost always play the note as a C-sharp, even if C-sharp is not in the mode of the tune. This may be in large part because playing B—C-sharp—D makes for an easier fingering sequence. The C-sharp goes by quickly enough that its altered pitch does not seem all that apparent. But this use of C-sharp is an important element of style, not just a fingering convenience. If you play such notes as C-naturals, they often just sound "wrong" to someone with an ear that is finely tuned to traditional Irish music. On the Boehm-system flute, fingering C-natural in such situations is no harder than fingering C-sharp——in fact sometimes it is easier. Therefore, Boehm-system flute players may forget to alter C in this way, since it has no particular fingering benefit for them.

For examples of this use of C-sharp, see *The Battering Ram* on p. 335, *The Cliffs of Moher* on p. 337, and *Hardiman the Fiddler* on p. 346.

Note that if you use the *tight triplet* technique (described on pp. 256-257 in Chapter 18) in these B—C—D sequences, then you will be playing C-natural instead of C-sharp.

MOST WHISTLES SOUND ONE OCTAVE HIGHER THAN WRITTEN

The most common and useful tin whistle is the small one in D. This instrument plays one octave higher than the flute, fiddle, pipes, etc. When reading tune transcriptions, this whistle sounds one octave higher than the notated music.

The much larger low D whistle, which plays one octave lower than the small D whistle (i.e. at the same pitch as the flute) is becoming increasingly popular. When reading music notation, this whistle plays the notes as written.

Whistles come in a variety of other keys. For the purpose of music notation, these "non-D" whistles are considered to be *transposing* instruments, that is "instruments for which the music is written in another key or octave than that of their actual sound."[viii] (By this definition, the small D whistle is technically a transposing instrument.) All the whistles are treated as if they were D whistles even though they produce music that is either higher or lower in pitch level than that of the small D whistle.

For example, the C whistle is one whole step lower in pitch than the small D whistle. The lowest note of a C whistle is, naturally, a C, and is played with all six tone holes covered, the fingering that produces D on a D whistle. For the purpose of music notation, this lowest note of *any* whistle is considered to be a D. Therefore, when reading a tune you would use the exact same fingerings, no matter what key of whistle you choose to play it on. Let's say you are playing a tune that is in D Ionian. If you play it on a C whistle, you use the same fingerings that you would use to play it on a D whistle, but the music comes out in C Ionian.

Using Non-D Whistles to Play Tunes that are in "Difficult" Modes

Now, here's a different situation. Let's say there is a great tune in D Dorian that you want to play on the whistle, along with other musicians. Playing in D Dorian is usually impractical on the D whistle because in this mode you often encounter F-naturals, which are difficult to finger. (You'll learn why in Chapter 5.)

To solve this problem, you can play the tune on a C whistle, playing it as if it were in E Dorian (using different fingerings of course), a mode that is very well suited to the whistle. Since the C whistle is a whole step lower than the D whistle, and since you are now playing the tune in a mode that is a whole step *higher* than where it is notated, these two factors cancel each other out and the tune "comes out" in D Dorian, right where you want it to be.

In case you are having trouble following this, let's use music notation to illustrate. Below is the first part of *Tuttle's Reel*, in D Dorian. Note the mode signature for D Dorian: no flats. (The key signature for D minor, i.e. D Aeolian, has one flat.)

*Figure 1-5. The first part of **Tuttle's Reel**, which is in D Dorian.*
(A complete version of this tune, in D Dorian, appears on p. 355.)

Note that there are a number of F-naturals in this tune. Though it is possible to play them on a D whistle, using half-hole fingerings, it is rather difficult. It is much easier to play it on a C whistle by fingering the tune as if it were in E Dorian, as notated on the next page. Note the mode signature.

*Figure 1-6. The first part of **Tuttle's Reel**, transposed up to E Dorian.*
(A complete version of this tune, in E Dorian, appears on p. 354.)

 Track 5

Played this way on a C whistle, the tune will sound in D Dorian, as shown in Figure 1-5. This strategy also solves the problem of the low C in bar 4 of Figure 1-5, which is too low for the D whistle.

TONGUING AND SLURRING

To **tongue**, in the musical terminology of wind instruments, means to use an action of the tongue to articulate or separate notes. You can use the tongue to stop and to start the flow of air.

To **slur** means to connect two or more notes such that only the first note of the group is articulated. A slurred group of notes is played using an uninterrupted, continuous stream of air. Only the first note of a slurred group is articulated by the use of tonguing or **throating**. (*Throating* is my term for the use of glottal stops and diaphragm action to articulate or separate notes. For a detailed discussion of throating, see p. 274 in Chapter 20.)

Note: Some people use the word *slur* (or *smear*) to mean a gradual, continuous pitch change. I call such pitch changes **slides**. Chapter 9 is devoted to an exploration of slides.

I follow common practice for notating slurs: an arched line above or below the noteheads of the slurred group. The arched line itself is called a slur. The first, and *only* the first, note under the slur is articulated. The rest are smoothly connected to this first, articulated note.

All notes that are *not* under a slur are articulated with tonguing or throating.

A typical example of slur notation is shown below.

Figure 1-7. An example of the use of slur notation.

 Track 6

29

In this example, the letter "t" (for *tongue* or *throat*) appears below each note that is articulated. Notice that only the first note of each slurred group is articulated. (These "t"s do not normally appear in written music. They are placed in this example only to help clarify the meaning of slur notation.)

THE CLASSIFICATION OF INSTRUMENTAL IRISH MUSIC

Broadly speaking, instrumental Irish music can be divided into two categories: *dance music* and *non-dance music*.

Non-Dance Music

Non-dance music includes slow airs, marches, planxties (tribute pieces) and the other compositions of O'Carolan and other harpers, which have found a home in the repertoires of traditional musicians, as well as a handful of tunes that are simply called "pieces." Breandán Breathnach writes that "pieces"

> . . . are derived from double or single jigs. These pieces were devised simply by filling in intervals in the original tunes with elaborate runs and embellishments. They were played rather deliberately, somewhat at waltz tempo, for which dance, in fact, they could quite easily be adapted. Settings of these pieces are quite commonly met with in the Munster manuscripts of a century or more ago. They are usually associated with the parent tune, the one described as 'the jig way,' the other as 'the piece way.' Pipers played some long descriptive pieces, the most well known being *Máirseáil Alasdruim* which commemorated the battle fought at Cnoc na nDos in 1647, and *The Battle of Augrim*, commemorating the defeat of the Jacobite forces in 1691. In these pieces, the assembly of the troops and the march into battle, the noise and frenzy of the fight, and the cries of women lamenting over the slain are imitated. In another of these pieces, *Fiach an Mhada Rua* or *The Fox Chase*, the sounds of the hounds, horns, and horses are imitated.[ix]

Dance Music

The bulk of instrumental Irish music played today is dance music. Most of this music is made up of the three most common dance tune types: *reels, double jigs,* and *hornpipes.* Other tune types which may be common, depending on the particular region, are *slip jigs, single jigs, slides,* and *polkas,* as well as *set dances, flings, highlands, schottisches, germans, barn dances, mazurkas, varsoviennes, strathspeys,* and *waltzes.* Of course, Irish music is widely played outside of Ireland as well, and local preferences for tune types no doubt vary considerably.

Many of the Irish dance tunes commonly played today originated during the 20th century. There certainly are many older tunes, but they do not form quite as large a part of the common repertoire as we might imagine.

Dance tunes typically have two sections, or *parts*, of eight measures each, though many tunes have more than two parts. Most players label these parts the "A part," the "B part," etc. An older convention is to call the A and B parts the *tune* and the *turn*, respectively. Typically each part is played twice before moving on to the next one, though there are many exceptions to this. Tunes are called *single* when the parts are played only once, i.e. ABAB, etc., as opposed to *double*, i.e. AABBAABB. When tunes are played single it is typically due to the fact that the first four bars of each part are either exactly the same or only minimally different from the second four bars.

Breandán Breathnach's *Folk Music & Dances of Ireland* [x] includes very extensive information on the history of some of these dance tune types, as well as the dances that go with them, and I recommend the book highly. The following information on jigs, reels, hornpipes, and set dances is based largely on information found in his book. For information on the rest of the tune types, I consulted with Caoimhin Mac Aoidh, a fiddler and fiddle teacher from Co. Donegal and the author of the fine book *Between the Jigs and Reels—The Donegal Fiddle Tradition*.[xi]

The *jig*, in its various forms, seems to be the oldest of the current Irish dance tunes. There is limited evidence suggesting that some jigs derive from ancient clan marches and songs, while others may have been adapted from older dance tunes. Many of today's jigs appear to have been composed by pipers and fiddlers of the 18th and 19th centuries.

It is widely agreed that the *reel* developed in Scotland around the middle of the 17th century and from there made its way into Ireland. Many older Irish reels are Scottish in origin.

The *hornpipe* is of English origin. It assumed its present meter and form around 1760 when it changed over from 3/2 time to 2/2 time. It was often performed during stage productions, being played and danced between the acts and scenes of plays.

Polkas and *slides* are particularly popular in *Sliabh Luachra*, which encompasses parts of the counties of Kerry and Cork. The polka, a fast dance tune in 2/4 time, is present in the northern half of the country as well. In the northern counties these tunes are played in a more even rhythm than in the south.

The distinction between *slides* and *single jigs* is a subtle and delicate one. Both have a characteristic quarter-note - eighth-note rhythmic pattern. The difference lies in the timing and beat emphasis of performance. Single jigs are played only slightly slower than slides and with less rhythmic emphasis. To understand a slide better, Caoimhin Mac Aoidh recommends listening to Padraig O Caoimh, Denis Murphy, Julia Clifford, and Gerry McCarthy. To understand a single jig better, he suggests listening to John Gordon, John Timony, John McGee, or Pat Kelly.

Slip jigs are in 9/8 time. They are played all over Ireland but are particularly popular in Co. Donegal. In the west, and particularly the southwest of Donegal, it would not be unusual for a dozen or so slip jigs to be played in any one session.

Set dances, also called *long dances*, are pieces of music intended to accompany a particular solo step dance. The dance usually carries the same name as the tune. Set dances are usually in a jig or hornpipe meter and usually have two parts. Sometimes the meter changes when going from one part to the other. Very often one of the parts, usually the second, is longer in form than the other part or parts, often comprising twelve bars instead of eight. Set dances are called *table dances* in West Limerick, a name which arises from the custom of the skilled solo dancer performing his or her steps on the kitchen table or the dismantled half-door instead of on the clay floor of the house.

Highlands, *schottisches*, *flings*, and *highland flings* are different names for the same tune type. They are in 4/4 time and almost invariably derive from Scottish strathspeys. In the northern parts of Ireland they are often played with additional emphasis on the on-pulse notes, a remnant of their Scottish parentage. They are normally played at tempos somewhere in between those of hornpipes and reels. While they have been played all over Ireland, in the last half of this century their popularity has been focused mainly in Ulster, and particularly Co. Donegal.

Barn dances and *germans* are also two names for the same type of tune, though the term "german" seems to be restricted to west and central Co. Donegal and is probably a shortening of "german schottische." This name distinguishes the german from the "highland schottische," or as it is more commonly known, the *highland* (see the paragraph above). Germans are in 4/4 time and are played at the tempo of a hornpipe. They are characterized by a particular and very determined rhythm: a recurring set of two or sometimes three quarter notes at the end of certain phrases, usually the fourth and eighth. In their geographic spread, barn dances are similar to highlands, though they now appear to be on the increase outside of Ulster.

Mazurkas are dances of Polish origin which appear to have been come to Ireland via associations between continental armies. They are in 3/4 time. There are probably not more than fifteen mazurkas played in the entire Irish repertoire today, and they are almost entirely restricted to Co. Donegal. Vague references are sometimes seen to a type of tune called a *varsovienne*. Apparently this is understood to mean a single tune, *Shoe the Donkey*, in its many forms. In truth it is simply a mazurka under a different name. Native Irish speakers in Co. Donegal often called the varsovienne a "reverse of Vienna," in confusion with the term "reverse," meaning to play in octaves.

The *strathspey* is a tune of Scottish origin in 4/4 time. In Ireland it is generally played slightly slower than a hornpipe and with a strongly dotted rhythmic pattern. Strathspeys are widespread in the province of Ulster, particularly in Co. Donegal. Such great fiddlers as Michael Coleman, Andy McGann, and Paddy Reynolds have played and recorded them.

Waltzes in Ireland are largely continental imports. Most of them have entered the traditional repertoire as song airs and through military regiments and ballroom influences. More recently, waltzes have come to Ireland through the Scottish and Cape Breton traditions. They are in 3/4 time and are played throughout the country.

DANCE-TUNE TYPES

To fully understand the variety of tune types found in traditional Irish music we first need to be clear on the ideas of *pulse*, *meter*, and *subdivision of pulse*.

PULSE

All Irish tunes, except for most slow airs, have a steady recurring beat where we are inclined to tap our feet. This is the *pulse*, the heartbeat of the music.

METER: DUPLE OR TRIPLE

As you listen to a wide variety of Irish music you will find that the pulses in most tunes are grouped in pairs. You would count them, "**one**, two; **one**, two." The first pulse in each pair is stronger. It carries more stress or weight than the second pulse.

In some other tunes the pulses come in groups of three. You would count them, "**one**, two, three; **one**, two, three." Again the first pulse of these groups of three carries the most weight.

This regular, consistent grouping or patterning of the pulse is called *meter*. If the pulses of the tune are grouped in pairs, we say the tune is in *duple meter*. If the pulses of the tune are grouped in threes, we say the tune is in *triple meter*. *Quadruple meter* can be said to occur in Irish music, in tunes such as slides and some marches, but these tunes can also be felt to be in duple meter. The question of quadruple meter vs. duple meter is mostly one of how one chooses to notate a tune, not of how one hears or feels it.

Many other kinds of meter exist, but they are not found in Irish music.

DON'T CONFUSE METER AND TEMPO

Some people confuse the words *meter* and *tempo*. *Tempo* simply means the speed at which a piece of music is played. This can be described subjectively, with phrases such as "moderately fast," "very slow," etc., or can be quantified as a number of beats per minute (bpm). Bpm numbers are shown on metronomes.

SUBDIVISION OF THE PULSE: SIMPLE OR COMPOUND

In all Irish tunes which have a pulse, that pulse is rhythmically subdivided into either two, three, or four shorter notes of equal duration. When the pulse is subdivided into two or four notes, we call this a *simple* subdivision. When the pulse is subdivided into three notes, we call this a *compound* subdivision.

SIMPLE DUPLE METER: REELS, POLKAS, HORNPIPES, SOME MARCHES, AND OTHERS

When a tune in duple meter has a simple subdivision of the pulse (i.e. subdivision by two or four) we say it is in *simple duple* meter. Reels, polkas, hornpipes, and some marches fall into this category, as do schottisches, highlands, flings, highland flings, germans, barn dances, and strathspeys.

The pulse of a *reel* is normally notated as having the duration of a half note. Its pulse is subdivided into four eighth notes, and the time signature is 2/2. (Some transcribers use 4/4, but 2/2 is a better choice as it reflects the reality of the pulse.) Reels make use of a wide variety of combinations of eighth, sixteenth, and quarter notes, but eighth notes predominate, as shown below.

Figure 1-8. Typical reel rhythms.

Notice that the stems of the eighth and sixteenth notes that comprise one pulse are joined together by a common beam (a thick, horizontal line that connects the stems of a group of notes). This shows visually that these beamed notes are contained within one pulse.

The pulse of a *polka* is normally notated as having the duration of a quarter note. Its pulse is subdivided into four sixteenth notes or two eighth notes, and the time signature is 2/4. Polkas make use of a wide variety of combinations of sixteenth, eighth, and quarter notes, as shown below.

Figure 1-9. Typical polka rhythms.

Notice that the stems of the eighth and sixteenth notes that comprise one pulse are joined together by a common beam. This shows visually that they are contained within one pulse.

Some *marches* are in simple duple meter, such as the march *Lord Mayo*. These marches are usually notated in 2/2 with a half-note pulse, as are reels, but they tend to use longer note values than reels do. The opening of *Lord Mayo*, shown below, illustrates some typical march rhythms.

Figure 1-10. The opening bars of the march **Lord Mayo.** *(A complete version of this tune appears on p. 357.)*

Other marches are in compound duple meter and are notated in 6/8 or 12/8.

 Track 7

Hornpipes are part of a special group of tune types that make use of an overtly uneven subdivision of the pulse. Our notation system doesn't do a good job with these kinds of tunes and fairly severe compromises are necessary in writing them down. I begin to address this subject later in this chapter, and do so in greater depth in Chapter 14, *Rolls in Tunes with Overtly Uneven Subdivisions of the Beat*. For the moment, suffice it to say that hornpipes are best notated in the manner of reels, in 2/2 with a half-note pulse. The pulse is predominantly subdivided into four eighth notes, though sixteenth notes, quarter notes, and eighth note triplets are also used.

COMPOUND DUPLE METER: DOUBLE JIGS, SINGLE JIGS, SLIDES, AND SOME MARCHES

When a tune in duple meter has a compound subdivision of the pulse (i.e. subdivision by three), we say it is in *compound duple* meter. Double jigs, single jigs, slides, and some marches fall into this category.

In double jigs, single jigs, and slides, the pulse is notated as having the duration of a dotted quarter note. That pulse is subdivided into three eighth notes. The time signature used for double jigs and single jigs is 6/8. Slides are often notated in 12/8, but sometimes in 6/8. Compound duple marches can be notated in either 6/8 or 12/8.

Double jigs make use of a variety of combinations of eighth, sixteenth, and quarter notes, but running eighth notes predominate, as shown below.

Figure 1-11. Typical double jig rhythms.

Notice that the stems of the eighth and sixteenth notes that comprise one pulse are joined together by a common beam. This shows visually that they are contained within one pulse.

Single jigs also make use of a variety of combinations of eighth, sixteenth, and quarter notes, but quarter note-eighth note couplets predominate over running eighth-note patterns. Musically they sound quite similar to double jigs, but are more "open" sounding due to their lower rhythmic density.

Figure 1-12. Typical single jig rhythms.

Slides make use of a variety of combinations of eighth notes, quarter notes, and dotted quarter notes, but they do not feature many sixteenth notes. They tend to be played a good bit faster than jigs. They are usually notated in 12/8 time.

Figure 1-13. Typical slide rhythms.

SIMPLE TRIPLE METER: WALTZES AND MAZURKAS

When a tune in triple meter has a simple subdivision of the pulse (i.e. subdivision by two or four), we say it is in *simple triple* meter. Waltzes and mazurkas fall into this category.

Waltzes make use of a variety of half, quarter, and eighth notes, and not many sixteenth notes. Quarter and eighth notes predominate. They are notated in 3/4 time with a quarter-note pulse.

Some Irish tunes in this meter were not meant for accompanying the dance of the waltz, so should perhaps not be called waltzes. An example of this is the well-known harp tune *Tabhair dom do Lámh* (Give Me Your Hand) by the harper Rory "Dall" Ó Catháin (ca. 1550 – ca. 1640). (A complete version of this tune appears on p. 358.)

Below we see some typical waltz rhythms.

Figure 1-14: Typical waltz rhythms.

Notice that the stems of the eighth notes that comprise one pulse are joined together by a common beam. This shows visually that they are contained within one pulse.

Mazurkas are similar to hornpipes in that they, too, are part of the special group of tune types that make use of an overtly uneven subdivision of the pulse. Mazurka notation issues are therefore much the same as those of hornpipes, and are addressed in Chapter 14.

COMPOUND TRIPLE METER: SLIP JIGS

When a tune in triple meter has a compound subdivision of the pulse (i.e. subdivision by three), we say it is in *compound triple* meter. Only slip jigs and hop jigs fall into this category.

Slip jigs and *hop jigs* make use of a variety of combinations of sixteenth, eighth, quarter, and dotted quarter notes, but eighth notes predominate. They are notated in 9/8 time.

Figure 1-15. Typical slip jig rhythms.

The following table summarizes some of the information given above.

Meter	Tune Types	Time Signatures
Simple Duple Meter	Reel	2/2
	Polka	2/4
	Hornpipe	2/2 or 4/4
	March	2/2 or 4/4
	Schottische, Highland, Fling, Highland Fling	4/4
	German, Barn Dance	4/4
	Strathspey	4/4
Compound Duple Meter	Double Jig	6/8
	Single Jig	6/8
	Slide	12/8 or 6/8
	March	6/8 or 12/8
Simple Triple Meter	Waltz	3/4
	Mazurka, Varsovienne	3/4
Compound Triple Meter	Slip Jig, Hop Jig	9/8

Table 1-1. Summary of meters, tune types, and time signatures.

THE ESSENTIALLY MELODIC NATURE OF IRISH MUSIC

In traditional Irish music, melody is king. A solo rendition of a tune is complete in and of itself, and functions perfectly well without accompaniment.

The great flute player Matt Molloy was quoted as follows in a 1979 interview:[xii]

> The real art form, as far as traditional music is concerned, is actually playing solo, that's what it's about. It's the interpretation that you can give a melodic line, the basic line there of a tune. You stand or fall on your interpretation of that particular piece. It's no use playing it the same way I play it. Or me taking something and playing it similar to someone else. You have to put your own particular stamp on it. And be that good, bad, or indifferent, at least it's you. It's your personality. Ultimately that's what you stand or fall on.

Harmonic accompaniment, other than the drone of the pipes, appears to be a 20th-century phenomenon, one that may have begun in America "where Irish musicians were a staple element of minstrelsy, musical theater, and vaudeville during the 19th century."[xiii] Percussive and harmonic accompanists must be very careful to support and not to overpower or restrict the melody.

36

THE LEGACY OF IRISH BAGPIPING

The Irish bagpiping tradition has played a seminal role in the development of the playing styles of all other melodic instruments used in traditional Irish music today, especially in the areas of articulation and ornamentation. Being wind instruments, the flute and the tin whistle bear a more direct relationship to the pipes than do the string or free reed instruments. By gaining some knowledge of the nature, history, and evolution of piping in Ireland, you will gain crucial insight into the aesthetics of traditional Irish flute and tin whistle playing.

The modern Irish pipes are referred to as the *uilleann pipes*, the *union pipes*, or simply the *Irish pipes*. *Uilleann*, apparently a form of an old Irish word for "elbow," makes reference to the right arm's pumping of a bellows which fills a bag, held under the left arm, which in turn provides a continuous supply of air to the instrument. The melody pipe is called the *chanter*. Three *drone* pipes supply a constant accompaniment by sounding a note that is in unison with the low note of the chanter, usually D, as well as notes one octave and two octaves below this pitch. The *regulators* are specialized, keyed chanters that make possible the occasional additions of one, two, or three harmony notes to the melody and drones. The keys of the regulators are usually played with the heel or wrist of the lower hand.

Figure 1-16. Declan Masterson playing the uilleann pipes at the 1991 Willie Clancy Summer School, Milltown Malbay, Co. Clare. The seated listener is Drew Hillman.

The origin of the name *union pipes* is not known. "Union" may refer to the joining of the regulator pipes to the chanter and drones, or it may be a corruption of *uilleann*.[xiv]

According to *Na Píobairí Uilleann*, an association of uilleann pipers based in Ireland,

> The history of piping in Ireland extends over a span of thirteen centuries. The earliest references are in the ancient law tracts and annals. Some high crosses have carved depictions of early pipes (10th century) and from the 15th century onwards references become more frequent. All of these pipes were mouth-blown instruments.

> The distinctively Irish form of bagpipe, the union or uilleann pipes, is believed to have originated about the beginning of the 18th century. . . The present form, with three drones and three regulators, came into being at the beginning of the 19th century.

> Piping was at its height in pre-famine Ireland (pre-1847) and was not confined to any social stratum. Social changes in the second half of the 19th century led to the decline in piping and by the beginning of the 20th century the last of the old pipers were mostly destitute, finding refuge in workhouses.[xv]

THE PASTORAL BAGPIPE

The history of the uilleann pipes is a developing field of study. At the time of this writing, research indicates that the uilleann pipes' closest ancestor was probably the *pastoral bagpipe*. Brian E. McCandless, in his article *The Pastoral Bagpipe*,[xvi], writes:

In the early eighteenth century, in Ireland, the British Isles, and the Colonies, there existed a bagpipe that shared characteristics of the modern Irish, or uilleann, bagpipe and of Scottish bellows-blown bagpipes. Very little is known about this bagpipe, its makers, or its players; knowledge of it, and its traditions died out by about 1900. . . Basic questions remain surrounding its invention, use, and nation of origin. A tutor and tunebook first published in London in 1746 by an Irishman, John Geoghegan, for this instrument referred to it as the Pastoral or New Bagpipe. It has been recently suggested that Mr. Geoghegan was the same piper Geoghegan (or Gahagan) known to have performed in Dublin's taverns and theaters at the end of the eighteenth century. Whoever he was, he gave us the earliest documentation about a pipe that was, at the very least, an early form of the uilleann bagpipe.

The pastoral pipes had a chanter much like that of the uilleann pipes, but it had an added footjoint which gave it a range that extended one whole step lower than that of the uilleann pipes. This added footjoint had holes in its sides in addition to the hole at the bottom formed by the end of the bore. Unlike the uilleann piper, the player of the pastoral pipes could not create momentary interruptions of the flow of air through the chanter, because, due to the side holes of the footjoint, there was no way to completely stop air from flowing through the chanter, even when the bottom of the bore was closed on the leg. Thus the melody was a constant, unbroken stream of sound. All articulation, by necessity, was created *solely* by movements of the fingers.

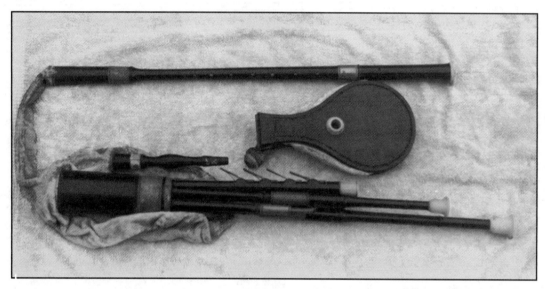

Figure 1-17. A modern set of pastoral pipes by Hugh Robertson. The bellows are from an original set. The pastoral pipes had two drones, one regulator pipe, bellows, and bag. Note especially the chanter, at the top of the photo, with the foot joint extension.

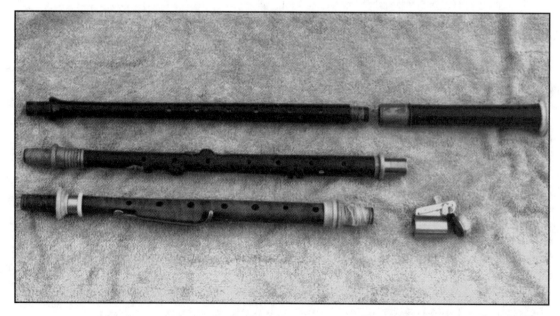

Figure 1-18. Three pipe chanters. From top to bottom: 1. Chanter from a set of pastoral pipes by Robertson with the foot joint detached, 2. Chanter from a set of uilleann pipes in C-sharp by Coyne. 3. Chanter from a set of uilleann pipes in D by Taylor with foot valve detached.

Before such research, it was widely thought that the uilleann pipes had evolved from the *píob mór*, an early Irish form of mouth-blown bagpipe that closely resembled the current Scottish highland pipes. Just how the uilleann pipes had supposedly evolved from the very different *píob mór* was unknown. Discoveries regarding the pastoral pipes have largely supplanted this hypothesis.

The demise of the *píob mór* and the ascendance of the uilleann pipes were however closely related, according to L. E. McCullough:

> At some unverifiable point in the late 17th or early 18th century, the mouth-blown bagpipe of Ireland (píob mór) began to be supplanted in the country's musical life by a new type of bagpipe operated by a bellows (píob uileann). Some commentators have explained the demise of the píob mór as resulting from a Penal Law proscription that classified it as a military instrument of war. The bellows-blown bagpipe, it is said, was quieter and could be played indoors where it would not be heard as easily by hostile authorities. Also, it had to be played sitting down and could not very well be used as a marching instrument. However, the píob mór was used at non-military occasions, such as weddings, wakes, dances, and sporting events, and continued to appear sporadically in public performances during the first few decades of the 1700s. Thus its progressive disappearance during the 18th century was more likely due to the fact that a more versatile bagpipe with a Western European tonality and scale system had to be developed to cope with the demands of the newly-emerging idiom of dance music being created and performed by Irish musicians on fiddles and flutes.[xvii]

The *píob mór*, like the pastoral bagpipe, had no capacity for momentary interruptions of the flow of air. Thus, their melodies were constant, unbroken streams of sound. Any articulations, by necessity, were created *solely* by movements of the fingers.

Figure 1-19. A piper playing the píob mór at the Glens Feis, probably at Ballycastle, Co. Antrim, ca. 1904 – 1906. The costume was designed by F. J. Biggar (died 1927), a member of the Gaelic League, as his interpretation of traditional Irish dress. The kilt may have been saffron colored.

The implications of this can be understood most clearly when imagining the player of such a bagpipe playing two consecutive melody notes of the same pitch. Since the flow of air cannot be interrupted, you can see that the second note can only be produced by *articulating* it with a fingering technique. The varied use of these fingered articulations became an integral and sophisticated element of Irish bagpipe music.

Irish flute and whistle players quite easily and directly adopted the pipers' finger articulations as their own, even though they *do* have the ability to interrupt the flow of air by using their tongue, glottis, and abdominal muscles. These finger articulations go by various names, but are most commonly referred to as *cuts* and *strikes* by players of the flute, whistle, and uilleann pipes. I address cuts and strikes in depth in Chapters 7 and 8.

THE UILLEANN PIPES' ABILITY TO INTERRUPT THE AIR FLOW

The developing uilleann pipes dispensed with the added footjoint of the pastoral pipes, giving its chanter a low note of D. When the player placed the bottom of the chanter on the leg *and* covered all of the finger holes, air could not flow through the chanter and it fell silent. Thus was born the distinctive ability of the uilleann pipes to play separated notes as well as connected notes: *staccato* as well as *legato*. (For definitions of these terms see Chapter 20, pp. 274-275.) This gave the instrument expressive possibilities that many believe made its music the most highly developed form of piping in the world.

AN INHERITED LEGATO AESTHETIC

Still, uilleann piping was deeply affected by the pastoral bagpipe and *píob mór* traditions. It inherited a fundamental and deeply held aesthetic from these ancestral bagpipe traditions, and combined it with its staccato capability to create a new synthesis, one that is also shared by the Irish flute and tin whistle: **The music, in all its variety, springs forth from an underlying foundation of legato playing. The appropriate use of staccato playing exists in relation to that foundation, and takes on its meaning in contrast to it.**

This legato aesthetic is essentially different from that of modern classical music. The classical wind player is taught that all notes are to be tongued unless there is an indication in the notated music, such as a slur, to do otherwise. Most Irish players use tonguing and throating intuitively as an expressive device *against a general backdrop of slurring*. Classically trained musicians who wish to learn to play traditional Irish music must come to understand this critical distinction.

Tonguing in fact is used extensively in both classical and Irish traditions, but in each it is thought of in a completely different way. Much of the tonguing and throating used in Irish flute and tin whistle playing goes unnoticed, because on the whole traditional players use a very connected kind of tonguing and throating that does not take the music away from its fundamentally legato nature.

It seems to me that the traditional Irish musician has much more variety of articulation available to her than does the classical wind player. In classical wind instrument playing, notes are *either* articulated *or* slurred. In Irish traditional music notes can be both articulated *and* slurred, because of its fingered articulations: the cut and the strike. Classical wind players do not have a common practice of fingered articulations.

I explore these subjects in depth in Chapter 20, *Tonguing, Multiple Tonguing, and Throating*.

WHERE DO YOU BREATHE?

The flute and whistle are the only instruments of traditional Irish music that are not suited to non-stop playing. They share a vast repertoire of tunes with the fiddle, pipes, accordion, banjo, concertina, etc., and the tunes have no built-in breathing places. We must create our own by leaving out notes or shortening longer notes. I address this subject in depth in Chapter 21, *Musical Breathing*.

LILT, OR SWING

Irish dance music is rarely if ever played in an absolutely even rhythmic fashion, i.e. with all eighth notes being exactly identical in duration. This is true of many varieties of folk, ethnic, and popular musics. Classical players, who are generally used to playing fairly straight, tend to notice this uneven quality right away. Musicians who are used to playing unevenly sometimes are not aware that they are not playing straight.

This pattern of variance is often referred to as the *lilt* or *swing* (or sometimes *sway*) in a player's style. Each player has her own quality and degree of lilt and it varies with the speed of playing, mood, whom she is playing with, whether or not she is playing for dancers, and many other factors.

Classically trained musicians who are new to traditional Irish music often find the lilt of Irish music to be very elusive. Lilt is an aspect of the music that cannot be learned in an analytical, self-conscious fashion. It cannot be written down. It can only be internalized by immersion, by ear, just as an accent in speech is picked up unconsciously. It helps to feel these rhythms in your body, so if you have an opportunity to learn to dance to Irish music it will no doubt be very helpful.

Lilt is an element of musical personality and it naturally differs from player to player. If you do a lot of listening, it will emerge in your playing over time.

Variance of Stress or Weight

Lilt involves not only the variance of duration, but also the variance of the stress or weight that is given to certain notes. The notes that are given more stress and longer duration are the notes that fall on more important subdivisions of the beat. To make this more clear, let's look at reels and jigs.

Reels are usually notated in 2/2 time, with each half-note pulse subdivided into four eighth notes. If you say the word *generator* over and over you will notice that you do not give each syllable absolutely the same weight and duration. There is a lilt inherent in the delivery of the word. The first syllable gets the most weight and duration. The third gets a bit less, but still more than the second and fourth which are roughly equal to each other. This pattern of varying duration and stress could be represented thus: **GEN**-er-at-or, **GEN**-er-at-or, **GEN**-er-at-or, **GEN**-er-at-or. The use of boldface and capitalization indicates added stress and duration. This resembles the lilt of reels.

Jigs are notated in 6/8 time. The measure contains two dotted-quarter-note pulses which are each subdivided into three eighth notes. Now say the word *energy* over and over and notice the lilt inherent in that word: **EN**-er-gy, **EN**-er-gy, **EN**-er-gy, **EN**-er-gy. The first syllable gets the most stress and duration. It borrows some time from the second, which gets the least amount of stress and duration (notice its smaller type size). The third syllable is stronger and longer than the second, getting approximately its normal one-third share of the available time. Musically, it functions as a *pick-up note* that leads you into the next pulse. This scheme resembles the lilt of jigs.

Playing "on the Front of the Beat"

Lilt is heard in the uneven subdivision of the pulse and the variance of stress. It is also heard in another way. If you listen carefully, you will notice that traditional Irish musicians tend to play "on the front of the beat." That is, they tend to place on-pulse notes a very slight bit early. This lends the music a feeling of "leaning forward," of forward motion and momentum. Some Irish musicians speak of a feeling of "lift" on the downbeat.

By contrast, blues musicians, to give one example, often do the opposite. They tend to play on the back of the beat, placing on-pulse notes a very slight bit late. This creates a "laid-back" feeling.

Sometimes you may notice that an Irish player who is tapping her foot seems to be playing a little ahead of the beat that her foot is setting. This is probably not evidence of sloppy foot tapping, but instead shows how she is playing on the front of the beat.

In an ensemble setting, different players may not always swing to the same degree and in the same ways. If they are very experienced playing together, they will intuitively find a way to fit their "swings" together to create a group lilt that gives great cohesion and energy to their sound.

"Even" Playing is Rarely Really Even

Throughout this book I notate jigs, reels, and the like in even eighth notes and I often recommend playing the notes in an "even" fashion when you are learning the basic physical motions and coordination of a new technique. In these situations I believe it is best to practice slowly in a truly even rhythm, along with a metronome. Once you are comfortable with a technique, it is fine to use it in accordance with whatever lilt you may normally employ.

The faster an Irish player plays the more even her playing tends to become. If this didn't happen, then fast playing would sound too stilted.

TUNES WITH AN OVERTLY UNEVEN SUBDIVISION OF THE BEAT

Then there are tunes that are played in an overtly uneven fashion, such as hornpipes, mazurkas, schottisches, flings, barn dances, and germans. These tunes are normally played much more unevenly than reels, jigs, etc. There is no consensus on how to notate them. I prefer to notate them with even eighth notes and occasional triplets, a notational style which does not reflect the reality of their sound, but which I believe is the best compromise. I elaborate upon the reasons for this opinion in Chapter 14.

NATURE AND MUSIC SEEK A BALANCE

As you begin to pay attention to the lilt of good players, you will notice that it is changeable and flexible. There are some times when a heavier swing is called for and others when a more even delivery is appropriate. Even within a single tune there is such variance. If you adopt a "signature lilt" and adhere to it at all times, your playing will seem rigid and contracted, instead of flexible and expansive. Aim to be supple and let your lilt adjust itself to the nature of the moment. Let the music breathe.

As you can see, lilt is a complex and elusive thing, comprised of many interactive elements. It is not hard to hear it, but it is difficult to describe it in words.

AN IMPORTANT ELEMENT OF PERSONAL AND REGIONAL STYLES

Lilt is clearly an important element of personal style. It is sometimes an identifiable element of regional styles as well. For example, Galway players, such as Paddy Carty, tend to play more evenly than Sligo players, such as Seamus Tansey. However, such generalizations are of limited use because they tend to break apart as you listen closely to individual players, especially in modern times as the definitions of regional styles are blurring due to decreasing isolation.

[i] Mary Larsen, "Martin Hayes, A Lilt All His Own," *Fiddler Magazine*, Spring 1994: p. 9.

[ii] Robert Jourdain, *Music, the Brain, and Ecstasy* (New York: Avon Books, 1997), p. 281–2.

[iii] Willi Apel, *Harvard Dictionary of Music*, (1944; 20th printing, Cambridge, MA: Harvard Univ. Press, 1968), p. 640.

[iv] Willi Apel, p. 452.

[v] Breandán Breathnach, *Folk Music & Dances of Ireland*, (Dublin: The Talbot Press, 1971), p. 14.

[vi] John Smith and Joe Wolfe, in the International Congress on Acoustics, Rome, Session 8.09, pp. 14-15, describe cross fingering in this way: "Opening successive tone holes in woodwind instruments shortens the standing wave in the bore. However, the standing wave propagates past the first open hole, so its frequency can be affected by closing other tone holes further downstream. This is called cross fingering, and in some instruments is used to produce the 'sharps and flats' missing from their natural scales." In the case of C-natural, the most commonly used cross-fingering on the flute and tin whistle has T2 and T3 covering their holes and all other holes open.

[vii] "Half-holing" refers to the practice of only partially covering a tone hole in order to play a pitch that is in between the pitches produced by fully covering the tone hole in question and fully uncovering that tone hole.

[viii] Willi Apel, p. 756.

[ix] Breandán Breathnach, p. 35.

[x] Breandán Breathnach, *Folk Music & Dances of Ireland*, (Dublin: The Talbot Press, 1971).

[xi] Caoimhin Mac Aoidh, *Between the Jigs and Reels - The Donegal Fiddle Tradition*, (Nure, Ireland: Drumlin Publications, 1994).

[xii] This is from an interview with Matt Molloy by Sean McCutcheon, a flute player from Montréal, that took place on September 26, 1997. I found it on Brad Hurley's website, "A Guide to the Irish Flute", <http://www.firescribble.net/flute/molloy.html>.

[xiii] L. E. McCullough, *The Complete Tin Whistle Tutor* (New York: Oak Publications, 1976), p. 4.

[xiv] L. E. McCullough, from his "Historical Notes" in Patrick Sky's *A Manual for the Irish Uilleann Pipes*, (Pittsburgh: Silver Spear Publications, 1980), p. 5.

[xv] Na Píobairí Uilleann, <http://www.iol.ie/npuhome.htm> (5 September, 1998).

[xvi] Brian E. McCandless, "The Pastoral Bagpipe," *Iris na bPíobairí (The Pipers' Review)* 17 (Spring 1998), 2: p. 19-28.

[xvii] L. E. McCullough, from his "Historical Notes" in Patrick Sky's *A Manual for the Irish Uilleann Pipes*, (Pittsburgh: Silver Spear Publications, 1980), p. 5.

chapter 2: the language analogy

Many writers have explored the common ground between music and spoken language. Though they have a great deal in common, in important ways the two are fundamentally different. Words are symbols that represent real objects, actions, and ideas. Musical sounds, when not coupled with lyrics, are not involved with the symbolic representation of anything.

Yet when musical sounds are put together they take on intricate and multidimensional relationships with each other that resemble the patterning of speech; and when we speak, we "perform" the sounds of language in real time. The similarities between music and spoken language are indeed many.

FOOD FOR THOUGHT

Since spoken language is such a rich and omnipresent aspect of our daily lives, examining its resemblance to music can yield potent insights. In this chapter, I will introduce some of these ideas as food for thought, notions to chew on as you progress through the book. Then, in Chapter 23, after exploring the depths of ornamentation, variation, blowing, phrasing, articulation, the use of the breath, and the playing of slow airs, we will revisit the analogy.

VERY SIMILAR, BUT DIFFERENT

Lest we go off the deep end with this fascinating parallel, let's first look at some of the fundamental differences between music and spoken language.

As mentioned above, words refer directly to things in the external world. Instrumental music refers to nothing outside itself. We often associate things of the outside world with instrumental music, for example by connecting a tune with its title. We may become inspired by the outside world to create music. But these external connections are not directly communicated by the music itself.

Almost all Irish music has a regular pulse and the durations of its notes are regular subdivisions of that pulse, lilt notwithstanding. The pitches of Irish music are discrete, contained in simple modes, and easily identifiable. Sometimes we slide into or out of a pitch or alter it in other ways, but these inflections refer to known pitches.

In speech there is a feeling of rhythm but not a recurrent pulse, unless we are reciting verse or chanting. The durations of syllables are usually not proportional to each other, and the pitched inflections we use are not stable, discrete, and identifiable as part of any consistent pattern or musical scale.

Now let's look at some parallels.

KEEPING THE BIG PICTURE IN VIEW

One of the prime challenges for the novice musician is to elevate her focus from the small details of individual notes and the technical challenges of basic playing to a broader view in which she can hear and understand musical phrasing, structure, and meaning.

Compare individual notes to syllables. The articulation of a note is like the beginning consonant or vowel of a syllable: discrete, well-defined, and hard; or soft and smoothly connected to the previous syllable. Syllables link together to form longer words, just as three-note groupings in a jig might form a melodic "word." Several words join together to form a phrase, a complete thought. Note groupings connect to form a musical phrase, a structure that creates direction and motion.

Phrases join to form a sentence. Punctuation delineates the phrases, clarifies their relationships, and gives the sentence finality. "Question and answer" in speech are reflected by "anticipation and resolution" in music. Musical phrases form melodic progressions that embody a complete musical statement, such as a complete A part or B part of a tune, which are punctuated by pauses, breathing, and cadence.

Sentences join to form paragraphs, or stanzas of poetry. A and B parts, sometimes more parts, form musical stanzas or paragraphs to make a complete musical poem or story. Medleys of tunes can be seen as longer, more complex story or poem structures.

To make sense of a poem or story, one cannot focus solely on the sounds of individual syllables or words. We are so thoroughly familiar with our native language that we scarcely notice such tiny things. We automatically focus foremost on the level of meaning in all its subtle shadings. Only by conscious decision do we examine the mechanics of consonants, vowels, and articulations.

This must also be our goal in playing music: *to master the technical aspects to such an extent that we naturally enter into the playing experience at the level of meaning.* If you cannot do that yet as a player, you certainly can, and do, as a listener. Bring the depth and breadth of your listening to your playing. Don't get completely caught up in the details of what you are doing. As you do the necessary detail work, at the same time stand back and hear the poetry of the music. This will guide your technical work and keep you on course toward expressive, eloquent playing. Just as we must function simultaneously on several levels in daily life (e.g. performing the complex physical, visual, auditory, and tactile tasks of driving a car while planning the next day's work and listening to music on the radio), so we must learn to give our attention to music at multiple levels at the same time.

A STRANGER IN A STRANGE LAND

Coming to this music without growing up in it is very much like learning to speak a foreign language in a foreign country. You are immersed in the language and eventually you reach a point where you can think in that language, no longer translating in your mind. You learn the grammar to a sufficient extent that you can begin to converse freely. You may not speak like a native right away. In fact you may spend years polishing up your grammar, syntax, and vocabulary. But, you have reached a critical point: you know the language well enough to eliminate the step of mental translation. This is the key to fluency—in language and in music.

BREATHING

When we speak, our breath, the flow of air through our bodies, is the medium for the sound of our voice. As flute and whistle players, our breath is the substance of the sound of our music. A fiddler breathes to get oxygen. We breathe for that purpose, but also to breathe life into our music.

As I noted in Chapter 1, the flute and whistle are the only instruments of traditional Irish music that are not suited to nonstop playing. We must interrupt the flow of sound in order to breathe, just as we do when speaking.

When we speak, we have an intuitive, automatic sense of when it is appropriate to breathe. We do not disrupt meaning by breathing in the middle of a phrase. In fact, we use the necessity of breathing to shape our speech and enhance its clarity and meaning. We use it for punctuation. We know that pausing gives emphasis to the next words we speak.

The musician's use of space enhances musical meaning in very much the same ways. Many musicians forget to use space in these meaningful ways, but wind players and singers cannot avoid leaving spaces in their music. It is up to us to learn to use the necessary creation of these spaces in an articulate way. That means learning to leave out notes, and shorten longer notes, in ways that contribute to our interpretation of the music. We will explore this subject in depth in Chapter 21, *Musical Breathing*.

TONGUING

In speech, we use our tongue to produce a vast spectrum of consonant sounds and to color and shape our vowel sounds. The tongue is capable of amazingly fine nuance. In playing the flute and whistle we can use our tongues to produce a similarly wide array of articulations and tone colors with seemingly endless gradations of quality. We will explore this subject in depth in Chapter 20, *Tonguing, Multiple Tonguing, and Throating.*

A SINGLE, LINEAR VOICE

When we speak, we have only one voice. We cannot speak in "harmony" with ourselves, expressing several different ideas at the same time, the way a pianist can harmonize her own melodies. The same is true of flute and whistle playing. We play one note at a time. We have a single voice. This is also the intrinsic nature of traditional Irish music. A tune is complete in itself as a single, unaccompanied melody.

A COMMON VOCABULARY

Music and language share a common vocabulary. Think of how the following words have meaning in describing both speech and music: intonation, inflection, delivery, attack, rhythm, tone, nuance, phrasing, accent, cadence, expression, lilt; eloquent, articulate, melodious, singsong, muted, brash. The personality of a speaker, and a musician, are revealed as much through these aspects of speaking and playing as through verbal or musical content.

CROSS-FERTILIZATION AND INSPIRATION

Instrumentalists the world over draw inspiration from the expressiveness of singers, who use the most natural of all instruments, the human voice. In Irish music this emulation finds its highest form in the playing of slow airs (see Chapter 22, *On Playing Slow Airs*). When playing slow airs, instrumentalists ideally know the lyrics of the air intimately and are guided by them in their musical expression.

Singers also are inspired to imitate instruments. In Irish music this finds its highest form in the art of *lilting*, the singing of instrumental tunes using the texture of nonsense syllables to evoke the articulations, ornamentation, and rhythms of instruments. Traditionally, singers lilt tunes for dancing when instrumentalists cannot be present.

⬧ section 2 ⬧

———

the instruments

chapter 3: the irish or simple-system flute and the modern flute

The *Irish flute*, despite the implication of this commonly used name, is not an instrument indigenous to Ireland. Other names heard in Irish circles are the *concert flute*, the *timber flute*, and the *fheadóg mhór* or "big whistle." These terms refer to the type of transverse flute favored by the vast majority of traditional Irish flute players, past and present: the classical wooden flute of the 19th century and modern instruments closely based upon it. The development of this instrument represented the last major stage in a long, continuous evolution which included the renaissance, baroque, and earlier flutes. The modern flute, based on Theobald Boehm's new-system flute of 1832, represents a radical break from that evolution.

THE OLDEST INSTRUMENT?

It appears that the flute is very ancient indeed. With the 1996 discovery of a Neanderthal bone flute segment estimated to be between 43,000 and 82,000 years old, the flute is, as of this writing, the oldest known musical instrument. Measurements of the tone holes on this bone flute segment show that it had a diatonic scale, the same basic scale as the Irish flute and tin whistle.

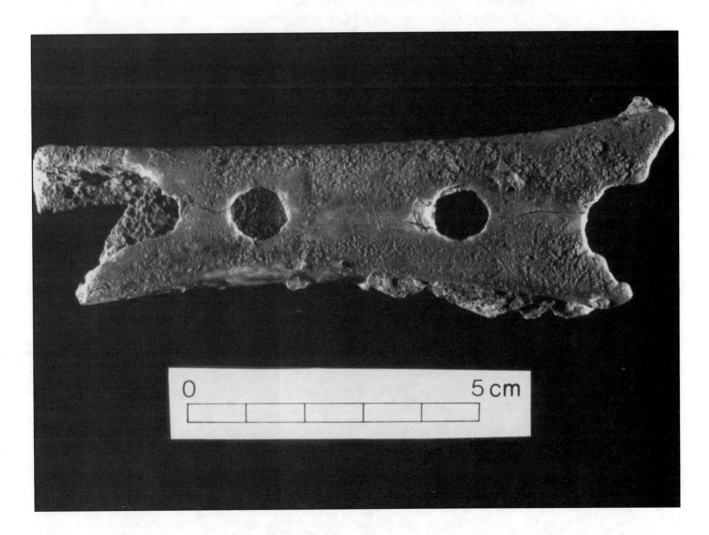

Figure 3-1. A segment of a Neanderthal flute, made from the femur of a cave bear, found in 1996 in Slovenia. Note the two intact tone holes and the two broken ones at the ends of the fragment.

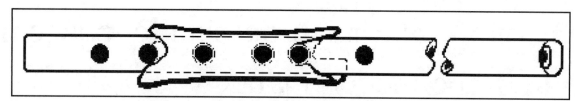

Figure 3-2. Based on a great deal of research and study, here is one idea, put forth by Bob Fink, for the original form of the Neanderthal bone flute.[i]

In Renaissance Europe, flutes were keyless, made in one piece, and had a cylindrical bore throughout. They were difficult to play in tune, especially above the middle of the second octave, having what is now considered a limited range.

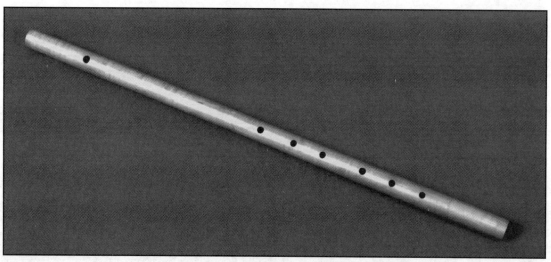

Figure 3-3. A copy in pear wood, by Boaz Berney, of a renaissance flute by Sigmund or Arsazius Schnitzer, Nürnberg, Germany, made in the first quarter of the 16th century. The original is in the Biblioteca Capitolare, Verona, Italy.

With the advent of the Baroque period, the flute was redesigned with a cylindrical head, a conical body, and a three- and later four-jointed construction. A seventh hole was added with a key for playing E-flat. These changes improved its octave tuning, extended its usable range, and changed its voice. Improved chromatic cross-fingering capability allowed composers to write music for the flute in a variety of scales based on various tonal centers.

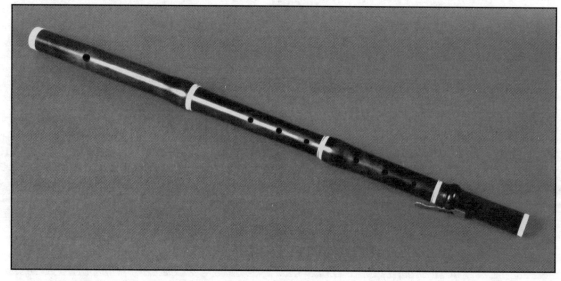

Figure 3-4. A baroque flute made by Folkers & Powell in stained boxwood and imitation ivory. Based on an original flute in boxwood and ivory by Godfridus Adrianus Rottenburgh, Brussels, ca. 1770.

The Classical and Romantic periods saw the addition of more keywork and, especially in England, larger embouchure and tone holes. While larger tone holes and other design factors made the use of cross-fingering less practical, the additional keys provided another, easier means to play chromatic music. These flutes were louder and had now acquired yet another voice due to their increased production of harmonics. Many post-baroque flutes also included a tuning slide that helped flutists play at a wider variety of pitch levels. The older renaissance and baroque flutes tended to be pitched anywhere from A=392 to A=430, well below A=440, the standard for most Irish session playing today.

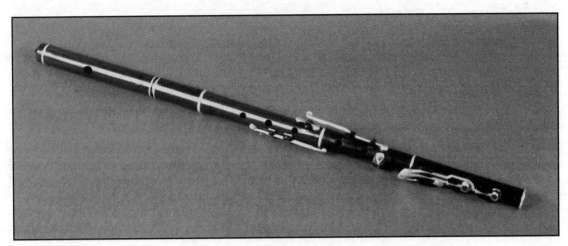

Figure 3-5. An eight-key classical flute in cocuswood and silver by Rudall and Rose, serial # 4973. Made in London, 1844.

THE SIMPLE-SYSTEM

All of these pre-modern style flutes (apparently even the Neanderthal flute) are called *simple-system* flutes, referring to their common basic fingering system. In this book, I use the term simple-system flutes the way it is now mainly used in Irish music circles: for post-baroque and pre-Boehm flutes.

Simple-system flutes have six tone holes that are covered and uncovered solely by the fingers, that is with no mechanical keywork intervening between the fingers and the holes. Covering all these holes yields a low D. Uncovering them one by one from low to high results in a scale in the key of D major (see the fingering charts in Appendix C).

The basic fingering system of the simple-system flute is identical to that of the tin whistle and is almost the same as that of the uilleann pipes. This is no doubt a factor that helped make the simple-system flute a natural choice for traditional Irish musicians. Techniques of piping and tin whistle playing were easily adapted to the simple-system flute. To this day, there is a great deal of overlap among players of these three instruments.

Many simple-system flutes have various combinations of supplementary keys that operate on additional holes, keys that make chromatic music more practical and which sometimes extend the range of the instrument. But still, the primary six finger holes of the instrument are touched only by the fingers.

NEW IRISH FLUTES

With the growth in popularity of the flute in traditional Irish music, and of Irish music in general, flute makers in Ireland and other countries since the 1970s have been making flutes designed specifically to fulfill the musical and aesthetic requirements of Irish traditional music. These then are *Irish flutes* in a truer sense. They are typically made with from zero to eight keys and range from relatively low priced beginners' instruments to expensive and exquisite models rivaling the work of the best of the 19th-century makers.

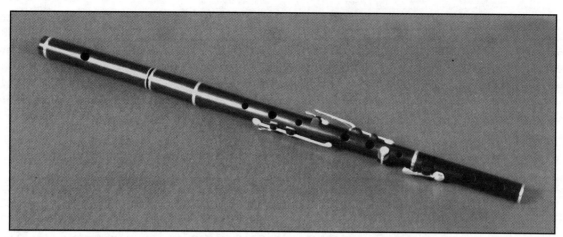

Figure 3-6. A six-key flute, in cocuswood and sterling silver, made by Patrick Olwell in Massies Mill, Virginia, 2000.

These Irish flutes are usually based on the simple-system flutes of 19th-century England, with their large bores, finger holes, and embouchure holes. The development of the English style of flutes was due in part to the championing of such instruments by English virtuosi such as Charles Nicholson the Younger (1795–1837), who made popular a sound and style of playing that featured a powerful, rich, and hard-edged tone, a sound which has been favored, by and large, by Irish musicians ever since. Matt Molloy, perhaps the greatest Irish flutist of our time, epitomizes this sound, and his brilliant playing has been tremendously influential among younger Irish flute players.

Some players, while greatly inspired by Molloy's playing, feel drawn to the more muted and subtle qualities of the smaller-holed flutes that were produced in the 18th and 19th centuries by French and some American makers. These design differences caused the flutes to produce and emphasize overtones differently, which, in turn, accounts for their differences in tonal quality. It could be argued that smaller-holed flutes respond more quickly to finger movements. Before acquiring an expensive flute it would be wise to become aware of the qualities you are most drawn to so that you can find a flute that allows you to bring those qualities forth.

THE USE OF THE KEYS

The keys that are present on many simple-system flutes are not needed for the playing of the bulk of traditional Irish music, a vast body of tunes that are shared by all of the traditional Irish melody instruments. In fact many simple-system flute players who have keyed flutes do not use the keys. But keys can be useful to those players who wish to play tunes that have some altered tones or tunes that are in modes such as D Dorian or G Dorian, many of which are from the repertoires of stringed instruments such as the fiddle and tenor banjo.

HOW DID IRISH PLAYERS COME TO ADOPT THE SIMPLE-SYSTEM FLUTE?

Classical-era flutes were not made with traditional Irish flutists in mind. They are instruments that were made in Europe and America for the classical and band musicians of the day. But clearly, traditional Irish musicians found the instrument very well suited to their music. According to common thought, the advent and eventual domination of the revolutionary Boehm-system flute among the classical musicians of the mid to late 19th century caused a great many simple-system flutes to be cast aside, which made them attainable by less affluent musicians. This phenomenon made possible the widespread acquisition of simple-system flutes by traditional Irish musicians who could not otherwise have afforded good quality instruments. Simple-system piccolos were similarly popular, though they have fallen out of favor among Irish traditional musicians in more recent times.

Harry Bradshaw writes, in the liner notes to *Fluters of Old Erin*, a compilation of Irish flute, piccolo, and whistle recordings of the 1920s and 30s,[ii]

> These discarded flutes made their way by many circuitous routes into the hands of traditional players. Where such sources did not exist, resourceful individuals made flutes and whistles from the elder or boor tree, hogweed stems, wooden spokes, legs of chairs, and, in more recent times, bicycle pumps!

There is evidence of some limited use of the baroque flute in polite Irish society by musicians playing traditional Irish music as early as 1724. John Neal, the Dublin publisher of the earliest surviving book of traditional Irish tunes, entitled *A Collection of the Most Celebrated Irish Tunes, Proper for the violin, German flute or hautboy,*[iii] was a flute player himself who seemed to have strong ties to both classical and traditional music.

By the mid 20th century, good simple-system flutes became rare, even though some makers had continued to make them throughout the waning years of the 19th and into the early 20th century. S. C. Hamilton writes that in the late 19th century ". . . many makers, realizing the increasing importance of the Boehm flute, began to make cheap simple-system flutes for amateur use, taking advantage of new developments in mass production. The 'German' flutes so common in Ireland date from this period."[iv]

MODERN FLUTES ENTER THE IRISH TRADITION

The simple-system flute is the favored flute of the vast majority of Irish flute players. However, it is possible to play Irish music quite well on modern flutes, as evidenced by such players as Paddy Carty of Co. Galway, Paddy Taylor of Co. Limerick, Noel Rice of Co. Tipperary, and Irish-American flutist Joannie Madden, of the group *Cherish the Ladies.*

Paddy Carty and Paddy Taylor are known for playing the Radcliff-system flute, though they both started out on simple-system flutes. The Radcliff flute, introduced by John R. Radcliff (1842-1917) in 1870 and based on the 1851 Carte model, was basically a wooden, closed-hole, Boehm flute with an altered fingering system that resembled more that of the simple-system flute. As such, it still featured keywork that intervened between the fingers and the holes and the Boehm flute's tonal and intonation characteristics.

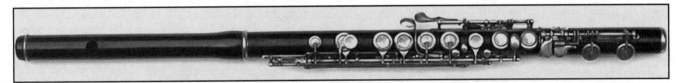

Figure 3-7. A Radcliff-system flute made in ebonite and silver by Rudall Carte in London, 1891.

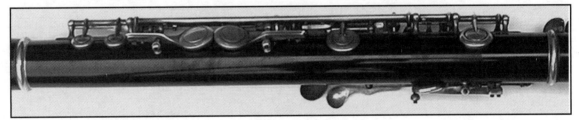

Figure 3-8. The top-hand keywork on the above-pictured Radcliff flute, showing the two thumb keys.

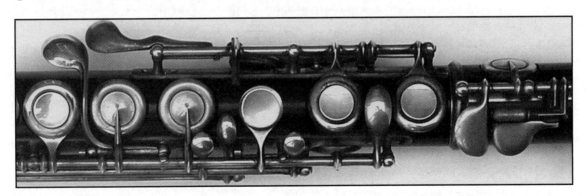

Figure 3-9. The bottom-hand keyword on the above-pictured Radcliff flute.

Players of the modern flute should not feel inhibited from learning the art of Irish flute playing. Throughout history, traditional musicians have adopted instruments that were commonly available to them, and there is no question that the modern flute has become the dominant flute of the West. By the 1940s, 50s, and 60s, simple-system flutes had become very difficult to obtain at reasonable prices, the modern Irish flute makers having not yet emerged. During this period, some traditional players, such as Paddy Carty, Paddy Taylor, and Noel Rice, turned to more modern flutes because these were the only good flutes they could acquire. However, things have changed quite a bit since then. Now it is not difficult to obtain a good quality simple-system flute.

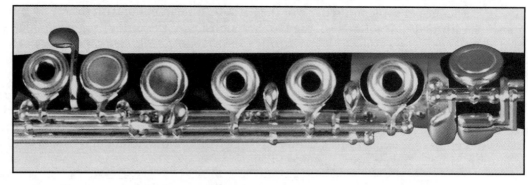

Figure 3-10. The bottom-hand keywork on a modern Boehm-system flute by Chris Abell. The complete flute appears in Figure 3-12.

In my view, the knowledge and sensitivity of the musician are far more important than the particulars of the instrument they have at hand or choose to play. However, I feel that Boehm-system flute players who decide to commit themselves to a deep exploration of Irish traditional music should sooner or later seriously consider making the switch to a simple-system flute. Those who cannot afford to do so can at least get a tin whistle.

ADVANTAGES OF THE SIMPLE-SYSTEM FLUTE IN IRISH MUSIC

Most players of traditional Irish music, including some who have tried both, prefer the simple-system flute over modern flutes. There are some techniques that are important to expressive Irish flute and tin whistle playing that are not well suited to, or even possible on, the Boehm-system and related modern flutes (such as the Radcliff flute) because of the keys that intervene between the player's fingers and the tone holes. Some of these techniques involve sliding fingers gradually on or off the tone holes. I address these in depth in Chapter 9. Such sliding techniques are very natural on the simple-system flute, tin whistle, and uilleann pipes but are more challenging and much more limited in scope on the modern flute, and are virtually impossible on closed-hole modern flutes. Other simple-system techniques involve *shading* or affecting only portions of certain tone holes, such as *Varying the Strength of the Strike*, described in Chapter 10, pp. 175-177, and *Partial Hole Finger Vibrato*, described in Chapter 18, pp. 247-249. These subtle effects are not possible on the modern flute.

In addition, the modern flute's homogeneous, wide-open sound, one of the great achievements of Theobald Boehm in his re-invention of the flute for the classical music of his time, is not a quality that is generally sought after among traditional Irish musicians. The "reedy" sound of the conical-bored, wooden, simple-system flute suits the music to a tee. The tonal variations that naturally occur among the notes of the simple-system flute, tin whistle, and other traditional instruments, especially the uilleann pipes, are qualities that are generally cherished in the aesthetic of traditional Irish music.

One of my students recently brought this point home to me in new way. She is an accomplished Boehm-system flutist who has chosen to learn Irish music on the simple-system flute. In noting how quickly she was able to learn tunes by ear, I remarked that she must be thoroughly familiar with musical intervals. She said that she was, but what helped her more was the fact that the sound of each note on the simple-system flute has a unique timbre or "personality" that she can recognize. The sounds of F-sharp, A, and C-natural for instance are quite different from each other, and the two octave registers have characters that are distinct as well. I asked her if she thought it would be harder for her to learn tunes from me by ear if we were both playing modern flutes. She said that it would.

Traditional musicians rejoice in the musical asymmetries of the simple-system instruments, what classical flutists might consider to be tonal "oddities" or inconsistencies. Most traditional musicians are not after a homogeneous sound.

Still, the choice of instrument remains a very personal one. Not all players share the predominant aesthetic preference for the sound and capabilities of the simple-system flute. A highly skilled and musically sensitive player can mold the sound of almost any good flute to suit her personality and the way that she hears the music she loves. Modern players such as Joanie Madden and Noel Rice have pioneered new techniques in the adaptation of the modern flute to traditional Irish music and have done so splendidly, due to their deep knowledge of and sensitivity to the music. I discuss these techniques in depth in Appendix B.

For those players who are exclusively committed to the modern flute, yet wish to pursue Irish music in depth, there are some options that may be attractive. There are Boehm-system flutes made of wood, both older instruments and new ones such as those made by Chris Abell, which sound somewhat more like simple-system flutes. Abell and others also make wooden headjoints for metal modern flutes which bring forth the warm tonal qualities reminiscent of the older instruments.

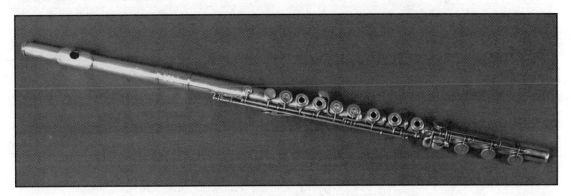

Figure 3-11. A modern Boehm-system flute made in silver by the William Haynes Company, Boston, Massachusetts, serial # 44166, 1978.

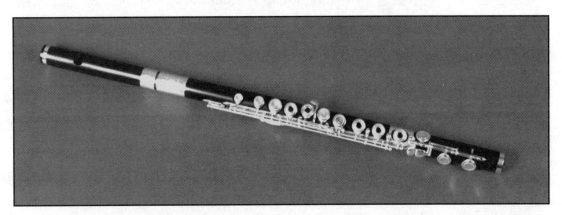

Figure 3-12. A wooden Boehm-system flute, in African blackwood (grenadilla) and sterling silver, by Chris Abell, Asheville, North Carolina, 2001.

Boehm himself wrote that:

> The silver flute is preferable for playing in very large rooms because of its great ability for tone modulation, and for the unsurpassed brilliancy and sonorousness of its tone. But on account of its unusually easy tone-production, very often it is over-blown, causing the tone to become hard and shrill; hence its advantages are fully realized only through a very good embouchure and diligent tone-practice. For this reason wooden flutes on my system are also made, which are better adapted to the embouchures of most flute players; and the wood flutes possess a full and pleasant quality of tone, which is valued especially in Germany.[v]

It is interesting to note that the effect on flute tone of wood vs. other materials is a hotly debated issue. There are scientific studies that conclude that the material of the flute has no impact on tone, that instead tonal differences are due to such factors as hole size, bore size, bore finish, and tone-hole chamfering (the beveling on the inside and outside of the tone holes).

NEW, IMPROVED HEADJOINTS FOR SIMPLE-SYSTEM FLUTES

Simple-system flute players may also want to look into having new headjoints made for their instruments. I currently play a 19th-century simple-system flute by Firth, Pond & Co. and have a custom made Abell headjoint that is significantly superior to the original headjoint, giving the instrument better responsiveness and overall sound.

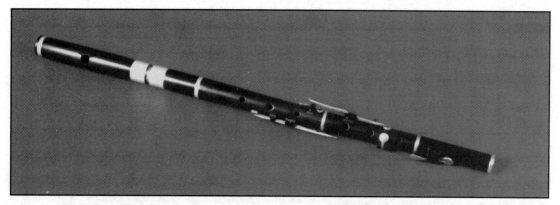

Figure 3-13. The author's flute. Made by Firth, Pond & Co., New York City, between 1847 and 1863. Cocuswood with six German silver keys. Shown here with a replacement headjoint made by Chris Abell in 1997.

ANOTHER BRANCH OF THE IRISH FLUTE TRADITION

According to S. C. Hamilton,[vi] the flute bands and fife and drum bands that are still active in Northern Ireland form another branch of the flute's traditional use in Ireland. The idea of group flute playing in such bands was most likely introduced by the British Army. High-pitched flutes, or fifes, in B-flat or high D are most commonly favored as their shrill sound carries well over that of a group of drummers. Some of these bands are quite large and employ a wide variety of sophisticated keyed simple-system and Boehm-type flutes in various sizes.

Many villages, even in the south of Ireland, had small fife and drum bands that played at various public events. This tradition had nearly died out by the 1930s, though there has been a small revival through competitions organized by Comhaltas Ceoltóirí Éireann.

THE PICCOLO

The piccolo was quite commonly used in traditional Irish music in the early 20th century and perhaps earlier, but it fell out of fashion after the 1930s. One notable exception was piccolo player John Doonan who made a piccolo LP, *Flute for the Feis*, in 1977.[vii]

Included in Harry Bradshaw's excellent compilation of flute, piccolo, and whistle recordings of the 1920s and 1930s, *Fluters of Old Erin*,[viii] are four tracks that feature or include the piccolo, performed by Paddy Finlay (1884–1950), Tommy Breen (1882–1971), John Sheridan (1899–1943), and Dan Sullivan's Shamrock Band. This band recorded 106 78-rpm record sides between 1926 and 1934, many of them featuring piccolo playing by Owen Frain, Dan Moroney, and Murty Rabbett.

Most commonly, the simple-system piccolo was made to play one octave higher than the flute, although some piccolos were made in E-flat and other nearby keys. A piccolo or fife, especially in its high register, can cut through in a dance band full of louder instruments such as banjos, accordions, and drums. In the days before amplification, that capability must have been quite an asset for a wind player.

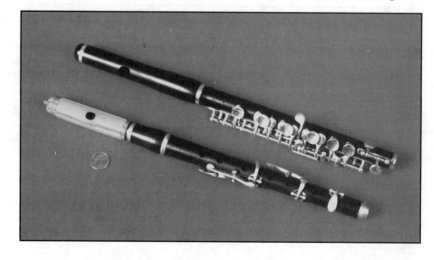

Figure 3-14. A modern piccolo, top, by Zentner and a simple-system six-key piccolo, bottom, by H. F Meyer, Hanover, Germany, ca. 1880, made of cocuswood and ivory with German silver keywork. (A US dime appears for size reference.)

The piccolo can be played with a beautiful sweet and round tone as well. I, for one, would certainly welcome the piccolo back into the fold.

MORE RESEARCH NEEDED

The very early history of the flute in traditional Irish music remains largely mysterious. S. C. Hamilton ably explores this fascinating topic at length in his book *The Irish Flute Player's Handbook*.[ix] The earliest known visual portrayal of the use of the flute in traditional Irish music appears to be a painting by Maclise entitled *Snap Apple Night* or *All-Hallow Eve in Ireland*, ca. 1833, which depicts a festive gathering in Co. Cork.[x] On the right edge of the painting are a fiddler, a flute player (partly hidden by the fiddler), and an uilleann piper playing together.

Figure 3-15. "Snap-Apple Night" or "All-Hallow Eve in Ireland" by Co. Cork artist Daniel Maclise (1806–1870). The painting was first exhibited in 1833.

Figure 3-16. A detail from the above-mentioned painting showing a wooden flute player. He or she appears to be playing a very small flute or piccolo.

As of this writing, the earliest known evidence of the flute's use in traditional Irish music is the above-cited reference to the "German Flute" in the title of John and William Neal's *A Collection of the Most Celebrated Irish Tunes, Proper for the violin, German flute or hautboy*, published in Dublin in 1724.[xi] According to Nicolas Carolan, who compiled the facsimile edition, this fascinating volume is

. . . the earliest body of Irish music to emerge from eight or nine thousand years of music making in the country, and the indications are that it is a first-hand collection. . . The bulk of the collection seems to derive from a harper or harpers. Whether of known or unknown composition, the tunes, with one or two possible exceptions, are of native origin. They are melodies of songs in Irish, celebrate native patrons, and in some cases show sympathy with the Irish side of the wars of 1688–91, a sympathy surprising in a collection made for sale in the heart of Dublin at this period.[xii]

The Neals were very active "musicians, musical instrument makers, music sellers and publishers, and music impresarios, who in the first half of the eighteenth century dominated the Dublin music trade from their shop in Christ Church Yard."[xiii] John Neal was described as playing the German flute by about 1714. "If by this is meant, as is probably the case, the one-keyed conical flute developed in France in the late seventeenth century, he would have been among the first in Ireland to do so."[xiv]

Also very notable is the Neals' 1724 publication, which unfortunately does not survive, of *Irish and Scottish tunes for the flute.*[xv]

Their other publications include a book of *Scottish tunes for the violin*, as well as a number of volumes of popular airs and minuets from England and the continent, and contemporary classical music by the likes of Handel.[xvi]

Also of great interest is the reference to the German Flute in the subtitle of the 1804 uilleann pipe tutor and tunebook, *O'Farrell's Collection of National Irish Music for the Union Pipes.*[xvii] The subtitle reads:

> Comprising a Variety of the Most Favorite Slow & Sprightly Tunes, set in proper Stile & Taste, with Variations and Adapted Likewise for the German Flute, Violin, Flagelet, Piano & Harp, with a Selection of Favorite Scotch Tunes, Also a Treatise with the most Perfect Instructions ever yet Published for the Pipes.

In his introduction to the facsimile edition,[xviii] Patrick Sky writes that the book

> . . . represents a number of probable firsts: the first significant collection of Irish dance tunes collected and written down by a traditional musician and performer - not a scholar; first tutor for the Union pipes; and finally the first Irish dance music collection by an Irishman, containing the earliest examples of many of the tunes that are in our current repertory.

[i] Drawing by Bob Fink, from Fink, "The Neanderthal Flute," Crosscurrents #183 1997, Greenwich Publishing, Canada. Also <http://www.webster.sk.ca/greenwich/fl-compl.htm>.

[ii] Harry Bradshaw, from the liner notes to *Fluters of Old Erin, Flute, Piccolo and Whistle Recordings of the 1920s and 30s* (Dublin: Viva Voce 002, 1990).

[iii] John & William Neal, *A Collection of the Most Celebrated Irish Tunes, Proper for the violin, German flute or hautboy*, first published 1724, facsimile edition by Nicolas Carolan (Dublin: Folk Music Society of Ireland, 1986).

[iv] S. C. Hamilton, *The Irish Flute Players Handbook* (Coolea, Ireland: Breac Publications, 1990).

[v] Theobald Boehm, *Die Flöte und das Flötenspiel* (1871); trans. Dayton C. Miller as *The Flute and Flute-Playing* (New York: Dover Publications, 1964), pp. 54–55.

[vi] Hamilton, p. 37.

[vii] John Doonan, *Flute for the Feis* (Ossian, OSS 42, 1977).

[viii] *Fluters of Old Erin, Flute, Piccolo and Whistle Recordings of the 1920s and 30s* (Dublin: Viva Voce 002, 1990).

[ix] Hamilton, p. 37.

[x] Hamilton, p. 33.

[xi] John & William Neal, *A Collection of the Most Celebrated Irish Tunes, Proper for the violin, German flute or hautboy*, Dublin, 1724. Facsimile edition compiled by Nicolas Carolan, Dublin: Folk Music Society of Ireland, 1986.

[xii] John & William Neal, p. xxvi–xxvii.

[xiii] John & William Neal, p. xii.

[xiv] John & William Neal, p. xiv.

[xv] John & William Neal, p. xxi.

[xvi] John & William Neal, p. xxi.

[xvii] O'Farrell (first name unknown), *O'Farrell's Collection of National Irish Music for the Union Pipes,* (London: John Gow, 1804). Compiled, edited and reconstructed by Patrick Sky, (Chapel Hill, North Carolina: Grassblade Music, 1995).

[xviii] O'Farrell, p. ii.

chapter 4: the tin whistle

The tin whistle also goes by the names *pennywhistle, whistle,* and sometimes *tin flute*. In Irish it is known as the *fead-óg* or *feadán*. It is undoubtedly the most affordable of the traditional melody instruments of Irish music, and for that reason probably the most widespread.

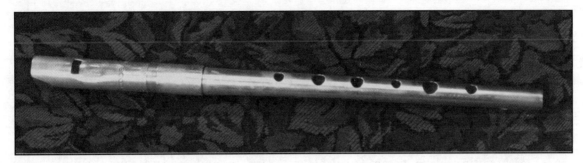

Figure 4-1. A tin whistle in D made by Michael Copeland, ca. 1995, Conshohocken, Pennsylvania.

A FIPPLE FLUTE

The tin whistle is an end-blown, vertically-held, six-hole *fipple flute*, in the same family as the recorder and numerous other fipple flutes found throughout world musical traditions.

In fipple flutes, tone is produced by blowing air through a special mouthpiece that makes use of a small plug or block (the fipple), made of wood or other material. Sometimes the fipple is instead built into the shape of the mouthpiece itself, as is the case with the one-piece plastic mouthpieces of Generation and similar brands of factory-made whistles. A small air channel is created between the fipple and the inside wall of the instrument. The air stream is shaped by and directed through this channel to a sharp edge or lip that splits the airstream, causing the air column to vibrate and produce sound.

A VERY LONG HISTORY

L. E. McCullough, in his book *The Complete Tin Whistle Tutor* [i] gives a fascinating summary of the history of the tin whistle, tracing its origins back to whistle-like instruments that are described in written records in Ireland dating as far back as the third century A.D. The *feadán* is mentioned by name in the 11th-century Irish poem "Aonach Carman" contained in the *Book of Leinster*,[ii] as is the *cuiseach*, an instrument made of reeds or corn stalks from which the pith had been removed.[iii]

There is no doubt that this simple type of fipple flute has been hand-crafted by ancient peoples around the globe for many centuries. Much attention has come in recent years to the 12th-century bone whistles unearthed in the old Norman quarter of Dublin. Certainly, Irish people made their own whistles out of bone, wood, or reeds before factory-made tin whistles came onto the scene. Current knowledge implies that the whistle, in something like its present form, came into use in traditional Irish music before the simple-system flute.

The manufactured tin whistle seems to have had its origins, at least in part, in the *flageolet*, a wooden fipple flute that reached its peak of popularity in Europe during the Renaissance and Baroque periods and which underwent a revival in the late 1700s and early 1800s. Flageolet maker Andrew Ellard was active in Dublin from 1819 to 1838 and Joseph and James Corbett made flageolets in Limerick between 1801 and 1814.[iv]

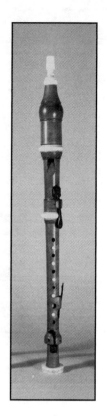

Figure 4-2. Anonymous 19th-century flageolet, from the Dayton C. Miller flute collection, Library of Congress, Washington, DC. The instrument was made in two sections. The upper section has the mouthpiece and fipple, a C-natural key, and a two-part sponge chamber (for absorbing breath condensation). The lower section has E-flat and F-natural keys and ivory finger studs. Made of boxwood with silver keys and ivory ferrules, finger studs, and mouthpiece.

At present, the earliest known evidence of the flageolet's use in traditional Irish music seems to be the reference to the "flagelet" in the subtitle of the 1804 uilleann pipe tutor and tunebook *O'Farrell's Collection of National Irish Music for the Union Pipes.*[v] The subtitle reads:

> Comprising a Variety of the Most Favorite Slow & Sprightly Tunes, set in proper Stile & Taste, with Variations and Adapted Likewise for the German Flute, Violin, Flagelet, Piano & Harp, with a Selection of Favorite Scotch Tunes, Also a Treatise with the most Perfect Instructions ever yet Published for the Pipes.

MANUFACTURED TIN WHISTLES

Inexpensive manufactured tin whistles became available in Ireland certainly no later than the mid-1840s with the introduction of instruments such as the English-made Clarke tin whistle. Unlike the flageolet, which was made of wood turned on a lathe, these whistles were made out of sheet tin rolled around a mandrel and could be produced, and purchased, at very small expense, hence the name pennywhistle. This name may also have come from street musicians who would play tunes on the whistle in exchange for the pennies of passersby.

The tradition of Irish people making their own whistles has persisted even into our time. L. E. McCullough writes that

> . . . uilleann pipemaker Patrick Hennelly of Chicago recalled that as a young lad in Mayo, he often made musical instruments from ripe oat straws simply by pushing out the pith and then fashioning the lip and fingerholes with a penknife, and, indeed, the basic structural principles of such instruments must have been discovered fairly early and by many people.[vi]

HIGHER REGARD FOR THE TIN WHISTLE

It appears that, until the 1960s, the tin whistle was not taken very seriously by most people in Ireland, being seen more as an introductory instrument for aspiring pipers and flute players and a good starting instrument for children. The Irish music revival of the 1960s and 70s, however, brought to light such masterful whistle players as Seán Potts, Mary Bergin, Paddy Maloney, Micho Russell, and Donncha Ó Bríain, who showed the world how highly developed and expressive tin whistle playing could be.

In response, there has been a tremendous flowering of innovation in tin whistle making, especially since the 1980s, resulting in a standard of quality never seen before. Now it is possible to buy fine hand-crafted whistles made of metal, wood, or plastic that are capable of responding to the finest nuances of a masterful player. Inexpensive whistles also abound in a wider variety than ever before.

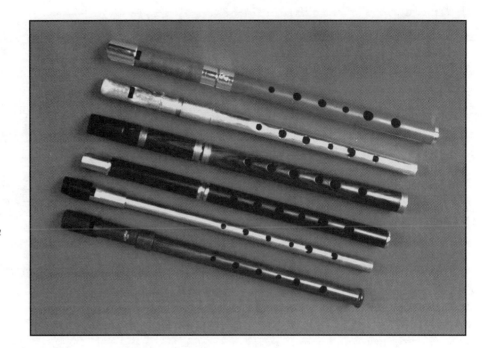

Figure 4-3. Six tin whistles in D. From top to bottom: Abell, Copeland, O'Riordan, Schultz, Sindt, and Susato. All of these have tuning slides and all have cylindrical bores except the Copeland, which has a conical bore.

A VARIETY OF SHAPES, SIZES, KEYS, AND PRICES

The small whistle in the key of D, an octave higher than the simple-system flute, is by far the most popular and useful. No whistler should be without a good, small D whistle. Whistles are made in a wide variety of keys, including low-D whistles that can play in unison with flutes.

There is a very broad array of whistles available today. Some have cylindrical bores and others are conical. There are many inexpensive mass-produced whistles and an ever-growing selection of fine, more expensive, hand-made instruments. Improved mouthpieces for inexpensive whistles are being made, and handmade whistles often come with several differently pitched bodies that can each be used with a single headjoint.

Figure 4-4. A set of three whistles bodies, in the keys of C, D, and E-flat, that share a single headjoint. Made by Chris Abell in grenadilla and silver.

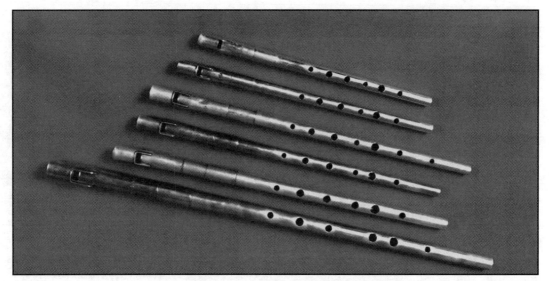

Figure 4-5. Not quite a complete set of whistles by Michael Copeland. From top to bottom: D, C, B-flat, A, G, and low D. Note that this particular B-flat whistle has a seventh hole which gives it a low note of A-flat.

It is prudent for many to start off with an inexpensive instrument. But if you decide to make a commitment to more serious playing, you owe it to yourself to get a good handmade instrument, one that plays well in tune and will respond well and quickly to the subtleties of your playing. While these instruments cost quite a bit more than the mass-produced ones, they are still a bargain compared to other high-quality musical instruments.

THE ACCESSIBLE MODES

The tin whistle is somewhat limited outside of its home key and several closely related modes. (For information on modes, see Chapter 1.) One can obtain chromatic notes by the half-covering of tone holes and by using cross-fingerings, but these techniques are impractical for some musical situations. This is one reason why whistles in keys other than D can come in very handy. For instance, one can play D Dorian tunes by playing them as if they were in E Dorian on a tin whistle in the key of C. (For more on this subject, see Chapter 1.)

On a D whistle, one can easily play, without half-hole fingerings, in the following modes that are commonly used in Irish music:

> D Ionian (major) and D Mixolydian
> E Dorian and E Aeolian (natural minor)
> G Ionian (major)
> A Mixolydian and A Dorian
> B Aeolian (natural minor)

TIN WHISTLES ARE SIMPLE-SYSTEM INSTRUMENTS

As stated in the previous chapter and elsewhere, the tin whistle and simple-system flute share the same fingering system, one which is almost the same as that of the uilleann pipes. As a result, fingering techniques on the flute and whistle are nearly identical, and both are very closely related to those of the uilleann pipes.

[i] L. E. McCullough, *The Complete Tin Whistle Tutor* (New York: Oak Publications, 1987), pp. 6–8.

[ii] Gearóid Ó hAllmhuráin, *A Pocket History of Traditional Irish Music* (Dublin: O'Brien Press, 1998), p. 13.

[iii] Breandán Breathnach, *Folk Music & Dances of Ireland* (Dublin: The Talbot Press, 1971), p.5.

[iv] McCullough, p. 8.

[v] O'Farrell (first name unknown), *O'Farrell's Collection of National Irish Music for the Union Pipes* (London: John Gow, 1804). Compiled, edited and reconstructed by Patrick Sky (Chapel Hill, North Carolina: Grassblade Music, 1995).

[vi] McCullough, p. 6.

chapter 5: holding and blowing the tin whistle

A Physical Relationship, and Much More

The first time you pick up your tin whistle, flute, or any musical instrument and hold it in your hands, you have begun a physical relationship with it that will hopefully last for years. If you are a beginner, you now have the golden opportunity to form good habits and avoid bad ones. If you have already formed some unfortunate ones, now is the time to discover what they are and begin your liberation from them.

Playing music is an athletic activity. As people learn to play, they train groups of muscles to work in exquisite coordination to perform the most subtle and complex maneuvers, sometimes in extremely brief moments of time. Playing the flute or whistle in particular is also a demanding aerobic activity. In this chapter, and in Chapter 6, we will explore the particular nature of the sustained deep breathing that Irish flute and tin whistle playing require. For now I will simply observe that keeping yourself in good shape with regular aerobic exercise will only enhance your playing. This is especially true for beginners who are still learning to use their air supply efficiently.

Playing music is also a mental, emotional, and spiritual activity. We tend to talk about these as separate aspects of creativity, labeling them with separate words, but in fact playing music is a completely unified experience. At its center is a beautifully subtle interaction between one's self and one's instrument. As you mature as a musician, you become more and more skilled at sensitively expanding that interaction outward to include other musicians and listeners. And finally, your sense of the core experience changes. You reach a point where you feel that you are not creating the music yourself, but that you have tuned yourself so well that you have *become* an instrument and music is simply flowing through you. All master musicians experience this.

But you must begin with the physical aspect of your relationship with the whistle or flute, and mastering it will take time. You will need to adopt the attitude of *always* "tuning in": always noticing the nature of the sounds you are producing and what is happening in your body when you produce them, always noticing the connections between your sound and your body. It may seem obvious, but many people forget that *when you play you must always listen*: to your sound, which you hear through the air and through your bones, and to the sensations of your own body. Starting with this core of inner sensitivity, you learn to expand your listening attitude outward, and ultimately other people will find it a joy to play music with you, dance to your music, and listen to you.

This attitude of focusing on sound and the physical sensations within your body requires a quiet, undistracted mind. Most of us can achieve this inner quiet in moments here and there. As you bring your attention and intention to practicing this, you will find that you can sustain internal quietness for longer periods of time. For many, closing the eyes while playing helps considerably.

Physical and mental relaxation are both essential to this process and, of course, are woven into one another. When you begin by giving your attention to physical relaxation, mental relaxation tends to follow.

Of course there is a difference between being physically relaxed and being limp. When you sit or stand in a relaxed manner there are many muscles that are working to hold you up. But none of them are overly tense, and those that don't need to work are relaxed. This state of balance, with no distraction caused by unnecessary muscle tension, is what I mean by physical relaxation.

A Brief Note on Posture

As a whistle or flute player, your starting point for a relaxed body and the optimal use of your energy is an upright spine. This is central to allowing the free movement of your diaphragm and allowing the relaxation of your air passages, shoulders, arms, neck, and head. When you play sitting down make sure to keep both feet flat on the floor. Of course, the same holds true for playing while standing.

We'll talk a bit more about posture as it relates to breathing later in the chapter. Now let's look at how to hold the whistle in a relaxed and secure way.

THE FINGER HOLES, AND A CHOICE FOR LEFT-HANDED PEOPLE

The six finger holes of the tin whistle are covered and uncovered by the middle three fingers of your two hands. Most people find that it feels most natural to use their dominant hand for the three holes at the bottom of the instrument, i.e. the holes furthest from the mouthpiece. Since most of us are right-handed, that means using the right hand for these bottom three holes.

If you are left-handed you may feel it is more natural for you to use your left hand for these bottom holes. Many left-handed people do play this way, while some others use the right-handed hold.

However, I offer a word of caution here for left-handed people, especially those who think that they may one day play the flute or uilleann pipes (or another woodwind instrument). These other instruments are not as symmetrical as the tin whistle and are almost always designed to be played right-handed. Many flute embouchure holes are designed to be blown into from one direction only, and the keywork on multi-keyed flutes is most definitely right-handed. You can go to the expense of having an instrument builder make you a left-handed instrument, but it may cost a pretty penny.

So, I advise you to give the right-handers' way a fair try and see how it feels. Switch back and forth and experiment a bit in this early stage if you wish. But don't delay very long in making a decision and sticking with it. We establish important neural pathways and connections from the earliest stages of learning and practicing a new instrument.

FINGERING NOTATION

In this book I will call the hand nearest the whistle mouthpiece the *top hand*. The hand nearest the other end, the foot of the whistle, I will call the *bottom hand*. Either of these can be the right or left hand, though, by far, most people play with the left hand as the top hand and the right hand as the bottom hand.

I call the top-hand index finger T1, the top-hand middle finger T2, and the top-hand ring finger T3. Similarly, I call the bottom-hand index finger B1, the bottom-hand middle finger B2, and the bottom-hand ring finger B3. See Figure 5-1 on the next page.

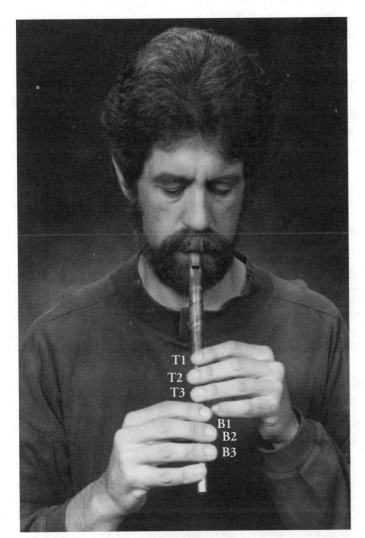

Figure 5-1. The whistle right-handed hold (left) and the left-handed hold (right), with fingering indications.

COMFORT AND STABILITY: THE ATTRIBUTES OF A GOOD WHISTLE HOLD

When you hold your whistle you want to be comfortable, as relaxed as possible, and have no worries, conscious or subconscious, about dropping the instrument. You also want to keep the whistle still while your playing fingers do their jobs.

RESTING POSITION FOR THE PLAYING FINGERS

When any of the six playing fingers are not in motion or covering their holes they should be in *resting position*, gently curved and hovering, relaxed, very near their holes, about one-third to one-quarter inch above them. When you are relaxed, this is the position your fingers will naturally want to assume. In resting position, your playing fingers are poised and ready for action.

THE FOUR ANCHOR POINTS OF THE TIN WHISTLE

Now comes one of the most crucial elements of your physical relationship with the whistle. When you learn to hold the instrument so that you can be relaxed throughout your hands, wrists, arms, and upper body, and never be in fear of dropping it, then you open the way for establishing the habit of physical and mental relaxation that is essential for being fully musical.

The six fingers we use to cover and uncover the finger holes (see Figure 5-1 above) should have *absolutely nothing* to do with holding or stabilizing the instrument. Their *only* job (and a huge job it is, as you will see as you work your way through this book) is to freely interact with the finger holes. Don't burden them with anything else!

When you use the four anchor points to hold, support, and stabilize the whistle, your playing fingers can be relaxed and free. The four anchor points are:

     1. Your lips
     2. Your top thumb
     3. Your bottom thumb
     4. Your bottom pinky

Figure 5-2. The proper way to hold the tin whistle. All fingers are relaxed, and in this case the playing fingers are in resting position above their finger holes. The whistle is held stable using the four anchor points and the whole body is relaxed.

We will examine these four anchor points in turn. But first, try this exercise to quickly establish the basic hold.

HAVE A SEAT: QUICKLY ESTABLISHING THE BASIC HOLD

1. Sit at a table and pull your chair right up close to the edge. Place this book before you on the table, an inch or two from the edge and place the bottom of the whistle squarely on the table top right before you. Sit high enough that, leaning over the edge of the table, you can position your head so that just the tip of the mouthpiece is held gently, centered between your lips. Holding the whistle this way (no need to blow), remove your hands. The whistle is gently held upright.

2. Now, approach the whistle with your top hand and, without your thumb touching the whistle, gently lay T1, T2, and T3 on their respective finger holes (see Figure 5-1 if you need to be reminded of where they go). Cover the holes not with your fingertips but with some part of the fleshy pad of the first joint of each finger. Your hand should remain very relaxed. Your fingers should be fairly flat but hopefully will have a gentle arch to them. Completely straight fingers are usually a sign of tensed muscles. Of course, the size and shape of hands and fingers vary considerably, as do the sizes of whistles in different keys, so you will have to work out your own way to comfortably cover the holes. Your top-hand pinky should just hang in the air, relaxing comfortably however it will, not touching the whistle at all. It is the only finger that gets to just come along for the ride and snooze.

3. Once your fingers are comfortable, make sure the thumb of your top hand is relaxed, and allow it to touch the underside of the whistle wherever it will rest most naturally. That is its optimal spot.

4. Next, approach the whistle with your *bottom* hand and, without your bottom thumb touching the whistle, gently lay B1, B2, and B3 on their respective finger holes. Once again, use the fleshy pads of your fingers to cover the holes as described above. As with the top hand, your bottom fingers should be fairly flat but will have a gentle arch to them as well, especially B2.

5. Once those fingers are comfortable, make sure the thumb of your bottom hand is relaxed and allow it to touch the whistle wherever it will rest most naturally. That is *its* optimal spot.

6. Now, lay the relaxed pinky of your bottom hand on the body of the whistle, somewhere below the B3 hole, wherever it wants to lay. If your hands are small it may only touch the body of the whistle with its tip. That's all right. It is important though that it be squarely *on* the whistle, not slipping off. You will probably need to experiment some with the bottom hand position in order to find the most comfortable way to cover the finger holes and rest the pinky on the whistle body.

If, with this relaxed hold, your bottom pinky simply will *not* reach the whistle, then you may want to explore anchoring with B3, covering its hole, as an alternative to anchoring with the pinky, when you are playing notes higher than E. But be aware of the flattening effect that this may have on the pitch of the notes you are playing, a factor which will vary from whistle to whistle.

7. Now, with all of your fingers in place and keeping them very relaxed, straighten out your poor aching back and simply lift the whistle with you. This is it: the basic hold.

Now we'll examine the mechanics of this more closely.

THE FIRST ANCHOR POINT: THE LIPS

The whistle should never touch your teeth. Place the whistle in the center of your lips, not off to one side or the other. I will explain the reasons for this soon.

There is no need to squeeze *at all* with your lips. Doing so will create unnecessary and potentially harmful tension in your face, head, and neck. Simply place the tip of the mouthpiece between your lips. If you are relaxed you will feel the slight weight of the mouthpiece resting on your lower lip.

Only the tip of the mouthpiece should be placed between the lips, just enough of it so that your lips can make an airtight seal around the windway (the opening in the tip of the mouthpiece that forms the beginning of the air channel). Most of the inexpensive whistles have a straight windway. Note that if you have a whistle with an arched or curved windway, you may have to place the mouthpiece a tiny bit further into your mouth in order to be sure you are completely sealing the entire perimeter of the windway with your lips.

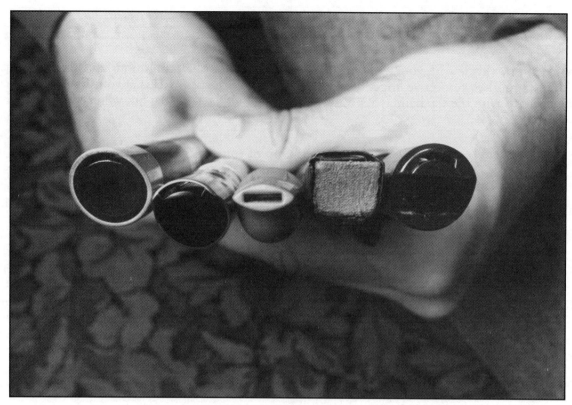

*Figure 5-3. The straight and curved windway openings of several different models of whistles.
Left to right: Abell, Copeland, Generation, Clarke, Susato.*

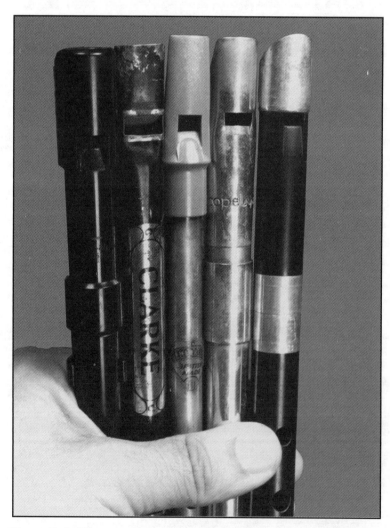

*Figure 5-4. The mouthpieces of several different models of whistles.
Left to right: Susato, Clarke, Generation, Copeland, Abell.*

Regardless of the shape of the windway, make sure there is no air escaping from your lips that is not traveling through the whistle.

Everyone's lips are different, but for me I need only place about one-quarter inch of the mouthpiece between my lips to achieve this seal. Experiment and find out how this works for you.

Now remove the whistle but keep your lips as they were when sealing the windway. When you blow air through your lips you will see that this kind of blowing resembles the way you might cool down a teaspoonful of hot soup held a few inches away from and below your lips, or the way you might try to gently alter or blow out a candle flame a few inches away and below your mouth, or the way you might spit out a watermelon seed. Feel the shape of the airstream with your hand.

As you get comfortable with the whistle you are going to learn to use the opening, or *aperture*, between your lips to help control and shape the flow of air. Now is the time to realize something important: **You will often want to blow a stream of air through the whistle that is *narrower* than the windway.** I'll explain the reasons for this later in the chapter.

You will control the size and shape of the airstream by changing the size and shape of the aperture between your lips. *If you place the whistle too far into your mouth, your lips will have no way to shape the airstream.* Try placing the whistle in too far, blow some air, and you will see what I mean. If you play this way, as many people unfortunately do, the shape of your airstream will be invariable, limited to the size and shape of the windway itself. You will see soon that a more focused airstream can be very useful.

Now try this. While holding the whistle as shown in Figure 5-2, blow air *straight* through the windway of the whistle. Sit or stand up straight, looking straight ahead, and keep your arms and upper body relaxed. If you do these things, you will find that you are holding the whistle at an angle approximately like that shown in Figure 5-5 below.

Figure 5-5. Holding the whistle at a proper angle so there is no kink or bend in the airstream.

Still looking straight ahead, notice that if you now raise or lower your hands, and thereby change the angle of the whistle in relation to your torso, two things happen. First, the air stream now has a kink or bend in it. The air has to go around a bend as it escapes the aperture between your lips and enters the windway. Playing this way will reduce the responsiveness of your whistle and adversely affect its tone and volume. Second, if you hold the whistle at one of these incorrect angles for very long you will begin to feel tension and fatigue developing in your arms, shoulders, upper back, and perhaps elsewhere.

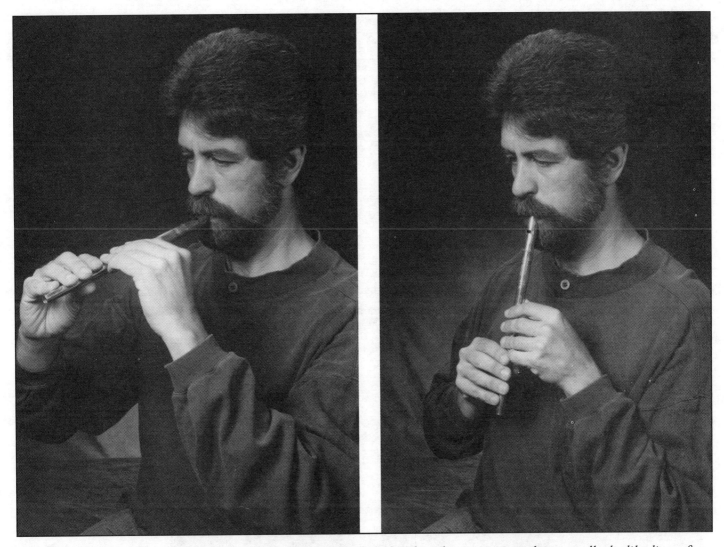

Figure 5-6. Two incorrect holding angles which cause a kink or bend in the airstream and, eventually, bodily discomfort.

Experiment with this angle, paying attention to preserving a straight airflow through the whistle and the relaxation of your body. As everyone's body is different, your correct holding angle may not be exactly the same as mine, but it should be close. As you find your correct position, close you eyes and *remember how it feels*. Take your time. You can also form a mental image of it by taking a look in a mirror. Do you see raised shoulders or other signs of tension?

You may not always play looking straight ahead. It is natural enough to find yourself looking a bit downward at times while you play. But notice that when you do so you need to adjust your upper body so that you are still blowing your air straight through the whistle. Notice also that this posture tends to close your throat a bit and restrict the capacity of your lungs. It is certainly better to play looking straight ahead and with an erect, upright posture. Similarly, twisting your body towards the right or left while playing restricts your lung capacity and puts stress on your spine.

Once you have fully explored this holding angle, let's take a look at a different one. See Figure 5-7 on the following page.

Figure 5-7. The whistle held in line with the spine and the direction of airflow.

Notice that the whistle is held straight up and down. The tip is not pointing to the left or right. The instrument is in line with the spine and the direction of airflow. This angle is also important in achieving the optimum responsiveness, tone, and volume of your instrument.

THE SECOND ANCHOR POINT: THE TOP THUMB

If you need to, return now to our table top exercise to re-establish the basic hold (see pp. 66-67).

The job of your top thumb is three-fold.

First, it helps to support the weight of the whistle, along with your bottom thumb and lower lip.

Second, it serves to maintain the position of the top hand. When playing C-sharp, the thumb will be the only part of the top hand that is touching the instrument. If it were not touching, then after every C-sharp you would have to re-establish your top-hand position.

Third, it supplies a tiny, but necessary, amount of opposing force to T1, T2, and T3, making it much easier for them to seal their holes securely.

The thumb's exact placement on the back of the whistle is unimportant. What is important is that it is as relaxed as possible and is not causing any strain to the rest of the hand. There is no reason to squeeze with your thumb. If you are squeezing with your thumb you are also squeezing with at least one of your other top hand fingers. This means undue hand tension, which you must eliminate.

The Third Anchor Point: the Bottom Thumb

The job of your bottom thumb is also three-fold.

First, it helps to support the weight of the whistle, along with your top thumb and lower lip.

Second, it serves to help maintain the position of the bottom hand, a job that is shared in this case by the bottom pinky. When playing the notes from G up to C-sharp, inclusively, B1, B2, and B3 will be off the whistle and the bottom thumb and pinky maintain the bottom hand's position.

Third, it supplies a tiny but necessary amount of opposing force to B1, B2, and B3, making it much easier for them to seal their holes securely.

As with the top thumb, the bottom thumb's exact placement on the back of the whistle is unimportant. What is important is that it is as relaxed as possible and is not causing any strain to the rest of the hand.

The Fourth Anchor Point: the Bottom Pinky

This seems to be the most controversial anchor point, though all of the fine, experienced whistle players I have seen use it, or in some cases B3 as an alternative to the bottom pinky. Whereas the thumbs and lips are obvious anchor points, most novices don't think of using the bottom pinky. Not using it, or another approach that accomplishes the same result, gives rise to several kinds of problems and unconscious compensations.

The weight of the whistle is ably supported by the lower lip and the thumbs. The thumbs exert a small upward force on the whistle. A small downward force is needed to balance the hold and make the instrument secure. If you do not use the bottom pinky to supply that downward force, it must be supplied by one or more of the playing fingers, or by clamping down with the lips on the mouthpiece, both of which are bad ideas. The playing fingers need to be completely unencumbered to do their myriad of playing jobs. Trying to hold the whistle securely in place with the lips compromises the embouchure and causes facial tension, plus it just doesn't work very well. Remember that unnecessary tension inhibits musicality. The term *embouchure*, used mainly in connection with the flute and brass instruments, refers to changes made in the disposition of the lips and mouth to affect the sound and response of the instrument.

Players who don't anchor with the bottom pinky (or alternately, B3) unconsciously compensate for not doing so. The situation is not very problematic while playing D, E, or F-sharp, but once B1, B2, and B3 are off their holes, the whistle becomes more and more unstable as more of the top hand playing fingers are lifted from their holes. Without the bottom pinky on the whistle, as you move from G to A to B it becomes increasingly difficult to hold the whistle steady and secure. When playing C-sharp, with all of the playing fingers off the whistle, you get into real trouble. In these situations many players unknowingly use the side of their B1 finger to exert some downward force, or squeeze the whistle between B1 and the bottom thumb. Needless to say, this is an awkward and clumsy strategy. Using the bottom pinky prevents these problems and insures that the whistle is always steady and secure.

The only time when the bottom pinky should be lifted off the whistle is when performing something called a strike on the note E. This subject is covered in Chapter 8.

Note that if you play the Boehm-system flute, now or in the future, your bottom pinky will usually operate the E-flat, C-sharp or C-natural key and thus becomes a playing finger. Some players of keyed simple-system flutes make frequent use of these keys as well. When you use these keys you ordinarily have all or almost all of your other playing fingers on the flute as well, so the steadiness of the instrument should not be an issue. However, on the flute you may prefer to use your bottom thumb as an anchor point instead of your bottom pinky. For more on this, see *An Alternate Anchor: Using the Bottom Thumb Instead of the Bottom Pinky* on pp. 91-92 of Chapter 6.

Take Care of Your Body

Like any other athletic activity, playing the whistle, though it may seem quite harmless, subjects you to the stresses of very repetitive movements and postures and certain immobile body positions. Holding unnecessary muscle tension or assuming and holding uncomfortable positions can lead to physical pain and problems. *Always listen to your body.* It wants to relax.

Posture and Breathing

With any wind instrument it makes sense to have full and unimpeded use of your lung capacity. This is especially true considering the nonstop nature of most traditional Irish music. With the tin whistle you need to be able to inhale deeply and very quickly in order to not interrupt the flow of the music.

Having an upright spine enables you to use your diaphragm to breathe deeply and to relax your entire air passage. Don't stoop over when playing. If you are sitting, sit forward on the edge of your chair. Some people find that it helps their playing posture to imagine that they have a string pulling up from the top of their head or their breastbone toward the ceiling. Think of being as tall as you can.

Get Comfortable with Fingering and Playing the Notes of the Low Octave

Before you proceed further in this chapter it would be wise to make sure that you can comfortably and reliably finger and sound all the notes in the low octave of the whistle. A fingering chart for the tin whistle appears in Appendix C on pp. 452-453.

Start with C-sharp (all holes open) and work your way down the D-major scale, adding fingers one at a time, making sure that each finger is sealing its hole completely before adding another finger. Completely sealing the holes is not something that comes naturally at first to most people. It takes some practice to develop the needed tactile sensitivity, control, and coordination.

To sound the low-octave notes you need to blow with a moderate force, enough to fill the instrument and produce a solid, low tone, but not so forcefully that you jump up into the second octave. Some experimentation will reveal a way of blowing that is usable for now.

Be sure to learn the names of the notes so you can automatically associate them with their fingerings. Even if you don't read music and never intend to, you really do need to know the names of the notes so that you can communicate with other musicians. This will also help you be able to think more clearly about the music you play.

Practice playing through all the possible combinations of notes, not just the adjacent ones, and learn to move the necessary groups of fingers together as coordinated units. These tasks are more difficult for some people than for others. Be patient with yourself. Try working out some simple tunes by ear, such as easy nursery rhymes that you learned as a child. My book, *The Essential Tin Whistle Toolbox*, contains exercises specifically for this purpose.

Adjusting the Overall Pitch of the Whistle

Some whistles are made in two pieces to allow for easy adjustment of the overall length of the whistle for tuning purposes. You can adjust your overall pitch higher (by pushing in to shorten the whistle) or lower (by pulling out to lengthen the whistle) to match the pitch of other instruments. Experiment and find a position that works well most of the time. You can then fine-tune the instrument as required. Note that excessive lengthening of the whistle's length will adversely affect the *intonation* (or "in-tuneness") of the intervals of the whistle's own scale.

Clearly, when you shorten or lengthen the whistle you are raising or lowering all of its notes. However, it is not obvious, yet very important to know, that this pitch change is not uniform. The pitch of certain notes changes more than the pitch of others. For any given note, the closer the lowest uncovered tone hole is to the foot of the whistle, the smaller the change in pitch.

Here is an example. On my small D whistle, with the tuning slide closed (i.e. fully pushed in) the distance from the cutting edge of the fipple to the center of the B3 hole is about 8.5 inches. This is the length of the vibrating air column that produces low E, B3 being the lowest uncovered tone hole. The distance from the cutting edge of the fipple to the center of the T1 hole is about 4.25 inches. This is the length of the vibrating air column that produces C-sharp in the low register, T1 being the lowest uncovered tone hole. If I pull out the tuning slide by one-quarter inch, I increase the lengths of these air columns to 8.75 inches and 4.5 inches respectively. In the case of E, this is a lengthening of about 2.9%, while for C-sharp this is a lengthening of about 5.9%. It follows that lengthening the whistle by one-quarter inch will lower the pitch of the C-sharp (the higher note) quite a bit more than it will lower the pitch of the E (the lower note). If you lengthen your whistle as far as it will safely go, you will experience this effect in the extreme.

If you have a one-piece whistle with a plastic mouthpiece that is glued onto a metal tube, you may be able to melt the glue so that the mouthpiece becomes movable. Try dipping the mouthpiece into very hot water to melt the glue, taking care not to melt the plastic. Then remove the mouthpiece and clean the molten glue out of it and off of the metal tube. When you put the mouthpiece back on, you will hopefully be able to adjust it in order to correct the overall pitch of the whistle.

TAKING A BREATH WHILE PLAYING

You will take frequent and quick breaths while playing the whistle. When you take a breath keep the whistle in place. Let the mouthpiece rest on your lower lip and open your mouth just a tiny bit so you can take air in quickly.

CLEARING THE WINDWAY

If the tone sounds stuffy or you can't produce any sound, there is probably a build-up of saliva or condensation in the windway of the whistle. This happens quite routinely, especially when you are salivating more than usual, such as soon after eating. It also happens more when the whistle is cold. There are two good ways to clear the windway.

One is to simply inhale *through* the whistle, keeping the whistle at your mouth as in normal playing and not opening your mouth. This way you will suck back in the moisture that is causing the problem. This is the method to use when you don't want to interrupt your playing. It is not a good way to get a fast, deep breath, however.

The other way is to stop playing, place a finger over the window of the mouthpiece, and blow forcefully enough through the whistle to clear out the clogging moisture. If you don't place your finger over the window you will produce quite a loud and shrill noise.

Figure 5-8. Covering the window of the mouthpiece while blowing to clear the windway.

75

Make Sure You Completely Cover the Holes

If you get squeaking or weak sounding notes, air may well be leaking out of some finger hole or holes. The more holes you are trying to cover the more likely you are to experience this difficulty. This is a very common problem for beginners. As you place more fingers on the holes, very often one or more fingers that are already covering holes will shift a bit without your knowledge and an air leak will result. Before long this problem will disappear.

The Two Registers, or Octaves, of the Tin Whistle

In traditional Irish music we confine ourselves to playing in the lower two octaves of the instrument's range. It is possible to play into the third octave, but such notes, which are quite loud and shrill, are not called for in traditional Irish playing. If you wish to explore them, feel free, but warn your neighbors first.

A quick glance at the fingering chart shown on pp. 452-453 reveals that the fingerings for the two registers are basically the same. The ways that you alter and control the airstream determine the register and the intonation of any given note.

"Kicking Up" into the Second Octave

Whistle players commonly say that you just "blow harder" to move from the first to the second octave. What actually happens when one blows harder in this way is something quite subtle and complex, though it is something that most players learn to do unconsciously, as I did.

By the way, it's interesting to know that when you "kick up" into the second octave you are forcing the air column inside the whistle to vibrate at the first overtone of a fundamental note. When you play in the low octave you are playing fundamental notes. I won't get into the physics, acoustics, and music theory of these matters here. If you are curious, I recommend that you read one of the many good books that address those subjects.

When I examine how I move from the lower octave to the upper octave I find that there are three, and sometimes four, different subtle changes happening at the same time that combine to provide the necessary increase in air speed. By the way, it is an increase in air *speed*, and not air volume or pressure, that is required.

Let's look at the example of moving from low E to high E, blowing a continuous stream of air with no tongue or throat articulation on either note.

First, I notice that my abdominal muscles push out my air a very slight bit harder.

Second, I notice a change in my throat. Looking in the mirror I see my Adam's apple rise and retreat a bit into my neck. This throat change is more dramatic than the abdominal one. I decrease the amount of space inside my throat by changing the shape of the back of my tongue, which in turn forces the air to travel faster through my throat. Reducing the diameter of this air passage by even a few millimeters has a large impact on the speed of the air traveling through it.

Third, I notice a very slight narrowing of the shape of the aperture between my lips, which forces the air to travel faster through them.

A fourth change that can be used, though it is not used in this example, is to give the higher note an attack with a quick puff of air from a tongue or throat articulation.

The first two changes, in the abdomen and the throat, happen quite automatically. Even in beginning whistle classes I have found that absolute novices do these things naturally and without awareness, when prompted to move a note from the low to high octave. (Actually it was a student in one of these classes that noticed the throat change and pointed it out to me. I had been unaware of it for over twenty years.)

As you notice the changes that happen in your throat, take care to just observe them. Don't try to tighten your throat more than it naturally does on its own, or you could inadvertently introduce undue muscle tension.

The third change, the aperture or embouchure change, doesn't come naturally to all players. First of all, many whistle players, as mentioned above, hold the mouthpiece too far inside their mouth to be able to affect the airstream in this way. Some others use aperture changing techniques quite naturally and unconsciously. All players should become aware of these techniques because they are very useful, in more ways than just helping to produce the octave jump.

Tin Whistle Embouchure

These aperture changing techniques can be properly called tin whistle embouchure.

A commonly held myth is that the tin whistle is just a "blow and go" instrument, one that can offer great sophistication in fingering embellishment possibilities but is strictly primitive when it comes to blowing. When you take a closer look and do some experimentation, you discover instead that there are unexpected possibilities in nuance and fine control in the blowing of the instrument, particularly with fine handmade whistles. Inexpensive, mass-produced whistles tend to be less responsive to embouchure.

The whistle's range of dynamics and tone colorations is smaller, to be sure, than that of the flute and many other instruments, but it is significant nonetheless. The use of these possibilities, whether conscious or not, is one of the things that distinguishes fine whistle players.

The abdominal breath support and throat narrowing combine to speed up the flow of air that arrives at the front of the mouth. Now, with embouchure changes, you can further speed up the air flow *without* having to blow more forcefully, thus using your air supply more efficiently. This means you won't run low on air as soon. Plus, you can *focus* the airstream.

Both the speeding up and the focusing of the air stream help correct for pitch. Try this. Blow a low E and then increase the air speed, *only* with the abdomen and throat, just by the *minimum* amount required to cause the jump into the second octave. You'll hear that the high note is very flat in pitch. More air speed is required to bring it up to the correct level. That means, if you are *not* using embouchure, that you need to support the breath more with your abdominal muscles and/or narrow your throat more to create enough air speed to bring the note up to the correct pitch level. If you use embouchure to aid in the process, you don't have to expend as much energy with your abdomen or use up as much air to achieve the same result.

Narrowing the airstream with the lips also has the added benefit of giving the tone of the instrument more focus and clarity. This effect can be heard when playing notes in the low octave as well as the high. I also notice that when blowing with a more focused airstream that a fine whistle will respond more quickly to finger movements.

Your lips can narrow the airstream in both the horizontal and vertical dimensions. I was recently surprised to find, upon checking in a mirror, that the narrowing I do occurs as much or more in the vertical axis as in the horizontal. The muscles used are much the same as the ones used in controlling flute embouchure, i.e. the muscles of the lips and the lower cheek areas. There is no need for tension in your upper cheeks.

Playing a Whistle in Tune

As you now see, after trying the pitch experiment described above, the tin whistle does not play in tune of its own accord. It is a variable-pitch instrument.

Electronic tuning machines attempt to measure the fundamental frequency of a note and compare it to the pitch standard that we call *equal temperament*. This provides us with a useful starting point, a good way to establish whether *overall* we are playing our whistle sharp or flat of the generally accepted standard pitch level of A440. Once we have warmed the whistle up to room temperature, and then to breath temperature, then adjusted our tuning slide or mouthpiece so it seems we are playing at the right overall pitch level, next we need to attend to the intonation of the individual notes that we play.

You may have noticed that when different players try out the same whistle, one may make it sound more in tune to your ear than other players do. No whistle has inherently perfect intonation; or perhaps it is more accurate to say the meaning of "in tune" is subjective. It necessarily changes from situation to situation and it often involves compromise when playing with other people. Experienced players do their best to play what sounds sweet to their ear in any given situation. That personal judgment of good intonation usually does not conform to equal temperament. Instead, we tend to prefer the sound of "pure intervals." It may be more useful to think of playing in-tune intervals rather than in-tune notes, for it is the relationship between notes that we are really tuning.

For instance, sometimes the third degree of the Ionian mode (or major scale)—let's consider F-sharp in the D-Ionian mode—sounds better to our ears, in relation to D (the tonic note), if it is played slightly flat of an equal tempered F-sharp. In another mode, such as E Dorian, a sweet or correct sounding F-sharp may be sharper that than the sweet F-sharp of D Ionian. Why this is so is a long story, one written about much by others, having to do with pure intervals and the harmonic series. I won't delve far into this controversial area. Suffice it to say that equal temperament is a rather artificial, though very useful, system that is not based closely on the natural harmonic series. It was developed initially for keyboard instruments. When given a choice, our ears usually prefer the sweeter, pure intervals.

When we play unison melodies with fixed-intonation equal-tempered instruments, such as accordions, concertinas, and keyboard instruments, we need to adjust to them, or at least compromise. When we are accompanied by instruments such as guitars and bouzoukis, we may also need to make some adjustments. The open strings of fretted string instruments are not always tuned to equal temperament, but their frets do produce equal tempered intervals. This is a tricky area. As always, let your ear lead the way.

Add to these considerations the fact that whistle makers have had their own differing opinions and aesthetics about how to adjust the inherent intonation of their instruments. (With inexpensive, mass-produced whistles, similar choices have been made, but there are also quality-control problems inherent in the manufacturing process that often result in poorly tuned and inconsistent instruments.)

You may have noticed that with old simple-system flutes, F-sharp tends to be flat, A tends to be sharp, C-natural tends to be sharp, and C-sharp tends to be flat. At least that's how these notes sound compared to equal temperament. Those same pitch "distortions" are typically found in tin whistles and uilleann pipes. A very similar pattern is even observed in Irish fiddling. Since fiddlers determine their intonation by finger placement, and by comparison of fingered pitches to those of the open strings, these pitch "distortions" are clearly a matter of choice, though probably an unconscious or conditioned one. It seems that there is a kind of natural intonation "profile" or "dialect" that is inherent in the design of the simple-system instruments (flute, whistle, uilleann pipes, even the Neanderthal bone flute mentioned in Chapter 3) which is also inherent in the nature of traditional Irish music, and no doubt in other musical traditions as well.

We can certainly say that tin whistles do not naturally play in an equal-tempered scale. It is tempting to surmise that at least some of the intonation oddities of tin whistles were, and are, in fact intentional. Most of us prefer the subtle intonation "personality" that the simple-system instruments share. It takes time and experience to learn how to play the tin whistle and simple-system flute "in tune," but the kind of "in-tuneness" that most of us strive for, consciously or not, is not the same as the equal-tempered ideal that Boehm worked so hard to achieve in his new flute. Boehm-system flute players who succeed in sounding traditional do so, I feel, in part by emulating the simple-system intonation profile.

If you are a beginner, it will be hard for you to judge the intonation of a whistle, and hard to know how well it fits your own emerging aesthetic. You may want to start out on an inexpensive whistle. Once you gain experience and if you decide that whistle playing is important enough in your life, you would be well advised to invest in a good, hand-made instrument. Try out different models and ask more experienced players to try whistles out for you and give you their feedback.

All of this boils down to the fact that you yourself must make a whistle play in tune, to your own standards, by controlling your embouchure. To make a note sharper you must increase the speed of the airstream, and to make a note flatter you must decrease that speed. These adjustments can be made by subtle and quick changes in your throat, mouth, and lips. If you are listening well and you care about intonation, you can probably learn to make these adjustments unconsciously, especially as you get to know your whistle and its intonation profile more intimately. As always, listening is the key to success.

An Advanced Technique for Adjusting the Dynamics of High-Register Notes

It is possible to play the notes of the high register, from E on up, more quietly than usual without the pitch going flat. While playing one of these notes, roll your T1 finger very slightly off its hole, toward the foot of the whistle. This will uncover just a tiny bit of the top edge of the T1 hole, making the pitch of the note go sharp. To compensate for this, simultaneously blow a slower stream of air. The pitch will, as a result, assume its correct place and the note will sound quieter than usual. This is a difficult balancing act, especially when the music is moving fast. With lower pitched whistles, the T1 hole is larger and the technique is consequently easier to use. One could use this technique with the flute as well, but there are better ways to control flute dynamics.

Get to Know Your Whistle

Now that you are aware of a wide range of blowing and embouchure techniques you can explore them on your whistle and discover how it responds. Try the following experiments, first without tongue or throat articulations. Introduce articulations later if you like and see what effect they have.

• Find the *minimum* amount of air-speed change required to kick a given note up into the second octave.

• Listen to how flat the upper-register notes are when played this way.

• Try this on different notes and notice how things change, especially in your throat, as you move up and down the scale.

• Find out how much more air speed is necessary to bring the high-register notes into good tune with the low-register ones. Try blowing them *too* sharp and see how that feels. Explore the limits, and always listen.

• Try tuning the high-register notes with embouchure, and then without using embouchure. Notice the differences in tone quality when you do and don't use embouchure to tune the notes.

• Try playing some long notes and move in and out of using embouchure to alter the tone quality. Try to do this while keeping the pitch stable and see how your air usage changes.

If you are new to the whistle these may be difficult experiments. But try them, and return to them as your experience deepens.

The use of these air control techniques will eventually become second nature to you. Irish music often requires us to change rapidly, and sometime repeatedly, between the two registers. You will discover ways to use these techniques, and the tonguing techniques described in Chapter 20, to enhance your agility and fluidity as a player.

Long Tones

There is a warm-up exercise that is of special benefit to flute players which can be helpful for whistle players too, though it may not seem so at first. If you would like to read about it, turn to the section *Long Tones: Another Very Useful Exercise* on pp. 103-104 in Chapter 6.

Breathing, and Leaving Out Notes

As you have probably observed, there are virtually no breathing places built into traditional Irish music. We have to create them. With very few exceptions, such as some places in slow airs and other slow and moderate tunes, it does not work to sneak a breath between notes. Doing so almost always disrupts the flow and energy of the music, drawing attention to your breathing and away from the music. Whistle players must learn how to leave out notes, and shorten longer notes, in a musical and tasteful way. When this is done well, most listeners will not even notice your breathing.

This is a crucial subject for whistle and flute players. An in-depth discussion of it requires knowledge of ornamentation. Therefore I have placed Chapter 21, *Musical Breathing*, after the chapters on ornamentation. If you wish, you may skip ahead and look at that material at any time, however you will get more out of it once you have worked your way through the intervening parts of the book.

MANY BREATHING ISSUES ARE THE SAME FOR FLUTE AND WHISTLE PLAYERS

At this point please turn to the next chapter and read the following six sections, which appear on pp. 93-96: *Normal Breathing: Shallow and Automatic; Flute and Whistle Breathing: Deep and Controlled; Exercise: Get Acquainted with Your Diaphragm; Resistance Is Needed for Slow Breath Release; Flute Embouchure Offers Much More than Just Resistance;* and *Why the Tin Whistle is Limited in Comparison with the Flute*. Breathing and embouchure issues are more complex and involved in flute playing than in tin whistle playing, so I have placed these sections in the flute chapter, but the information given in them is very important for tin whistle players as well.

BREATHING EXERCISES

Good breath control is essential in tin whistle playing. Playing the larger whistles sometimes requires even more air than flute playing does. For some useful breathing exercises, see the section called *Breathing Exercises* on p. 104 in the next chapter.

SUBTLE BREATH PULSE OR WEIGHT

The flow of air that you blow is much like the hair of the fiddler's bow as it travels across the string. Just as a fiddler can change the pressure and speed of her bowstrokes to emphasize certain notes and to impart rhythmic stress, weight, or impulse, you can give such life to your music with changes in the qualities of your breath. Just as a fiddler can "lean into" the bow, you can "lean into" the breath.

We have much more capability in this regard on the flute than we have on the whistle, but even very subtle touches, as are possible on the whistle, can help bring your music to life beautifully. One way that good handmade whistles show their worth is that they offer you more capability to lean into the breath without adversely affecting pitch.

I elaborate upon the subject of subtle breath pulse in Chapter 10 in the sections *Rhythmic Emphasis Within the Long Roll* and *It's Alive—It Has a Pulse*, which appear on pp. 173-174. I suggest you work your way through the book to that point before delving into this aspect of breath and embouchure control.

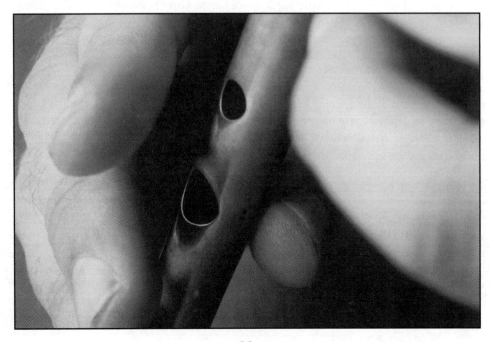

chapter 6: holding and blowing the flute

Throughout this chapter and the rest of this book, when I use the word "flute" I am referring to the Irish, or simple-system flute. If you are uncertain as to what I mean by this, please refer to Chapter 3.

A PHYSICAL RELATIONSHIP, AND MUCH MORE

The flute and the tin whistle have a great deal in common. If you have not yet read Chapter 5: *Holding and Blowing the Tin Whistle*, please turn to it now and read the first section, entitled *A Physical Relationship, and Much More*. This information is very important for both flute and tin whistle players.

A BRIEF NOTE ON POSTURE

As a flute player, your starting point for a relaxed body and the optimal use of your energy is an upright spine. This is central to allowing the free movement of your diaphragm and the relaxation of your air passages, shoulders, arms, neck, and head. Whether you play sitting or standing, make sure to keep both feet flat on the floor. If you are seated, sit forward on the edge of the chair. Most right-handed players find it helpful to place the left foot somewhat forward of the right foot when standing, the opposite being true for left-handed players. There is more about posture as it relates to breathing later in the chapter.

TAKE CARE OF YOUR BODY

When playing the tin whistle, it is easy to keep one's spine completely straight. Not so, unfortunately, with the flute. Since the instrument extends out to one side, the player's upper body is extended and twisted somewhat in that direction. This necessarily stresses the spine. Since this is a given of flute playing, and since we often play for hours on end, it is smart to avoid making the situation even worse by dropping the foot of the flute too far down or stooping over. It's a good idea to stop playing every now and then to move about to loosen up and give your spine a rest. Remember that playing the flute is an athletic activity that subjects your body to some peculiar stresses and asymmetrical postures. Holding unnecessary muscle tension or assuming and holding uncomfortable positions can lead to physical pain and problems. *Always listen to your body.*

PUTTING YOUR FLUTE TOGETHER

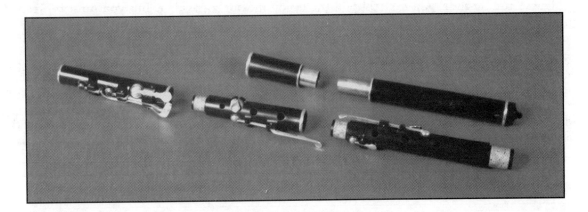

*Figure 6-1. A flute disassembled. In the top row, left to right, are the barrel and headjoint.
In the bottom row, left to right, are the footjoint, the bottom hand's joint, and the top hand's joint.*

If a flute does not have a tuning slide, it will not have a barrel. If you do have a tuning slide, keep the two parts of it assembled (not as pictured above) and push the slide together completely when you are done playing and put the flute in its case. This helps to keep the sliding surfaces of the parts clean.

Some flute makers combine into one piece the first two, second two, or all three of the pieces shown in the bottom row of this photo.

The flute pictured above has cork on its tenons. Sometimes tenons are wrapped with thread. Take good care of your corked or thread-wrapped tenons, as they are relatively delicate and vulnerable. Be sure corks are always well greased. Put the pieces of the flute together with a gentle turning motion to reduce stress on the tenons.

If you are playing an old flute for the first time, make sure that it is in as good a condition for playing as possible.

ADJUSTING THE TUNING SLIDE

Many flutes have a metal sleeve inside all or part of the barrel and headjoint that allows for easy adjustment of the overall length of the flute for tuning purposes. Most flute makers who include tuning slides design their instruments to play optimally with the tuning slide pulled out slightly. This allows you to adjust the overall pitch sharper (by pushing in the slide, shortening the flute) or flatter (by pulling out the slide, lengthening the flute) to match the pitch of other instruments. I recommend starting with your tuning slide pulled out slightly.

It is clear that when you shorten or lengthen the flute by adjusting the tuning slide you are raising or lowering all the notes of the flute. Not so obvious, but very important to know, is the fact that this pitch change is not uniform. The pitch of certain notes changes more than the pitch of others. For any given note, the closer the lowest uncovered tone hole is to the foot of the flute, the smaller the change in pitch.

Let's look at a real world example. On my flute, with the tuning slide closed (i.e. fully pushed in), the distance from the end of the headjoint cork to the center of the B3 hole is about 17 inches. This is the length of the vibrating air column that produces low E, B3 being the lowest uncovered tone hole. The distance from the end of the headjoint cork to the center of the T1 hole is about 9 inches. This is the length of the vibrating air column that produces C-sharp in the low register, T1 being the lowest uncovered tone hole. If I pull out the tuning slide by one-half inch, I increase the lengths of these two air columns to 17.5 inches and 9.5 inches, respectively. In the case of E, this is a lengthening of about 2.9%, while for C-sharp this is a lengthening of about 6.2%. It follows that pulling out the tuning slide by one-half inch will lower the pitch of the C-sharp (the higher note) quite a bit more than it will lower the pitch of the E (the lower note). If you pull your tuning slide out as far as it will safely go, you will experience this effect in its extreme.

Overall pitch is also affected by several other factors, including the position of your lower lip on the flute. I discuss this later in the chapter (see pp. 99-100). As you refine your embouchure, you may need to experiment with the position of your tuning slide. You will eventually find a position for it that works well most of the time. You can then fine-tune the instrument as required.

If you do not have a tuning slide, you can still pull the headjoint out somewhat. But you must be very careful that you don't pull it out so far that the joint becomes loose or wobbly. This distorts the shape of the bore and may put you in danger of having your flute fall apart while playing.

Once I played an old William Hall flute that had no tuning slide. I sometimes had to pull out the headjoint quite a bit to play in tune with other musicians. In 1980, using this flute, I was on a concert tour performing with the great fiddler Kevin Burke. He noticed that I liked to play with my eyes closed, tuning into the music and tuning out much of the outside world. Once, in the middle of a fast reel, Kevin let out a sudden blood-curdling scream that startled me so severely that I jumped and my flute came apart at the headjoint. Kevin would spring this trick on me whenever he thought I least expected it, and it always worked. I was an easy target.

When you assemble your flute, if you have a joint between the three top and three bottom finger holes, begin by lining up the six finger holes in a straight line. Initially line up the center of the embouchure hole with the line formed by connecting the centers of the six finger holes. Then, offset the center of the embouchure hole a small bit from this line by turning it in toward your mouth. This makes the instrument more comfortable to hold for most people. The maximum embouchure hole offset you will probably want to use can be seen by lining up the far edge of the embouchure hole, i.e. the edge that is opposite your lips, with the line formed by connecting the centers of the six finger holes.

The degree of offset is something to experiment with over time. A very small adjustment can make for major changes in your physical relationship with your flute. Since you will tend to position the flute consistently in relation to your lips, rotating the embouchure hole *toward* you has the effect of rotating the finger holes out and *away* from you. This in turn has a major impact on the orientation of your fingers, hands, arms, and upper body.

If your flute has a joint between the two groups of three finger holes, you have another option to experiment with. You can leave the six finger holes aligned in a straight line. But if you have small hands, short fingers, short arms, a flute with a large outer diameter, or any combination of these things, you may find that you are more comfortable offsetting the joint containing the lower three finger holes slightly toward you.

THE FINGER HOLES, AND CONSIDERATIONS FOR LEFT-HANDED PLAYERS

The six finger holes of the flute are covered and uncovered by the middle three fingers of your two hands. Most people find that it feels most natural to use their dominant hand for the three holes at the bottom of the flute, i.e. the holes furthest from the embouchure hole.

Therefore, if you are left-handed, you may feel it is more natural for you to use your left hand for these bottom holes, in which case the flute will extend out to your left side instead of to your right. If you have a flute without keys, this may seem like a perfectly fine way to proceed. But the keywork on multikeyed flutes is very definitely designed for right-handed use. Yet, some left-handed people do play the flute this way, an example being the great Irish flute players Cathal McConnell and Seamus Tansey.

However, if you are new to the flute I would advise you to try the right-handed way of playing. If this feels workable to you, so much the better. I say this for several reasons. First of all, even if playing left-handed seems to work fine on your current flute, you may move on to other flutes in the future. And some embouchure holes, even on keyless flutes, are not undercut symmetrically but are designed to be blown into from one direction only. It may be possible to find a flute maker who will make you a left-handed instrument, complete with left-handed keywork. This would no doubt be quite an expensive option.

Having said these things, I have to admit that, not being left-handed myself, I really cannot relate to the challenge of being left-handed and playing right-handed. You'll have to decide for yourself whether it is something worth considering. I know that when I try to hold my flute left-handed my brain seems to turn inside out and I shudder at the thought of ever having to play that way. But then I have been playing right-handed since 1973.

COMFORT AND STABILITY: THE ATTRIBUTES OF A GOOD FLUTE HOLD

When you hold your flute, you want to be comfortable, as relaxed as possible, and have no worries, conscious or subconscious, about dropping it. You also want to keep the flute quite still while your playing fingers do their jobs. A wobbling or jiggling flute can disturb the embouchure. Shortly we will examine the anchor points of the flute hold and how to establish them.

There are two very different ways of holding the flute that are in common usage among Irish flute players. The one I use and recommend I call the *normal hold* as this is the kind of hold used by most flutists, including classical and baroque players.

Figure 6-2. Playing the flute using the normal hold.

The other way of holding the flute I call the *piper's hold* since it resembles in some important ways the hold that uilleann pipers use with their vertical chanters.

The difference between the two lies in the top hand position. With the piper's hold, the thumb of the top hand pushes the flute against the player's lower lip. In the normal hold, it is the base of the top hand's T1 finger that performs this function.

Figure 6-3. Playing the flute using the piper's hold. Note the top hand position.

During my first few years of playing I used the piper's hold, but later made the switch to the normal hold. My initial motivation for making the change was that I became interested in using the B-flat key on my flute. That required the use of my top thumb, something that was impossible using the piper's hold. Usage of some of the other keys was also awkward with this hold.

Though I had thought that I was quite comfortable using the piper's hold, I realized later that the normal hold was more relaxing for my left hand. I will elaborate on this point later in the chapter, once I have discussed the anchor points for holding the flute.

FINGERING NOTATION

In this book, I will call the hand nearest the embouchure hole the *top hand*. The hand nearest the other end, the foot of the flute, I will call the *bottom hand*. Either of these can be the right or left hand, though more people by far play with the left hand as the top hand and the right hand as the bottom hand.

I call the top-hand index finger T1, the top-hand middle finger T2, and the top-hand ring finger T3. Similarly, I call the bottom-hand index finger B1, the bottom-hand middle finger B2, and the bottom-hand ring finger B3. This notation system works equally well for right-handed and left-handed players.

*Figure 6-4. The right-handed hold (above) and the
left-handed hold (below), with fingering indications.*

THE FIVE ANCHOR POINTS OF THE FLUTE

If you have read the section in the previous chapter on the tin whistle anchor points, you will see that things are quite different when it comes to the flute.

As stated above, I recommend the normal hold over the piper's hold. *Everything that follows pertains to the normal hold.*

Learning the anchor points is one of the most critical elements of your physical relationship with the flute. When you learn to hold the flute so that you can be relaxed throughout your hands, wrists, arms, and upper body and never be in fear, consciously or subconsciously, of dropping the instrument, then you open the way for establishing the habit of physical and mental relaxation essential for being fully musical.

The six fingers we use to cover and uncover the finger holes (see Figure 6-4) should, with one exception, have *absolutely nothing* to do with holding or stabilizing the flute. Their *only* job (and a huge job it is, as you will see as you work your way through this book) is to freely interact with the finger holes.

The one exception to this involves the top-hand index finger, or T1. The base or bottom joint of that finger is one of the primary anchor points for holding and supporting the flute. Its role in supporting the instrument, however, need not impede its freedom to perform its fingering tasks.

PRIMARY AND SECONDARY ANCHOR POINTS

There are two different approaches to anchoring the flute that are in common use. I will elaborate here the one that I prefer. Another approach, which you may prefer, is briefly described on pp. 91-92 in the section entitled *An Alternate Anchor: Using the Bottom Thumb Instead of the Bottom Pinky.*

Of the five anchor points, three are primary and are essential to holding and supporting the weight of the flute.

The three primary anchor points are:

1. Your lower lip

2. The base or bottom joint of your top-hand index finger, i.e. T1

3. Your bottom pinky

The two secondary anchor points do not play a role in supporting the weight of the flute, but are important for other reasons which I will talk about later in the chapter. They are:

1. Your top thumb

2. Your bottom thumb

Figure 6-5. Here you can see the three primary anchor points: the lower lip, the base of T1, and the bottom pinky.

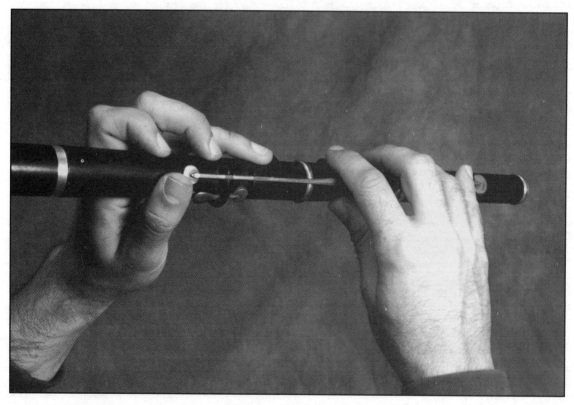

Figure 6-6. Here you can see the two secondary anchors, the top and bottom thumbs, as well as another view of the T1 and bottom pinky anchors.

EXERCISE: DISCOVERING YOUR NORMAL HOLD

Following the 20 steps in the exercise below will help you begin to find your optimal way of holding your flute. There are so many variables involved: the sizes and shapes of your fingers, hands, arms, shoulders, and neck, the outer diameter of your flute, its length and weight, the sizes of its finger holes, etc. It will take some time to become comfortable with your flute. This exercise is quite lengthy and involved. I recommend taking your time with it and returning to it often.

You can stand or sit for this exercise. Take care to maintain relaxation at all times. It can be helpful to face a mirror. *The following describes the right-handed hold. You may reverse the hands if you wish for the left-handed hold.* If you are sitting, you may place this book on a table in front of you. If you are standing, place the book somewhere nearby within easy view, perhaps on a music stand.

1. Face straight ahead. Rest the headjoint of the flute on your left shoulder and hold the foot of the flute cradled in the palm of your right hand in front of you. Hold the flute so that the tone holes are facing the ceiling. Rest your right elbow against your abdomen if you like. Allow your left arm to droop relaxed by your side. The weight of the flute is being supported only and entirely by your left shoulder and right hand.

2. Now, raise your left arm and place only the fingertip of T1 on its hole. No other part of your left hand is touching the instrument. Allow your left thumb to rest, relaxed, under the flute, not touching it. Your fingers are relaxed and curved. Now adjust your left arm so that the back of your hand, your wrist, and your forearm form a fairly straight line. (This is strictly temporary.)

3. Next, place the fingertip of T2 on its hole. Both T1 and T2 remain curved and relaxed. Your left thumb is still not touching the flute. Note that if you have long fingernails you may not be able to place the tips of these fingers on their holes. I recommend keeping your nails short, at least on your left hand.

4. Now, no longer trying to maintain the straight line that you have formed with your left hand, wrist, and forearm, slowly rotate your left wrist to the left, that is toward your body or counterclockwise, keeping T1 and T2 nicely arched with their fingertips on their holes, until the base of T1 comes into contact with the flute, somewhere along T1's bottom joint. The tips of T1 and T2 will naturally shift on their holes as you rotate your wrist. Allow your left thumb to swing under the flute if it has not already done so. It is still not touching the flute. Allow your left wrist to drop and relax naturally. It will be bent in somewhat, toward your chest, when you are playing.

5. Now, let your left thumb come into contact with the flute wherever and however it most naturally wants to, keeping it relaxed. The weight of the flute is still completely supported by your left shoulder and right hand. If you have a B-flat thumb key, do not rest your left thumb on the key itself. Do not squeeze with your thumb and T1 *at all*. Stay relaxed.

6. Next, allow T3 to drop onto its hole, however it will. For most people this finger will be much less arched than T1 and T2 and it may be nearly flat. The fleshy part of the pad of the finger will probably be covering the hole instead of the fingertip. Let your left pinky relax and hang in the air wherever it will, nicely curved. Do not place it on the flute or hold the top of it against the underside of the flute. It should be ready to operate the G-sharp key if you have one. If you don't have one on your present flute, you may have one on a future flute.

7. At this point, take stock of your left hand. *Relaxation is the top priority.* Experiment with changing which part of the base of T1 comes into contact with the flute. Keeping your playing fingers on the flute, try shifting the T1 contact point around, allowing your left thumb and wrist to move in accommodation. Try moving your playing fingers around a bit with each new trial placement of the base of T1. Find what is most comfortable for you. Allow your left wrist to relax and drop. Its position will change anyway once you put the flute up to your mouth.

8. The foot of the flute is still resting in the palm of your right hand. Now find a shelf or some support that is about shoulder height or a bit lower and rest the foot of the flute safely and securely upon it so that you can remove your right hand. Let your right arm hang down and totally relax it for a few moments.

9. Now raise your right arm, forming a fairly straight line with the back of your hand, your wrist, and forearm. Don't raise your shoulder. Allow your right thumb to hang somewhere in the air below the flute, not touching the flute, as you place the fleshy pad of the top joint of B3, the ring finger of your right hand, onto the bottom finger hole of the flute. The finger should be fairly flat with a slight arch to it.

10. Now let B1 fall naturally onto its finger hole, placing the fleshy pad of its first joint upon the hole. In doing this you may need to adjust the orientation of your right arm. Your bottom thumb is still not touching the flute.

11. Next place the fleshy pad of the top joint of B2 onto its hole. To do this, you will probably need to have more of an arch to this finger than you do with B1 and B3, due to its greater length. As a result, you may find that you cover the hole with a part of B2 that is closer to its tip. Now that you have all three of these fingers on the flute, adjust them as a group and find the most comfortable way to dependably cover and seal the holes. Some people prefer to straighten out B2 to match the arching of B1 and B3. In most cases, this will result in B2 covering its hole with an area of the finger that falls between the first and second joints of the finger. For some people, this is a problem, making it difficult for them to seal the hole, but others do just fine this way. Experiment and see what works for you.

12. Next, allow your right thumb to float up and come into contact with the flute, wherever it will most naturally.

13. Now, allow your right hand pinky to rest comfortably on the body of the flute, wherever it will. If you have an E-flat key, you may be able to rest the pinky on the key. If it is relaxed, it shouldn't accidentally depress the key, especially if you rest it near the fulcrum of the key instead of on its touch. (On the Boehm-system flute, this key is depressed most of the time, but this is rarely workable on the simple-system flute. Depressing this key often makes certain notes too sharp, particularly E.) If your pinky is relatively short, it may not reach the flute easily without adversely affecting the relaxed positions of B1, B2, and B3 that you have just established. In this case you may want to consider using the right thumb as an anchor instead. See *An Alternate Anchor: Using the Bottom Thumb Instead of the Bottom Pinky* on the next page.

14. Make whatever adjustments you would like to your right hand position. Experiment a bit and get comfortable.

The weight of the flute is still supported completely by your left shoulder and the shelf or support where the foot of the flute is resting. That is about to change. Keep all of your playing fingers on their holes and your thumbs and right pinky on the flute as you perform the rest of these steps.

15. Get ready to lift the flute off the shelf or support, still keeping the headjoint on your shoulder. To do this you are going to temporarily use your right thumb to help support the weight of the flute. Go ahead and do this now.

16. The next step is to prepare to lift the headjoint off of your shoulder. When you do this you will be supporting the majority of the flute's weight with the base of T1 and your left thumb. When you're ready, go ahead and do this.

17. Now bring the headjoint near to your mouth. Maintaining relaxation, allow the positions of your wrists to shift naturally as needed. Gently feel the near edge of the embouchure hole with the bottom edge or ridge of your lower lip, the place where the smooth skin of your lower lip meets the normal skin. You may slightly moisten this area of the flute with your tongue if you wish. Move your head slightly left and right, lightly brushing with your lip the near edge of the embouchure hole, and get a sense of its width and shape. When you're ready, place the center of the near edge of the embouchure hole against the center of the bottom edge or ridge of your lower lip. It may help you to look in a mirror as you do this. You're not going to do any blowing just yet.

Now you have established a contact point between your lower lip and the flute. Without moving anything very much, if at all, you are now going to make a few subtle changes in how you are supporting the flute. Make sure that all your playing fingers, your thumbs, and your right pinky are still in place.

18. Exerting a small bit of pressure with the base of T1, gently but firmly press the flute in against your lower lip and jaw. At the same time, with your right pinky exert a small amount of pressure in opposition to T1. Your jaw is, of course, also exerting a small force in opposition to T1. The axis of the flute should be parallel to your lips. In other words, the foot of the flute should not be pushed forward and away from you or pulled back in towards you.

19. You have now established the three primary anchor points: the lower lip, the base of T1, and the right pinky. Your thumbs are no longer needed to support the weight of the flute. If everything is set up right, at this point you could lift all of your playing fingers and both of your thumbs off the flute and still hold it solidly and securely with just the three primary anchor points. Before you try this you may need to once again adjust the contact point between the base of T1 and the flute. When you feel you are ready, give it a try.

20. Once you've found your most comfortable playing position, close your eyes and try to memorize how it feels. Take your time. When you open your eyes, look at the geometry of your fingers, hands, and arms and form a mental image of it. Look in a mirror and take in the entire picture of your upper body with the flute.

RESTING POSITION FOR THE PLAYING FINGERS

When any of the six playing fingers are not in motion or covering their holes, they should be in *resting position*, hovering relaxed very near their holes, about one-third to one-quarter inch above them. When you are relaxed, this is the position your fingers naturally want to assume. In this position, your fingers are close enough to their holes that you may at times feel your breath gently escaping from the finger holes. In resting position, your playing fingers are poised and ready for their next action.

A CLOSER LOOK AT THE THUMBS

Though the top thumb is not needed to support the weight of the flute, it is needed for other reasons. It helps to maintain the position of the top hand, as does the base of T1. When playing C-sharp the thumb and T1 will be the only parts of the top hand that are touching the instrument.

The thumb also supplies a tiny but necessary amount of opposing force to T1, T2, and T3, making it much easier for them to seal their holes securely.

If you have a B-flat key, the top thumb operates it and the thumb needs to be free to move for this purpose. This is an important reason why the top thumb should not be used to support the weight of the flute or to help insure its stability.

The thumb's exact placement on the back of the flute is unimportant. What is important is that it be as relaxed as possible and not be causing any strain to the rest of the hand. There is no reason at all to squeeze with your thumb. If you are squeezing with your thumb, you are also squeezing with the base of T1 and creating potentially harmful muscle tension in your left hand and arm. If you find yourself doing this, you *must* reevaluate how you are supporting the flute with T1 and find a better hand position that frees up your thumb. If this is a persistent problem, you may want to experiment with offsetting the embouchure hole in a different way (see *Alignment of the Finger Holes and Embouchure Hole* on p. 83).

Like the top thumb, the bottom thumb serves to help maintain the position of the bottom hand, a job that is shared in this case by the bottom pinky. When playing the notes from G up to C-sharp, B1, B2, and B3 will be off the flute and the bottom thumb and pinky maintain the bottom hand's position.

The bottom thumb also supplies a tiny but necessary amount of opposing force to B1, B2, and B3, making it much easier for them to seal their holes securely.

As with the top thumb, the bottom thumb's exact placement on the underside of the flute is unimportant. What is important is that it be as relaxed as possible and not be causing any strain to the rest of the bottom hand.

AN ALTERNATE ANCHOR: USING THE BOTTOM THUMB INSTEAD OF THE BOTTOM PINKY

There are players who prefer to anchor with the bottom thumb instead of the bottom pinky. This method was strongly advocated by Richard Shepherd Rockstro in his 1890 treatise.[i] I do not feel that this provides me as solid and secure a hold on the flute, but you may find that it works better for you, especially if your hands or fingers are too small to permit your bottom pinky to comfortably rest on the flute.

With this kind of hold the bottom thumb must provide a small amount of force that opposes the force of the base of T1. To accomplish this, you must place the thumb more on the side of the flute nearest to your chest, not as much on the underside of the flute. In this position the bottom thumb will be pushing the flute lightly away from your body. For most players, it will work best to place the thumb on the side of the flute between B1 and B2.

If you frequently use the bottom pinky to operate one or more keys, you may prefer this approach. Though the bottom pinky is no longer supplying a force opposing T1, some players who use this hold still touch the pinky to the flute for further stabilization.

A Further Comment on the Piper's Hold

I mentioned earlier that I felt the normal hold is more comfortable for the top hand than the piper's hold. With the normal hold, the weight and pressure that come to bear on the base of T1 are naturally transferred into and distributed throughout the rest of the hand, wrist, and forearm. It seems to me that with the piper's hold this weight and pressure are born much more by the top thumb alone, which is often put into an abnormally extended position. After playing for long periods of time with the piper's hold, I found that my thumb often became sore.

Uilleann pipers do use a hold similar to this, that is with the fingers of the top hand fairly flat, covering the finger holes with the fleshy pads of the fingers. But for them, the top thumb is not bearing weight and pressure. In fact, it is left free to cover and uncover the thumb hole on the back of the chanter. The tin whistle is held vertically like the chanter of the uilleann pipes, and its hold, which is very similar to that of the uilleann pipe chanter, also places no significant weight or stress on the top thumb. This piper's type of hold is natural for the tin whistle but is unnatural for the flute in my opinion.

Resting the Flute on the Shoulder—a Painful Posture

Some Irish flutists rest the end of the headjoint on their shoulder. This position causes them to keep their left shoulder unnaturally raised and their neck twisted and tilted severely to the left. It contorts their spine and constricts their air passages. I suppose it is one way, though a poor one, to compensate for not having found a suitable way to establish the T1 anchor point, for the weight of the flute is instead born by the left shoulder, which also provides opposing force to the lower jaw.

Getting Comfortable with Your Flute

It can take some time to get used to holding a flute. For many, it feels quite unnatural at first. If the anchor points are not working for you yet and you feel some apprehension, even in the back of your mind, that you might drop your flute, you may unconsciously start to compensate by gripping the flute in one way or another. Gripping has no part in a good flute hold. Relaxation is key. Try very hard to prevent gripping from creeping in.

Stay aware of the sensations in your body and be on the lookout for tightness and tension. If you are tight, tense, or sore try to understand why. Go through the exercise, *Discovering Your Normal Hold* again (see pp. 89-91), proceeding slowly step by step, and notice where problems arise. Experiment with the offset of the embouchure hole in relation to the finger holes (see *Alignment of the Finger Holes and Embouchure Hole* on p. 83). Try offsetting the lower three finger holes if your flute offers that capability. You can also try turning your head slightly to the left, letting your shoulders follow its lead. This is a position that most people adopt unconsciously but perhaps you have not done so. When you turn in this way, your shoulders are rotated somewhat to the left in relation to your pelvis.

A surprisingly large amount of our nervous system is devoted to *proprioception*, or body-position memory. In addition to nerves that tell our muscles what to do and nerves sending sensations to the spine and brain, there are huge bundles of nerves monitoring body position. These systems can be taught, which is why repeating a motion works. The more often you achieve your natural flute hold, and tell yourself that you have found it, the easier it will be to find it the next time. Fortunately, right ways to hold the flute feel better than wrong ways.

If troubles persist, consult with an experienced flute player or teacher. The hold is somewhat different for the modern flute, but the same principles apply on the whole.

TIME TO PUT AWAY YOUR POWDERED WIG

Johann Georg Tromlitz, in his 1791 treatise *The Virtuoso Flute-Player*[ii] offers this valuable advice for the working flutist:

> When the weather is very hot, and one perspires freely, one commonly loses one's embouchure in the course of playing, since the flute slips away from the place on the chin where it is supposed to rest, on account of the perspiration which prevents it from making firm contact, and impedes the progress of the piece. Quantz suggests a remedy: in such cases one should touch one's powdered hair or wig, and wipe the powder that sticks to the fingers onto that part of the chin so as to stop up the pores, and one will be able to play on without interference. But this is not correct; the powder does not stop up the pores, and the perspiration keeps on flowing, and now it mingles with the powder to form a viscous and slippery dough, far more injurious to the secure placement of the flute than perspiration alone. When I meet with this problem I wipe the perspiration away and continue to play. Meanwhile the most intelligent course is not to play any long, difficult and non-stop pieces during such hot weather.

NOW, ON TO POSTURE AND BREATHING

With any wind instrument, it makes sense to have full and unimpeded use of your lung capacity. This is especially true considering the nonstop nature of most traditional Irish music. With the flute, you need to be able to inhale deeply and very quickly in order to not interrupt the flow of the music.

Having an upright spine enables you to fully use your diaphragm, to breathe deeply, and to relax your entire air passage. Don't stoop over when playing. Some people find that it helps their playing posture to imagine that they have a string pulling up from the top of their head toward the ceiling or sky. You can also imagine this string pulling up from your chest or sternum. Imagine being as tall as you can.

Though it is impractical and uncomfortable to keep the flute absolutely parallel with the floor, it should not slant down too far. It is best to keep the flute in line with the lips so that the horizontal line of the aperture between your lips is parallel to the axis of the flute. Otherwise the embouchure can suffer. A slight tilt of the head is natural.

The following information on breathing and embouchure comes from various people, experiences, and resources I have encountered over the years, including in particular Walfrid Kujala's excellent book *The Flutist's Progress*.[iii]

NORMAL BREATHING: SHALLOW AND AUTOMATIC

There is no more normal an activity than breathing. We are always breathing, but we rarely attend to it.

Normal breathing is fairly shallow. At rest, we inhale and exhale about a pint of air. In between the exhale and the next inhale we pause for a brief period of repose, roughly equal in the length to the inhale and exhale phases. It's a regular cycle: inhale, exhale, rest; inhale, exhale, rest.

FLUTE AND WHISTLE BREATHING: DEEP AND CONTROLLED

In flute and whistle playing, an entirely different kind of breathing is required. We must learn to quickly take in a much greater quantity of air, sometimes as much as *eight* pints, in a half a second or less. We must also learn to release the air in a very slow and controlled manner. The pace of flute and whistle breathing is irregular, being determined by the phrasing, dynamics, and register of the music. And, *especially* in Irish music, there is no rest period between one exhalation and the next inhalation.

When playing the flute or whistle, you should inhale through your mouth rather than your nose. You can take in air much more quickly this way. It is not necessary to open your mouth very far.

You can inhale through both your mouth and nose, but if you do you will have to then close off your nose on the exhale so you don't waste valuable air that should be traveling only through the instrument. I had always thought this approach to be an unnecessary complication. But in contending with asthma, I have actually found it to be quite useful for me. It takes a good bit of practice to reach the point where it becomes second nature to inhale through both the mouth and nose and exhale only through the mouth.

Try this simple, powerful visualization technique to help your body learn how to take very deep, quick breaths. With your hand find the spot near the base of your throat where your collarbones come together and form a "V". Feel that soft, indented area of your throat with your fingers. Now, imagine that there is a hole there. Put your flute in position and take a quick, deep breath, imagining that you are taking in all of your air directly through that hole, not through your mouth (or nose). Feel the breath hit the back of your lower throat as it rushes in. Something about this visualization cues the body to open the throat, which enables you to take in more air in the short amount of time that is available to you.

BREATHING, AND LEAVING OUT NOTES

As you have probably observed, there are almost no breathing places built into traditional Irish music. We have to create our own. With very few exceptions, such as some places in slow airs and other slow and moderate tunes, it does not work to sneak a breath between notes. Doing so almost always disrupts the flow and energy of the music, drawing attention to your breathing and away from the music. We flute players must learn how to *leave out* notes, and shorten longer notes, in a musical and tasteful way. When this is done well, most listeners will not even notice that you are breathing.

This is a crucial subject for whistle and flute players. An in-depth discussion of it requires knowledge of ornamentation. Therefore, I have placed Chapter 21, *Musical Breathing*, after the chapters on ornamentation. If you wish, you may skip ahead and look at that material at any time. However, you will get more out of it once you have worked your way through the intervening parts of the book.

EXERCISE: GET ACQUAINTED WITH YOUR DIAPHRAGM

Breathing is activated by changes in air pressure within the lungs. Expanding the chest capacity causes the air pressure within the lungs to drop in relation to atmospheric pressure, and as a result air rushes in (inhalation). Reducing chest capacity causes the air pressure within the lungs to increase, and so air rushes out (exhalation). Two actions can increase chest capacity and thereby cause inhalation: raising the ribcage, and lowering the floor of the lungs by contracting, or lowering, the diaphragm. The diaphragmatic action is vastly more effective, though both come into play.

If you are unfamiliar with the action of your diaphragm, try this exercise. Lie on your back and breathe normally through your mouth, placing your hand on your abdomen. Feel your abdomen rise as you inhale and fall as you exhale. When you inhale, your diaphragm contracts and draws itself down (toward your feet), expanding your lungs and pushing against the abdominal organs, which in turn push against the abdominal wall, causing your hand to rise. When you exhale, the diaphragm relaxes and rises, allowing the lungs to contract, and your abdominal wall falls back.

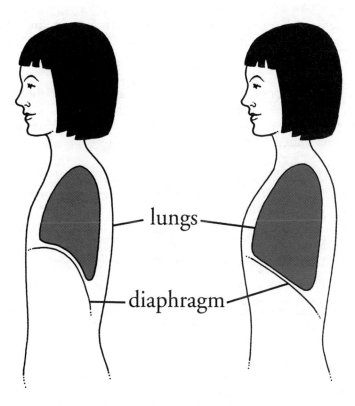

Figure 6-7. Left: During exhalation, the diaphragm relaxes and ascends, taking on a domed shape. The lungs deflate and the chest cavity contracts. Right: During inhalation the diaphragm contracts, flattens and descends. The lungs inflate and the chest cavity expands.

Try this again, now taking deeper and slower breaths. Feel how your abdomen expands much further. Continue deep, slow breathing and restrict the movement of your ribcage by pressing down on it with your hands. There is not a major change. Now press your hands firmly against your abdomen and try to continue deep breathing by elevating your ribcage only. Your air capacity is greatly reduced this way.

To feel how your back also moves when you breath, place your hands under your waist area and get a friend to place their hand on your abdomen just below your ribcage. Take a deep, slow breath and notice how you can feel the expansion in your back as well as your front.

Now roll over onto your stomach and place your hands by your sides. Have a friend place their hands on your shoulder blades and provide some moderate weight. Again take a slow, deep breath and feel the chest expansion in your back.

When you exhale, your diaphragm relaxes and rises. It does not "push" the air out of your lungs. The muscles of your abdominal wall and ribcage act in tension with the diaphragm to accomplish this and give support to the breath, helping to control the rate and pressure of exhalation.

RESISTANCE IS NEEDED FOR SLOW BREATH RELEASE

If we are to release our breath in a slow, controlled manner, something must resist its natural outrushing. In flute playing, this is almost entirely achieved through *embouchure*, the disposition and manipulation of the lips to control air flow. By creating a very small opening between the lips, the volume of air escaping can be reduced while its speed is increased. This makes for more efficient use of your limited reservoir of air.

You can observe a similar phenomenon when using a garden hose with an adjustable nozzle. As the opening in the nozzle is made smaller the water is focused into a narrower stream which is forced to shoot out of the hose faster. In the case of the garden hose, the volume of water passing through it remains constant. Playing the flute or whistle is a more subtle pursuit than watering a garden: we can control both the speed of air flow *and* its volume.

Keep your chest expanded while your abdominal muscles are contracting during the exhale. If, after expending all the air you can with your diaphragm, you find that you still need more, you can exhale a little more by contracting your ribcage. Hopefully you will create breathing places frequently enough that you will not find yourself in such need.

You can also use the back of the tongue to reduce the amount of space in the throat, thus causing the air to move faster. Many classical flutists feel that this "closed throat" adversely affects tone. The glottis can be used to create resistance as well, a technique which is used by singers. However, glottal resistance does not seem to be used by flute and whistle players, though the glottis is used by many of them, instead of or in addition to the tongue, for purposes of articulation.

The flute and whistle themselves provide virtually no air resistance. Many other wind instruments, such as oboe, clarinet, and other reed and brass instruments, do provide air resistance.

Flute Embouchure Offers Much More than Just Resistance

Through the use of embouchure, coupled with breath control, we can govern and continuously vary the speed, volume, shape, and direction of the airstream. We can also change the distance between the escaping air and the cutting edge of the embouchure hole.

Why the Tin Whistle is Limited in Comparison with the Flute

It is the control of these last three variables, the shape and direction of the airstream and the distance of the airstream from its cutting edge, that give the flute player a much broader range of dynamic and tonal expression than a tin whistle player can have. The tin whistle's windway, not the whistle player's lips, directs the air flow to the whistle's cutting edge. The direction and distance of the air flow in relation to this cutting edge are fixed by the physical dimensions of the whistle's windway and mouthpiece, though the shape of the airstream is somewhat controllable with embouchure. On the bright side, these same limitations make the whistle a much easier instrument to learn to play.

The Essential Mystery of Flute Embouchure

It is impossible to explain every nuance of flute embouchure or to design a teaching method that will work for everyone. Ultimately each player has to discover her own way. The most important element of success in this regard is *listening*. Listen to the sounds you produce, notice their character, and, noticing what is happening in your body when you produce them, try to understand and feel the relationship between the sound and your body. If you do this diligently, you will over time develop a very fine sensitivity to the subtle movements and disposition of your lips, tongue, and facial muscles and how they affect the sounds of your flute.

A Closer Look at Relaxation

Certainly by now you've noticed that I am an ardent advocate of relaxation. As stated in the last chapter, there is a difference between being relaxed and being limp. When you sit or stand in a relaxed manner there are a great many muscles that are working to hold you up. But none of them are overly tense, and those that don't need to work are relaxed. So it is with playing music in general, and with flute embouchure in particular.

Relaxation is key, but there are some muscles that have work to do. If you are new to flute playing, you will be encountering some new uses of facial muscles and it will take time for you to get those muscles in shape. Consequently, they may get tired or sore in the process. Be gentle and patient with yourself. For most people, the production of beautiful flute tone remains a very elusive goal for quite some time. These new skills are difficult to master, not only because our muscles are untrained, but because it is impossible to see all of the subtle and interactive physical changes that are taking place in the lips, face, and mouth.

Walfrid Kujala, in his book *The Flutist's Progress*, gives an excellent orientation to basic flute embouchure which I will summarize here.[iv] Although he was writing about the modern flute, his advice applies to the simple-system flute as well.

In forceful blowing, such as blowing out candles or inflating balloons, it is natural to puff out your cheeks, something you can do only when all of your facial muscles are relaxed. In flute playing, since some of these muscles are relaxed and others are at work, you cannot puff out your cheeks in this way.

The muscles of the lower cheeks are among those that have work to do. The upper cheeks, however, can and should remain fairly relaxed. According to Kujala, "for the most supple embouchure, there should be just enough firmness to deter inflation of the lower cheek area without preventing slight air spaces from developing in the upper cheeks."[v]

To get the feeling of basic embouchure, he recommends the following three-step exercise, done without the flute.

1. Moisten your lips, form a very small opening between them with your teeth slightly apart, and blow with just enough strength to keep the cheeks inflated.

2. Place the tips of your forefingers just below the corners of your mouth and press the base of those fingers over the lower cheeks so that the air is squeezed out of those areas.

3. Now remove your fingers and try to seal off the air access to those same areas, this time by firming up and slightly pulling the corners of your mouth *from below*. It should feel almost as if you were trying to tuck the corners of your mouth against your lower teeth.

When you do this your lips should still form a normal mouth shape, that is an ellipse pointed at the corners. Your mouth should not assume a bowl shape, with a flat upper lip that emphasizes the smiling muscles. Check for this in a mirror.

Once you have organized your mouth this way, hold your hand six to eight inches away from and slightly below your mouth and blow a narrowly focused jet of air at your hand. You can think of this as being similar to the way you might cool down a teaspoonful of hot soup, or the way you might try to gently alter or blow out a candle flame. There is also a similarity to the way that you spit out a watermelon seed.

Make the jet of air move up and down your hand only by adjusting your lips, without moving your head up and down. When you move your lips in this way notice that you are also moving your lower jaw very slightly in and out. This is how you will adjust the angle of the airstream with the flute and we will explore it more, later in the chapter. Notice also how the air hits your hand. Try to focus the airstream so that it hits the smallest possible area.

THE NEXT STEP: ADDING THE FLUTE HEADJOINT

So that you are not distracted with the challenges of holding your whole flute, do the following exercise with just the headjoint. Stand in front of a well-lit mirror.

1. Hold the headjoint with your two hands. Hold it near the cap with your top hand and hold it at the open end with your bottom hand. If you wish you can seal off the bore at the lower end with your hand, but do so securely. This will make it produce a lower, more soothing sound. But be careful: If your seal is leaky you will not get a good sound from the headjoint.

2. Moisten the near edge of the embouchure hole with your tongue.

3. Without pressing the headjoint against your lower lip, gently feel the near edge of the embouchure hole with the bottom edge or ridge of your lower lip, the place where the smooth skin of your lip meets the normal skin of your chin area. Repeatedly, move your head slightly left and right, lightly brushing the edge of the embouchure hole with the ridge of your lower lip, and get a sense of the hole's width and shape. When you're ready, still without pressing

the headjoint against your lip, gently place the center of the near edge of the embouchure hole against the center of the bottom edge or ridge of your lower lip.

4. Once you have found this position, press the headjoint into your lower lip. Press it firmly, but not too hard. You should not press it so hard that your lip is fully compressed and you feel the headjoint pushing directly against your lower teeth. Your lip should form a cushion between the flute and your lower teeth. Your lower lip should now be covering one-fourth to one-third of the embouchure hole itself. Take a look in the mirror and check this. You will probably need to tilt your head down to see this clearly.

5. Now, just so you'll know what *not* to do, go ahead and press the headjoint in too hard, so that your lip *is* fully compressed and you feel the headjoint pushing directly against your lower teeth. This is not very comfortable and you don't want to play this way. Now, back off the pressure so that the headjoint is firmly but comfortably in place again. You can feel that not very much pressure is required.

6. Now, form your mouth as you did in the last exercise and blow a very narrow stream of air, aiming it at the sharp wedge that is formed by the far side of the embouchure hole. This wedge will split the air into two parts, as shown in Figure 6-8, below.

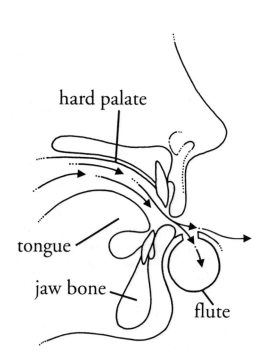

Figure 6-8. The mouth and flute headjoint in cross section, showing how the anatomy of the mouth directs and shapes the airsteam, and how the airstream is split by the far edge of the embouchure hole.

If you are lucky, you will get a tone right away, but few of us are so lucky. If you are not getting a tone, perhaps your airstream is not being split by the far edge of the embouchure hole. Vary the angle of the air with your lips, like you did when blowing against your hand. Hopefully you will find an angle that produces a tone. You may have experimented in this fashion when trying to get a sound by blowing across the top of a bottle.

If you still don't produce a tone, several things could be amiss. First, your airstream may be too off-center (in the left-right plane) in relation to the far edge of the embouchure hole. Check again in the mirror. With many people the aperture between the lips does not naturally form exactly in the center of their lips. If this is the case with you, you may need to adjust the location of the spot where you anchor the flute against your lower lip.

Second, the aperture between your lips may be too large, in which case you will be blowing a stream of air that is too diffuse. In fact, if you are a beginner, it would be very surprising if your aperture is not too large. Remember the analogy of the garden hose and try to make the opening of your "nozzle" smaller. This involves new muscle skills, ones that don't seem to be called for in other normal life activities. It can take quite a lot of time to gain fine control of these muscles.

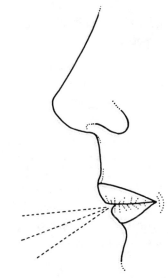

*Figure 6-9. The aperture formed by the lips is
too large and the airstream is too diffuse.*

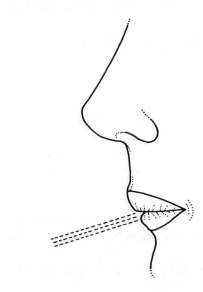

*Figure 6-10. The aperture formed by the lips is
smaller and the airstream is more focused.*

Third, it could be that you are not blowing fast enough to get the airstream up to a minimal effective speed.

If you are getting a high, squeaky tone, try blowing more gently and see if the tone drops down to a lower pitch.

If you still can't get a sound, don't despair. This is difficult for many of us. Be patient and keep trying. Getting together with an experienced flutist or flute teacher will certainly help.

THE DEGREE OF LOWER LIP COVERAGE AFFECTS OVERALL PITCH AND TONE

I stated above that when you press the flute to your lower lip it should be covering about one-fourth to one-third of the embouchure hole. This is a general starting place and you may find at some point that you will want to change how your lower lip contacts the flute.

Once you have been playing for some time, take notice of where you tend to fall in terms of overall pitch. If you tend to always be a bit flat, your tuning slide is always pushed in, and your tone tends to be small or weak, you can change that by planting the flute so that you cover less of the embouchure hole with your lower lip. This will not only raise your overall pitch but will enable you to play louder when desired and strengthen your tone.

Of course, it is possible to be off in the other direction as well. In that case you will tend to be sharp overall and have a hard-edged tone that lacks in suppleness and depth.

TIME TO PUT IT ALL TOGETHER

Now it is time to start putting everything together. Assemble your flute and find your comfortable hold. Check your posture. Relax your mouth. Have a nice yawn to help you open up your throat. Have a sigh to relax your diaphragm and abdomen.

Establish the contact between your lower lip and the embouchure hole. Keep all of your playing fingers off their holes, in resting position. Now, blow gently as you did in the previous exercise. Once you get a tone it should be a low C-sharp. If it sounds too high gradually decrease your air speed and see if the tone drops down into the low register.

Blow a nice long tone. Make it as clear, open and centered a sound as you can. Take a deep breath and play it again. Repeat this and be sure to *listen*! Imagine a beautiful, clear flute tone and keep that musical ideal in your mind's ear as you play, listening to yourself and comparing your actual sound with your ideal, striving for that ideal.

You have now begun a process of tuning *yourself* that will last for many years.

ONLY HALF AN INSTRUMENT

The flute is an instrument, but in truth it is only half of the instrument. The other half is you: your lips, mouth, tongue, air passages, lungs, diaphragm; your fingers, hands, arms, shoulders; your whole body; your breath; your ears; your mind, your soul, your inspiration. The flute is a very sophisticated tool that allows you to sing in a way that you never could before.

The flute is ultimately a tool of transformation. The flute makes possible a unique musical voice and language, one that is beyond words. As you become fluent and eloquent in that language, which you learn through playing the flute, it exists and lives in your mind, even when you are away from your flute. Using the flute, you transform the creations of that language into actual sound that others can hear, feel, and understand as they translate it into their own beauty within their own imaginations, in their own ways.

BACK TO BUSINESS

Getting back now to playing notes, place T1 on its hole and blow. The pitch is now B. Spend some time getting familiar with this sound. Now add T2. The pitch drops to A. Spend some time here. Add T3. The pitch drops to G. Experiment in this way with each of these notes and proceed on down the scale to low D.

Keep striving for the clarity, openness, and centeredness of your ideal flute sound. Your striving for that sound will call up your body's own wisdom and over time your embouchure will gradually develop of its own accord. Knowledge gained from books such as this can help, but will get you nowhere if you are not listening to yourself and continually striving for your ideal sound. This ideal sound will mature and become more clear to you the more you listen to masterful flute players. Understanding better now the necessity of your "elders," the masters of your new language, you have taken your place in a lineage.

EACH NOTE HAS A DIFFERENT EMBOUCHURE

The fact that each note has a different embouchure is not something that you consciously need to know. As long as you hold your ideal sound in your mind's ear and listen attentively to yourself, your body will discover that in order to produce that strong clear tone, the lips have to accommodate themselves slightly differently for each of the flute's different notes. Steadfast listening, while keeping your ideal sound in mind, will guide your lips in this regard. A little awareness of news from outside sources never hurts though.

So far, we have been working only with the notes of the low octave. These are the fundamental notes of the flute. The notes of the second octave are the first overtones of these lower, fundamental notes. I won't get into the physics, acoustics, and music theory of these matters here. If you are curious about it, I recommend that you read one of the many good books on those subjects.

An Illustrative Exercise: Working with Low G and High G

While the difference in embouchure between two adjacent notes is very subtle indeed, the difference in the embouchures of, say, a first-octave G and a second-octave G is quite dramatic.

To move from a fundamental note to its first overtone, we need first of all to increase the airspeed. Play a low G and then, keeping your embouchure unchanged, blow faster by forcing the air out harder with your abdominal muscles and by narrowing the throat with the back of your tongue. This may take some experimentation if you are unfamiliar with these muscles. To get familiar with the back of your tongue, begin to say the letter K. You will feel the back of your tongue close off some of the space in your throat.

For now slur these notes together, that is, keep the air flow uninterrupted; don't use any tongue or throat articulation. Move slowly back and forth between the low G and high G in this way. The high G probably sounds louder and rougher than the low G. I'm guessing that it is farther away from your ideal sound than the low G is.

Embouchure Refinements

In order to make the high G approach your ideal sound several refinements of the embouchure are needed. There are a number of different approaches to describing these. I prefer once again the approach taken by Walfrid Kujala in *The Flutist's Progress*,[vi] which I draw from on the following two pages.

We have already seen how it is necessary to increase the air speed to move from the low G to the high G. To better control the sound of the high G we need to *decrease the distance* between the opening of the lips and the far edge of the embouchure hole.

We can experience this easily through a crude exercise. Without changing the force of your blowing, play a low G, and press the flute very hard with T1 into your lower lip, adding a little upward push and the tiniest inward rotation of the flute. This brings the lip aperture closer to the embouchure hole's far edge, which, in turn, should cause the low G to jump up to the high G. As you try this, watch in a mirror and observe that the flesh of your lower lip rolls further out, covering more of the embouchure hole.

Kujala's DIREKT

Of course there is a far better way to achieve this same result. Kujala writes that this better method

> . . . calls for a forward pressure of the lips, the lower lip taking the lead as if you were combining a delicate kiss and a pout. Remember, though, that when you try this. . . the grip you maintain at the corners of your mouth with your normal . . . embouchure should prevent the center of your lips from actually getting the puckered appearance we usually associate with a kiss. This friendly opposition of . . . techniques creates a tension that is adjustable through a remarkably wide range of gradations and refinements. . . . [vii]

This embouchure maneuver, which Kujala calls the *distance reduction kissing technique* or *DIREKT*, naturally results in four things:

1. A smaller aperture between the lips,

2. A greater coverage of the embouchure hole by the lower lip,

3. A reduction in the distance between the lip aperture and the far edge of the embouchure hole, and

4. A raising of the angle of air travel relative to the far edge of the embouchure hole.

The air is now being blown more *across* the hole and less down *into* it, though the airstream is still being split by the sharp wedge formed by the far edge of the embouchure hole.

This leads us to three general observations about flute embouchure:

1. In general, for high notes you use a smaller aperture between your lips than you do for low notes.

2. In general, for high notes you cover more of the embouchure hole with your lower lip than you do for low notes.

3. In general, for high notes you blow more across the embouchure hole and for low notes you blow more down into the embouchure hole. See Figure 6-11 below.

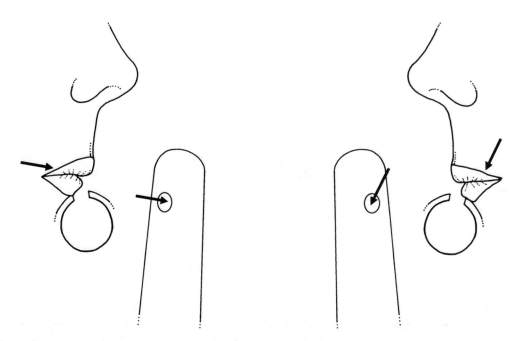

Figure 6-11. The two different airstream angles described in 3 above. On the left, the airstream is angled up a bit for playing high notes. On the right, the airstream is directed more down into the flute for playing low notes.

Some other changes happen naturally as well. There is a very slight upward and outward movement of the jaw which occurs as a natural result of the forward motion of the lower lip. It's best not to think of intentionally moving your jaw, just let it happen as a result of the lip movement.

Furthermore, Kujala observes that *DIREKT*

> . . . influences the lips to increase their pressure against one another, and this becomes more pronounced as you play even higher. This increased compression causes the corners of the mouth to react, making them appear tighter. But do not be misled. The tightening action of the corners is a reaction, not an action. That is, this is an effect, not a cause, so don't consciously tighten your lips beyond their normal tendency.[viii]

Try out these new ideas by shifting back and forth between the low and high octaves on the other pitches of the D-major scale. Notice the subtle changes required of your embouchure to approach the ideal sound on each of these different scale degrees.

By now you have noticed that the embouchure changes we are talking about are minute. They should be invisible to the casual observer. Many of them are invisible even to us as we watch carefully in a mirror. You must learn to rely upon and develop your tactile sensitivity. Closing your eyes may help you to tune in.

Once you have gained some facility with forming and changing your embouchure, give the following exercise a try. It is an excellent one for becoming aware of embouchure changes and is also a great embouchure warm-up.

Play a low D and gradually, without articulating, change to the D an octave higher. This second D is the first overtone of the fundamental note (low D). By continuing to change your embouchure in this way you can reach the second overtone, which is an A a fifth higher than the second D. Continuing to change your embouchure you can reach several of the higher overtones. The third one is a D two octaves higher than the fundamental. The fourth is an F-sharp above that and the fifth is an A above that. If you can reach the fifth overtone, you are doing extremely well. Note that some of these overtones, especially the F-sharp, sound out of tune to our ears.

Once you can play these tones, try climbing up *and* down the series of overtones in a controlled way. This may require quite a bit of practice and your facial muscles will get tired. Don't overtax them. Try this exercise starting on other notes of the scale, such as low E, F-sharp, G, etc.

As you gain more control, you can try moving among these overtones with specific rhythms, creating simple slow melodies using only the overtones of the fundamental. When you are able to do this you will have gained a fine degree of embouchure control. Two examples of such exercises are shown below, and you can make up your own. Those shown below in Figure 6-12 are played on the fundamental note of low D, but you can transpose them using any of the low register notes as fundamental tones. Try playing these note sequences slurred, articulated, and with combinations of slurs and articulations. (The small circles above these notes indicate that they are played as overtones, or harmonics.)

Figure 6-12. Two examples of embouchure exercises using the overtones of low D.

LONG TONES: ANOTHER VERY USEFUL EXERCISE

Here is a warm-up that very effectively tunes your embouchure and wakes up your breathing apparatus. Classical wind players use this type of exercise in a wide variety of ways to work on tone.

Starting with B in the first octave, take a deep, full breath and play a long, steady note using the kind of tone that you most like. Around the middle of your breath, drop cleanly down to A. Maintain the same steady tone quality until you reach nearly the end of your breath. Repeat this, listening closely to your tone. Now continue in the same way, this time playing A and moving down to G. Proceed in this manner down the scale to D. Next, start again, this time with B in the second register and work your way all the way down to low D. This sequence is shown below.

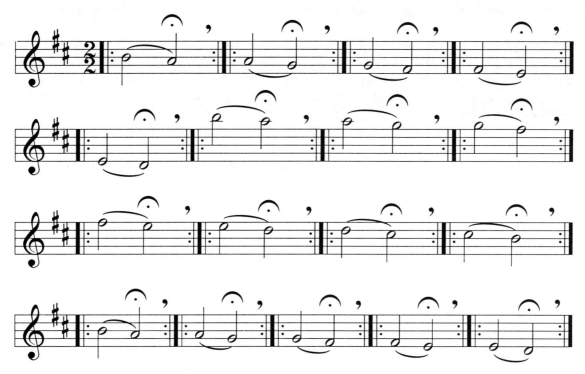

Figure 6-13. A long tones exercise.

Of course, there are myriad ways you can apply the principle of this exercise. You can play three- or four-note descending patterns. You can use ascending patterns. You can move by larger intervals. You can use different rhythms. If you would like to see a very complete treatment of this, take a look at *A Trevor Wye Practice Book for Flute, Volume 1: Tone.*[ix] This is a book for modern flute but it will give simple-system flute players plenty of ideas to work with.

BREATHING EXERCISES

In *The Flute Book,*[x] Nancy Toff gathers together eight breathing exercises from various modern flute teachers, all of which can be helpful for developing breath capacity and control for Irish flute and whistle players. I will paraphrase four of them here. If you wish to explore more exercises I suggest you consult her book.

For the first exercise, stand erect with your feet slightly apart and inhale slowly and deeply through your mouth, expanding your abdomen. Slowly exhale. Repeat this, gradually increasing the frequency and reducing the duration of your breaths until you are panting. Place your hands on your hips so that you can feel expansion both in the front and back of your abdomen.

In this next exercise, which Nancy Toff calls "The Hiss," stand and place your hands on your hips, as above. Inhale, form a flute embouchure, and hiss like a snake as you exhale. This hiss, along with support from the abdominal muscles, restricts the airflow, and helps you develop those muscles.

Noted flute teacher Sarah Baird Fouse has developed an exercise called "The Thinker." Sitting in an armless chair, place your elbows on your knees with your jaw resting gently in your cupped hands. This posture constricts your abdominal muscles, something you want to avoid when playing. But in this posture your abdomen can only expand at waist level. When you breathe deeply you cannot fail to feel these crucial muscles working.

Finally, with your flute (or whistle), play a middle register note as long as you can and time yourself. An easy way to do this is to set a metronome at 60 beats per minute and count the clicks, which occur once each second. If you do this frequently and keep a written record of your time, you should see progress as your breathing muscles and your embouchure develop.

The question may have already arisen in your mind: how does one play a given note and keep it in tune at all gradations of loudness or softness? The basic principle here is:

1. For loud playing one blows a faster air stream through a smaller opening, while

2. For soft playing one blows a slower stream of air through a larger opening.

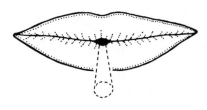

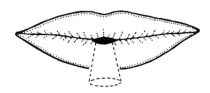

*Figure 6-14. Top: With a smaller aperture you can produce a faster airstream, enabling you to play louder.
Bottom: With a larger aperture you can produce a slower airstream, enabling you to play more quietly.*

This leads you necessarily to the realization that these different facets of embouchure are all highly interactive, that changes in one aspect affect the nature or requirements of others, that there is no one, fixed set of size, shape, speed, angle, and distance "embouchure settings" for any given note. Not only that, the aspects of a note's embouchure often change in the *course* of the note, especially when in playing slow tunes you want to change the tone color, loudness, or both at the same time during a single note.

ROLLING THE HEAD OR THE FLUTE: RELEASING A NOTE GENTLY

When you wish to get softer as you end the last, long note of a phrase, you of course use the dynamic embouchure technique described just above. In addition, you can roll or lean your head back just a bit as the note fades away. This changes the angle of air travel which helps to keep the note from drifting flat at the end and adds to your dynamic shaping ability.

This rolling-in and rolling-out technique can be use to correct for pitch in other situations too, but be careful not to use it to the exclusion of developing the ability to correct for pitch with your embouchure. Since it is not as subtle a movement, it cannot be used with the speed and accuracy that you can use embouchure pitch correction. Using the two techniques together can be very useful however.

ARE SIMPLE-SYSTEM FLUTES INHERENTLY "OUT OF TUNE"?

This question begs another: what does it mean to play "in tune"? The answer is not so simple.

Electronic tuning machines attempt to measure the fundamental frequency of a note and compare it to the pitch standard that we call equal temperament. This provides us with a useful starting point, a good way to establish whether *overall* we are playing our flute sharp or flat of the generally accepted standard pitch level of A440. Once we have warmed the flute up to room temperature, and then to breath temperature, then adjusted the tuning slide and our embouchure so it seems we are playing at the right overall pitch level, next we need to attend to the intonation of the individual notes we play.

Some of the information in the following paragraphs was given in the last chapter but it bears repeating here, especially if you are not a whistle player and did not read the last chapter. As is the case with whistles, when different players try out the same flute, one may make it sound more in tune to your ear than the others do. No flute has inherently perfect intonation; or perhaps it is more accurate to say that the meaning of "in tune" is subjective. It necessarily changes from situation to situation and it often involves compromise when playing with other people. Experienced players do their best to play what sounds sweet to their ear in any given situation. That personal judgment of good intonation very often does not conform to equal temperament. Instead, we tend to prefer the sound of "pure intervals." It may be more useful to think of playing in-tune intervals rather than in-tune notes, for it is the relationship between notes that we are really tuning.

For instance, sometimes the third degree of the Ionian mode (or major scale)—let's consider F-sharp in the D-Ionian mode—sounds better to our ears, in relation to D (the tonic note), if it is played slightly flat of an equal-tempered F-sharp. In another mode, such as E Dorian, a sweet or correct sounding F-sharp may be sharper than the sweet F-sharp in D Ionian. Why this is so is a long story, one much written about by others, which has to do with pure intervals and the harmonic series that we explored when playing the *Working with Harmonics* exercise, above. I won't delve very far into this controversial area in this book. Suffice it to say that equal temperament is a rather artificial, though very useful, system that is not based closely on the natural harmonic series. When given a choice, our ears usually prefer the sweeter, pure intervals.

When we play unison melodies with fixed-intonation equal-tempered instruments, such as accordions and concertinas, we need to adjust to them or at least compromise. When we are accompanied by instruments such as guitars, bouzoukis, keyboards, etc., we may also need to make some adjustments. The open strings of fretted string instruments are not always tuned to equal temperament, but their frets do produce equal-tempered intervals. This is a tricky area. As always, let your ear lead the way.

It is impossible to know exactly how 19th-century simple-system flute makers thought about the problem of intonation, and why they made the design decisions they did. We do know that they were building instruments to play throughout three octaves. Irish flute players, almost without exception, use only the lower two octaves.

In these flutes, the third octave notes had a natural tendency to play sharp. One theory is that, in order to adjust those pitches flatter, design decisions were made that had an impact on the intonation of some the lower-octave notes. You may have noticed that, with these old flutes, F-sharp tends to be flat, A tends to be sharp, C-natural tends to be sharp, and C-sharp tends to be flat. In addition, the low D is often flat. At least that's how these notes sound compared to equal temperament. Add to these complexities the fact that there was not a standard pitch level in those days. The pitch of the note A ranged somewhat above and below our present standard of 440 Hz.

Though we cannot understand the exact reasons behind the intonation profiles of these old flutes, it is interesting to note that the same kinds of pitch "distortions" mentioned above as being typical of simple-system flutes are also typical of the uilleann pipes and tin whistle, and are even observed in Irish fiddling. Since fiddlers determine their intonation by finger placement, and by comparison of fingered pitches to those of open strings, these pitch "distortions" are clearly a matter of choice, though probably an unconscious or conditioned one. It seems that there is a kind of natural intonation "profile" or "dialect" that is inherent in the design of the simple-system instruments (flute, whistle, uilleann pipes, even the Neanderthal bone flute mentioned in Chapter 3). It is also inherent in the nature of traditional Irish music regardless of the instrument on which it is played. No doubt this is true in other musical traditions as well.

We can say for certain that simple-system flutes do not naturally play an equal-tempered scale. It is tempting to surmise that at least some of the intonation oddities of simple-system flutes were in fact intentional. By radically redesigning the flute, Theobald Boehm really created a new instrument, one that came very close to having an equal-tempered scale. His invention sparked a storm of experimentation and controversy among the flute makers and players of his time, and well into ours. I think that the more equal-tempered intonation of the Boehm flute is one of the factors that, to most Irish flute players, makes it sound "odd" when used for Irish music. Those who succeed in getting a traditional sound on the Boehm-system flute do so in part, I feel, by emulating the intonation profile of simple-system instruments.

Most traditional Irish musicians prefer this subtle intonation personality that the simple-system instruments share. It takes time and experience to learn how to play the simple-system flute and tin whistle "in tune," but the kind of "in tuneness" that most Irish musicians strive for, consciously or not, is not the same as the equal-tempered ideal that Boehm worked so hard to achieve in his new flute.

THE F-NATURAL AND C-NATURAL KEYS CAN HELP INTONATION

As mentioned above, F-sharp and C-sharp tend to be a bit flat on many simple-system flutes. Depressing the F-natural key while playing F-sharp will raise its pitch a bit. This can be very useful when tempo and fingering sequence allow for it. Depressing the C-natural key while playing C-sharp will raise that note's pitch somewhat as well.

THE CHALLENGE OF EVALUATING THE INTONATION OF A FLUTE

If you are a beginner it will be hard for you to judge the intonation of a flute, and hard to know how well it fits your own emerging aesthetic. Try out flutes by different makers and ask more experienced players to try them for you and give you their feedback. Unfortunately, there are lots of poorly made flutes out there, waiting to fall into the hands of the unaware.

If you are lucky you may find a good antique flute that you can afford. Hopefully it will be in good enough repair for you to judge its qualities. S. C. Hamilton offers excellent, comprehensive guidelines on how to evaluate and buy an antique flute in his book *The Irish Flute Players Handbook*.[xi]

Antique flutes do not improve with age like old violins do. You really should give equal consideration to new flutes. Some of the new builders that are making flutes specifically for Irish music are optimizing their instruments for two-octave playing, which simplifies some of the design challenges.

ULTIMATELY, GOOD INTONATION IS UP TO YOU

This whole discussion boils down to the fact that you yourself must make your flute play in tune, to your own standards, by controlling it with your embouchure. Such embouchure adjustments are made by exceedingly subtle and quick changes in your throat, mouth, lips, and jaw. If you are listening well and care about intonation, you will eventually learn to make these adjustments unconsciously, especially as you get to know your own flute and its intonation profile intimately. As always, listening is the key to success.

TONE COLORS

Along with subtle changes in embouchure, you can experiment with the shaping of the mouth, tongue and throat. By forming different vowel sounds (but of course not voicing those sounds while playing) you can achieve a variety of tone colors. Though many Irish flute players do not use a wide palette of tone color and dynamics, others do, and many more could if they let their imaginations go a bit farther and gained some more understanding of these techniques. I find that forming the mouth as you would when saying "ooo" helps to produce a rich, full, open tone. Forming the mouth as if saying "eee" produces something quite different, a harder, edgier, more penetrating tone. Of course, when playing and forming the "eee" shape inside the mouth, your lips remained fairly closed to form the embouchure. If you were to voice the sound when shaping your mouth and lips this way, i.e. saying "eee" with the lips shaped as if you were saying "ooo," you would hear a sound something similar to the German "ü" or "ö."

SUBTLE BREATH PULSE OR WEIGHT

The flow of air that you blow is much like the horse hair of the fiddler's bow as it travels across the string. Just as a fiddler can change the pressure and speed of her bowstrokes to emphasize certain notes and to impart rhythmic stress, weight, or impulse, you can give such life to your music with changes in the qualities of your breath. Just as a fiddler can "lean into" the bow, you can "lean into" the breath.

I elaborate upon this in Chapter 10, in the sections *Rhythmic Emphasis Within the Long Roll* and *It's Alive—It Has a Pulse* which appear on pp. 173-174. I suggest that you work your way through the book to that point before delving into this aspect of breath and embouchure control.

HEAVY BREATH PULSING

Heavy breath pulsing appears to come from a relatively old style of loud playing that emphasizes forceful and driving rhythm over smooth lyricism. It is a style that is great for dancing, and makes one think of the days before amplification when flute players in céilí bands had to work hard to be heard alongside the accordion, pipes, banjo, drums, and other louder instruments.

In its extreme, the breath pulses have a strong pronounced attack. Players such as Eddie Cahill and Kevin Henry, who use breath pulses almost continuously and rarely slur notes together, make little use of fingered articulations and ornaments. For more on this subject see p. 292 in Chapter 21.

THE HARD D

Uilleann pipers sometimes give the bottom note of the chanter, the low D, a hard, loud, ringing sound by forcing more than the usual amount of air through the chanter. This *hard D* is a sound dear to the hearts of Irish flute players as well. On the flute, the hard D is played very loud and sometimes has a harsh edge to it. It is produced by blowing a very fast stream of air through a very small aperture, leaning hard into the note with your breath. You can hear examples in the recordings of Matt Molloy, Conal Ó Gráda, John McKenna, and many others. Some feel that it is easiest to produce a fine, ringing, hard D on simple-system flutes that have D as their lowest note.

If you have trouble getting a good hard D, check to make sure that your flute's keys have pads that are sealing tightly. The cut of the embouchure hole also plays an important part in this. If the embouchure hole is very large, it may be more difficult to get a good hard D.

A FINAL THOUGHT ON TONE PRODUCTION AND EMBOUCHURE

The subtleties of tone production and embouchure must be learned by feel over a long period of time, as a result of much conscious practice, and a lot of unselfconscious playing. If you can imagine the sound you want, you are more than halfway there. It is as if just holding your desired sound in your mind's ear will awaken an inner ability and wisdom that will eventually carry out the necessary physical changes to produce the sound. Training your muscles and mind in these ways takes a lot of time. Be patient and gentle with yourself.

[i] Richard Shepherd Rockstro, *A Treatise on the Construction, the History, and the Practise of The Flute, Including a Sketch of the Elements of Acoustics and Critical Notices of Sixty Celebrated Flute Players* (Buren, the Netherlands: 1986, Frits Knuf), Part III, p. 420–424.

[ii] Johann Georg Tromlitz, *Ausführlicher und gründlicher Unterricht die Flöte zu spielen* (Leipzig: Adam Friedrich Böhme, 1791); trans. and ed. Ardal Powell as *The Virtuoso Flute Player* (Cambridge: Cambridge University Press, 1991), p. 52.

[iii] Walfrid Kujala, *The Flutist's Progress* (Evanston, Illinois: Progress Press, 1970).

[iv] Walfrid Kujala, p. 13.

[v] Walfrid Kujala, p. 13.

[vi] Walfrid Kujala.

[vii] Walfrid Kujala, p. 71.

[viii] Walfrid Kujala, p. 72.

[ix] Trevor Wye, *A Trevor Wye Practice Book for Flute,* 6 vols. (Kent: Novello & Co. Ltd., 1981), pp. 1:5–21.

[x] Nancy Toff, *The Flute Book* (Oxford: Oxford University Press, 1996), p.84–5.

[xi] S. C. Hamilton, *The Irish Flute Players Handbook* (Coolea, Ireland: Breac Publications, 1990), pp. 202–5.

❖ section 3 ❖

——

ornamentation

introduction to ornamentation

Traditional Irish music is a living aural tradition, one that is continually evolving. Styles and techniques of ornamentation among Irish flute and whistle players are very diverse. It would be a mistake to think that anyone can reduce them to a uniform catalog of rules.

In your exploration and study of ornamentation, and during the development of your own personal ornamentation style, it is *essential* that you do a great deal of listening to excellent players, in person when possible. Establish this habit early. This book will allow you to better understand what you hear and see in their playing.

I find that the closer I look at the details of ornamentation in my own playing, and in the playing of people who have styles different from my own, the more I realize that there are subtle differences in many aspects of ornamentation and articulation that happily coexist within the living Irish tradition. This stylistic diversity is part of what makes Irish music so vital. Yet there *is* a common ground amid the diversity, and that is where one should start one's study. A full understanding of the art of ornamentation, and the development of one's own ornamentation style, requires years of playing and attentive listening.

After about 30 such years I have formed some clear opinions on how best to think of and execute the building blocks of Irish flute and whistle ornamentation, as well as its more complex structures. In this book I take quite a bit of time and care to present all of these as clearly and comprehensively as I can, for this is an area where the available teaching materials have proven inadequate and where there is a great need for completeness and clarity.

ABOVE ALL, AN AURAL TRADITION

Traditional Irish music has always been passed along and learned by ear. It is therefore understandable that no clear consensus has emerged on how to conceptualize ornamentation techniques so that they can be clearly conveyed in words and in music notation. I hope that my innovations with the concepts and notation of these techniques will bring us closer to such a consensus.

But amid all of this ink on paper, let us never forget the central and critical importance of learning and passing along this music by ear. Music notation is an excellent servant, a very elegant box of tools, and I encourage everyone to learn to use it. But it was never meant to become our master. Beware of becoming dependent upon music notation. (For more on this see Chapter 1.)

TOO MUCH BORROWING FROM CLASSICAL MUSIC

Most people who have attempted to codify traditional Irish flute and whistle playing have borrowed concepts and notation practices from classical music. This works fairly well in some areas, and not well at all in others.

Ornamentation is an area where this borrowing has not served us well. In many years of teaching, I have encountered a great many players who are mystified by ornamentation techniques. Most of them have not had personal access to good players. Struck by the beauty of what they hear on recordings, but missing important knowledge, they often turn to books in their search for insight. The books available before this one borrowed too much from the language and notation of classical music in an attempt to define techniques and concepts that exist outside of the palette of classical music. The more or less foggy and incomplete explanations that these books provide offer some help, but unfortunately many of them also create and perpetuate misunderstandings about Irish flute and whistle ornamentation.

Most of this confusion has arisen from the vague and liberal use in these books of the *grace note*, as a term, as a concept, and as a notation practice. I feel that such use of grace notes has severely limited our thinking and it is the single biggest factor in constraining many people's understanding of ornamentation to what I feel is a fairly primitive level. In the following chapters, I bring to light the confusions that this has caused and lay out a new and accurate way to understand and notate Irish flute and whistle ornamentation. The concept of the *articulation* is the key that lets us venture much further.

What Is Ornamentation?

When I speak of ornamentation in traditional Irish music I am referring to ways of altering or embellishing small pieces or cells of a melody that are between one and three eighth-note beats long. These alterations and embellishments are created mainly through the use of special fingered articulations and inflections, not through the addition of extra, ornamental or grace notes.

The modern classical musician's view of ornamentation is quite different. *Ornamentation, A Question & Answer Manual*, a book written to help classical musicians understand ornamentation from the baroque era through the present, offers this definition: "Ornamentation is the practice of adding notes to a melody to allow music to be more expressive."[i]

Classical musicians naturally tend to carry this kind of thinking with them as newcomers to traditional Irish music. However, as long as they overlay the "added note" concept onto Irish ornamentation, they will be unable to gain fluency in the language of Irish music.

More than "Ornamental"

The word *ornament* implies a musical element that could just as well be left out, leaving the essence of the music perfectly intact. Many ornaments used in Irish music do fit that description, but there are others that do not, that are essential or intrinsic to the life of the tune. Stated another way, there are places in many tunes that cannot sound "right" without the use of ornamentation.

Ornaments are among the tools we use in the larger pursuits of variation and interpretation. Returning to the language analogy I introduced in Chapter 2, *ornamentation* corresponds to the many ways you can enunciate, pronounce, and deliver individual syllables and words. *Variation* corresponds to the particular ways that you choose to combine words into phrases and use idioms and slang. *Interpretation* corresponds to how you combine phrases into sentences and paragraphs, how you reveal and express your personality, your soul, and your view of the world through your command of language.

Ornamental techniques join together with the air-management techniques of tonguing, slurring, and breath control to give the player a vast variety of tools for musical expression.

Hats Off to the Pipes

As stated in Chapter 1, Irish flute and tin whistle ornamentation techniques have their origins in the tradition of the uilleann pipes, the current bellows-blown bagpipe of Ireland, whose music developed out of the older pastoral bagpipe and *píob mór* traditions. The nature of the playing capabilities of these antecedent bagpipes sheds important light upon why many uilleann pipe, Irish flute, and tin whistle techniques have evolved as they have. With these older bagpipes, in order to articulate or separate notes of the same pitch it was necessary to use fingered articulations. These articulations have come down to us in the forms of the *cut*, the *strike*, and the multi-note ornaments that make use of cuts and strikes.

Of course Irish flute and tin whistle traditions have also developed independently of piping, so the differences between the uilleann pipes and our mouth-blown flutes and whistles are very important as well.

ARTICULATION OR ORNAMENTATION?

Many players use glottal and diaphragm techniques in place of tonguing. From here forward, for simplicity's sake, I will group these techniques together under the term *throating*. I discuss this in depth in Chapter 20.

Tonguing and throating are usually grouped under the moniker of *articulation*. For our purposes I identify an articulation as *that extremely brief sound component of a note that defines its beginning or attack*.

So far, I have been freely using the term *articulation* as if it were a part of a vocabulary that is commonly accepted for describing Irish music. But in fact, this is not so. This is something that I hope will change.

Cuts and strikes, the fingered articulations referred to above, are commonly referred to by Irish musicians as ornaments. Since it is such a long-established custom to call them ornaments, I feel I must do so as well. But it is truly more accurate to define them as articulations. They are very brief sounds that define the attacks of notes. Since cuts and strikes are so central to flute and whistle ornamentation, the ramifications of defining them as articulations are quite far-reaching.

Cuts and strikes are special articulations that have their own pitch element, so I refer to them as *pitched articulations*. They sound ornamental to our ear because of their pitch element. Other articulations that do not have a pitch element, such as tonguing and throating, do not sound as ornamental to our ears (rapid multiple tonguing/throating being another matter).

ORNAMENT CATEGORIES

Most of the ornaments are **fingered ornaments.** I divide these into two groups: *single-note ornaments* and *multi-note ornaments*.

The single-note ornaments are the pitched articulations (the *cut* and the *strike*) and a class of pitch inflections called *slides*.

Multi-note ornaments include *rolls, cranns, trills, finger vibrato,* and a few others. There are many varieties of rolls and cranns.

After examining this, we'll look at the **non-fingered ornaments:** multiple tonguing/throating and breath vibrato. And finally, in Chapter 19, we'll examine ornamentation through the use of small melodic variations.

I strongly recommend that you progress through the chapters in this section in order, for the information in later chapters is built upon that of the earlier chapters.

IT'S FINE TO BE SELECTIVE

In this book I will introduce you to a great many expressive techniques, especially in the area of ornamentation. But remember, there is no need to incorporate all of these techniques into your personal style. At a well-stocked salad bar you don't necessarily include every possible ingredient in your salad. There are some techniques in this book that I very rarely use, and some that I never use. The transcriptions of the playing of great flute and whistle players given in Section 8 show this selectivity very clearly.

The development of a personal voice requires years of experience. Over time, and with dedication, you will find an ever clearer view of yourself through your music.

i Valery Lloyd and Carole L. Bigler, *Ornamentation, A Question & Answer Manual,* (Van Nuys, California: Alfred Publishing Co., 1995), p. 8.

preface to single-note ornaments

The single-note ornaments are **cuts, strikes,** and **slides.**

Cuts and strikes also fall into the category of articulations, along with tonguing and throating. Cuts and strikes are *pitched articulations* while tonguing and throating are *nonpitched articulations.*

Multiple tonguings or throatings can function as multi-note ornaments and will be considered in Chapter 20.

The slide is an *inflection.* It has too long a duration to be considered an articulation in my view, though you can certainly play very quick and subtle slides.

Single-note ornaments and articulations can be utilized alone, and some can be combined and played simultaneously, or "stacked," in a variety of ways to give the player a very wide palette of ways to express single notes.

chapter 7: cuts

The first and most important single-note ornament to learn is the **cut**. The cut is by far the most-used ornament in this music and we will spend quite a bit of time exploring the many contexts in which we can use it. Other names sometimes heard for the cut are *chip*, *grace*, *grace note*, and *upper grace note*.

The movement of the cut is a very small and quick lift of a finger completely off its hole and the immediate replacement of that finger. When executed well, the movement of the cut can be almost invisible. The finger barely needs to lift from the hole, though it does completely uncover it. It is very important to keep your hands relaxed when learning and using cuts. Don't fall prey to the temptation to tense up while trying to make your cuts quick and crisp.

The sound of the well-executed cut is extremely brief, so brief that a listener does not perceive it as having an identifiable pitch, duration, or rhythmic identity. The well-played cut is therefore not perceived as a *note* but as an *articulation*.

The cut forms the attack of a note and gives that note emphasis. I call the note that it articulates its *parent note*. Though a good cut doesn't seem to have a pitch, it in fact does and that pitch is always higher than that of its parent note. This higher pitch is part of what gives the cut its unique qualitative identity. A cut is a *pitched articulation*.

A cut can range from being very subtle to very emphatic, depending upon the melodic context, the quality of the breath used, and whether or not (or how) you tongue, throat, or slide at the same time you cut. (Slides are described in Chapter 9.)

CORRECTING A MAJOR MISCONCEPTION

Unfortunately, everything I have seen in print regarding cuts supports the idea that cuts are to be thought of and perceived as notes unto themselves. However, this notion doesn't fit with what one hears when listening to a good player using cuts.

Though it may seem like a small or subtle distinction at first, regarding cuts as articulations leads to a completely different and more accurate understanding of their nature and function. It is well worth the time and effort to delve deeply into this matter and understand it well since the cut is such a critical element of the language of traditional Irish music, and since the way we think about music has a tremendous impact on how we play it. Often with Irish music it is very important to pay close attention to the details. The cut is a tiny thing, yet it can convey a great deal in energy and expression when it is executed well.

TRY SOME CUTS

First, try some cuts. Play a low G. (Later on you can do this same exercise on high G.) While holding a low G, and without tonguing or throating at all, try to create little "blips" in the sound by lifting and quickly replacing the T2 finger, keeping the T3 finger down. Keep the finger lift as small and quick as you can, and make sure to keep your hand and body relaxed. (For a key to these fingering indications see Figure 5-1 on p. 65 and Figure 6-4 on p. 86.)

These blips have a pitch somewhere around B. The exact pitch will vary from instrument to instrument. It's just fine for it to be out of tune. Ultimately, when you're more experienced, your cuts will be so quick that the ear won't perceive them as having an identifiable pitch.

Keep a steady, slow beat by setting a metronome at a comfortable tempo somewhere around 60 beats per minute, or by tapping your foot, and try to place the blips exactly on those beats, not before and not after.

This is not easy. If you are new to this your blips are probably not very short. Most likely you can hear each one's beginning and ending and easily discern its pitch. So which do you place on the beat, the beginning or end of the blip? For now make sure the end is on the beat, and as you practice, keep drawing the beginning closer and closer into the beat. See Figures 7-1 through 7-4.

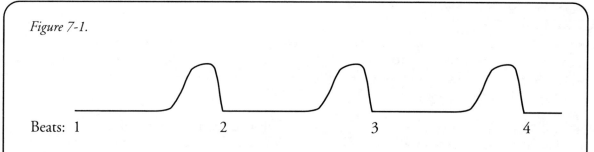

Figure 7-1.

Beats: 1   2   3   4

A beginner's cuts. The ends of the cuts are placed on the beat. At this stage, the blips are long and sound like notes. The beginnings of the blips anticipate the beat or pulse.

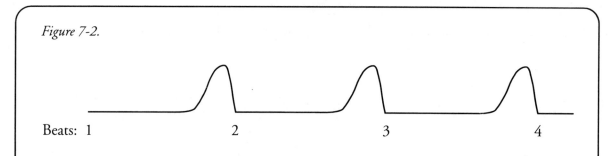

Figure 7-2.

Beats: 1   2   3   4

Making progress. The ends of the cuts are still placed on the beat but the beginnings are drawn in closer to the beats. The cuts still sound like notes.

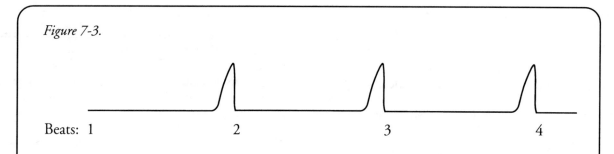

Figure 7-3.

Beats: 1   2   3   4

Further Progress. The cuts are getting shorter. The beginnings of the cuts are drawn in closer to the beats, and the cuts are sounding less like notes unto themselves.

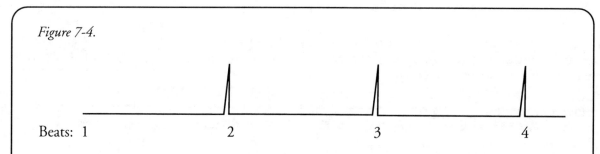

Figure 7-4.

Beats: 1   2   3   4

Well-played cuts. They are short enough that the ear does not perceive them as having beginnings and endings, duration, or pitch. They no longer anticipate the beat but are placed right on the beat. They sound like articulations.

If you're tapping your foot, don't speed up. Using a metronome instead is highly recommended. Make the blips as crisp and brief as you can.

Now, instead of hearing alternating G notes and blips, *adjust your thinking* and imagine that each blip forms the beginning of a G note. Each G note lasts one beat. Now you hear only a succession of G notes and each one is initiated by a blip. Thinking this way, these blips no longer have independent identities as *notes*. Each is merely the attack, the articulation of its parent G note.

Be patient! It will take a long time to gain the skill to play cuts well. Keep that ideal sound in your mind's ear. It will guide your muscles as they learn to do their job.

TAKE HEED!

I cannot overemphasize the importance of learning to place cuts (and strikes, described in the next chapter) *precisely* on the beat. Think about it: Since cuts and strikes are the articulations of their parent notes, I'm simply saying that it is of paramount importance to be able to place notes on their beats, in a good solid rhythm. As you advance in your skill you will not always want to place every note strictly on a beat or a subdivision of a beat, but you will always need to be able to, especially when playing tunes at fast tempos.

THE CUT IS *NOT* A NOTE

The well-played cut is not a note, for the simple reason that it is not *perceived* as a note.

A cut is more properly thought of as a verb than as a noun. When you cut a slice of bread from its loaf, you "articulate" that slice with the action of your knife. The cut can only be seen in its *effect*: that is, the new edge of the slice of bread. The cut does not exist independent of its slice of bread.

To cut is to articulate a note in a special way. To tongue is another way to articulate a note. While it's true that every articulation does occupy a tiny bit of time, if that duration is brief enough, a listener will not perceive it as having a duration, and therefore will not hear it as being a note unto itself. The listener will also not perceive it as having an identifiable pitch. *These are the secrets of the cut and the strike.*

The cut and strike, the pitched articulations we use in this music, seem magical. Their musical qualities exist as they do because they are so brief that they fall below a certain threshold of human perception. It is these *perceptions* that are truly important, not the fact that these articulations do have tiny, measurable durations. If they fall below that duration perception threshold, then in effect they are not notes.

When the cut is understood simply as a way to articulate a note, it follows that the cut will fall exactly upon the location in time where its parent note is placed.

So it is in this music. When you cut a note, the cut does not come before the beginning of the note, it *is* the beginning of the note, it defines the leading edge of the note. It is of crucial importance that you understand this concept. You will not be able to execute such brief and precise cuts at first, or perhaps for a long time, but as long as you are hearing that sound in your mind's ear and are striving for it, you will gradually come to master it.

NEITHER IS THE CUT A GRACE NOTE

Figure 7-5. The conventional, misleading, way of notating a cut as a grace note.

In my experience, all who have written about Irish flute and whistle ornamentation have defined the cut as a kind of grace note. Some don't even call it a cut, but just call it a *grace* or *grace note*. In addition to adopting this classical music term to define or name the cut, almost universally these writers have used grace notes to notate them.

For several reasons, the practice of equating cuts with grace notes, in both verbal description and musical notation, is very misleading. Cuts, when executed well, do not sound like grace notes.

WHY IS IT MISLEADING TO EQUATE CUTS WITH GRACE NOTES?

Grace notes, as understood in classical music traditions from the baroque to the present, have a definite pitch and are meant to be heard as such. The notated pitch determines the fingering to be used for grace notes and they are expected to be "in tune."

A well-played cut, while it does have a pitch, is an event of such short duration that the listener should not be able to discern its actual pitch. The pitch of a cut is sometimes not in the mode of the melody or even in tune with any of the twelve tones of the chromatic scale. A cut fingering should be chosen for its responsiveness, clarity, and its qualitative effect, not for the pitch it produces.

Grace note notation implies that the grace note is meant to be heard as distinct from the principal note.

The cut is an articulation. It should not be heard, or thought of, as an entity distinct from its parent note.

Grace notes are understood to have a duration and must "steal time" from another note or rest. Due to the visual placement of the grace note before the principal note and before its beat, grace note notation implies that the grace note steals time from the note or beat preceding the principal note.[i]

The cut is a way to attack a note. It occurs right on a beat, not before it. It's best to think of it as having no duration. Think of the cut as the leading edge of the parent note, the beginning of the parent note's envelope, or the attack of the parent note.

CUT FINGERINGS: AN IMPORTANT CHOICE IS AT HAND

In my opinion, a cut should almost always sound as well defined and crisp as possible. (I'll elaborate on this shortly.) Using the optimum fingerings is a great help in achieving this. To this end I use somewhat different fingerings than most players do. There is actually quite a bit of variance among players in their choice of cut fingerings.

In my method, for each of the notes D, E, F-sharp, G, and A, in both octaves, the lowest covered hole remains covered (i.e. the covered hole that is furthest from the embouchure or mouthpiece). You perform the cut by quickly uncovering and re-covering the next hole up. Therefore D is cut with B2, E with B1, F-sharp with T3, G with T2, and A with T1. The exception to this rule occurs when cutting B. You cut B with T1 as this is the only finger available for the job.

Why do I prefer cutting with the finger above the lowest covered hole? Cutting on the lowest covered hole, while achieving a good quick response, produces a cut that is very close in pitch to that of its parent note. This closeness of pitch lessens the definition of the cut note's attack. I feel that it is almost always better to maximize the clarity and definition of that attack. But there may be times when you would like to use a gentler sounding cut. At those times you may cut with the finger on the lowest covered hole. Note however that you cannot do this when you are descending to a cut note. In such cases that hole must be covered just to *arrive* at that note. For example, when descending from G to F-sharp and cutting the F-sharp, you cannot perform the cut with B1 because B1 must cover its hole just to get you to the F-sharp. B1 cannot do both jobs because the arrival at the note and its cut occur simultaneously. If this is hard to understand now, it will become clear as you work through this chapter.

You may wish to explore other cut fingerings and their qualitative effects. Feel free to do so but beware of the sluggish response that many of them have. This is a more of a hazard on the flute than on the whistle, and the high register of the flute is particularly prone to this problem. Uilleann pipers have more options because their instrument is exquisitely responsive to nearly all such fingerings.

Now, let's get back to trying out my recommended cut fingerings.

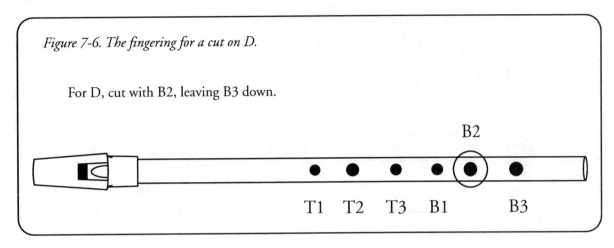

Figure 7-6. The fingering for a cut on D.

For D, cut with B2, leaving B3 down.

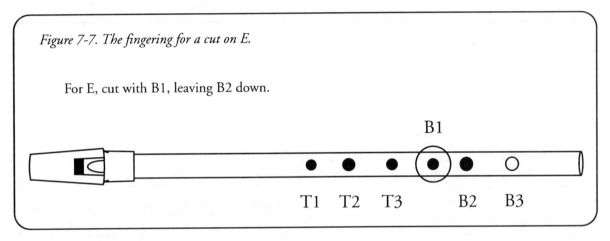

Figure 7-7. The fingering for a cut on E.

For E, cut with B1, leaving B2 down.

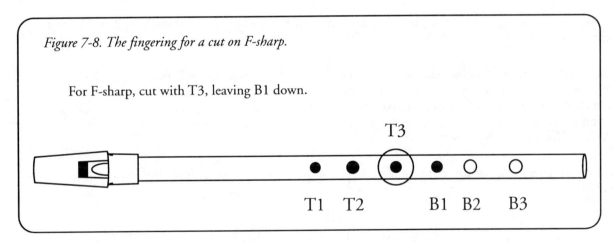

Figure 7-8. The fingering for a cut on F-sharp.

For F-sharp, cut with T3, leaving B1 down.

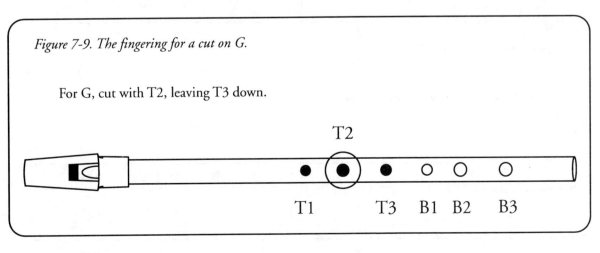

Figure 7-9. The fingering for a cut on G.

For G, cut with T2, leaving T3 down.

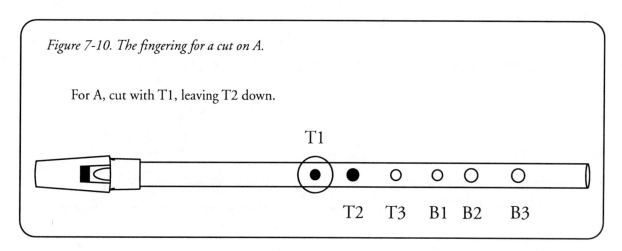

Figure 7-10. The fingering for a cut on A.

For A, cut with T1, leaving T2 down.

T1

T2 T3 B1 B2 B3

The exception to this rule is that for the note B you have no choice but to cut with T1, leaving no finger down.

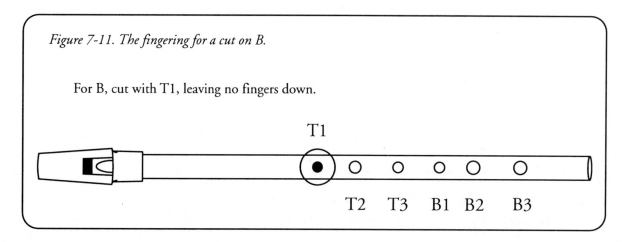

Figure 7-11. The fingering for a cut on B.

For B, cut with T1, leaving no fingers down.

T1

T2 T3 B1 B2 B3

There are some instances when one needs to use different cut fingerings (see *Cuts on Notes that Descend by an Interval Larger than a Second* on pp. 126-129.)

There are ways to play or simulate cuts on low register C and C-sharp though not many players use them. For C there is a strike fingering that simulates the sound of a cut (see Figure 8-8 on p. 140 in the next chapter). Some players, such as flute player Conal Ó Gráda, make use of a fingering pattern that is not a true cut but produces a sound like a cut on C-natural. This is discussed in the introduction to the transcription of Conal Ó Gráda's recording of the slip jig *Ride a Mile* on p. 420 of Section 8.

For low C-sharp there is a cut fingering that seems to work on some instruments but not on others. This fingering is shown below.

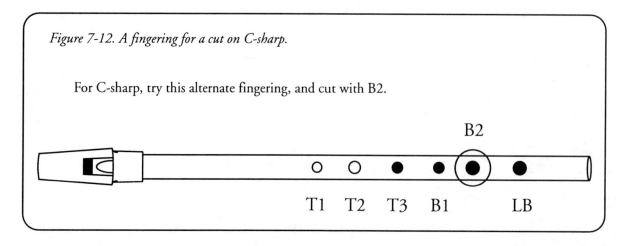

Figure 7-12. A fingering for a cut on C-sharp.

For C-sharp, try this alternate fingering, and cut with B2.

B2

T1 T2 T3 B1   LB

THE CUT FINGERINGS MOST COMMONLY USED

Quite a few players use another approach to cut fingerings, shown below, and this is what you will encounter in most other instruction books.

For D, E, F-sharp, and G they cut with T3.

For A and B they cut with T1.

The attraction of this approach is that you need only learn to cut with two fingers, T1 and T3. (For the notes F-sharp, A, and B note that these are the same as my recommended cut fingerings.)

> *However, note well this rule*: **the farther removed the cutting finger is from the lowest covered hole, the less responsive and more sluggish is the cut.**

This holds true for whistles, but even more so for flutes and the larger whistles with their more voluminous air columns. You'll usually find that sluggish cut fingerings sound even more sluggish in the second octave of both flutes and whistles.

The particulars of the various cut fingerings and the sounds they produce will vary somewhat from instrument to instrument, but the above rule holds true overall.

DON'T BE FOOLED!

Be careful in your choice of cut fingerings! Until you have gained the ability to execute short, crisp cuts you may well have trouble hearing the difference in response among the fingering options. Also, you may be playing relatively slowly now and not realize that the faster you play the more important it will be to have crisp, clean, responsive cuts. The extra work you put in now to learn my method will pay off a great deal in the future. It's even worth it to re-learn this method if you have learned another. That's what I did.

A word of caution to whistle players: With the whistle you may feel that the difference in clarity and responsiveness is not a big enough one to justify the extra work entailed in learning to cut with my fingerings. However, if you think you may someday wish to play the flute you would be well advised to learn my method so that you can avoid re-learning your fingerings later. My fingerings produce significantly cleaner cuts on the flute, especially in the second register.

For players of keyed simple-system flutes: It is possible, depending upon the number of keys your flute has, for you to cut notes such as E-flat, F-natural, G-sharp, B-flat, and C-natural. When playing any of these notes using your keys, cut them with the same finger that you would cut the note which is a half step lower. For example, to cut an E-flat use the same finger that you would use to cut a D.

A NEW CUT NOTATION

Since a cut is an articulation, I notate it as a slash placed over its parent note.

Figure 7-13. A new symbol for a cut.

This is a simple, clean notation that reflects the reality of the cut's sound and function. There is only one note here, not two. There is no indication or implication of pitch or duration for the cut. The notation is similar visually to other markings, such as staccato markings or accents, which are placed above the note they affect.

As stated in Chapter 1, much of the foundation of flute and whistle ornamentation technique and style came to us through the traditions of the uilleann pipes and its antecedents, the pastoral bagpipe and the *píob mór*. With these older bagpipes there was a constant flow of air through the chanter.

When two notes of the same pitch are played, the second one must be articulated in some way. Since these pipers had nothing analogous to tonguing or throating, i.e. the techniques with mouth-blown wind instruments of stopping and re-initiating the air flow with the tongue or in the throat (see Chapter 20), they used a finger articulation, such as a cut, to articulate the second note.

With the flute and whistle we have several choices in this situation. We can cut, tongue, throat, or both cut *and* tongue or throat. (Another ornament called a *strike* can also be used like a cut in this situation, though cuts are much more commonly used. This subject will be addressed in the next chapter.) Until you have a good handle on cuts, I recommend that you mainly cut without also articulating the note with tonguing or throating. Tonguing or throating your cuts at this point may mislead you into thinking that you have more precise control of your cuts than you actually do.

Now let's try using cuts to articulate notes of the same pitch (i.e. repeated notes).

Exercise 7-1. Practicing cuts on repeated Ds.

Play a series of Ds. Tongue or throat only the first one. Without interrupting the flow of air, articulate the rest of them only by cutting them with B2. Keep a steady, slow beat by setting a metronome at a comfortable tempo somewhere around 60 beats per minute, or by tapping your foot. Each beat of the metronome, or foot tap, represents one eighth note, as notated above. Try to place the cuts right on the beat. Note that if you are playing D in the second register (an octave above the low D) and you are venting the note by uncovering the T1 hole, the cut will produce a pitch that is lower than its parent note. Try these exercises in both octaves.

Exercise 7-2. Play a series of Es. Proceed as in Exercise 7-1, cutting with B1.

Exercise 7-2. Practicing cuts on repeated Es.

Exercise 7-3. Play a series of F-sharps. Proceed as in Exercise 7-1, cutting with T3.

Exercise 7-3. Practicing cuts on repeated F-sharps.

Exercise 7-4. Play a series of Gs. Proceed as in Exercise 7-1, cutting with T2.

Exercise 7-4. Practicing cuts on repeated Gs.

Exercise 7-5. Play a series of As. Proceed as in Exercise 7-1, cutting with T1.

Exercise 7-5. Practicing cuts on repeated As.

Exercise 7-6. Play a series of Bs. Proceed as in Exercise 7-1, cutting with T1.

Exercise 7-6. Practicing cuts on repeated Bs.

If the cut seems like a fairly simple thing at this point, that's good. However, cuts are used in many different contexts and that makes their use more challenging.

THE NEXT CHALLENGE: CUTS ON STEPWISE ASCENDING NOTES

You will often want to use a cut to draw attention to a note, to make your phrasing ideas more clear, not just to separate repeated notes. Let's say you want to cut a G that comes right after an F-sharp.

Figure 7-14. Ascending from F-sharp to G and cutting the G.

The movement from F-sharp to G is called *stepwise* because it is the smallest distance we can move within the natural whistle or flute scale, i.e. one *step* up or down the ladder of pitches. In this case the length of that "step" is the interval of a semi-tone. In the case of D to E the length of the step is the interval of a whole tone.

Getting back to our example, to move from F-sharp to G while cutting the G you have to do two very different things *simultaneously*. You lift B1 off its hole to change notes. At the same time you cut the G with T2. T3 stays on its hole the entire time.

123

Stated another way, you lift both T2 and B1 *at exactly the same moment*, i.e. right on the beat, while leaving T3 down. But you replace the cutting finger, T2, immediately while you leave B1 off its hole.

Remember that the cut is an articulation. It initiates the G and therefore defines the location of the note and the beat. It is not a *note* or grace note that comes before or after the beat.

MUSICAL ALCHEMY: TURNING THREE NOTES INTO TWO

Let's break this down. Try the following slow-motion exercise and don't worry for the moment about the fact that at first the cut won't sound like a cut. Especially if you're playing a flute, you may want to look in a mirror so you can see your fingering more clearly.

Play an F-sharp. Without tonguing, lift B1 and T2 simultaneously and hold them both off the finger holes for a moment while you continue to blow. This will produce a B-ish sort of note. Don't worry if it's out of tune. Still blowing, and without tonguing, replace T2. Do all this on a single breath and without tonguing or throating. Do this repeatedly, making *sure* to lift B1 and T2 simultaneously.

Played this way the cut is elongated and so doesn't sound like an articulation. What you hear as you play this exercise is three notes: F-sharp, a B-ish note (the cut stretched out in time), and G.

Once you get comfortable with this exercise start replacing T2 a little bit sooner each time. Soon it will begin to sound like you are playing only two notes instead of three. Recognize that you are cutting the G now, instead of playing a B-ish note between the F-sharp and G. You are placing this cut right on a beat. You are using it to articulate the G. You could have tongued the G, but instead you are using a finger ornament, the cut, to articulate it. As you repeat this, begin to feel a rhythmic pulse and place the cut note right on a beat. Try it in both octaves.

Exercise 7-7. F-sharp to a cut G.

Track 9

Now you see that although cutting is fairly simple, combining the cut with other simultaneous finger movements is not so simple, at least at first. Eventually you will be able to cut notes in any context without giving it a thought.

STRETCHING THE BRAIN A LITTLE FURTHER

When doing this exercise with F-sharp and G you are dividing the fingering labor between your two hands. When doing many of the exercises that follow the work is done with only one hand. Some people find that to be a bit more challenging.

Do these exercises in the same manner. Start in slow motion, out of rhythm. Gradually replace the cutting finger a bit sooner each time until you begin to hear two notes instead of three. Then find a pulse and place the cut note right on the beat. Try these exercises in both octaves.

Exercise 7-8 is just like exercise 7-7 but it is done with the notes D and E. Play D. Simultaneously lift B3 and B1. Replace B1. All the labor is in the bottom hand.

Exercise 7-8. D to a cut E.

Exercise 7-9 is done with the notes E and F-sharp. Play E. Simultaneously lift B2 and T3. Replace T3. Here we get to divide the labor between the two hands again, as in exercise 7-7.

Exercise 7-9. E to a cut F-sharp.

Exercise 7-10 is done with the notes G and A. Play G. Simultaneously lift T3 and T1. Replace T1. All the labor is in the top hand.

Exercise 7-10. G to a cut A.

Exercise 7-11 is done with the notes A and B. Play A. Simultaneously lift T2 and T1. Replace T1. All the labor is in the top hand. This situation feels different because there is no stationary finger between the two moving fingers. You must cut B with T1.

Exercise 7-11. A to a cut B.

TRY USING SOME CUTS IN A TUNE

Before we explore more contexts for cuts, let's put to practical use the cuts we have just been practicing, that is cuts on repeated notes and cuts on stepwise ascending notes. Figure 7-15 shows a version of *The Lonesome Jig* (also known as *The Rolling Waves, McGuire's March,* or *Maguire's Kick*) which makes use of only these types of cuts. Try playing through it, playing the cuts that are indicated. For now, do not tongue or throat at the same time that you cut. Next, play the tune through with no cuts. This will show you how even the use of fairly simple cuts goes a long way in bringing a traditional sound to your playing.

125

*Figure 7-15. A version of **The Lonesome Jig** which makes use of cuts only on repeated notes and stepwise ascending notes.*

Track 10

In the above tune setting, cuts occur only on strong beats or pulses. As you will see soon, cuts occur in other places as well. Now let's continue exploring other contexts for using cuts.

CUTS ON NOTES THAT ASCEND BY AN INTERVAL LARGER THAN A SECOND

Of course you will encounter melodies in which you will want to cut a note that ascends by an interval larger than a second, not stepwise but "leapwise." Try these cuts. With almost all of them you will once again be dividing the labor between the two hands. But now there are more fingers to lift simultaneously. Try these in both octaves.

Exercise 7-12. Move from D to F-sharp, cutting the F-sharp. Simultaneously lift B3, B2, and T3, leaving B1 down. Replace T3.

Exercise 7-12. D to a cut F-sharp.

Track 11

Exercise 7-13. Move from D to G, cutting the G. Simultaneously lift B3, B2, B1, and T2, leaving T3 down. Replace T2.

Exercise 7-13. D to a cut G.

Track 12

126

Exercise 7-14. Move from D to A, cutting the A. Simultaneously lift B3, B2, B1, T3, and T1, leaving T2 down. Replace T1.

Exercise 7-14. D to a cut A.

Exercise 7-15. Move from D to B, cutting the B. Simultaneously lift all six fingers. Replace T1.

Exercise 7-15. D to a cut B.

Exercise 7-16. Move from E to G, cutting the G. Simultaneously lift B2, B1, and T2, leaving T3 down. Replace T2.

Exercise 7-16. E to a cut G.

Exercise 7-17. Move from E to A, cutting the A. Simultaneously lift B2, B1, T3, and T1, leaving T2 down. Replace T1.

Exercise 7-17. E to a cut A.

Exercise 7-18. Move from E to B, cutting the B. Simultaneously lift all five fingers. Replace T1.

Exercise 7-18. E to a cut B.

Exercise 7-19. Move from F-sharp to A, cutting the A. Simultaneously lift B1, T3, and T1, leaving T2 down. Replace T1.

Exercise 7-19. F-sharp to a cut A.

Exercise 7-20. Move from F-sharp to B, cutting the B. Simultaneously lift all four fingers. Replace T1.

Exercise 7-20. F-sharp to a cut B.

Exercise 7-21. Move from G to B, cutting the B. Simultaneously lift all three fingers. Replace T1.

Exercise 7-21. G to a cut B.

THE NEXT CUTTING CHALLENGE: CUTS ON STEPWISE DESCENDING NOTES

Let's say you're moving from G to F-sharp and you want to cut the F-sharp. Cutting a stepwise descending note like this presents a different challenge. Once again you need to perform two different finger movements simultaneously. But this time you'll be cutting while putting *down* another finger.

Exercise 7-22. G down to a cut F-sharp.

Track 15

Place B1 onto its hole to change from G to F-sharp and, at exactly the same moment, i.e. right on the beat, lift the cutting finger, T3, and then immediately replace it on its hole.

As before, it is very useful to break this down into a slow motion exercise. The cut will be elongated and won't sound like a cut at first. Again, you may find it helpful to do this in front of a mirror so you can see your fingering clearly.

Play a G. Without tonguing, place B1 down on its hole and simultaneously lift T3 off its hole. This will produce an A-ish note. (If you hear a short F-sharp between the G and the A-ish note you are lifting T3 a little late.) Then replace T3 on its hole to complete the cut. Do all this on a single breath and without stopping the air. As you play this exercise you hear three notes: G, an A-ish note (the cut stretched out in time), and F-sharp.

Play this repeatedly. Once you get comfortable with this exercise start replacing T3 a little bit sooner each time. As before, it will begin to sound like you are playing only two notes instead of three. Recognize that you are cutting the F-sharp now, instead of playing an A-ish note between the G and F-sharp. You are placing this cut right on a beat, using it to articulate the F-sharp. As you repeat this, begin to feel a pulse and place the cut F-sharp right on a beat. Try it in both octaves.

STRIKES CAN BE USED IN PLACE OF CUTS ON DESCENDING NOTES, BUT BEWARE

I will note briefly here that strikes can be used in the place of cuts on descending notes. The next chapter is devoted to strikes and I address this topic there. However, I want to caution you now not to neglect learning cuts on descending notes. They sound very different from strikes and I feel they usually sound better. I also observe that traditional players use cuts much more often than strikes in these situations. You should have both techniques at your command.

CONTINUING TO LEARN CUTS ON STEPWISE DESCENDING NOTES

Here are some more descending stepwise cut exercises. Do these in the same manner that we just did Exercise 7-22. Start in slow motion, out of rhythm. Gradually replace the cutting finger a bit sooner each time until you begin to hear two notes instead of three. Then find a pulse and place the cut note right on the beat. Try both octaves.

Exercise 7-23 is done with the notes E and D. Play E. Simultaneously put down B3 and lift B2. Replace B2. All the labor is in the bottom hand.

Exercise 7-23. E down to a cut D.

Exercise 7-24 is done with the notes F-sharp and E. Play F-sharp. Simultaneously put down B2 and lift B1. Replace B1. All the labor is in the bottom hand.

Exercise 7-24. F-sharp down to a cut E.

Exercise 7-25 is done with the notes A and G. Play A. Simultaneously put down T3 and lift T2. Replace T2. All the labor is in the top hand.

Exercise 7-25. A down to a cut G.

Exercise 7-26 is done with the notes B and A. Play B. Simultaneously put down T2 and lift T1. Replace T1. All the labor is in the top hand.

Exercise 7-26. B down to a cut A.

CUTS ON NOTES THAT DESCEND BY AN INTERVAL LARGER THAN A SECOND

Here we come to a category of cuts in which it is necessary to use cut fingerings different from the ones we have been learning. This is necessary when descending to a cut note by an interval larger than a second, but *only* when both notes are in the same octave, or register, of the flute or whistle. When descending from a note in the second octave to a note in the first octave, and cutting the lower note, the standard cut fingerings can and should be used.

Let's look first at the example of going from F-sharp down to D and cutting the D.

Exercise 7-27. F-sharp down to a cut D.

 Track 16

Normally we would cut D with B2. But, just to get from F-sharp to D you have to put down B2 and B3. Clearly it is impossible to do that and simultaneously cut with B2. So you must cut with a different finger. The next best option, yielding the best sounding available cut, is to cut the D with B1, the lowest finger available for the job. Note that, when playing an F-sharp, B1 is also the lowest finger that is covering a hole.

A GENERAL RULE

This is the general rule for getting the best cuts in all such situations (i.e. when descending to a cut note by an interval larger than a second when both notes are in the same octave): cut with the lowest available finger. Note that this will always be the lowest finger covering a hole when playing the higher of the two notes.

For the sake of completeness, in the following exercises you will find each of these cuts described. In practice some of these cuts are awkward or do not speak well (especially in the second octave) and are not often played. Generally, the larger the descending interval, the less useful the cut.

It is worth mentioning, before proceeding to work through these special cuts, that there is another option in performing cuts of this kind. You may want to use it especially on some of the more awkward cuts that you will encounter in the following exercises, and it is really the only way to effectively cut a note when descending from C-sharp. If you make the higher note short, by stopping the air with your tongue or throat, during the brief silence thus created you can put down the fingers required to play the lower note and *then* cut it as you articulate it, using the normal cut fingering. For example, let's say you are moving from low B down to low E and cutting the low E. You would play the B, make it short, then during the brief silence thus created you would put down T2, T3, B1, and B2, i.e. the fingers needed to play low E. Then, on the next beat, you would articulate the E, with tongue or throat, and, *at the same time*, cut it with B1. Making a note short like this is conspicuous, so be sure that it is musically appropriate.

If you are very clever, during the brief silence described above you could put down T2, T3, B2, and *not* B1, waiting to put down B1 until you articulate the E with your tongue or throat. This achieves the same effect with slightly less effort, as you are putting down B1 only once, i.e. to execute the cut.

Now we'll proceed with the exercises.

Exercise 7-28 is done with the notes G and D. Play G. Simultaneously put down B1, B2, and B3 and lift T3. Replace T3. In the upper register you will want to vent the D (i.e. lift T1) as you cut it.

Exercise 7-28. G down to a cut D.

Exercise 7-29 is done with the notes A and D. Play A. Simultaneously put down T3, B1, B2, and B3 and lift T2. Replace T2. In the upper register you will want to vent the D (i.e. lift T1) as you cut it.

Exercise 7-29. A down to a cut D.

Exercise 7-30 is done with the notes B and D. Play B. Simultaneously put down T2, T3, B1, B2, and B3 and lift T1. Replace T1. This is a fairly impractical cut which may not work well on some instruments, especially in the second octave. In the upper register you cannot vent the D (i.e. lift T1) because you need this finger to perform the cut.

Exercise 7-30. B down to a cut D.

Exercise 7-31 is done in the low register with the notes C-natural and D. Play C-natural. On most flutes and whistles, finger this by covering holes with T2 and T3. Simultaneously put down T1, B1, B2, and B3 and lift T3. Replace T3. (If you need to add lower fingers to get the C-natural in tune this cut will still work.)

Exercise 7-31. C-natural down to a cut D.

131

Exercise 7-32 is done with the notes G and E. Play G. Simultaneously put down B1 and B2 and lift T3. Replace T3. Try both registers.

Exercise 7-32. G down to a cut E.

Exercise 7-33 is done with the notes A and E. Play A. Simultaneously put down T3, B1, and B2 and lift T2. Replace T2. Try both registers.

Exercise 7-33. A down to a cut E.

Exercise 7-34 is done with the notes B and E. Play B. Simultaneously put down T2, T3, B1, and B2 and lift T1. Replace T1. This may not work well on some instruments, especially in the upper register.

Exercise 7-34. B down to a cut E.

Exercise 7-35 is done in the low register with the notes C-natural and E. Play C-natural. On most flutes and whistles, finger this by covering holes with T2 and T3. Simultaneously put down T1, B1, and B2 and lift T3. Replace T3. (If you need to add B1 and/or B2 to get the C-natural in tune this cut will still work. If you need to add B3 you will have to lift it simultaneously with the cut.)

Exercise 7-35. C-natural down to a cut E.

Exercise 7-36 is done with the notes A and F-sharp. Play A. Simultaneously put down T3 and B1 and lift T2. Replace T2. Try both registers.

Exercise 7-36. A down to a cut F-sharp.

Exercise 7-37 is done with the notes B and F-sharp. Play B. Simultaneously put down T2, T3, and B1 and lift T1. Replace T1. This may not work well on some instruments in the upper register.

Exercise 7-37. B down to a cut F-sharp.

Exercise 7-38 is done in the low octave with the notes C-natural and F-sharp. Play C-natural. On most flutes and whistles, finger this by covering holes with T2 and T3. Simultaneously put down T1 and B1 and lift T3. Replace T3. (If you need to add B1 to get the C-natural in tune this cut will still work. If you need to add B2 or B3 you will have to lift them simultaneously with the cut.) Note that, in this case, T3 is the normal finger for cutting F-sharp.

Exercise 7-38. C natural down to a cut F-sharp.

Exercise 7-39 is done with the notes B and G. Play B. Simultaneously put down T2 and T3 and lift T1. Replace T1. This may not work well on some instruments in the upper register.

Exercise 7-39. B down to a cut G.

Exercise 7-40 is done in the low register with the notes C-natural and G. Play C-natural. On most flutes and whistles, finger this by covering holes with T2 and T3. Simultaneously put down T1 and lift T2. Replace T2. (If you need to add B1, B2, or B3 to bring the C-natural into tune you will have to lift them simultaneously with the cut.) Note that, in this case, T2 is the normal finger for cutting G.

Exercise 7-40. C natural down to a cut G.

TRY USING ALL TYPES OF CUTS IN A TUNE

Now that we have worked through all of the different classes of cuts, let's put them to use in a tune. Figure 7-16 (on the next page) shows a version of the slip jig *The Boys of Ballisodare* that makes use of them all. You should try following the phrasing I have indicated for the purpose of practice. For example, the second slur in measure 4 forces you to cut the E, and the D in the next measure, with T3 instead of the normal cutting fingers. Similar cuts occur in measures 8, 12, and 16.

Also, in measures 4 and 12 we encounter a situation we haven't yet discussed. We will touch on it here but will discuss it in more depth in the next section, *Cutting and Tonguing or Throating at the Same Time.* A C-natural is followed by a cut B. In cutting the B, all fingers are momentarily off the instrument. The cut sounds more clear and distinct if you make the C-natural short, by stopping the air with the tongue or throat, and then articulate the cut B. The dot above the C-natural is called a *staccato* marking, a symbol used in classical music to indicate that you should separate the indicated note from the next note. (For more information on this term see p. 274 in Chapter 20.) Try the B cut with and without articulation and see what you think. It can be played both ways, but I think you'll find that articulating the cut B makes the fingering sequence a bit easier to execute as well as making the cut B more distinct.

*Figure 7-16. A version of the slip jig **The Boys of Ballisodare** that makes use of examples of every class of cuts.*

 Track 17

CUTTING AND TONGUING (OR THROATING) AT THE SAME TIME

A cut is usually used to give special emphasis to a note. As an articulation, the cut seems to command more attention than a tongue or throat articulation. Perhaps this is because of the pitched element of the cut.

It follows that tonguing or throating *and* cutting a note will give that note still more emphasis. Be careful when you try this—good timing is critical. Know that when you cut and tongue or throat at the same time, your cutting finger needs to be in the air, not still on the instrument, at the instant that you tongue or throat. If you cut slightly after you tongue or throat you will hear the cut an instant late and the result will be some kind of double articulation.

A word of caution here: If you do not have a good handle on the accurate timing of your cuts, tonguing or throating them may hide that fact from you. For example, if you tend to cut late, as many novices do, you will hear (if you are *not* tonguing or throating, and if you are paying attention) the start of the parent note and *then* the cut. These two things should coincide.

If your cut is late, the problem will be especially apparent when you are approaching the cut note from a pitch above or below. If you are tonguing or throating that same cut, however, you are momentarily stopping the sound and introducing another rhythmic factor into the equation. That can obscure your perception of what you are actually doing. Stated another way, if you tend to cut slightly late and that late lift of the cutting finger happens during the brief silence introduced by tonguing/throating, you will not know it.

There are other factors as well that play into the effect of articulations and combined articulations. Primary among these is the quality of the breath one uses. One can, with great subtlety, "lean into" or "back off of" the breath, much as a fiddler can add or release pressure from her bow stroke. Much more is possible with this technique on the flute than on the whistle, though good handmade whistles can do more in this regard than most of the mass-produced ones.

You can begin to see why the possibilities here are vast for the expressive musician. We will discuss such subjects in more depth later.

DELAYING THE CUT, OR CUTTING IN THE MIDST OF A NOTE

Once you have mastered your articulations you may on occasion want to play around with their timing for expressive effect. For example you may sometimes choose to cut not at the start of note but in the midst of it.

In slow airs the sense of pulse can be highly changeable, elastic, or even nonexistent. This is a form of music in which the player emulates *sean nós* (old-style) singing. In slow airs, cuts and other articulations may be used mid-note without regard to any underlying pulse. Chapter 22 is devoted to the subject of playing slow airs.

DELAYING THE CUT BY PLACING IT ON A SUBDIVISION OF THE PULSE

In tunes other than slow airs, i.e. tunes with a regular pulse, players almost always apply this technique by cutting halfway through the duration of the note in question, or at least on some regular subdivision of the beat. That way they don't disturb the underlying pulse of the music that is so essential to its forward motion.

For an example of this, look at the first measure of the slip jig *Hardiman the Fiddler*. In Figure 7-17 note that there is a cut defining the attack of the first note, a quarter-note A.

*Figure 7-17. The first two measures of the slip jig **Hardiman the Fiddler** with a cut placed at the onset of the first note. (For a complete version of the tune see p. 346.)*

Track 18

This is the way we have been learning to apply cuts.

One could, instead, place a cut halfway through the duration of the first note. I have shown this in Figure 7-18 by re-writing the quarter-note A as two eighth notes tied together and placing the cut on the second eighth note.

*Figure 7-18. The first measure of the slip jig **Hardiman the Fiddler**. The first note, which had been notated as a quarter-note A, is now notated as two tied eighth notes. The second of these eighth notes is articulated with a cut.*

By viewing the situation this way we can see that this is still the way we have been learning to apply cuts. The cut still forms the articulation, the attack, of a note. In this case it is simply the second of two eighth notes instead of the first.

Most musicians, however, will still think of this cut as coming in the middle of a quarter note. After all, if they were to play this passage without using a cut they would most likely play a quarter note, not two eighth notes. For that reason I prefer to use the notation shown in Figure 7-19 for this kind of situation.

Figure 7-19. The clearest way to notate what is played in Figure 7-18.

Track 19

Here the quarter-note notation is restored, since this is the way most musicians think of the tune, and the cut symbol is placed halfway between the start of the quarter note and the following eighth note, showing where the cut happens in time. When you encounter this kind of cut notation remember that the cut is meant to be placed on a subdivision of the beat.

TINY DELAYS OF THE CUT

On occasion a player will place a cut just a very tiny bit after the attack of a note, but not nearly late enough to suggest any rhythmic subdivision of the note. The cut still sounds like it belongs to the beginning of the note, but there is something just a little "different" about it, something more "ornate" or rhythmically active in it. This kind of delay can of course happen as the result of sloppy playing. But you can hear it sparingly and effectively used in the music of such great players as Matt Molloy and Seamus Egan. When you listen very closely to this (especially if you are able to play a recording at slower than normal speed) you can hear the arrival of the parent note just an instant before the cut.

"DOUBLE GRACES" AND THE *CASADH*

I think that these two special applications of delaying the cut are what some authors are actually referring to when they vaguely describe "double graces" or "double grace notes." I think this is also what Geraldine Cotter calls the *casadh* (Irish for *twist* or *turn*) in her book *Geraldine Cotter's Traditional Irish Tin Whistle Tutor*.[ii] Her description and notation of the *casadh* are sketchy and vague. I have not been able to find any other mention of the term *casadh* in the literature.

A VARIANT: ELONGATING THE CUT

Sometimes, when cutting a repeated note it is pleasing to elongate the cut such that it becomes a new melody note.

Here are the first two measures of the second part of the reel *The Gravel Walk*. Notice the first two notes: two A eighth notes, the second of which is cut.

*Figure 7-20. The first two measures of the second part of the reel **The Gravel Walk** using a normal cut. (For a complete version of the tune see p. 351.)*

If you now elongate the cut it becomes a sixteenth note in its own right, as shown below. Note that the cut is stretched so that its beginning comes earlier. The end of the elongated cut now falls where the entire cut used to be, i.e. on the beat that defines the attack of the second A.

The cut fingering is still being used, not the normal fingering for C-natural. The C-natural produced this way may be a bit sharp, but it goes by quickly enough that this doesn't matter. It would be difficult to play such a brief C-natural using the normal cross-fingering, or the C-natural key on a keyed flute. This kind of C-natural, which in pitch falls between the equal-tempered C-natural and C-sharp, is sometimes referred to as "the piping C". See pp. 27 and 361-362 for more on this.

*Figure 7-21. A variation on the first two measures of the second part of the reel **The Gravel Walk**, created by elongating a cut.*

Since the normal cut and the variation produced by elongating the cut are so similar physically (with both you move the same finger, just with a slightly different timing), the "decision" to elongate the cut can be made very spontaneously. I put "decision" in quotes because this kind of action is not normally the result of conscious planning but simply improvisation that occurs on an intuitive level.

For a beautiful example of elongated cuts listen to Matt Molloy's recording of the reel *Griffin from the Bridge*.[iii] You will a find a transcription of this tune on pp. 398-399 in Section 8 with a discussion of his use of elongated cuts.

PREVIEW OF A FUTURE REFINEMENT

Once you have mastered the cut and the basic multi-note ornaments such as long rolls, there is another refinement of the cut technique that you can begin to learn and use to good musical effect. This is covered in the Chapter 10 in the section called *Varying the "Strength" of the Cut.*

[i] In the Baroque and Classical periods, grace notes, more properly termed *appogiaturas* or *accaciaturas*, were played on the beat, stealing time from the principal note. During the Romantic period, grace notes sometimes came to be played before the beat of the principal note. Classical musicians today, if they are not well acquainted with the performance practices of the period of the piece at hand, may be found to play grace notes either on the beat or before the beat. For more on this subject, see the book *Ornamentation, A Question and Answer Manual* (see Bibliography).

[ii] Geraldine Cotter, *Geraldine Cotter's Traditional Irish Tin Whistle Tutor*, 2nd ed. (Cork: Ossian Publications, 1989).

[iii] This is on Matt Molloy's 1987 recording, *Stony Steps*, Green Linnet GLDC 3041.

chapter 8: strikes

The second single-note ornament to learn is the **strike**. It is sometimes known by the names *tip, tap, pat,* or *slap*.

The strike is just like the cut in several important ways. The strike is a pitched articulation, not a note or a grace note. It is a way to attack a note and give it emphasis. Therefore, it follows that the strike, like the cut, will fall exactly upon the beat where its parent note itself is placed. Its duration is so brief that we don't hear it as having an identifiable pitch or rhythmic duration.

Unlike the cut, a strike's pitch is *lower* than that of its parent note. When it is played well, we can't identify its pitch, but qualitatively it feels different from the cut because of its lower pitch, and its particular attack. And while the strike produces a sound very similar to that of the cut, the physical motions required to produce these two articulations could hardly be more different.

THE PHYSICAL MOVEMENTS AND FINGERINGS OF THE STRIKE

The strike is well named, for its crisp sound is due to its percussive nature. In performing a strike one "throws" one's finger at its tone hole so that it hits the instrument at a high velocity. Due to that velocity, the finger bounces back of its own accord. As with the cut, your fingers must be relaxed, though not limp.

Unlike cut fingerings, strike fingerings seem to be almost universally agreed upon. As a rule, a strike on any given note is performed on the open tone hole closest to the embouchure or mouthpiece. For example, on the note E a strike is performed with B3. For F-sharp, you strike with B2, for G with B1, for A with T3, for B with T2, for C-natural (using the normal cross fingering) with T1, and for C-sharp also with T1. You cannot do a strike on D.

If you play the Boehm-system flute, the strikes on F-sharp and C-natural are fingered differently. For more on this, see Appendix B.

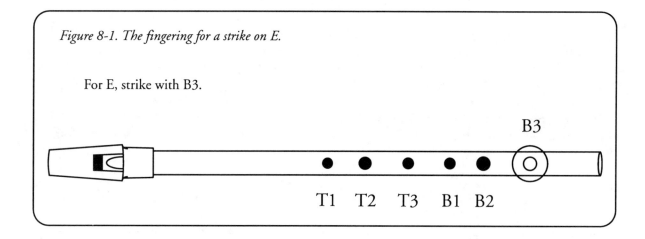

Figure 8-1. The fingering for a strike on E.

For E, strike with B3.

B3

T1 T2 T3 B1 B2

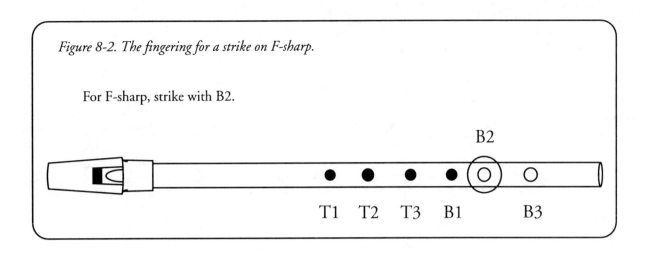

Figure 8-2. The fingering for a strike on F-sharp.

For F-sharp, strike with B2.

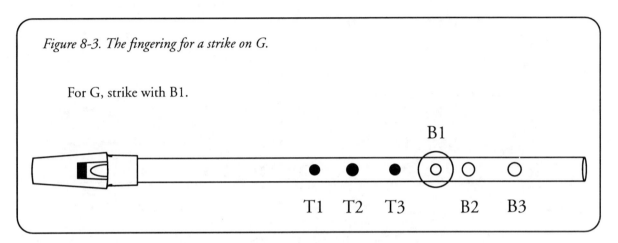

Figure 8-3. The fingering for a strike on G.

For G, strike with B1.

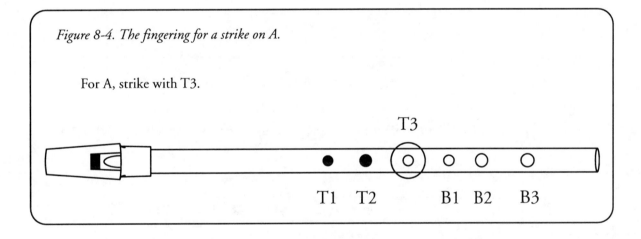

Figure 8-4. The fingering for a strike on A.

For A, strike with T3.

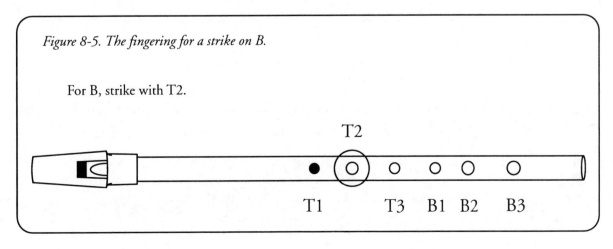

Figure 8-5. The fingering for a strike on B.

For B, strike with T2.

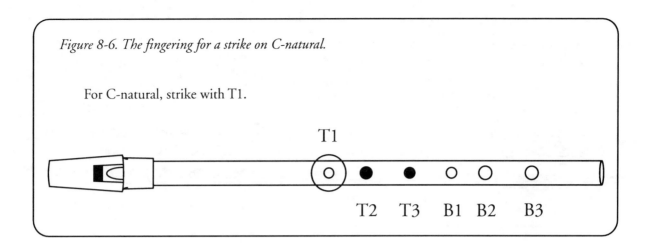

Figure 8-6. The fingering for a strike on C-natural.

For C-natural, strike with T1.

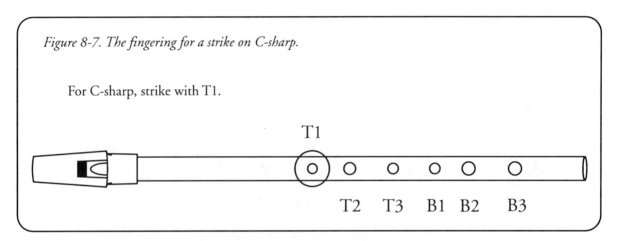

Figure 8-7. The fingering for a strike on C-sharp.

For C-sharp, strike with T1.

Using an alternate fingering one can perform a strike on C in the low register that produces a pitch higher than that of its parent note, making the strike sound like a cut. This, in fact, is the way to simulate a cut on C-natural, as shown in Figure 8-8 below.

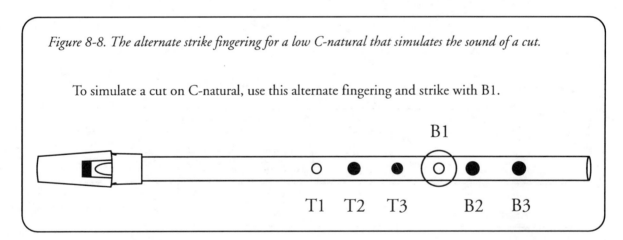

Figure 8-8. The alternate strike fingering for a low C-natural that simulates the sound of a cut.

To simulate a cut on C-natural, use this alternate fingering and strike with B1.

THE THREE PHASES OF THE STRIKE

The strike has a large, conspicuous motion, unlike the cut. That motion has three phases and each phase merges seamlessly into the next. That may make you suspect that the strike is hard to learn, but in fact I have found that for many people it is easier to master than the cut.

To understand the three phases of the strike you must first understand the idea of *resting position*.

When any of your fingers are not covering their respective tone holes they should be relaxed, resting approximately a quarter of an inch above the holes.

140

Figure 8-9. The bottom hand's fingers in resting position.

Often novices hold their fingers too high in the air, which indicates unnecessary muscle tension. With any instrument, it should be your goal to continually fine tune your physical relationship with it so that you gradually eliminate any unproductive muscle tension in your body.

Before beginning a strike, make sure that all fingers not currently covering holes are in resting position.

1. The first phase is the *preparation*. As the time for the impact of the strike approaches you raise the striking finger high into the air.

Figure 8-10. B1 in preparation for a strike on G.

141

As you are learning this, go ahead and raise the finger quite high. Once you have mastered the strike you may refine this to a somewhat smaller, more efficient motion.

2. The second phase is the *velocity* phase in which you propel your finger towards its impact, right on the beat, with its tone hole.

Figure 8-11. B1 in the velocity phase of the strike.

This impact creates the attack, the beginning of the strike's parent note.

3. Phase three is the *rebound* phase. Your finger bounces back of its own accord. You have no need to lift it. In recovery, it normally rebounds a bit past resting position and then naturally returns to it, ready for its next task.

A NEW STRIKE NOTATION

Since a strike is an articulation, I notate it by placing a V over its parent note.

Figure 8-12. The symbol for a strike.

This symbol graphically illustrates the downward velocity, impact, and rebound of the strike. This is a simple, clean notation that reflects the reality of the strike's sound and function. Neither pitch nor duration are indicated or implied. There is only one note here, not two. Just like the cut, and for the same reasons (see pp. 117-118), the strike is not a grace note. (Don't confuse this symbol with the *upbow* indication for bowed string instruments.)

I said it in the last chapter and I'll say it again because it is so important: **you must learn to place strikes and cuts precisely on the beat.** You will not always want to articulate every note strictly on a beat or one of its subdivisions, but you will always need to be able to, especially when playing tunes at fast tempos.

A metronome is an invaluable tool in raising your awareness of how you are really faring in this regard—that is if you listen to it! You'd be surprised how often I have seen a student turn on her metronome and then blithely play away, unaware that she is completely out of synch with it. It won't adjust to you—that's why it is so enlightening to use.

THE SIMPLEST AND MOST COMMON USE OF A STRIKE: ARTICULATING A REPEATED NOTE

Set your metronome at a comfortable tempo somewhere around 120 beats per minute. You are going to play along with the metronome in a cycle (or meter) of four beats, placing strikes on beat one of each group of four. Count out the four-beat pattern until you are comfortable with it. Then, on beat one, start playing a G (low or high register). Don't tongue or interrupt the flow of air after this point until you need to breathe.

Fingers B1, B2, and B3 should be in resting position. On beat four, begin the preparation phase of the strike. The velocity phase of the strike begins just a hair before beat one so that the impact occurs exactly *on* beat one. With that impact you have just defined the beginning of the next four-beat G note.

Keep going this way, articulating each four-beat G note with a strike, until you need to breathe.

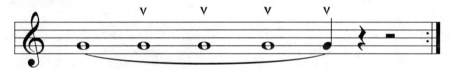

Exercise 8-1. Practicing repeated strikes on G.

Track 20

Take a breath, all the while maintaining your four beat count, and, catching the next beat number one, begin again. Pay attention! Are your strikes on the beat? If you're like most people you will tend to be early. If so, that's all right. Just notice it, and try to place the next one more precisely. Effective practice is at least 90% attention and focus.

This and the following exercises can be done in both the low and high registers.

Now do *Exercise 8-2* on F-sharp. You will be striking with B2.

Exercise 8-2. Practicing repeated strikes on F-sharp.

Next do *Exercise 8-3* on E. You will be striking with B3.

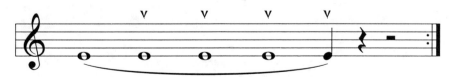

Exercise 8-3. Practicing repeated strikes on E.

Striking on E is the only occasion when it is necessary to lift the anchoring pinky of your bottom hand off your instrument. Due to our anatomy, you simply can't move your B3 finger in the way required without also lifting the pinky. Lift the pinky at the same time that you lift B3, moving both as a unit.

I recommend that you also bring the pinky down with the striking B3, both fingers again moving as a unit. The pinky then remains on the instrument while B3 hits the instrument, rebounds from it and settles back to its resting position.

This works well for two reasons. First, B3 can move more freely when the pinky moves with it, and second, the pinky returns to its anchoring spot immediately, not as a later and unnecessary step in the sequence of fingerings.

I find that when playing this strike on the flute, I need to move my B3 finger in a somewhat different way, not vertically straight down but with a lateral component to its motion.

Figure 8-13. B3 in preparation for the strike on E. The arrow indicates its lateral path as it comes down for impact.

Next do *Exercise 8-4* on A. You will be striking with T3.

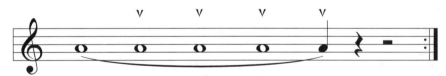

Exercise 8-4. Practicing repeated strikes on A.

Next do *Exercise 8-5* on B. You will be striking with T2.

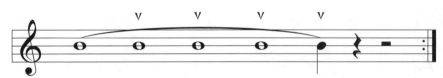

Exercise 8-5. Practicing repeated strikes on B.

144

Next do *Exercise 8-6* on C-natural. You will be striking with T1.

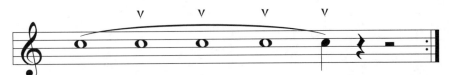

Exercise 8-6. Practicing repeated strikes on C-natural.

Next do *Exercise 8-7* on C-sharp. You will be striking again with T1.

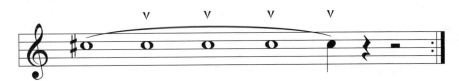

Exercise 8-7. Practicing repeated strikes on C-sharp.

THE USES AND LIMITATIONS OF THE STRIKE

The strike is sometimes used as an ornamental articulation of single notes, but most of the time the cut is chosen for that purpose instead. I suspect this is the case because the cut is more versatile than the strike. One cannot strike a note when ascending to it if the preceding note is in the same register (low or high). You can strike some notes when ascending to them across the register break. These are shown on the following page in Figure 8-14.

145

Figure 8-14. The possible ascending strikes.

Strikes can be useful for articulating certain notes that cannot be cut. On an instrument without a C key, you cannot cut a C-natural. As noted above you can simulate such a C-natural cut with a strike, as shown in Figure 8-8 (see p. 140). On a few instruments it is possible to cut a C-sharp, as shown in Figure 7-12 (see p. 120), but a C-sharp strike can be done on all flutes and whistles.

You can strike when descending, and of course on repeated notes. As noted earlier, you cannot strike a D.

By far the most important and common use of the strike is as an essential ingredient of a multi-note class of ornaments called *rolls*. We will examine rolls in Chapters 10 through 15.

Still, one can use the strike on its own to lovely effect in various contexts and you should have the technique at your disposal. Cathal McConnell is a flute and whistle player from Co. Fermanagh who makes use of strikes in a wide and intriguing variety of ways. For more on this, see the transcriptions of his playing of *Peter Flanagan's* and *The Long Slender Sally* in Section 8, pp. 400-404. Another example of the use of strikes to articulate notes that are not parts of rolls can be seen in the transcription of Desi Wilkinson's recording of the highland *Bidh Eoin* on pp. 411-412 in Section 8.

Let's say you're moving from G to F-sharp (low or high register) and you want to strike the F-sharp. To do so, you need to perform two different finger movements simultaneously. To move from G to F-sharp you will place B1 on its hole. At the same time, right on the beat, you will strike with B2. Both B1 and B2 will contact the instrument at the same moment but B2 will rebound off while B1 stays down. If your strike is late you will hear two distinctly articulated F-sharps.

I think you'll find that this is not as hard as performing stepwise descending cuts. With all stepwise descending strikes, both fingers that are moving are coming down onto the instrument, and they are always adjacent fingers.

Play Exercise 8-8 along with the metronome. Set your metronome for 60, or slower. You are going to play along with it in a cycle (or meter) of four beats, placing the strikes on beat two of each group of four.

Count out the four beat pattern until you are comfortable with it. Then, on beat one, play a low G for one beat. Without tonguing or interrupting the air flow in any way, move to F-sharp, attacking it with a strike on beat two. Hold the F-sharp for beats two and three. Then take a breath on beat four. Resume the same pattern again on beat one.

Exercise 8-8. Practicing strikes on F-sharp when descending from G.

Track 21

Try this in the high register too. Do Exercises 8-9 through 8-12 in the same manner.

Exercise 8-9. Now move from F-sharp to E while striking the E. Place B2 on its hole and at the same moment, right on the beat, you will strike with B3. Remember to let your bottom-hand pinky move with B3.

Exercise 8-9. Practicing strikes on E when descending from F-sharp.

Exercise 8-10. Next move from A to G while striking the G. Place T3 on its hole and, at the same moment, strike with B1. Interestingly, traditional players often strike G with B1 and B2 simultaneously. Try it—it does feel good.

Exercise 8-10. Practicing strikes on G when descending from A.

147

Exercise 8-11. Next move from B to A while striking the A. Place T2 on its hole and, at the same moment, strike with T3.

Exercise 8-11. Practicing strikes on A when descending from B.

Exercise 8-12. Next move from C-sharp to B while striking the B. Place T1 on its hole and, at the same moment, strike with T2.

Exercise 8-12. Practicing strikes on B when descending from C-sharp.

Note that there are examples of ascending strikes in Figure 8-14 (on p. 146) that use the same fingerings as some of the descending strikes given in Exercises 8-8 through 8-12. For example, Exercise 8-9 describes descending from F-sharp to a struck E (low or high register). These same fingerings work for the second example in Figure 8-14, ascending from a low F-sharp to a struck *high* E. The only differences are in how you blow.

By the way, you'll find that it is impractical to strike a B when moving down to it from C-natural.

TRY USING SOME STRIKES IN A TUNE

Before we explore more contexts for strikes, let's put to use the strikes we have just been practicing, that is, strikes on repeated notes and strikes on stepwise descending notes.

Figure 8-15 shows a version of the hornpipe *Bantry Bay* that makes use of only these types of strikes, as well as a variety of cuts. Play through it, with the strikes, cuts, and phrasing as indicated. As I have mentioned earlier, strikes are not used a great deal outside of the context of rolls, but for the sake of illustration I have included quite a few of them in this example. Afterwards, play the tune through without strikes and cuts and see how different the music feels.

148

Figure 8-15. A version of the hornpipe **Bantry Bay** using cuts,
and strikes only on repeated notes and descending stepwise notes.

 Track 22

To complete our strike explorations, try the following exercises.

STRIKES ON NOTES THAT DESCEND BY AN INTERVAL LARGER THAN A SECOND

Let's try striking E when descending from G. To move from G down to E, you put down B1 and B2. At the same moment strike with B3. All three fingers of the bottom hand will contact the instrument at the same moment but B3 will rebound off while the others stay down. Do this and the following exercises in the same manner as Exercises 8-8 through 8-12. In Exercises 8-13 through 8-17, remember to let your bottom-hand pinky move with the other fingers.

Exercise 8-13. Practicing strikes on E when descending from G.

 Track 23

149

Exercise 8-14. Now move from A to E while striking the E. Begin by playing A with T1 and T2 on their holes. Then move to E by placing T3, B1, and B2 on their holes and at the same time strike with B3.

Exercise 8-14. Practicing strikes on E when descending from A.

Exercise 8-15. Now move from B to E while striking the E. Begin by playing B with T1 on its hole. Then move to E by placing T2, T3, B1, and B2 on their holes and at the same time strike with B3.

Exercise 8-15. Practicing strikes on E when descending from B.

Exercise 8-16. Now move from C-natural to E while striking the E. Begin by playing C-natural with T2 and T3 on their holes. Then move to E by placing T1, B1, and B2 on their holes and at the same time strike with B3.

Exercise 8-16. Practicing strikes on E when descending from C-natural.

Exercise 8-17. Now move from C-sharp to E while striking the E. Begin by playing C-sharp with all holes open. Then move to E by placing T1, T2, T3, B1, and B2 on their holes and at the same time strike with B3.

Exercise 8-17. Practicing strikes on E when descending from C-sharp.

Exercise 8-18. Now move from A to F-sharp while striking the F-sharp. Begin by playing A with T1 and T2 on their holes. Then move to F-sharp by placing T3 and B1 on their holes and at the same time strike with B2.

Exercise 8-18. Practicing strikes on F-sharp when descending from A.

Exercise 8-19. Now move from B to F-sharp while striking the F-sharp. Begin by playing B with T1 on its hole. Then move to F-sharp by placing T2, T3, and B1 on their holes and at the same time strike with B2.

Exercise 8-19. Practicing strikes on F-sharp when descending from B.

Exercise 8-20. Now move from C-natural to F-sharp while striking the F-sharp. Begin by playing C-natural with T2 and T3 on their holes. Then move to F-sharp by placing T1 and B1 on their holes and at the same time strike with B2.

Exercise 8-20. Practicing strikes on F-sharp when descending from C-natural.

Exercise 8-21. Now move from C-sharp to F-sharp while striking the F-sharp. Begin by playing C-sharp with all holes open. Then move to F-sharp by placing T1, T2, T3, and B1 on their holes and at the same time strike with B2.

Exercise 8-21. Practicing strikes on F-sharp when descending from C-sharp.

Exercise 8-22. Now move from B to G while striking the G. Begin by playing B with T1 on its hole. Then move to G by placing T2 and T3 on their holes and at the same time strike with B1.

Exercise 8-22. Practicing strikes on G when descending from B.

Exercise 8-23. Now move from C-natural to G while striking the G. Begin by playing C-natural with T2 and T3 on their holes. Then move to G by placing T1 on its hole and at the same time strike with B1.

Exercise 8-23. Practicing strikes on G when descending from C-natural.

Exercise 8-24. Now move from C-sharp to G while striking the G. Begin by playing C-sharp with all holes open. Then move to G by placing T1, T2, and T3 on their holes and at the same time strike with B1.

Exercise 8-24. Practicing strikes on G when descending from C-sharp.

Exercise 8-25. Now move from C-sharp to A while striking the A. Begin by playing C-sharp with all holes open. Then move to A by placing T1 and T2 on their holes and at the same time strike with T3.

Exercise 8-25. Practicing strikes on A when descending from C-sharp.

BANTRY BAY, REVISITED

Now that we've practiced strikes on notes that descend by more than a second, let's try out a version of *Bantry Bay* that incorporates some of them. This version is the same as the previous one with the addition of some strikes of this type as well as one strike on an ascending note that crosses the octave break.

*Figure 8-16. A version of the hornpipe **Bantry Bay** using cuts, and a variety of strikes.*

 Track 24

152

ADDITIONAL STRIKE TECHNIQUES

Just as with cuts, one can strike and tongue at the same time. There are some examples of this in both of the versions of *Bantry Bay* presented above. See the discussion under *Tonguing and Cutting at the Same Time* (on p. 134 of the previous chapter), which applies equally to strikes.

It is also possible to strike in the midst of a note. See the discussion on pp. 135-136 of the previous chapter, which also applies to strikes.

PREVIEW OF A FUTURE REFINEMENT

As stated at the end of the last chapter, once you have truly mastered the strike and the basic multi-note ornaments such as long rolls, there is a refinement of the strike technique that you can begin to learn and use to very good musical effect. This is covered in Chapter 10 in the section entitled *Varying the "Strength" of the Strike,* pp. 175-177.

chapter 9: slides

NOT AN ARTICULATION

The **slide** is quite different from the cut and strike in several ways. First, it is not an articulation. It is an *inflection*. It is not played or heard as an "instantaneous" event like the cut and strike are. It is a continuous, moving alteration of a note's pitch. Some people refer to this as a *slur* or *smear*, but slur has another, more widely accepted meaning, as explained in Chapter 20. It is therefore best not to use the word slur for a slide. In the classical world, the slide is often referred to as a *portamento*.

For now, when I speak of the slide I am referring to a musical gesture that is accomplished using a finger technique. Note that pitch slides can also be accomplished by breath techniques, quite independent of the fingers. I'll get to that subject at the end of this chapter. Fingered slides however offer much more in speed and agility.

The cut and strike create the attacks of their parent notes and are therefore fixed in their temporal relationships to them. The slide exists independent of these considerations. The concept of a parent note is not always useful in regard to the slide. A slide can begin before the attack of a note, or after. It can be very brief or very long. It can be a way to move from one note to another and can therefore affect both notes. The slide is the free spirit of single-note ornaments and, as such, it can get carried away if you don't watch out, giving your playing a slurpy, even drunken feeling.

Slides can rise or fall in pitch. Rising slides are used much more often in Irish music than falling slides.

THE PHYSICAL MOVEMENT OF THE SLIDE

When you slide you are gradually, and sometimes only partially, covering or uncovering a finger hole in such a way that the pitch of the note you are playing at that moment rises or falls gradually. By the way, the word *slide* refers to what happens to the *pitch* of the affected note or notes, not necessarily what the finger *does* to achieve that sound. Sometimes you do slide the finger off the hole, but other times you may tilt, rock, or roll it slightly instead.

Sliding is easy and natural on the tin whistle, simple-system flute and uilleann pipes since the fingers come into direct contact with the finger holes. Sliding is possible, but not as natural, on open-hole Boehm-system flutes, because of the key mechanisms that intervene between the fingers and the tone holes themselves. Sliding is virtually impossible on the closed-hole Boehm-system flute. This difference is certainly one of the reasons why the simple-system flute is preferred by almost all Irish flute players. For more information on this see Appendix B.

AN ESSENTIAL PRINCIPLE

The finger movement of the slide should be one that leaves your hand in good playing position once the slide is complete. We will keep returning to that principle as we look at different kinds of slides.

TWO CLASSES OF SLIDES

Slides fall into two classes according to:

      1. their relationship to the melody, and

      2. the fingerings they require.

The **simple slide** directly connects two consecutive notes in a melody, "filling in" the interval between them. Clearly, this kind of slide moves in the same direction as the melody. In sliding from one melody note to the next, the only finger or fingers moving are the same ones that, in normal playing, you would use to simply go from the first note to the second. For example, when moving from A up to B using a simple slide, one simply removes T2 *gradually* from its hole.

The **added-finger slide** requires the involvement of an *additional* finger, one that is not normally used in moving from the first melody note to the next. The pitch slide does not occur within the interval formed by the two melody notes, but *outside* of this interval, and it moves in the direction opposite to that of the melodic movement. For example, when moving from G down to E and using an added-finger slide, you put down B1 and B2 in a normal fashion to move from G to E, and, at the *same* time, B3 covers all or part of its hole and immediately moves smoothly off of it to produce a pitch slide up to E from below. The melodic movement from G to E is downward, but the movement of the pitch slide is upward, moving up to E from below.

Both simple and added-finger slides can occur in rising and falling forms.

THE FIRST SLIDE: THE RISING STEPWISE SIMPLE SLIDE

Let's consider first the simplest and most natural application of the slide, the rising stepwise simple slide. By that I mean sliding from one note of a melody to the following note when that following note is higher by one step in the scale or mode. For example, see Figure 9-1.

Figure 9-1. Sliding up from E to F-sharp.

Track 25

In this slide, instead of simply lifting B2 off its hole, you gradually move B2 all the way off its hole, making the pitch gradually rise from E to F-sharp.

Do not draw B2 back toward your wrist. That would take your hand out of good playing position. Instead, scoop B2 up and away from your wrist and the hole, or putting it another way, simply straighten out B2 so that it gradually uncovers the far edge of the hole first. See Figure 9-2.

155

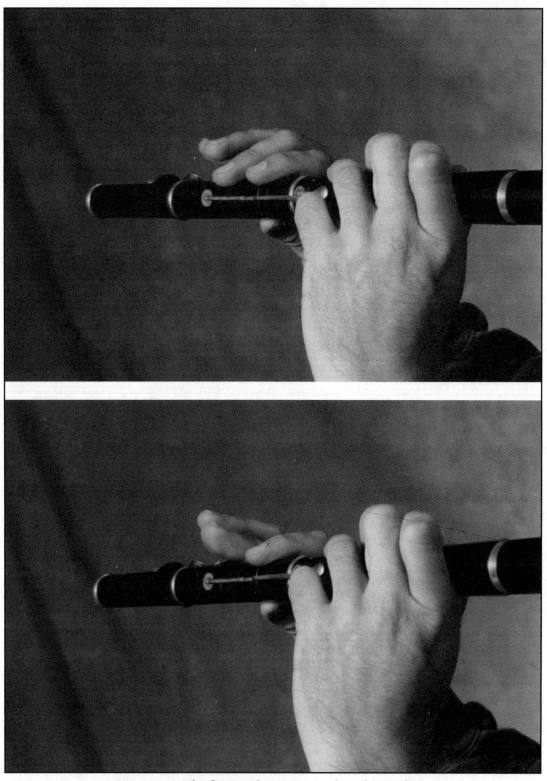

*Figure 9-2. The fingers playing an E, then the B2 finger
straightened out, having just completed a slide up to F-sharp.*

As with all finger movements, it should be your goal to fine-tune the motion so that there is no unnecessary or wasted effort. Feel free to experiment with your own ways of executing slides. Differences in hand size and shape as well as instrument and finger-hole sizes will combine in various ways and you'll need to find what works best for you under various circumstances. Just take care not to draw your hand away from the instrument and out of good playing position.

A SLIDE NOTATION

In Figures 9-3 and 9-4, I show my slide notation symbols for rising and falling slides.

Figure 9-3. The symbol for a rising slide.

Figure 9-4. The symbol for a falling slide.

The horizontal placement of the symbol could be stretched out to illustrate where the slide begins and ends if you want to be that precise, for example if you are transcribing a particular performance. How and when one slides is a very personal element of one's style.

SLIDING TO A HALF-HOLE POSITION

Picking up on the example shown in Figures 9-1 and 9-3 above, let's say you now want to slide from E to F-natural (see Figure 9-5).

Figure 9-5. Sliding from E to F-natural.

In this case you do not slide or tilt B2 all the way off its hole, but just enough to get to F-natural, holding the finger there in that position as long as you need to sound the F-natural. This requires precision and practice.

If you have a flute with an F-natural key (short and/or long keys) you may be able to very gradually depress the key to get a similar effect, though you will probably have better control by using a finger slide.

Sliding from B to C-natural is another example of this same technique, one that is used quite a bit by whistle players and to a lesser extent by flute players. The typical C-natural fingering (covering holes with T2 and T3) sometimes yields an out of tune and/or muted note, especially on mass-produced whistles. The half-hole fingering is often much more pleasing in tone and can be more in tune as long as your half-hole technique is good.

With some fingering sequences, it is highly impractical to half-hole the C-natural. But when ascending from B to C-natural the fingering is not difficult and the resultant slide can give a very pleasing effect. If the C-natural is followed immediately by another B, a fairly common occurrence, you can easily slide right back down to the B.

You can try both of these slides on the B–C-natural–B sequence that occurs in measures two and three of the jig *The Blarney Pilgrim*, shown on the next page in Figure 9-6.

Figure 9-6. The opening measures of **The Blarney Pilgrim**, with simple slides from B up to C-natural and back down to B. (For a complete version of the tune see p. 336.)

Track 26

To play a B to C-natural slide on the whistle I usually use a finger straightening technique like the one described above for sliding from E to F-natural. However, on the flute I do this differently. I roll my T1 finger away from the embouchure hole, so that the edge of the hole nearest the embouchure is uncovered just a bit, leaving the other edge of the hole covered. You can use this technique on the whistle if you wish. To slide back from C-natural to B, I simply reverse this movement.

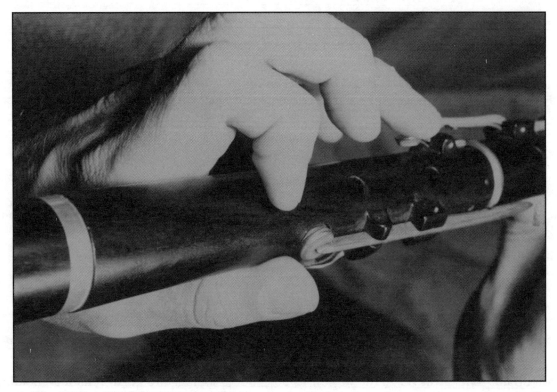

Figure 9-7. T1 rolled partially off its hole to complete a slide from B up to C-natural on the flute.

If you have a flute with a C key you may be able to very gradually depress the key to get a similar effect, though you will probably achieve better control by using a finger slide.

THE FALLING STEPWISE SIMPLE SLIDE

As mentioned above, falling slides are not used as much in Irish music as rising ones. Falling slides are usually more challenging than rising ones. It is more difficult to gradually and smoothly add a finger from mid-air to cover a hole than it is to gradually and smoothly remove a finger that is already on the instrument. Most falling slides require a lot of practice.

Interestingly, while rising half-hole slides are more difficult than rising stepwise slides, falling half-hole slides are easier than falling stepwise slides. It makes sense when you think about it. If you are already using a half-hole fingering to play a note, all you have to do to play the falling slide is ease your finger back to a position completely covering its hole. This is the kind of falling slide we encountered in Figure 9-6 (above).

For an example of a half-hole falling slide in a different context, let's look at the following excerpt from a variation on the beginning of the jig *The Cliffs of Moher*.

158

Figure 9-8. An excerpt from a variation on the beginning of the jig
The Cliffs of Moher. *(For a complete version of the tune see p. 337.)*

 Track 27

Take a close look at measure three. Finger the first C-natural in the normal way, using T2 and T3 to cover their holes. Finger the next C-natural by half-holing on the T1 hole. If you use your tongue to cut short the A that precedes this second C, thereby introducing a small silence before the second C, you should not hear a slide up to the C. Now, to play the following B, simply ease T1 down to completely cover its hole, producing a falling half-hole slide. Try using the phrasing that I have indicated, at least in measure three.

SLIDES THAT RISE BY AN INTERVAL LARGER THAN A SECOND

Slides that rise by an interval larger than a second (i.e. leapwise) are not that different from rising stepwise slides. I find that it works well to begin and perform the slide mainly with the highest moving finger, letting the rest of them follow along. For example, in sliding from E up to B, begin the slide with T2 and perform it mostly with that finger, letting T3, B1, and B2 follow along just a tiny bit later. Or perform the entire slide with T2 and simply lift the other fingers completely off their holes at the same time.

SLIDES THAT FALL BY AN INTERVAL LARGER THAN A SECOND

These are fairly challenging and are rarely heard in Irish music. To make such slides sound smooth in most cases you will need to gradually put down all the fingers in question together in a coordinated and smooth fashion. If you wish to pursue this you'll have to experiment with it a good bit.

ADDED-FINGER SLIDES FROM BELOW

So far we have looked at the class of *simple slides*, slides that connect melody notes, "filling in the gap" of the interval between the two notes. Sometimes it sounds lovely to use a slide that does not fill in that gap but that gives inflection to a note in another way.

This typically happens when, in descending from one melody note to another, you slide into the second note from below. For an example, let's look at the first few measures of the single jig or slide *The Star Above the Garter*. It gives a lovely nuance to the G in the third measure to slide up into it from below.

*Figure 9-9. The opening measures of **The Star Above the Garter** with an added-finger slide up to G followed by a simple slide up to C-natural. (For a complete version of the tune see p. 345.)*

 Track 28   Track 29

159

To perform this added-finger slide, you put down T3 to move from A to G and at the same time you use B1 to cover all, or better yet, only part of its hole, immediately easing it off its hole to produce the slide. I like to use the same "straightening" technique described on pp. 155-156 to perform this slide.

This putting down of B1 must be timed just right for it to produce the desired smooth effect, but with practice this soon becomes natural.

This gesture can be beautifully subtle, especially when the slide covers less than one step of the mode. This happens when you slide by covering only part of a tone hole.

Note that the slide up to C-natural later in the same measure is a rising simple slide on a note that ascends leapwise rather than stepwise. I would execute this slide by lifting T2, T3, B1, and B2 cleanly off their holes and at the same time half-holing with T1. This produces a subtle, quick slide from B to C-natural.

ADDED-FINGER SLIDES FROM ABOVE?

In the interest of completeness, it is possible to play an added-finger slide in the context of ascending melodic notes. This would be a falling slide that comes down to the higher melodic note from above. This is something I have rarely, if ever, heard in traditional Irish playing. If you wish to pursue it, have fun.

YET ANOTHER ORNAMENT: THE STRUCK SLIDE

In Figure 9-9, the first slide emphasizes the G in a graceful, soft-spoken way. If you want to emphasize it more assertively, you could cut at the end of the slide. But I think that is a bit strong in this case. If you want to give the note something a bit more special than just the slide, but still want it to treat it gently, you could try a **struck slide**, a variant on the slide that incorporates an aspect of the strike.

Let's look at the first slide example in Figure 9-9 again. You move from A to G by placing T3 on its hole. At the same moment, you slide up to G by covering the edge of the B1 hole and immediately tilting the finger off the hole to produce the slide.

To use a struck slide, B1 will approach its hole in a different way. As in the strike, raise B1 enough into the air so that it can come down onto the *edge* of its hole with some velocity, giving a hint of the percussive attack of the strike. This will be a subtle attack because you are striking only part of the tone hole, not the entire hole.

Then, instead of letting the finger rebound as in the strike, keep the finger on the instrument and immediately tilt it up to produce the slide. This takes some practice. It is a subtle effect, but it is noticeably different from the normal slide.

Another good place for a struck slide is the third to last note, a G, in Figure 9-6 on p. 158.

SLIDING INTO A CUT

Above, I mentioned sliding and cutting at the end of the slide. A better way to state this is to say you are sliding into a cut. In the example we just discussed, the G in the third measure of Figure 9-9, we can slide into a cut using an added-finger slide.

Of course you can do the same with simple slides too, as shown in the opening of *Willie Coleman's Jig*, shown in Figure 9-10 (below).

*Figure 9-10. The opening measures of **Willie Coleman's Jig**.*
(For a complete version of the tune see p. 344.)

Track 30

Here you slide into the G that begins the second measure and cut it when you arrive at the note.

Sliding into a cut has great evocative potential, so use it judiciously. Of course you can slide into multi-note ornaments that begin with cuts, such as some varieties of rolls that we will get to know in coming chapters. Get ready: sliding into rolls is very satisfying.

STOPPING THE AIR BEFORE OR AFTER A SLIDE

It is often useful to create a brief silence by tonguing or throating before or after a slide.

For example, let's say you slide from B up to the half-hole C-natural (using T1) and then wish go back down to B without sliding down to it. Having sounded the half-hole C-natural, stop the air briefly, move T1 fully back onto its hole and then sound the B. You have in effect silenced the slide back down to B. You can use the same technique when moving from any half-hole fingering to any other note.

Here's another useful application. Let's say you play an E and then want to slide up to G using a very subtle slide. Having sounded the E you can stop the air, take B2 entirely off its hole and at the same time straighten out B1 so that it is covering only part of its hole. Then resume your air and complete the small, microtonal slide up to G by gradually removing B1 from its hole. This idea can be applied whenever you want to use a very small slide.

BREATH SLIDES

You can make the pitch of a note slide down by decreasing the amount of air you are blowing through the instrument. As you do this you also make the instrument play more quietly, which can be a very nice effect.

You can do this with the whistle or the flute, but on the flute you have an additional breath technique that can affect a pitch lowering. You can "roll in" your embouchure, blowing more down into the flute to lower the pitch. You can combine this technique with that of decreasing the air flow. And, you can combine both of these techniques with the finger slide.

You can see that the possibilities for sliding are quite vast.

You could raise the pitch with similar breath techniques, but you don't hear that done much in Irish flute and whistle playing, except to return the pitch to normal after it has already been lowered.

preface to multi-note ornaments

You can cut, strike, tongue, or throat to articulate single notes. Some of these articulations can be combined or "stacked." And you can slide to alter the pitch shape of single notes. There are a great many ways to "deliver" a single note.

Most multi-note ornaments are constructed by combining in sequence, almost always slurred together, two, three, or four of these articulated notes in eighth-, sixteenth-, or, rarely, thirty-second-note durations. You can see that the number of possible combinations is enormous. Luckily for the player, only a fairly small number of these combinations are used in Irish flute and whistle music.

This is a living tradition though, and the current common practice will no doubt continue to evolve.

An Expanded Classification System

Through many years of listening and teaching, I have developed a system of understanding and classifying most of the variety of Irish flute and tin whistle multi-note ornaments that makes them easier to understand. I hope that many people will find my methods and innovations in naming, defining, and classifying multi-note ornaments to be a basis for more clarity, completeness, and deeper understanding.

Long and Short Forms of Rolls and Cranns

Rolls and cranns exist in long form (three eighth-note beats in duration) and short form (two eighth-note beats in duration). The classification of rolls as *long* and *short* is widely recognized and used by traditional players, though there is not a clear consensus on the exact nature of long and short rolls. The classification of cranns as long and short has not been as widely recognized.

In Chapters 10, 11, 16, and 17 I show as clearly and completely as possible what I mean by short and long rolls and cranns.

Condensed Rolls and Cranns

It is a frequent occurrence that rolls and cranns are compacted into a shorter than usual amount of time, while retaining all of their basic elements. I call such rolls and cranns *condensed*. I have found that the ways rolls and cranns are condensed is quite consistent. This has led me to describe and name a number of condensed rolls and cranns in Chapters 12, 13, 15, and 16.

Normal View and Exploded View

Throughout the following chapters you will encounter notated musical examples that are given in *normal view*, *exploded view*, or both.

Exploded view shows what happens inside of each multi-note ornament. Each of the ornament's constituent notes are depicted, complete with each note's articulation (cut, strike, or tongue/throat) and inflection (slide).

Normal view represents the multi-note ornament as a single note with a special symbol above it. This is how I commonly notate such ornaments, for example, in a collection of tune transcriptions. However, the *symbol* over the note tells you only half the story of the multi-note ornament. The *duration* of the note below the symbol tells you the other half.

This will become more clear as you work your way through the following chapters. Just remember to pay careful attention to both the symbol *and* the duration of the note below it.

chapter 10: long rolls

The **long roll** is the most commonly used multi-note ornament. There are a number of other kinds of rolls that I describe in Chapters 11 through 15.

The long roll is something very simple and lovely: *a group of three slurred eighth notes of the same pitch, each one having a different articulation.* The first note is either tongued, throated, or slurred into from a preceding melody note; the second note is cut; and the third is struck. In my notation, what I have just described looks like this:

Figure 10-1. A long roll on G, in exploded view.

Using an Accepted Symbol

There is a symbol in common usage for rolls in general. Pat Mitchell, in his book *The Dance Music of Willie Clancy*[i] writes that Breandán Breathnach devised this symbol to stand for rolls and cranns in his very influential series of tune collections *Ceol Rince na hEireann.*[ii]

Unlike Breathnach, I use the symbol very specifically, as shown in Figure 10-2, to indicate the *long* roll only. I depict other types of rolls and cranns differently, as you will see in later chapters.

Figure 10-2. The symbol for a long roll, and what it means.

Note that this crescent-shaped symbol is above a dotted quarter note. The long roll is three eighth notes in duration, the same length as a dotted quarter note.

Clearing Away Some Fog

Almost universally, the long roll has been described and taught as a five-note ornament. This is due to the prevailing custom of thinking of cuts and strikes as grace notes. Add the two grace notes to the three principal notes and you get five notes. The problem is, when you listen to a well-played long roll, *you only hear three notes!*

Cuts and strikes are not to be thought of as notes. We should think of them as articulations. Once that is understood it follows that the notion of the five-note long roll represents an unnecessary and misleading complication.

Figure 10-3 shows some examples of long roll notation taken from some published whistle and flute tutors.

Figure 10-3. Examples of misleading long roll notation taken from other flute and whistle tutors.

None of these examples look like what a long roll sounds like. None of them accurately conveys the rhythm of the long roll. They all imply that the exact pitch of the cut and strike are perceivable and significant. None of them show that the sounds of the cut and the strike are qualitatively different from each other. Even on other instruments, such as the fiddle and accordion, the cut and strike sound qualitatively different. If anyone, not already *knowing* what a long roll sounds like, tried to accurately reproduce what was notated in these examples they would get *nothing* that sounds like a long roll.

When one is first learning cuts and strikes and cannot yet make them brief enough, a long roll will indeed sound like it has five notes. Perhaps since everyone started out playing them that way we have retained some vestige of our old perceptions in our notation practices.

But why not notate them the way they sound when played *well,* especially since that notation is much simpler to read and write?

THE RHYTHM OF THE LONG ROLL

When learning to play long rolls, it is critically important to learn to play them absolutely dead even, without a lilt, each eighth note articulated right on its beat. You will not always want to play rolls so evenly, but you will need to be able to when playing tunes at very fast tempos. The evenly played roll is your solid base from which you can depart and experiment. A good player needs that firm foundation. Later we will discuss more of the reasons for playing rolls in non-even rhythms.

TRY SOME LONG ROLLS

Let's play the long roll on low G that is shown in Figures 10-1 and 10-2 on the previous page. Remember, you're simply going to play three eighth notes, tonguing or throating only the first one.

Set your metronome at a comfortable tempo somewhere around 60 beats per minute. You are going to play along with the metronome in a cycle (or meter) of four beats, each beat representing an eighth note. Count out the four beat pattern until you are comfortable with it. Then, on beat one, start playing a low G. Still playing, and without interrupting the air flow, cut the G on beat two, then strike the G on beat three. On beat four stop and take a breath if you wish. Try it a few more times. This is notated in Exercise 10-1, below. (As mentioned in Chapter 8, traditional players often strike G with B1 and B2 simultaneously.)

Exercise 10-1. Practicing long rolls on G, shown in exploded view.

Track 31

Notice the subtle differences among the three articulations and how they sound in sequence. Notice how the articulations progress down the instrument and away from you, from your mouth to T2, to B1. The roll has a direction of flow. Can you hear how the long roll resembles spoken language, or chant? Realize that you are playing only three notes of the same pitch, but that they are subtly different from each other. Note that the last finger down when you play a G stays still throughout the roll. The last finger will stay down like this for almost all rolls, when you use my cut fingerings. If you notice tension or gripping in your hands or fingers, find a way to relax.

Experiment with this as you wish and once you are ready, start again and keep the pattern going as shown in Exercise 10-1.

Remember that what you are now playing can also be written as shown in Figure 10-4.

Figure 10-4. Practicing long rolls on G, shown in normal view.

Try playing these rolls in the high octave too. These fingerings, and the ones for the other long rolls you are about to learn, are correct for both octaves.

CONGRATULATIONS!

You have now grasped what is one of the most pleasing and beautiful gestures in Irish music. Right now it is probably sounding rather stiff and pedestrian, but don't worry. You will come to experience how poetic it can be, and how fluid a long roll can feel, rippling down through your fingers.

The G long roll is probably the easiest one to play because the labor is divided between the two hands and you are using fingers that for most people are among their most agile ones.

The F-sharp long roll is the next easiest one. Set up the metronome as before and play these exercises in the same manner you played Exercise 10-1.

Exercise 10-2. Practicing long rolls on F-sharp, shown in exploded view.

Cut with T3 and strike with B2. Leave B1 in place.

Next, work with the E long roll. This can be one of the more challenging ones because all of the work is in one hand. Don't forget to lift your bottom-hand pinky when it's time to strike the E.

Exercise 10-3. Practicing long rolls on E, shown in exploded view.

Cut with B1 and strike with B3. Leave B2 in place.

165

You cannot do a roll on D because there is no way to strike a D.

THE SPORTING PITCHFORK

In this chapter, and in Chapters 11, 12 and 13, I will present two settings of the jig *The Sporting Pitchfork* to demonstrate how one can use the various forms of rolls in a musical context. As you play through these different versions of the tune you will get a deeper sense of the language of Irish music, and the breadth of variation, improvisation and interpretation that is possible within it. My primary purpose is to demonstrate the uses of all the different rolls, but I will be varying the tune settings in other ways as well. Bear in mind that I am presenting only my style of variation.

In Chapter 13, on pp. 207-209, in the section called *Summary: All Eight Settings of The Sporting Pitchfork*, you can see all eight settings of the tune presented together in a score format, so you can easily make measure by measure comparisons.

By the way, it is hard to say whether this tune is in D Mixolydian or G Ionian. The mode signature is valid for both.

Here's the first setting, which makes use of the three long rolls we have been learning, those on G, F-sharp, and E.

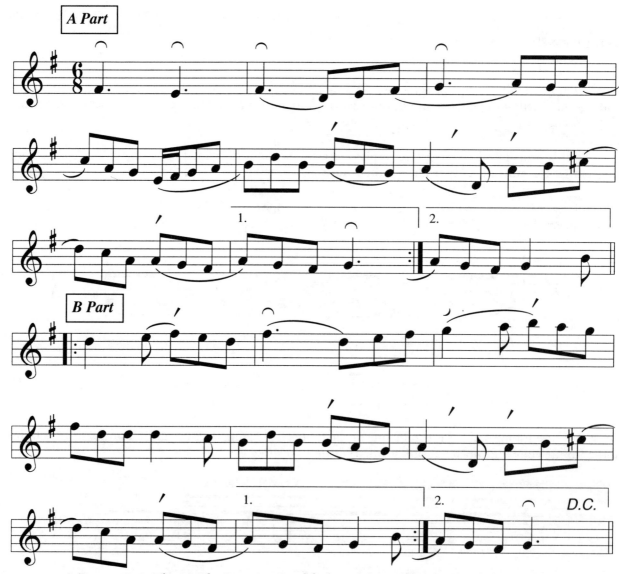

Figure 10-5. The jig **The Sporting Pitchfork** with long rolls on G, F-sharp, and E.

Track 32

166

TRY LONG ROLLS ON A AND B

Try the A long roll next. This is another of the one-handed rolls, for many people the most difficult one because of the strike with T3, the least agile of the hole-covering fingers for most people. Cut with T1 and strike with T3. Leave T2 in place.

Exercise 10-4. Practicing long rolls on A, shown in exploded view.

Now try the B long roll. Again, a one-handed roll. This one feels different because the cutting and striking fingers are adjacent, with no stationary finger between them. Cut with T1 and strike with T2. No finger stays down.

Exercise 10-5. Practicing long rolls on B, shown in exploded view.

ADD SOME A AND B LONG ROLLS TO *THE SPORTING PITCHFORK*

Now that you've have learned the five main long rolls, try them out in the following setting of *The Sporting Pitchfork*. Notice the various ways in which this version differs from that shown in Figure 10-5, above. For one thing, you can see that rolls can replace short melodic figures that center around one pitch area. There are other differences too. These kinds of variations are central aspects of improvisation in the language of Irish music.

You should know that I have put more long rolls into this setting of the tune than I normally would play, in order to provide more opportunities to practice them.

167

*Figure 10-6. The jig **The Sporting Pitchfork** with long rolls on B, A, G, F-sharp, and E.*

Track 33

LONG "ROLLS" ON C AND C-SHARP

You cannot do "proper" rolls on C or C-sharp because you cannot properly cut these notes. You can, however, simulate rolls on these notes, in the low register, by using strikes with special fingerings. Most players don't use these techniques.

Figure 8-8, on p. 140, showed how to simulate a cut on low C-natural. Figure 10-7, on the next page, shows how to use that fingering, plus another one, to simulate a C-natural long roll.

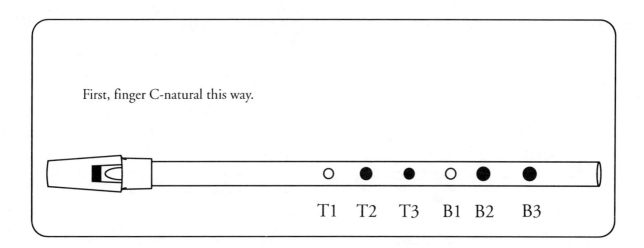

First, finger C-natural this way.

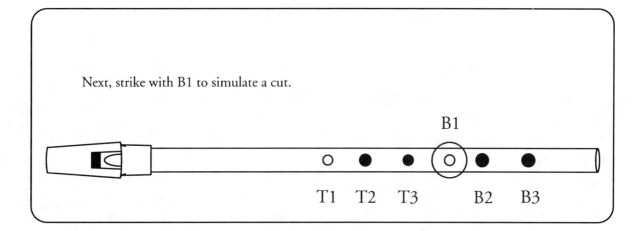

Next, strike with B1 to simulate a cut.

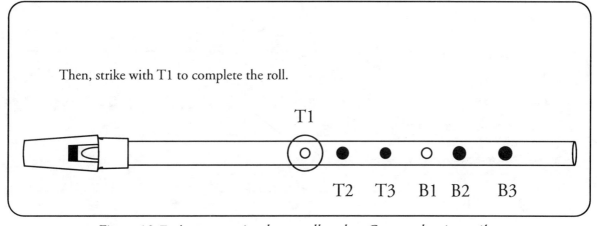

Then, strike with T1 to complete the roll.

Figure 10-7. An way to simulate a roll on low C-natural, using strikes.

Another set of fingerings, shown below in Figure 10-8, can also yield a C roll which, with some whistles, will be more in tune.

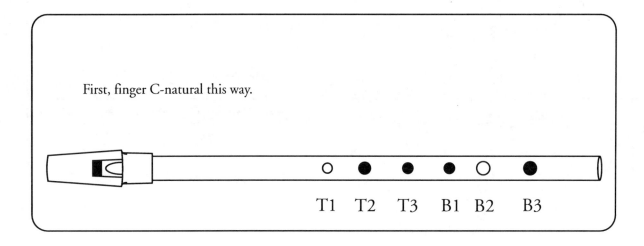

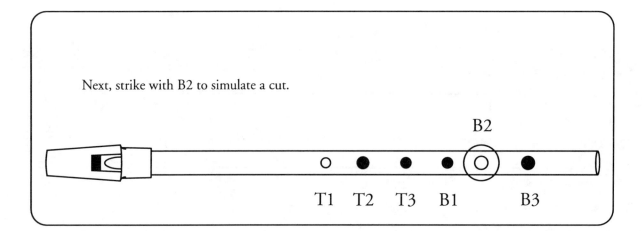

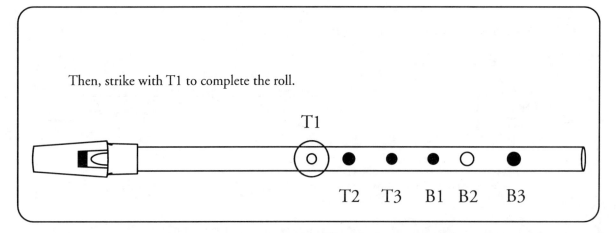

Figure 10-8. An alternate way to simulate a roll on low C-natural, again using strikes.

In a similar fashion, you can simulate rolls on low C-sharp, though these are weaker than C-natural rolls on most instruments. First, you can modify the fingerings shown in Figures 10-7 and 10-8 by keeping T2 off its hole to turn these into C-sharp rolls.

Figure 10-9, below, shows another fingering pattern to try.

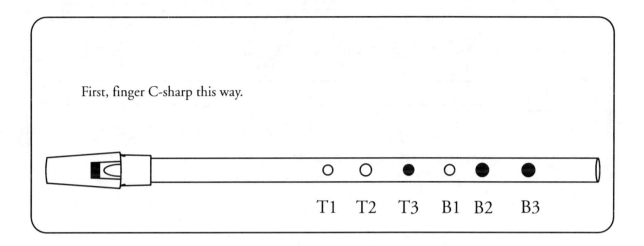

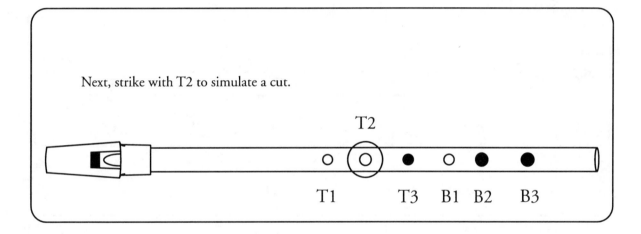

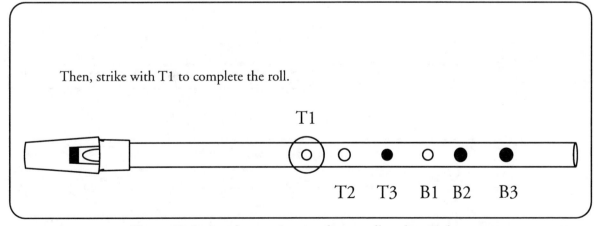

Figure 10-9. Another way to simulate a roll on low C-sharp.

Figure 10-10, below, shows yet another possibility.

First, finger C-sharp this way.

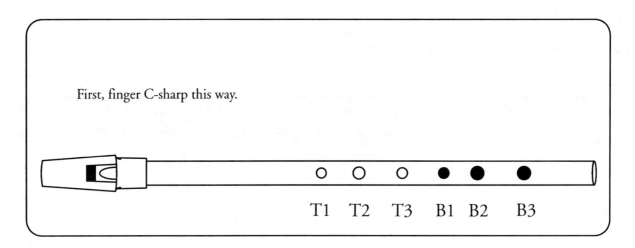

Next, strike with T2, or T2 *and* T3, to simulate a cut.

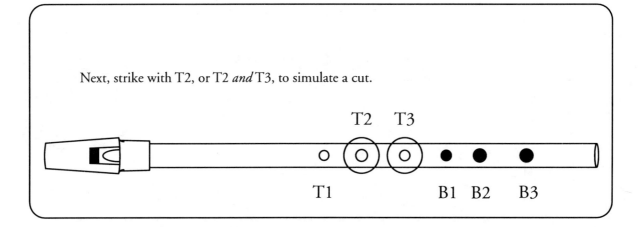

Then, strike with T1 to complete the roll

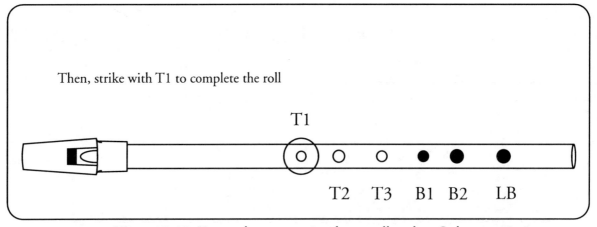

Figure 10-10. Yet another way to simulate a roll on low C-sharp.

172

SLOW AND STEADY

Over the months, as you practice your rolls, don't lose track of the steady beat. When you hear that a cut or strike is early or late, take note of that and return your focus to matching the beat. When you are able to stay on the beat consistently, stay with that comfortable tempo for a while and let your muscles really get to know the feeling of placing these articulations where they belong. In other words, practice doing it *right* for a while before going on to a faster tempo. After a while increase the tempo just a notch or two and see how that feels. If you can't handle it, return to the slower tempo. If you can do fairly well at the new tempo, stick with it until it feels comfortable and stay *there* for a while. And so on. Don't be in a rush. Our muscles learn more slowly than our minds it seems, but perhaps they remember things better in the long run. For more on this see *The Physiology of "Muscle Memory"* in Chapter 24, pp. 302-303.

CROSSING A THRESHOLD

As you do reach the point where you can play good, even, long rolls up to a normal playing speed you will notice something fascinating. The movements of the cut and strike, which at slower tempos were separate and discreet events within the roll, are now overlapping. When the tempo rises to a certain point the preparation for the strike can, and should, begin even before you perform the cut. Now you can see and feel the fluidity of the roll, how it is like water in a stream rolling over rocks, one part of the wave flowing up to a crest while just ahead the water is flowing down into a trough. The unbroken stream of your breath provides the smooth downstream flow that encompasses the up and down movements of your fingers. The poetic combination of these elements manifest in the sound of the roll itself, which is a pleasure to the listener's ears. But the player is the luckiest one, for she is able not only to listen to the roll but to feel and embody it as well.

RHYTHMIC EMPHASIS WITHIN THE LONG ROLL

As I have pointed out earlier, the flow of air that you blow is much like the horse hair of a fiddler's bow as it travels across the string. Just as a fiddler can change the pressure and speed of her bowstrokes to emphasize certain notes and to impart rhythmic stress, weight, or impulse, you can give such life to your music with changes in the qualities of your breath. Just as a fiddler can "lean into" the bow, you can "lean into" the breath.

We have much more capability in this regard on the flute than we have on the whistle, but even very subtle touches, as are possible on the whistle, can help bring your music to life beautifully.

One way that good handmade whistles show their worth is that they offer you more capability to lean into the breath without adversely affecting pitch. See also the sections *"Kicking Up" into the Second Octave* and *Tin Whistle Embouchure*, in Chapter 5 on pp. 76-77.

There are also subtleties in how you can play cuts and strikes that control how much emphasis they impart to their parent notes. We will explore these matters further, after we take a look at the idea of *pulse* in Irish music.

IT'S ALIVE—IT HAS A PULSE

In reels, single jigs, double jigs, slides, hornpipes, polkas, schottisches, flings, barn dances, germans, strathspeys, and marches there are two strong recurrent pulses which could be counted "**one**, two; **one**, two," etc. In musical terms, we say these types of tunes are in *duple* meter. Most people tap their feet to these pulses and "one" usually gets a bit more stress than "two." In slip jigs, mazurkas, and waltzes, there are three strong recurrent pulses, which of course are counted "**one**, two, three; **one**, two, three" and so on, with "one" getting a bit more stress than "two" or "three." In musical terms, we say these types of tunes are in *triple* meter.

In each tune type these pulses are subdivided into smaller units of time. In reels each pulse is subdivided into four parts, usually notated as eighth notes, and in jigs each pulse is subdivided into three eighth-note parts. In musical terms, we say that reels are in a *simple duple meter* and jigs are in a *compound duple meter*.

In reels, then, there are eight eighth-note beats per measure. The pulse we have been talking about falls on the first and fifth of these beats. But the third and seventh beats carry some special weight too, though not as much as the first and fifth. Thus, there are two pulses existing concurrently in reels, the primary pulse on one and five and a secondary pulse on three and seven. In jigs, the pulse falls on the first and fourth eighth-note beats and there is no secondary pulse. To keep things fairly simple we will only look at reels and jigs for now. See Figure 10-11 below.

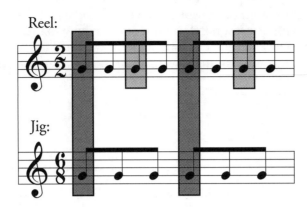

Figure 10-11. The pulse and its subdivisions in a reel and a jig. The dark shaded areas show the two pulses of the jig and the two primary pulses of the reel, which coincide. The lighter shaded areas show the two secondary pulses of the reel.

As I alluded to above, it is possible to give emphasis to the different notes of the long roll using the breath and differing ways of playing cuts and strikes. Why would we want to do this? Because rolls can occur in a variety of different contexts in relation to the pulse. In our practice of rolls so far we have only been playing them such that the first note of the roll falls on a strong pulse. This is one way that we encounter rolls in tunes, but very often a pulse coincides with the cut (second) note or the struck (third) note of the long roll instead. Soon I will give you a variety of examples.

I feel that rolls sound more musical when you give a bit of emphasis to the note that falls on the pulse. To this same end it helps to make the off-pulse notes a bit more gentle.

I have alluded to how you can accomplish this with breath emphasis. You can "lean into" the on-pulse note with your breath, blowing just a bit harder and louder, taking care not to appreciably raise the pitch of the note.

Now let's take a closer look at some subtleties of the cut and strike that can also help in this regard. Note that these are very advanced refinements that should only be attempted after you have achieved considerable mastery of regular cuts and strikes.

VARYING THE "STRENGTH" OF THE CUT

In the chapter on cuts we saw how the good cut must be brief enough to fall below a threshold of perception such that our ears do not perceive them as notes unto themselves. We didn't talk about the fact that the brevity of cuts, once below that threshold, can still vary. I find that, among cuts that do fall below that threshold, the shorter ones sound more subtle, or less emphatic to our ears. Thus, once you truly master the cut, you can vary its length to achieve differing degrees of strength. The shorter, less emphatic cuts are produced by a smaller lift of the finger. Since the lift covers less distance it can be shorter in time. These shorter cuts require a higher level of mastery of the physical movement involved.

When the cut note of a long roll falls on the pulse you should try using the longer, stronger cut. When the first or third note of the roll falls on the pulse, the cut (second) note necessarily falls on a weak beat. That is a time to use the shorter, less emphatic cut.

174

Here I want to introduce a new idea regarding the physical movements of the strike itself, not the speed of such movements. Thus far, in the velocity phase of the strike we have been hitting the tone hole full on with the striking finger to achieve a good, strong, percussive sound. It is possible however, by just slightly straightening the striking finger, to hit the tone hole in such a way that in the moment of impact you do not cover the entire hole. This results in a strike that sounds less emphatic, though it is no less crisp and precise.

You can use this subtler strike to good effect when the first note, or especially when the second note (i.e. the cut note) of the long roll falls on a pulse. When the cut note of the long roll falls on the pulse, the strike consequently falls on a weaker, off-pulse beat. Giving less emphasis to the strike in these cases has the effect of giving more emphasis where you want it, on the pulse.

Figures 10-12 and 10-13 below shows the B2 finger first in preparation for a strike on F-sharp, with the usual, gentle arch, and then in contact with the tone hole on impact, fully covering the hole.

Figures 10-12. B2 in preparation for a strike on F-sharp.

Figure 10-13. B2 in contact with its hole performing a normal strike.

Figures 10-14 and 10-15 show first the B2 finger in preparation for a strike on F-sharp, and then the finger in contact with the tone hole on impact, covering most of the hole but leaving the far edge of it unaffected. Notice how the finger is slightly straightened.

Figures 10-14. B2 in preparation for a strike on F-sharp.

Figure 10-15. B2 in contact with its hole, slightly straightened, performing a more subtle strike.

The angle of attack of the striking finger is of course continuously variable by making minute adjustments to the straightness of the finger. This allows you a wide range of variation in the strength of your strikes. Cathal McConnell is a player who employs strikes of a wide variety of qualities. See the transcription of his recording of the reel *Peter Flanagan's* in Section 8, pp. 400-402 and seek out his recordings to hear these techniques in action.

Unfortunately, varying the angle of attack of the striking finger does not give the same effect on Boehm-system flutes.

How Long Rolls Relate to the Pulse

Now that you know how you can control rhythmic emphasis within the roll, and why you would want to do so, here are some real-life applications.

In Irish tunes, the first note of a long roll quite frequently falls upon a primary pulse. For examples, see the beginning of the reel *The Banshee* in Figures 10-16 and 10-17 below:

*Figure 10-16. The first two measures of the reel **The Banshee** with long rolls on G. (For a complete version of the tune, see p. 348.)*

 Track 34

177

*Figure 10-17. The first two measures of the reel **The Banshee** with G long rolls, shown in exploded view.*

and the beginning of *Whelan's Jig* in Figures 10-18 and 10-19 below.

*Figure 10-18. The first two measures of **Whelan's Jig** with a
long roll on E. (For a complete version of the tune, see p. 344.)*

Track 35

*Figure 10-19. The first two measures of **Whelan's Jig** with the E long roll, shown in exploded view.*

Long rolls, however, do not always begin on a pulse, primary or secondary. For an example, see the beginning of the reel *The Drunken Landlady* in Figure 10-20 and 10-21 below. (A note to classical players: I do not intend for the notation of the first two notes in each measure of Figure 10-20 to imply emphasis on the start of the second note. Emphasis should instead be placed on the cut notes of these rolls, which fall on secondary pulses, as shown in Figure 10-21.)

*Figure 10-20. The first two measures of the reel **The Drunken Landlady** with long rolls on E, which
begin on the second eighth-note beat of the measure. (For a complete version of the tune see p. 349.)*

Track 36

*Figure 10-21. The first two measures of the reel **The Drunken Landlady**
with E long rolls, shown in exploded view.*

In Figure 10-21 you can clearly see that the second note of the roll, the cut note, falls upon a secondary pulse (i.e. the third eighth-note beat). The first and third notes of the roll fall on weaker nonpulse beats (two and four). Therefore, you may choose to give the second note of the roll, the cut note, some emphasis, as explained above, while slightly de-emphasizing the weight of the first and third notes of the roll. Here is a good place for one of those more subtle strikes.

Of course, the cut note of a long roll can fall on a reel's primary pulse as well. In Figures 10-22 and 10-23 you see the beginning of the reel *The Gravel Walk*. At the end of the first measure and crossing the barline into the second measure is a long roll on A. Notice that the cut note falls on the primary pulse at the beginning of the second measure.

*Figure 10-22. The first two measures of the reel **The Gravel Walk** with a long A roll beginning on the eighth eighth-note beat of the first measure. (For a complete version of the tune, see p. 351.)*

 Track 37

*Figure 10-23. The first two measures of the reel **The Gravel Walk** with a long A roll, shown in exploded view.*

Notice also the unusual notation in Figure 10-22. The roll symbol appears above an eighth note that is tied across a barline to a quarter note. The total duration of the two tied notes equals three eighth-note beats, the number of beats required for a long roll. There's really nothing unusual about this roll's sound and function in the music. It's just our convention of using barlines to divide our notated music up into regular, manageable chunks that forces us to notate this roll in an odd-looking way.

Rolls in which the second, or cut note falls on a pulse are unusual in jigs, but they do occur. (Remember that jigs have no secondary pulses.) Figures 10-24 and 10-25 show a variation on the beginning of *The Monaghan Jig* that yields just such a situation.

*Figure 10-24. The first two measures of a variation on **The Monaghan Jig** with a long roll on E beginning on the third eighth-note beat of the measure. (For a complete version of the tune, see p. 341.)*

 Track 38

*Figure 10-25. The first two measures of a variation on **The Monaghan Jig** with a long roll on E, shown in exploded view.*

In jigs, there are also times when the third note of a long roll, the struck note, falls on a pulse. Figures 10-26 and 10-27 show such a roll in the B part of the well-known jig *The Rose in the Heather*. Take a look at the long roll on E in the fourth measure. Here you could use a good strong strike and a gentler cut.

*Figure 10-26. The first four measures of the B part of **The Rose in the Heather** which includes a long roll on E beginning on the second eighth-note beat of the fourth measure. (For a complete version of the tune, see p. 342.)*

 Track 39

*Figure 10-27. The first four measures of the B part of **The Rose in the Heather** with long rolls, shown in exploded view.*

In a reel it can happen that the struck note of a long roll falls on either a primary or secondary pulse. In fact in Figures 10-16 and 10-17 the struck notes of the G long rolls fall on a secondary pulses. We hardly notice this, though, because the first notes of these rolls are falling on the stronger primary pulses. This is a very common occurrence in reels.

However, it is very unusual for the struck note of a long roll to fall on a primary pulse in a reel.

UNEVEN ROLLS

Once you feel you have gained enough control that you can consistently play the three notes of your long rolls dead even on their beats, you are ready to experiment with the internal rhythm of the roll.

Actually, the only kind of deviation from the even long roll that I often hear traditional players make is one in which the cut note is delayed. The struck note seems to stay on the third beat. Thus, the cut and the strike are squeezed closer together than in the even roll. This kind of roll can be heard among players of all instruments but is especially common among fiddlers, and when tunes are played at slow or moderate tempos. As the tunes speed up the rolls tend to even out.

The amount that the cut note is delayed is highly individual and changeable. However, it is rarely something as neat and orderly as simply dotting the first note of the roll, that is, placing the second note exactly halfway between beats two and three, as shown below in Figure 10-28.

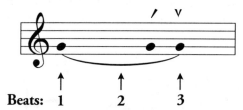

Beats: 1   2   3

Figure 10-28. Uneven rolls are rarely played as shown here, with the second note placed halfway between beats two and three.

Much more often the internal rhythm of the uneven roll is something more like what is shown in Figure 10-29 below.

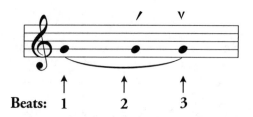

Beats: 1   2   3

Figure 10-29. Uneven rolls are usually played in a fashion similar to what is shown here, that is, the second note is placed closer to beat two than to beat three.

When you are trying to play in tight unison with another musician, there are a great many aspects of their playing that you will want to understand and match. One of them is surely the internal rhythm of their rolls. Hopefully they are listening to you with the same attention and care!

PREVIEW OF A SPECIAL CASE OF UNEVEN ROLLS

Certain types of tunes, such as hornpipes, mazurkas, and schottisches, are normally played with an *overtly* uneven subdivision of the pulse. That is, the notes tend to alternate "long–short, long–short". The lilt of jigs, reels, and the like is usually more subtle and often goes unnoticed.

A special situation comes up when playing rolls in these uneven kinds of tunes. The rolls are mostly played with the same kind of underlying unevenness. We'll take a close look at all of this in Chapter 14, *Rolls in Tunes with Overtly Uneven Subdivisions of the Beat*, once we've explored some other forms of rolls.

SLIDING INTO THE ROLL

One of the most pleasing things to do with all the varieties of rolls is to slide into its first note from below. This can be accomplished with either the simple type or added-finger type of slide, or with the struck slide, depending upon the musical context. It is usually best done in a subtle manner without "slurping" the pitch too much.

If you wish to notate sliding into a roll you could do so as shown below in the beginning of the reel *Roaring Mary*.

*Figure 10-30. Sliding into long rolls at the start of the reel **Roaring Mary**.*
(For a complete version of the tune, see p. 349.)

 Track 40

Note that you slide into the first long roll with a simple slide and into the second one with an added-finger slide, that could be a struck slide if desired. Also note how you can slide into the quarter-note high G in the second measure, which has a mid-note cut indicated.

i Pat Mitchell, *The Dance Music of Willie Clancy*, 2nd ed. (Dublin: Mercier Press, 1977), p. 12.

ii Breandán Breathnach, *Ceol Rince na hÉireann, Vol. 1* (Dublin: An Gúm, 1963).

chapter 11: short rolls

The **short roll** can be most easily grasped as a long roll missing its first note. Thus, the short roll is a group of two slurred notes of the same pitch, each one having a different articulation. The first note is cut, and the second is struck. What I have just described looks like this:

Figure 11-1. A short roll on G, shown in exploded view.

It is essential to understand that the short roll occupies only *two* eighth-note beats whereas the long roll occupies three (see Figure 11-2 below).

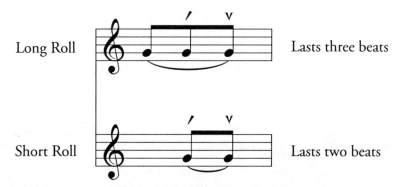

Figure 11-2. Comparison of long and short rolls.

As we examine more forms of the roll, you will see that some of them occupy three eighth-note beats, some occupy two, and two of them occupy only one eighth-note beat.

A NEW SYMBOL

I have modified the symbol in common usage for rolls to create a symbol specifically for the short roll. It is shown below in Figure 11-3.

Figure 11-3. The symbol for a short roll on G.

Note well that the short-roll symbol appears above a quarter note. The short roll is only two eighth notes in duration, the same duration as a quarter note.

Notice that the short-roll symbol is the long-roll symbol with a slash through it. This shows that the short roll is a shortened form of the long roll. The slash, being the symbol for the cut, also draws attention to the fact that a cut initiates the short roll.

182

Another way to look at the difference between long and short rolls is that the long roll starts with a "plain" note that gives you one eighth-note beat to prepare for doing a cut on the second note. The cut in the long roll is the easiest of all cuts, one that separates two notes of the same pitch.

The short roll doesn't allow you any preparation time. It starts with its cut right off the bat. That's one reason why the short roll is more challenging to play than the long roll. Since the short roll begins with a cut, most of the issues raised in the chapter on cuts, Chapter 7, apply equally to the short roll. For example, the challenges of cutting notes, when ascending or descending to them, apply to short rolls as well.

You will often find that you will want or need to tongue or throat the start of a short roll. In that case, you will be cutting and tonguing or throating at the same time. This is tricky until you've had a lot of practice. If you need clarification on this see the section *Cutting and Tonguing (or Throating) at the Same Time* in Chapter 7, p. 134.

Remember that when you cut and tongue or throat at the same time, your cutting finger needs to be in the air, not still on the instrument, at the instant that you tongue or throat. If you cut slightly after you tongue or throat you will hear the cut an instant late and the result will be a kind of jumbled double articulation.

NOW THAT THE FOG HAS CLEARED

By now you are thoroughly familiar with my opinion that cuts and strikes are articulations, not notes or grace notes of any kind. Thus you understand that the short roll is a two-note ornament, and not a four-note ornament as it has been almost universally described in published whistle and flute tutors. Figure 11-4 below shows some examples of unfortunate, ill-conceived short-roll notation taken from such books.

Figure 11-4. Examples of ill-conceived short-roll notation taken from published flute and whistle tutors.

All of these examples are incorrect and misleading. None of them look like what a short roll sounds like. None of them accurately convey the rhythm of the short roll. They all imply that the pitch of the cut and strike are perceivable and significant. If anyone, not already knowing what a short roll sounds like, tried to reproduce what is notated in these examples, they would not get anything that sounds like a short roll.

Why not notate them the way they sound when played *well*, especially when that notation is much simpler to read and write?

THE RHYTHM OF THE SHORT ROLL

This bears repeating: **it is critically important to learn to play your short rolls absolutely dead even, each eighth note articulated right on its beat.** You will not always want to play them so evenly, but you will need to be able to, especially when playing tunes at very fast tempos.

TRY SOME SHORT ROLLS

Try playing the short roll on low G that is shown on p. 182 in Figure 11-1. You're simply going to play two eighth notes, cutting and tonguing or throating the first one, then slurring into and striking the second one.

Set your metronome at a comfortable tempo somewhere around 60 beats per minute. You are going to play along with the metronome in a cycle (or meter) of three beats, each beat representing an eighth note. Count out the three-beat pattern until you are comfortable with it. Then, on beat one, cut a low G with T2 at the same moment that you tongue or throat it. (Remember: your cutting finger should be in the air at the moment you tongue or throat. If you cut slightly after you tongue or throat you will hear the cut an instant late.) Still playing, and without interrupting the air flow, strike the G with B1 on beat two. On beat three stop and take a breath if you wish. Try this short roll a few more times.

Experiment as you wish and once you are ready, start again and keep the pattern going (see Exercise 11-1, below).

Exercise 11-1. Practicing short rolls on G, shown in exploded view.

Track 41

Remember that what you are now playing can also be written as shown in Figure 11-5 below.

Figure 11-5. Practicing short rolls on G, in normal view.

Try playing these short rolls in the high register, too. These fingerings, and the ones for the other short rolls you are about to learn, are correct for both registers.

The G short roll is probably the easiest one to play because the labor is divided between your two hands and you are using fingers that for most people are among their most agile ones. The F-sharp short roll is the next easiest one. Set up the metronome as before and play these exercises in the same manner you played Exercise 11-1. Cut with T3 and strike with B2. Leave B1 in place.

Exercise 11-2. Practicing short rolls on F-sharp, shown in exploded view.

Next work with the E short roll. This can be one of the more challenging ones because all of the work is in one hand. Don't forget to lift your bottom hand pinky when it's time to strike the E. Cut with B1 and strike with B3. Leave B2 in place.

Exercise 11-3. Practicing short rolls on E, shown in exploded view.

The following setting of *The Sporting Pitchfork* makes use of the three short rolls we have just been practicing.

Figure 11-6. A setting of **The Sporting Pitchfork** using short rolls on G, F-sharp, and E.

 Track 42

185

You cannot do a short roll on D because there is no way to strike a D.

Try the A short roll next. This is another of the one-handed rolls, for many people the most difficult one because of the strike with T3, the least agile of the hole-covering fingers for most people. Cut with T1 and strike with T3. Leave T2 in place.

Exercise 11-4. Practicing short rolls on A, shown in exploded view.

Now try the B short roll, which is another one-handed roll. This one feels different because the cutting and striking fingers are adjacent, with no stationary finger between them. Cut with T1 and strike with T2. No finger stays down.

Exercise 11-5. Practicing short rolls on B, shown in exploded view.

Just as with the long roll, don't lose track of the steady beat as you practice your short rolls. When you hear that a cut or strike is early or late, take note of that and return your focus to matching the beat. When you are able to stay on the beat consistently, stay with that comfortable tempo for a while and let your muscles really get to know the feeling of placing these articulations where they belong. In other words, practice doing it right for a while before going on to a faster tempo.

ADDING SHORT ROLLS ON A AND B TO *THE SPORTING PITCHFORK*

The following setting of *The Sporting Pitchfork* adds the A and B short rolls to the G, F-sharp and E short rolls.

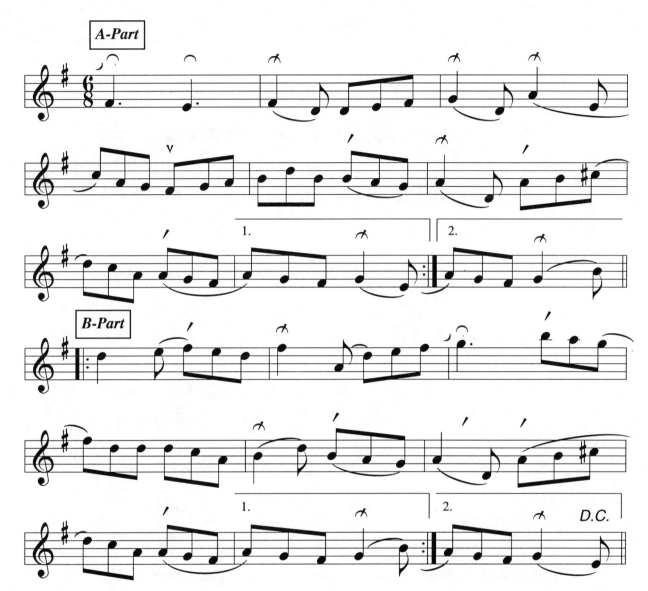

*Figure 11-7. A setting of **The Sporting Pitchfork** using short rolls on B, A, G, F-sharp, and E.*

Track 43

LESS TIME TO PREPARE FOR THE STRIKE

With long rolls, as you reached the point where you could play them well at a normal playing speed, you noticed that the preparation for the strike could begin even before you performed the cut. This lent a grace and fluidity to the feeling of playing the long roll.

With the short roll, things are a bit trickier. You rarely have the time or opportunity to start the preparation for the strike before the cut that begins the short roll. Often, the finger that will be striking is busy doing something else just before the short roll begins.

So, once you get short rolls up to speed you should begin the preparation for the strike at the same time that you perform the cut. Thus you will be lifting two fingers at approximately the same time, the cutting finger and the striking finger preparing to strike.

187

Whereas long rolls can be placed in a number of different ways relative to the pulse (see *How Long Rolls Relate to the Pulse* on pp. 177-180 in Chapter 10), short rolls seem to be appropriate in a more limited range of rhythmic placements. In reels, you never seem to hear them beginning on a beat that is not either a primary or secondary pulse. You could use them in this way, but I feel that when you do so they draw too much attention to non-pulse beats. An example of this awkward-sounding use of a short roll appears below in a variant on the beginning of *Lad O'Beirne's Reel*. (Note also the mid-note cut on G in the first bar.)

*Figure 11-8. A variant on the start of **Lad O'Beirne's Reel** demonstrating an awkward-sounding short roll that begins on a non-pulse beat. (For a complete version of the tune see p. 352.)*

 Track 44

A more musical way of playing this appears in Figure 11-9. Note that a short roll begins on a primary pulse in this example.

*Figure 11-9. A more musical variant on the start of **Lad O'Beirne's Reel**.*

 Track 45

Another way that many people play the beginning of this reel is shown in Figure 11-10 below.

*Figure 11-10. A more common way to play the start of **Lad O'Beirne's Reel**.*

 Track 46

In jigs, short rolls can be used starting on pulse or non-pulse beats, though it is uncommon to encounter them starting on non-pulse beats. Here is an example of a short roll starting on a pulse in the single jig *The Lonesome Jig*, also know as *The Rolling Waves, McGuire's March,* and *Maguire's Kick.* Note the mid-note cut in the first bar.

*Figure 11-11. A short roll in the second bar of **The Lonesome Jig**.*
(For a complete version of the tune see p. 126.)

 Track 47

In the next example, we see the appropriate use of short rolls starting on non-pulse beats, namely the second beat in the group of three. This is the beginning of the jig *Tripping Up the Stairs.* Care should be taken to play these short rolls gently so as not to overemphasize the non-pulse beats.

Figure 11-12. Short rolls in the opening bar of the jig **Tripping Up the Stairs**.
(For a complete version of the tune see p. 343.)

Track 48

Note that Figure 11-12 could also be notated using mid-note cuts in the fifth bar as shown in Figure 11-13 below.

Figure 11-13. The music of Figure 11-12 notated with mid-note cuts.

The following interpretation of the jig *The Frost is All Over* shows an example of a short roll starting on the third beat of a group of three eighth notes.

Figure 11-14. A variant on the opening bars of the jig **The Frost is All Over**.
(For a complete version of the tune see p. 338.)

Track 49

Once again, care should be taken not to overemphasize the cut of this short roll. The struck note should get more weight than the cut note.

A SHORT ROLL PRECEDED BY AN EIGHTH NOTE OF THE SAME PITCH, OR IS IT A LONG ROLL?

Sometimes a long roll may be interpreted as a short roll preceded by an eighth note of the same pitch, especially when the cut note of the long roll falls on a pulse and is thus emphasized. This is not really wrong, for the last two notes of a long roll are identical to the elements of a short roll. The only factor that really distinguishes these two interpretations is that the notes of any roll, according to my definition, are always slurred together. So, if all three notes in question are slurred together, I would say that there is a long roll being played. If only the last two notes are slurred together, then I would vote to call it a short roll preceded by an eighth note of the same pitch.

Figures 11-15 and 11-16 below show an example of this situation in which only the last two notes are slurred to thus form a short roll.

Figure 11-15. An example of a short roll preceded by an eighth note of the same pitch, shown in normal view.

Figure 11-16. The same example as Figure 11-15 shown in exploded view. This shows more clearly that only the last two notes are slurred, forming a short roll.

Figures 11-17 and 11-18 show the same musical example with all three E notes slurred together, thus forming a long roll on E. The distinction between the sounds of these two examples is really quite slight.

Figure 11-17. The same example notated with a long roll, shown in normal view.

Figure 11-18. The same example as Figure 11-17 shown in exploded view. This shows more clearly that the last three notes are slurred, forming a long roll.

Let's look at how both of these variants can be used in the same tune, in this case the first part of the reel *The Drunken Landlady*.

*Figure 11-19. The first part of the reel **The Drunken Landlady**.*
(For a complete version of the tune see p. 349.)

 Track 51

Comparing the beginnings of the first two measures, the short roll in measure two, with its articulated cut, gives a slight emphasis to the third eighth-note beat. The long roll in measure one has a smoother feeling because we slur into the cut note on the third eighth-note beat. It is a subtle variation, one that helps develop the rhythmic landscape of the tune.

UNEVEN SHORT ROLLS

Short rolls that occur in hornpipes, mazurkas, schottisches, or other tunes that are played with an overtly uneven underlying rhythm, are played to go along with that uneven rhythm. In these situations, the struck note is delayed but the cut note remains on the beat. We will cover that topic in depth in Chapter 14.

The kind of uneven playing that is discussed on pp. 180-181 in the previous chapter, i.e. long rolls in which the cut note is somewhat delayed, does not apply in the case of short rolls. Since the short roll begins with the cut note, that note cannot be delayed without serious damage being done. As we have seen from the examples above, when a short roll is used it is almost always placed so as to give emphasis and draw attention to the cut note. Therefore the cut's rhythmic placement must be accurate.

The cut note in the *long* roll can take on a variety of "characters." It can be strong and emphatic or it can be gentle and subtle. Since it is a note *internal* to the roll, it can be delayed. Not so with the cut in the short roll. It *initiates* the short roll and so cannot be delayed.

SLIDING INTO THE SHORT ROLL

This subject was discussed in regard to long rolls at the end of the last chapter. There is nothing much different about sliding into a short roll except that when you do so you are also sliding into a cut.

191

You can take the idea of sliding into a long roll to its extreme, resulting in a long roll variant that I call an *ascending roll*. Instead of lowering the pitch of the first note momentarily with a slide, in this case you actually play the *entire* first note one scale step lower than normal. Mary Bergin does this in *Old Joe's Jig,* which appears on her first recording.[i] Figures 11-20 and 11-21 show how the opening of *Old Joe's Jig* could be played without, and then with an ascending roll.

*Figure 11-20. The opening bars of **Old Joe's Jig** beginning with a long roll, shown in normal view. (For a complete version of the tune see p. 342.)*

Track 52

*Figure 11-21. The opening bars of **Old Joe's Jig** beginning with an ascending roll, which is shown in exploded view.*

Track 53

Is this an altered long roll, or is it really just a short roll preceded by an eighth note?

*Figure 11-22. The opening bars of **Old Joe's Jig** shown beginning with an ascending roll, which is notated using the short roll symbol.*

Good question. I don't have a good answer and I'm not sure that it matters very much. Since most players think of this place in the tune as a long roll on F-sharp, I suppose I would consider this ascending roll to be a variant on that idea. The fact that all three notes are slurred together further supports this.

But since there is an easy way to notate what is happening here using already existing symbols (as in Figure 11-22), I don't feel there's a reason to invent a new symbol for the ascending roll.

[i] Mary Bergin, *Feadóga Stáin: Traditional Irish Music on the Tin Whistle.* Shanachie Records 79006, 1979.

chapter 12: condensed long rolls

The **condensed long roll** contains all of the elements of the long roll, condensed in time from its normal duration of three eighth-note beats to a duration of only *two* eighth-note beats. In condensing the long roll, the only things that change are the duration of the roll and its internal rhythm.

The use of the term "condensed" to describe this form of long roll, as well as other forms of rolls and cranns shown in the following chapters, is my own invention. Condensed ornaments, however, have been around for a very long time.

Figure 12-1 shows the normal long roll and Figure 12-2 shows the condensed long roll.

Figure 12-1. A long roll on G, shown in exploded view.

Figure 12-2. A condensed long roll on G, shown in exploded view.

The long roll and the condensed long roll share all of the following characteristics:

1. Each is a group of three slurred notes of the same pitch;

2. Each note has a different articulation;

3. The first note is either tongued, throated, or slurred into from a preceding melody note;

4. The second note is cut; and

5. The third is struck.

The rhythm of the long roll is simply three eighth notes in succession. All three notes are equal in length. The total duration of the long roll is three eighth-note beats, or the equivalent of a dotted quarter note.

The rhythm of the condensed long roll is two sixteenth notes followed by one eighth note. Therefore the first two notes are each only half as long as the third note. The total duration of the condensed long roll is only two eighth-note beats, or the equivalent of a quarter note (undotted).

No New Symbol—a New Context Instead

The symbol for the condensed long roll is the same as the symbol for the long roll, because both contain the same elements. If the symbol appears above a dotted quarter note (three beats) the roll is a normal long roll. If the symbol appears over a regular quarter note (i.e. undotted, two eighth-note beats) then the roll is a condensed long roll. See Figure 12-3.

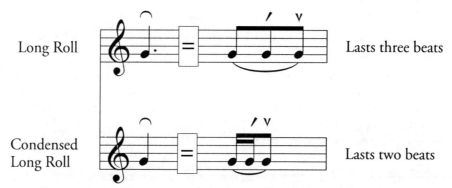

Long Roll — Lasts three beats

Condensed Long Roll — Lasts two beats

Figure 12-3. Comparison of the long roll and the condensed long roll.

Let's look at a musical example to make this more clear. Since a condensed long roll occupies only two eighth-note beats it can take the place of:

- a quarter note
- two eighth notes
- a short roll

Let's look at the beginning of *The Glen Allen Reel*. The tune begins with two eighth-note beats of G. Figure 12-4, below, shows those two beats of G played in four different ways.

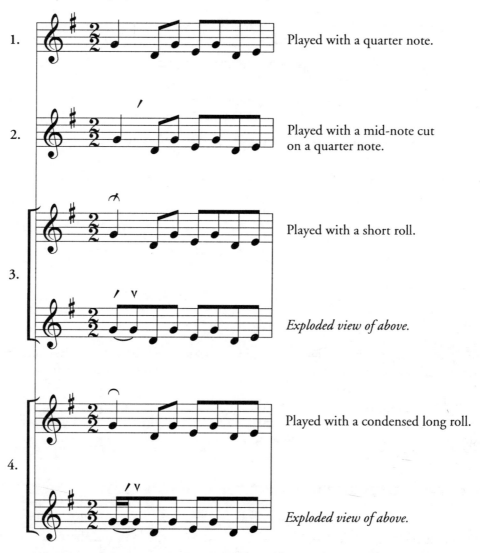

1. Played with a quarter note.

2. Played with a mid-note cut on a quarter note.

3. Played with a short roll.

   Exploded view of above.

4. Played with a condensed long roll.

   Exploded view of above.

*Figure 12-4. Four different ways to play the beginning of **The Glen Allen Reel**.*
(For a complete version of the tune see p. 350.)

Track 54

You can play a condensed long roll wherever you can play a short roll. Let's compare closely the short roll and the condensed long roll.

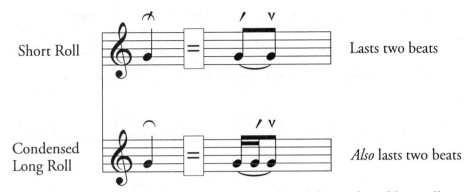

Figure 12-5. Comparison of the short roll and the condensed long roll.

Both occupy two eighth-note beats. With both, the strike comes right on the second beat. The differences are contained in the first eighth-note beat. During that first beat, the short roll has only one note and it is cut. During that same beat the condensed long roll has two notes of equal length and only the second one is cut.

Condensed Long Rolls Are Easier to Play than Short Rolls

Most people, once they understand condensed long rolls, find them easier to play and apply than short rolls. This is because, as with the regular long roll, there is a preparation note before the cut note. Therefore, the cut in the condensed long roll is always the easiest kind of cut, the cut between two notes of the same pitch. The various challenges shared by the cut and the short roll, discussed in the last chapter, are not issues with the condensed long roll.

Don't be tempted, though, to abandon the short roll in favor of the condensed long roll. You should have both under your belt. The qualities they impart to a tune are extremely different. Mary Bergin's clean, lean style is due in large part to her use of short rolls. Matt Molloy on the other hand, with his florid style, makes extensive use of condensed rolls, as well as other rhythmically condensed ornaments that we will get to in later chapters. Both approaches have their benefits and challenges. You should have all options available to you as you develop your own style of playing.

Thank Goodness the Fog is Gone

It's a good thing we have defined and understood cuts and strikes as articulations. Imagine how messy it would be to describe or notate the condensed long roll if we thought of cuts and strikes as grace notes. Maybe this is why none of the other flute or whistle tutors that I have seen make any mention of condensed rolls.

Try Some Condensed Long Rolls

With this ornament we are encountering sixteenth notes for the first time. Be sure that you are playing accurate, even sixteenth notes, not just a flurry of quick notes of an ill-defined nature. Try the following exercise to make sure you are on the right track.

Let's play the condensed long roll on low G that is shown in Figure 12-2 (see p. 193).

Set your metronome at a comfortable tempo somewhere around 60 beats per minute. You are going to play along with the metronome in a cycle (or meter) of three beats, each beat representing an eighth note. Count out the three-beat pattern until you are comfortable with it. Then, on beat one, play a low G. *Exactly* halfway between beat one and beat two, cut the G with T2. Still playing, and without interrupting the air flow, strike the G with B1 *exactly* on beat two. On beat three stop and take a breath if you wish. Try this condensed long roll a few more times.

Experiment as you wish and once you are ready, start again, and keep the pattern going (see Exercise 12-1, below).

Exercise 12-1. Practicing condensed long rolls on G, shown in exploded view.

Remember that what you are now playing can also be written as shown below in Figure 12-6.

Figure 12-6. Condensed long rolls on G, shown in normal view.

Try playing these condensed long rolls in the high register, too. These fingerings, and the ones for the other condensed long rolls you are about to learn, are correct for both registers.

The G condensed long roll is probably the easiest one to play because the labor is divided between your two hands and you are using fingers that for most people are among their most agile ones.

The F-sharp condensed long roll is the next easiest one. Set up the metronome as before and play these exercises in the same manner you played Exercise 12-1. Cut with T3 and strike with B2. Leave B1 in place.

Exercise 12-2. Practicing condensed long rolls on F-sharp, shown in exploded view.

Next, work with the E condensed long roll. This can be one of the more challenging ones because all of the work is in one hand. Don't forget to lift your bottom hand pinky when it's time to strike the E. Cut with B1 and strike with B3. Leave B2 in place.

Exercise 12-3. Practicing condensed long rolls on E, shown in exploded view.

The following setting of *The Sporting Pitchfork* makes use of the three condensed long rolls we have just been practicing.

*Figure 12-7. A setting of **The Sporting Pitchfork** using condensed long rolls on G, F-sharp, and E.*

Track 56

Remember that the long roll and condensed long roll use the same symbol. The difference is the duration of the note under the symbol. Note that there is a long roll followed by a condensed long roll in the first measure of Figure 12-7.

197

You cannot do a condensed long roll on D because there is no way to strike a D.

Try the condensed long roll on A next. This is another of the one-handed rolls, perhaps the most difficult one because of the strike with T3, the least agile of the hole-covering fingers for most people. Cut with T1 and strike with T3. Leave T2 in place.

Exercise 12-4. Practicing condensed long rolls on A, shown in exploded view.

Now try the B condensed long roll. Again, it is a one-handed roll. This one feels different because the cutting and striking fingers are adjacent, with no stationary finger between them. Cut with T1 and strike with T2. No finger stays down.

Exercise 12-5. Practicing condensed long rolls on B, shown in exploded view.

The following setting of *The Sporting Pitchfork* adds A and B condensed long rolls to the G, F-sharp, and E condensed long rolls.

*Figure 12-8. A setting of **The Sporting Pitchfork** using condensed long rolls on B, A, G, F-sharp, and E.*

 Track 57

HOW CONDENSED LONG ROLLS RELATE TO THE PULSE

Since condensed long rolls and short rolls are fairly interchangeable, the section in the last chapter called *How Short Rolls Relate to the Pulse* (see pp. 188-189) applies quite well to the case of condensed long rolls.

UNEVEN CONDENSED LONG ROLLS

Condensed long rolls that occur in hornpipes, mazurkas, schottisches, or other tunes that are played with an overtly uneven underlying rhythm are played to go along with that uneven rhythm. In these situations, the struck notes are delayed to match the underlying uneven subdivision of the beat. The cut note may or may not be delayed depending on the preferences of the player. We will cover this topic in depth in the Chapter 14.

This subject was discussed in regard to long rolls at the end of the Chapter 10. There is nothing much different about sliding into a condensed long roll.

THE DOUBLE-CONDENSED LONG ROLL

It is possible to condense the long roll from its original duration of three eighth-note beats down to only *one* eighth-note beat. I think of this as condensing the roll by *two degrees*, hence the name **double-condensed long roll.**

Figure 12-9 shows the double-condensed long roll.

Figure 12-9. A double-condensed long roll on G,
shown in exploded view.

The rhythm of this ornament is two thirty-second notes followed by one sixteenth note. However, when playing in a fast tempo most players will tend to even these notes out so that they resemble more a true sixteenth-note triplet, as shown below. In a sixteenth-note triplet, three notes of equal duration are played in the amount of time normally occupied by two sixteenth notes.

Figure 12-10. A double-condensed long roll on G,
played as a true sixteenth-note triplet.

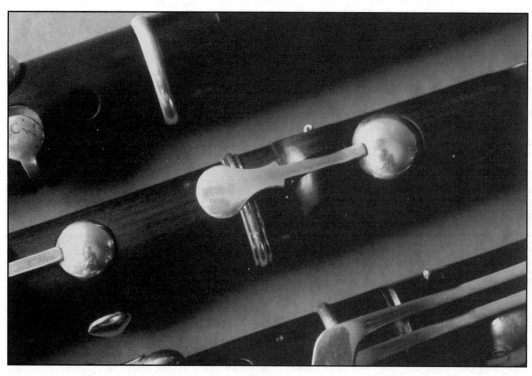

The symbol for the double-condensed long roll is the same as the one used for the long roll and the condensed long roll, because all three of these rolls contain the same elements. However, the symbol for the double-condensed long roll appears over an *eighth note*, since that is its total duration. Figure 12-11 (below) shows a comparison of the long roll, the condensed long roll, and the double-condensed long roll. Note well the durations of the notes that appear under each long roll symbol.

Figure 12-11. A comparison of the long roll, the condensed long roll, and the double-condensed long roll.

The double-condensed long roll is rarely heard, but there are some excellent examples of it in my transcription of Matt Molloy's version of the jig *The Humours of Drinagh*, which appears on pp. 395-397 in Section 8. Below, we can see how Matt Molloy uses this ornament in measure 11, the second time through the tune.

Figure 12-12. Matt Molloy's use of a double-condensed long roll in measure 11 of the second time through the jig
The Humours of Drinagh, *shown here in normal view. Note also the condensed short crann in m. 12.*

Here is the same excerpt shown in exploded view.

Figure 12-13. The same as above, shown in exploded view.

Matt Molloy plays this at quite a fast tempo. The rhythm of both the double-condensed long roll and the condensed short crann both resemble sixteenth-note triplets, as shown above in Figure 12-10. We will explore cranns in Chapter 16.

chapter 13: condensed short rolls

The **condensed short roll** contains all of the elements of the short roll, condensed in time from its normal duration of two eighth-note beats down to a duration of only *one* eighth-note beat. In condensing the short roll the only things that change are its duration and internal rhythm.

Figure 13-1 shows the normal short roll and Figure 13-2 shows the condensed short roll.

Figure 13-1. A short roll on G, shown in exploded view.

Figure 13-2. A condensed short roll on G, shown in exploded view.

The short roll and the condensed short roll share all of the following characteristics:

1. Each is a group of two slurred notes of the same pitch.

2. Each note has a different kind of articulation.

3. The first note is cut, and may be either tongued, throated, or slurred into from a preceding melody note.

4. The second note is struck.

As you know, the rhythm of the short roll is simply two eighth notes in succession. Both notes are equal in length. The total duration of the short roll is the equivalent of a quarter note.

The rhythm of the condensed short roll is two *sixteenth notes* in succession. Both of its notes are also equal in length. The total duration of the condensed short roll is only one eighth-note beat.

NO NEW SYMBOL—A NEW CONTEXT INSTEAD

The symbol for the condensed short roll is the same as the symbol for the short roll, because both contain the same basic elements. If the symbol appears above a quarter note (two beats), the roll is a normal short roll. If the symbol appears over an eighth note (one beat), then the roll is a condensed short roll. See Figure 13-3.

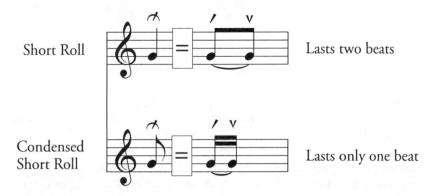

Short Roll — Lasts two beats

Condensed Short Roll — Lasts only one beat

Figure 13-3. Comparison of the short roll and the condensed short roll.

Let's look at a musical example to make this more clear. Figure 13-4 shows the beginning of the jig *The Humours of Drinagh*. Matt Molloy plays this on his first album[i] and sometimes uses a condensed short roll on the first note of the tune as shown below.

*Figure 13-4: The first two bars of the jig **The Humours of Drinagh** with a condensed short roll on F-sharp shown in normal view. (For a complete version of the tune see the transcription of Matt Molloy's recording on pp. 395-397 in Section 8.)*

Figure 13-5 shows the condensed short roll in exploded view:

*Figure 13-5. The first two bars of the jig **The Humours of Drinagh**
with a condensed short roll on F-sharp shown in exploded view.*

Condensed short rolls are very useful for ornamenting eighth notes in polkas. For example, see the excerpt from the first part of the polka *Maids of Ardagh* in Figures 13-6 and 13-7 below.

*Figure 13-6. A condensed short roll on F-sharp in the third bar of the polka **Maids of Ardagh**,
shown in normal view. (For a complete version of the tune see p. 356.)*

① *Track 58*

*Figure 13-7. A condensed short roll on F-sharp in the third bar
of the polka **The Maids of Ardagh**, shown in exploded view.*

Let's play the condensed short roll on low G that is shown in Figure 13-2 (see p. 202).

Set your metronome at a comfortable tempo somewhere around 60 beats per minute. You are going to play along with the metronome in a cycle (or meter) of two beats, each beat representing an eighth note. Count out the two-beat pattern until you are comfortable with it. Then, on beat one, cut a low G with T2 at the same moment that you tongue or throat it. (Remember: your cutting finger should be in the air at the moment you tongue or throat. If you cut slightly after you tongue or throat, you will hear the cut an instant late.) Still playing, and without interrupting the air flow, strike the G with B1 *exactly* halfway between beat one and beat two. On beat two, stop and take a breath if you wish. Try this short roll a few more times.

Experiment as you wish and once you are ready, start again and keep the pattern going (see Exercise 13-1 below).

Exercise 13-1. Practicing condensed short rolls on G, shown in exploded view.

Track 59

Remember that what you are now playing can also be written as shown in Figure 13-8 below.

Figure 13-8. Condensed short rolls on G, shown in normal view.

Try playing these condensed short rolls in the high octave too. These fingerings, and the ones for the other short rolls you are about to learn, are correct for both octaves.

The G condensed short roll is probably the easiest one to play because the labor is divided between your two hands and you are using fingers that for most people are among their most agile ones.

The F-sharp condensed short roll is the next easiest one. Set up the metronome as before and play these exercises in the same manner you played Exercise 13-1. Cut with T3 and strike with B2. Leave B1 in place.

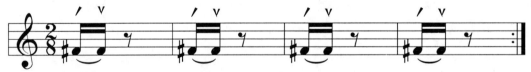

Exercise 13-2: Practicing condensed short rolls on F-sharp, shown in exploded view.

Next, work with the E condensed short roll. This can be one of the more challenging ones because all of the work is in one hand. Don't forget to lift your bottom-hand pinky when it's time to strike the E. Cut with B1 and strike with B3. Leave B2 in place.

Exercise 13-3. Practicing condensed short rolls on E, shown in exploded view.

USING CONDENSED SHORT ROLLS ON G, F-SHARP, AND E IN *THE SPORTING PITCHFORK*

The following setting of *The Sporting Pitchfork* makes us of the three condensed short rolls we have just been practicing.

*Figure 13-9. A setting of **The Sporting Pitchfork** using condensed short rolls on G, F-sharp, and E.*

Track 60

205

MORE CONDENSED SHORT ROLLS

You cannot do a condensed short roll on D because there is no way to strike a D.

Try the A condensed short roll next. This is another of the one-handed rolls, for many people the most difficult one because of the strike with T3, the least agile of the hole-covering fingers for most people. Cut with T1 and strike with T3. Leave T2 in place.

Exercise 13-4. Practicing condensed short short rolls on A, shown in exploded view.

Now try the B condensed short roll. Again, a one-handed roll. This one feels different because the cutting and striking fingers are adjacent, with no stationary finger between them. Cut with T1 and strike with T2. No finger stays down.

Exercise 13-5. Practicing condensed short short rolls on B, shown in exploded view.

ADDING CONDENSED SHORT ROLLS ON A AND B TO *THE SPORTING PITCHFORK*

The following setting of *The Sporting Pitchfork* adds the A and B condensed short rolls to the G, F-sharp, and E condensed short rolls.

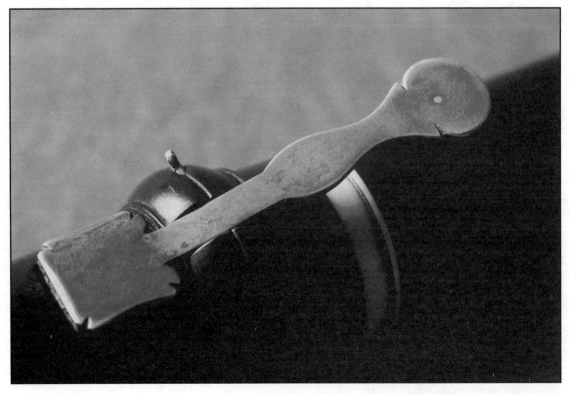

*Figure 13-10. A setting of **The Sporting Pitchfork** using condensed short rolls on B, A, G, F-sharp, and E.*

 Track 61

SLIDING INTO THE CONDENSED SHORT ROLL

This subject was discussed in regard to long rolls at the end of the Chapter 10. There is nothing much different about sliding into a condensed short roll except that when you do so you are also sliding into a cut.

SUMMARY: ALL EIGHT SETTINGS OF *THE SPORTING PITCHFORK*

On the following two pages you may view and compare all eight settings of *The Sporting Pitchfork* that are given in Chapters 10–13. The variations you see there represent only the tip of the iceberg of possibilities, and represent only my own style of playing.

These examples serve to illustrate some possible uses of various rolls, cuts, slides, phrasing, and general variation. I have put them in score form so that you can easily compare them. Long rolls are introduced in #1(on E, F-sharp, and G) and #2 (on E, F-sharp, G, A, and B); short rolls in #3 (on E, F-sharp, and G) and #4 (on E, F-sharp, G, A, and B); condensed long rolls in #5 (on E, F-sharp, and G) and #6 (on E, F-sharp, G, A, and B); and condensed short rolls in #7 (on E, F-sharp, and G) and #8 (on E, F-sharp, G, A, and B).

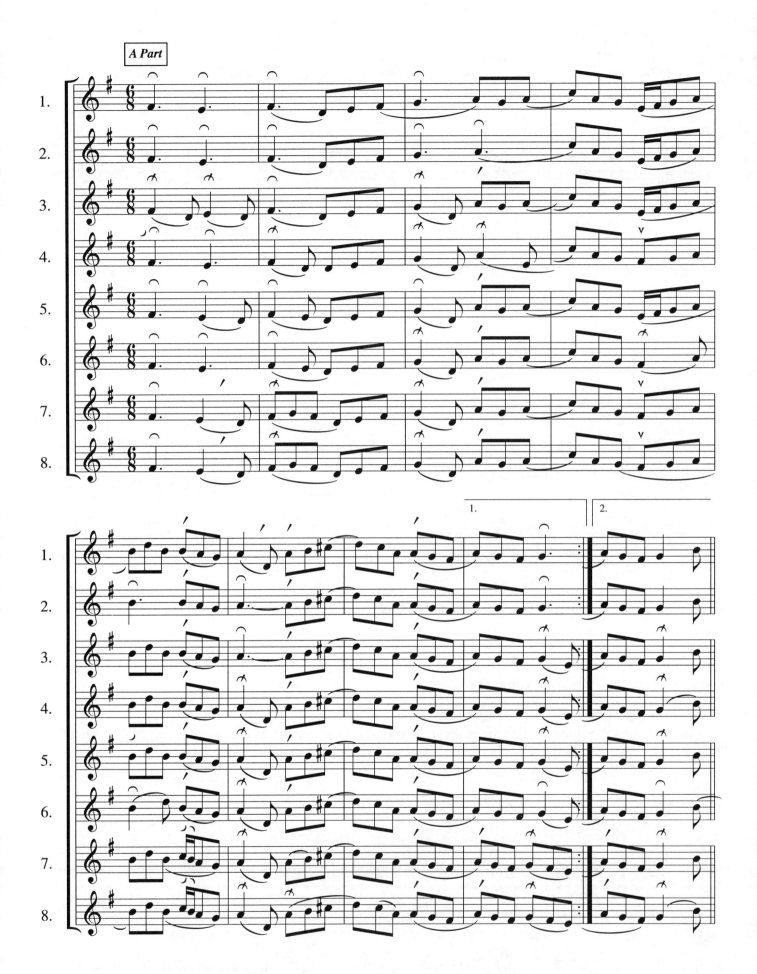

*Figure 13-11. The eight settings of the jig **The Sporting Pitchfork** given in Chapters 10 through 13 as figures 10-5, 10-6, 11-6, 11-7, 12-7, 12-8, 13-9, and 13-10.*

208

i Matt Molloy, *Matt Molloy*. Mulligan Music Limited, 1976. LUN 004.

chapter 14: Rolls in tunes with overtly uneven subdivisions of the beat

In Chapter 1, I wrote about the fact that Irish dance music is rarely if ever played in an absolutely even rhythmic fashion, i.e. with all the eighth notes being exactly identical in duration and weight. The unevenness, or *lilt*, in reels, jigs, and the like can be quite subtle and often goes unnoticed. For a detailed discussion of this, refer to pp. 40-42 in Chapter 1.

However, hornpipes, mazurkas, schottisches, germans, flings, and barn dances are normally played with an overt, intentional unevenness of rhythm that is not so subtle. Throughout the rest of this chapter I will speak only of hornpipes, but the information given also applies to these other tune types.

UNEVEN PLAYING: SUBTLE AND UNCONSCIOUS, OR OVERT AND CONSCIOUS

In reels, jigs, and the like I advocate playing rolls in an even rhythmic fashion, at least as a point of departure for other approaches.

In this context, by playing rolls "evenly" I mean playing them according to whatever subtle lilt you happen to be using. Most experienced Irish musicians think of this kind of playing as *being* even, even if it is technically not. The lilt that they use is usually unconscious, and they are therefore not thinking of the music as being uneven.

With hornpipes and the like, the uneven playing is overt and obvious, conscious and intentional. When playing rolls in such tunes you generally play them in the prevailing lilt. You therefore play them in a *consciously* or overtly uneven fashion. A close look at the case of hornpipes will shed more light on this.

HORNPIPE NOTATION: COMPROMISING WITH AN IMPOSSIBILITY

Hornpipes are usually notated as if they were played as a succession of even eighth notes, like reels, with occasional triplets. See the opening measures of the hornpipe *Bantry Bay* in Figure 14-1 below.

*Figure 14-1. The beginning of **Bantry Bay**, in typical "even-note" hornpipe notation.*
(For a complete version of the tune see p. 149 or p. 152 in Chapter 8.)

Note the long roll on G in the second complete measure.

Hornpipes are not usually played this evenly. They are instead played unevenly, with an overt lilt.

Occasionally you will see hornpipes notated in a dotted-eighth and sixteenth-note fashion. This is misleading, as Irish hornpipes are almost never played this unevenly. (See Figure 14-2, below.)

*Figure 14-2. The beginning of the hornpipe **Bantry Bay**, shown in an incorrect dotted notation. The long roll in the second complete bar is shown in exploded view.*

Sometimes, such as when playing slowly for step dancing, hornpipes are played such that the notes that are on the beat are twice as long as the off-beat notes. One could accurately notate this fashion of rendering a hornpipe as being in 12/8 time, as shown in Figure 14-3 (below).

*Figure 14-3. The beginning of the hornpipe **Bantry Bay**, notated in 12/8 time. The long roll is show in exploded view.*

Many experienced players would consider this a heavy-handed way of playing a hornpipe when playing in a session or another purely listening situation.

Experienced players feel the lilt or "groove" of a hornpipe somewhere in between the two extremes of a one to one ratio (even notes, as notated in Figure 14-1) and a two to one ratio (as notated in Figure 14-3). This lilt is a personal thing and it is influenced by tempo, mood, other players, and many other factors. A player might play a given hornpipe more evenly when she plays on the fast side and more unevenly when she plays it slower.

With hornpipes, conventional notation fails us. Don't be fooled into thinking that hornpipe rhythm is something complicated—it isn't. Just listen to well-played hornpipes. The rhythm makes perfect sense. It's doesn't *feel* complicated. It's just complicated, or rather impossible, using our conventional notation system, to write down hornpipe rhythm, which in reality often does not follow a *proportional* subdivision of the beat. This fact leads to some potentially confusing situations on paper.

Notice how the long roll on G manifests in Figure 14-3. It is still taking up three beats in a way, it's just that the "beats" are not all of the same length. In this case they are uneven to the extreme of having a two to one ratio in their durations.

Even though the convention of notating hornpipes in even eighth notes and eighth-note triplets (as in Figure 14-1) does not portray the way the tunes are actually played, I feel it is the best way to proceed given the impossibility of accurately notating hornpipe rhythm.

Notice that the long roll in Figure 14-1 occurs on a notated dotted quarter note, which is what we are accustomed to seeing. However, the same long roll, as notated in Figure 14-3, occurs over a tied quarter-note, eighth-note, quarter-note group, i.e. five eighth-note beats, as shown in Figure 14-4. This is just a bizarre artifact of a notational system that is not able to capture the true rhythmic nature of the music.

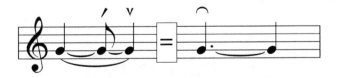

Figure 14-4. Bizarre long roll notation resulting from notating a hornpipe in 12/8 time.

This is simply a failure of notation. The G long rolls in Figures 14-1 (notated in 4/4) and 14-3 (notated in 12/8) represent the same sound. Both rolls occur over three beats. It's just that the beats are not even. In 4/4 the beats are portrayed too evenly and in 12/8 too unevenly. Uneven, non-proportional subdivision of the beat is something that makes our notation system put out garbage. Consequently, the "feel" of hornpipes must be learned by ear.

We see now why the even eighth-note style of hornpipe notation, as in Figure 14-1, is better. At least the long roll is portrayed as happening in the space of three eighth notes, not five.

Another reason why this is the better notation compromise is that condensed rolls, which occur frequently in hornpipes, are also portrayed in a sensible way.

Figure 14-5 shows the same excerpt from *Bantry Bay* with a condensed long roll in the place where we had been playing a long roll. Figure 14-6 shows the same excerpt with the condensed long roll in its exploded form.

*Figure 14-5. The beginning of **Bantry Bay**, shown with a condensed long roll in normal view.*

Figure 14-6. The same passage as Figure 14-5, with the condensed long roll shown in exploded view.

The *actual* rhythm of such a condensed long roll will depend upon the lilt that the player is using for the hornpipe. If the player is playing in a fairly uneven manner, then the rhythm of the condensed long roll will probably sound much like a true eighth-note triplet, i.e. with all three notes equal in length, as shown below in Figure 14-7.

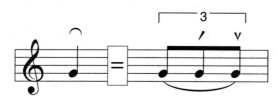

Figure 14-7. The way a condensed long roll may sound in a hornpipe that is being played in a fairly uneven manner.

Figures 14-8 and 14-9 show the same passage with a short roll.

*Figure 14-8. The beginning of **Bantry Bay**, with a short roll shown in normal view.*

Figure 14-9. The same passage as Figure 14-8, with the short roll shown in exploded view.

Again, the *actual* rhythm of such a short roll will depend upon the lilt that the player is using for the hornpipe. If the player is playing in a fairly uneven manner, then the rhythm of the short roll will probably also be in a rhythm close to a true eighth-note triplet, or, more properly, a quarter-note, eighth-note triplet, as shown below in Figure 14-10.

212

Figure 14-10. The way a short roll may sound in a hornpipe that is being played in a fairly uneven manner.

Figures 14-11 and 14-12 show the start of the tune with a condensed short roll.

*Figure 14-11. The beginning of **Bantry Bay**, with a condensed short roll shown in normal view.*

Figure 14-12. The same passage as Figure 14-11, with the condensed short roll shown in exploded view.

This is a somewhat different situation. Here, the roll in question occupies only the first part of the longer note–shorter note couplet. The unevenness of the lilt occurs only in the *relationship* between the two notes of the couplet. So here, the two sixteenth notes of the roll will be even.

However, if the player is playing in a fairly uneven manner, then the rhythm of the group of notes formed by the condensed short roll *plus* the following eighth note will probably sound much like a true eighth-note triplet, as shown below in Figure 14-13.

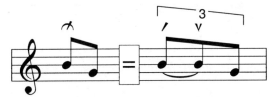

Figure 14-13. The way the group of notes formed by the condensed short roll plus the following eighth note (shown in the first complete measure of Figure 14-11) may sound in a hornpipe that is being played in a fairly uneven manner.

chapter 15: double-cut rolls

Double-cut rolls are very florid, rhythmically dense rolls in which the normal cut note of a roll is replaced by two cut notes, each with half the duration of the normal cut note. The two cuts of the double-cut roll are performed by two different fingers.

L. E. McCullough writes that double-cut rolls are often used by uilleann pipers.[i] He learned the technique from Chicago piper Joe Shannon, who first heard them used on the 78-rpm recordings of the great uilleann piper Patsy Touhy.

This double-cut technique may be applied to long rolls, short rolls, condensed long rolls, and condensed short rolls. Double-cut rolls are difficult to play and in my view are best used sparingly. Condensed double-cut rolls are particularly rare. Most players never use them at all. But, for the sake of completeness, you should at least know about them, even if you might never use them.

THE LONG DOUBLE-CUT ROLL

Let's look first at the long double-cut roll. The difference between a long roll and a long double-cut roll are shown below in Figure 15-1.

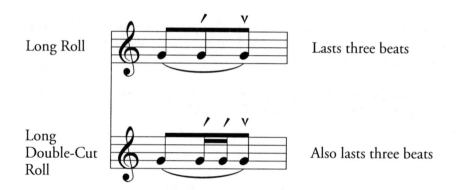

Figure 15-1. Comparison of the long roll and the long double-cut roll.

As you can see, most elements of the long roll are preserved in the long double-cut roll. The only difference between the two is that, while the second beat of the long roll is one cut eighth note, the second beat of the long double-cut roll is comprised of two cut sixteenth notes. Later you will see that the rhythmic structure of the long double-cut roll is the same as that of the long crann. (We will get to cranns in the next chapter.)

FINGERING THE DOUBLE-CUTS

The few flute and whistle tutors I have seen that mention double-cut rolls instruct you to use T1 and T2 to perform the cuts of all double-cut rolls, regardless of whether they are done on E, F-sharp, G, or A. The B double-cut roll cannot be done on whistles and unkeyed flutes because there is only one finger available for cutting B. However, on some keyed flutes one can do a double-cut roll on B by using the long C key to perform one of the two cuts.

While using only T1 and T2 for these double-cuts makes for less work learning finger skills, it does not make for the best sound. As we discussed in depth in Chapter 7, cuts need to be crisp and responsive. This is especially true in the case of double-cut rolls (and cranns) where the cuts come in such rapid succession. T1 and T2, being too distant from the lower holes of the flute or whistle, do not produce the most crisp, responsive cuts on E or F-sharp, especially in the second octave.

For the best, most responsive cuts, use your normal cutting finger for the first cut and then the next finger up for the second cut ("up" meaning towards the mouthpiece or embouchure hole). Following this rule means learning different double-cut fingerings for E and F-sharp. The commonly recommended fingerings (i.e. using T1 and T2) are correct for G and A.

I recommend using the normal cutting finger for the first cut because that cut is more important to the rhythmic definition of the roll, falling as it does right on the start of the second eighth-note beat. The second cut falls halfway between the second and third eighth-note beats, so it is better to use the weaker cut fingering for that one.

This approach to fingering double-cut rolls makes sense also because it is simply a variation on the way you already finger normal, single cut rolls. You perform the first cut just as you usually do. You simply add a second cut, using the next finger up, which falls, in time, halfway between the first cut and the strike.

Because the second cut of the double-cut rolls comes so quickly on the heels of the first one, you cannot play double-cut rolls well until you have mastered very quick, crisp cuts. I recommend that you not try double-cut rolls, or cranns, prematurely.

A NEW SYMBOL FOR THE DOUBLE-CUT ROLL

To indicate a double-cut roll I simply add two small cut symbols just to the right of the symbol for the roll. The symbol for the long double-cut roll is shown below in Figure 15-2.

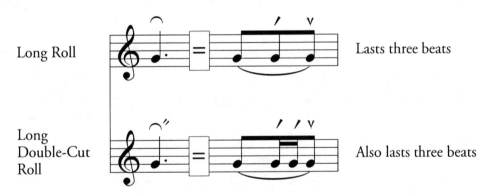

Figure 15-2. A new symbol for the long double-cut roll.

TRY SOME LONG DOUBLE-CUT ROLLS

Let's play the long double-cut roll on low G that is shown in Figures 15-1 and 15-2.

Set your metronome at a comfortable tempo somewhere around 60 beats per minute. You are going to play along with the metronome in a cycle (or meter) of four beats, each beat representing an eighth note. Count out the four beat pattern until you are comfortable with it. Then, on beat one, start playing a low G. Still playing, and without interrupting the air flow, cut the G on beat two with T2. Then, *exactly* halfway between beat two and beat three cut the G again, this time with T1. On beat three, strike the G with B1. On beat four, stop and take a breath if you wish. Try this a few more times.

Experiment with this as you wish and, once you are ready, start again and keep the pattern going, as shown below in Exercise 15-1.

Exercise 15-1. Practicing long double-cut rolls on G, shown in exploded view.

Track 62

Remember that what you are now playing can also be written as shown in Figure 15-3 below.

Figure 15-3. Long double-cut rolls on G shown in normal view.

Try playing these rolls in the high register too. These fingerings, and the ones for the other double-cut long rolls you are about to learn, are correct in both registers.

The G long double-cut roll is the easiest one to play because the labor is divided between your two hands and you are using fingers that for most people are among their most agile ones.

The F-sharp long double-cut roll is the next easiest one. Set up the metronome as before and play these exercises in the same manner you played Exercise 15-1. Play the first cut with T3, the second one with T2, and then strike with B2. Leave B1 in place.

Exercise 15-2. Practicing long double-cut rolls on F-sharp, shown in exploded view.

Next work with the E long double-cut roll. Don't forget to lift your bottom-hand pinky when it's time to strike the E. Play the first cut with B1, the second one with T3, and then strike with B3. Leave B2 in place.

Exercise 15-3. Practicing long double-cut rolls on E, shown in exploded view.

You cannot do a long double-cut roll on D because there is no way to strike a D. Later you will learn to crann on D instead.

Try the A long double-cut roll next. This is the only one-handed double-cut roll. Since there are only two fingers that you can cut with, those are the ones you use. Play the first cut with T1, the second one with T2, and then strike with T3.

Exercise 15-4. Practicing long double-cut rolls on A, shown in exploded view.

On whistle and unkeyed flutes, you cannot do a double-cut roll on B because there is only one finger with which you can cut a B. However, on certain keyed flutes you can use the long C key to play one of the two cuts required.

USING LONG DOUBLE-CUT ROLLS IN *THE SKYLARK*

The following setting of the reel *The Skylark* makes use of the long double-cut rolls we have just been practicing. For that purpose I've put in more of them than I would ordinarily use.

We will use this same reel throughout this chapter to practice three other forms of double-cut rolls. At the end of this chapter you will be able to view all four settings in a score format.

*Figure 15-4. A setting of the reel **The Skylark** using long double-cut rolls on A, G, F-sharp and E.*

Track 63

You can simulate long double-cut rolls on low C and C-sharp by adapting the fingering patterns shown in Figure 10-7 (see p. 169). Another possibility for a simulated low C-sharp long double-cut roll is show below in Figure 15-5.

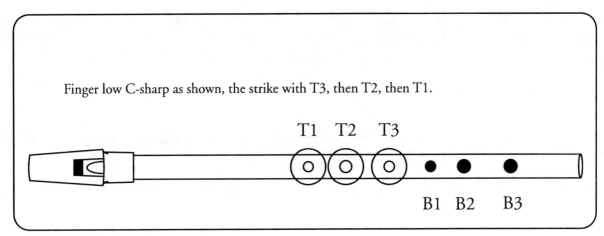

Finger low C-sharp as shown, the strike with T3, then T2, then T1.

Figure 15-5. Simulating a low C-sharp long double-cut roll using strikes.

THE SHORT DOUBLE-CUT ROLL

Now let's look at the short double-cut roll. The difference between a short roll and a short double-cut roll is shown below in Figure 15-6.

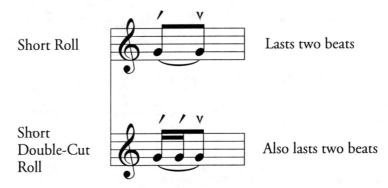

Short Roll — Lasts two beats

Short Double-Cut Roll — Also lasts two beats

Figure 15-6. Comparison of the short roll and the short double-cut roll.

Once again, most elements of the short roll are preserved in the short double-cut roll. The only difference between the two is that, while the first beat of the short roll is one cut eighth note, the first beat of the short double-cut roll is comprised of two cut sixteenth notes. Later you will see that the rhythmic structure of the short double-cut roll is the same as that of the short crann.

NOTATING THE SHORT DOUBLE-CUT ROLL

To indicate a short double-cut roll I add two small cut symbols just to the right of the symbol for the short roll, as shown in Figure 15-7.

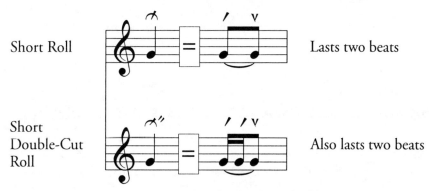

Short Roll — Lasts two beats

Short Double-Cut Roll — Also lasts two beats

Figure 15-7. A new symbol for the short double-cut roll.

TRY SOME SHORT DOUBLE-CUT ROLLS

Let's play the short double-cut roll on low G that is shown in Figure 15-7.

Set your metronome at a comfortable tempo somewhere around 60 beats per minute. You are going to play along with the metronome in a cycle (or meter) of three beats, each beat representing an eighth note. Count out the three-beat pattern until you are comfortable with it. Then, on beat one, cut a low G with T2 at the same moment that you tongue or throat it. (Remember: your cutting finger should be in the air at the moment you tongue or throat. If you cut slightly after you tongue or throat you will hear the cut an instant late.) Still playing, and without interrupting the air flow, cut the G again at the point *exactly* halfway between beats one and two with T1. On beat two, strike the G with B1. On beat three stop, and take a breath if you wish. Try this a few more times.

Experiment with this as you wish and, once you are ready, start again and keep the pattern going, as shown below in Exercise 15-5.

Exercise 15-5. Practicing short double-cut rolls on G, shown in exploded view.

Track 64

Remember that what you are now playing can also be written as shown in Figure 15-8 below.

Figure 15-8. Short double-cut rolls on G shown in normal view.

Try playing these rolls in the high register too. These fingerings, and the ones for the other short double-cut rolls you are about to learn, are correct for both registers.

Move on now to the F-sharp short double-cut roll. Set up the metronome as before and play these exercises in the same manner you played Exercise 15-5. Play the first cut with T3, the second one with T2, and then strike with B2. Leave B1 in place.

Exercise 15-6. Practicing short double-cut rolls on F-sharp, shown in exploded view.

Next, work with the E short double-cut roll. Don't forget to lift your bottom-hand pinky when it's time to strike the E. Play the first cut with B1, the second one with T3, and then strike with B3. Leave B2 in place.

Exercise 15-7. Practicing short double-cut rolls on E, shown in exploded view.

You cannot do a short double-cut roll on D because there is no way to strike a D.

Try the A short double-cut roll next. Play the first cut with T1, the second one with T2, and then strike with T3.

Exercise 15-8. Practicing short double-cut rolls on A, shown in exploded view.

On whistle and unkeyed flutes you cannot do a short double-cut roll on B because there is only one finger with which you can cut a B. However, on certain keyed flutes you can use the long C key to play one of the two cuts required.

The following setting of *The Skylark* makes use of the short double-cut rolls we have just been practicing. Once again, for practice purposes I've put in more of them than I would ordinarily use.

*Figure 15-9. A setting of the reel **The Skylark** using short double-cut rolls on A, G, F-sharp, and E.*

 Track 65

THE CONDENSED LONG DOUBLE-CUT ROLL

Now we're about to get into some really esoteric rolls.

The difference between a condensed long roll and a condensed long double-cut roll are shown in Figure 15-10.

Condensed Long Roll — Lasts two beats

Condensed Long Double-Cut Roll — Also lasts two beats

Figure 15-10. Comparison of the condensed long roll and the condensed long double-cut roll.

Once again, most elements of the condensed long roll are preserved in the condensed long double-cut roll. The only difference between the two is that, while the second sixteenth-note beat of the condensed long roll is one cut sixteenth note, the second sixteenth-note beat of the condensed long double-cut roll is comprised of two cut thirty-second-notes.

As you would by now expect, I indicate a condensed long double-cut roll by adding two small cut symbols just to the right of the symbol for the condensed long roll. Remember that the symbol for the condensed long roll is the same as that of the long roll; it appears, however, above a quarter note instead of a dotted quarter note. The symbol for the condensed long double-cut roll is shown below in Figure 15-11.

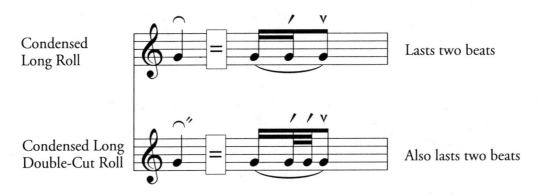

Condensed Long Roll — Lasts two beats

Condensed Long Double-Cut Roll — Also lasts two beats

Figure 15-11. A new symbol for the condensed long double-cut roll.

TRY SOME CONDENSED LONG DOUBLE-CUT ROLLS, IF YOU DARE

Let's play the condensed long double-cut roll on low G that is shown in Figures 15-10 and 15-11.

Once again, set your metronome at a comfortable tempo somewhere around 60 beats per minute. You are going to play along with the metronome in a cycle (or meter) of three beats, each beat representing an eighth note. Count out the three-beat pattern until you are comfortable with it. Then, on beat one, start playing a low G. Still playing, and without interrupting the air flow, cut the G *exactly* halfway between beats one and two with T2. Then, halfway between the first cut and beat two, cut the G again, this time with T1. Put another way, this second cut comes three-quarters of the way between beat one and beat two. Then, right on beat two, strike the G with B1. On beat three stop and take a breath if you wish. Try this a few more times.

Experiment with this as you wish and once you are ready, start again and keep the pattern going, as shown in Exercise 15-9.

Exercise 15-9. Practicing condensed long double-cut rolls on G, shown in exploded view.

Track 66

Remember that what you are now playing can also be written as shown below in Figure 15-12.

Figure 15-12. Condensed long double-cut rolls on G, shown in normal view.

Try playing these rolls in the high register too.

The F-sharp condensed long double-cut roll is the next easiest one. Set up the metronome as before and play these exercises in the same manner you played Exercise 15-9. Play the first cut with T3, the second one with T2, and then strike with B2. Leave B1 in place.

Exercise 15-10. Practicing condensed long double-cut rolls on F-sharp, shown in exploded view.

Next work with the E condensed long double-cut roll. Don't forget to lift your bottom hand pinky when it's time to strike the E. Play the first cut with B1, the second one with T3, and then strike with B3. Leave B2 in place.

Exercise 15-11. Practicing condensed long double-cut rolls on E, shown in exploded view.

Try the A condensed long double-cut roll next. Play the first cut with T1, the second one with T2, and then strike with T3.

Exercise 15-12. Practicing condensed long double-cut rolls on A, shown in exploded view.

On whistle and unkeyed flutes, you cannot do a condensed long double-cut roll on B because there is only one finger with which you can cut a B. However, on certain keyed flutes you can use the long C key to play one of the two cuts required.

USING CONDENSED LONG DOUBLE-CUT ROLLS IN *THE SKYLARK*

The following setting of *The Skylark* makes use of two of the condensed long double-cut rolls we have just been practicing. This setting is the same as the one shown in Figure 15-9 with two exceptions: there is now a condensed long double-cut roll on E in measure 3, and there is a condensed long double-cut roll on F-sharp in measure 15. I use condensed long double-cut rolls so rarely, since I prefer a fairly lean style, that I don't find many places where I feel it is appropriate to use them.

*Figure 15-13. A setting of the reel **The Skylark** using condensed long double-cut rolls on F-sharp and E.*

 Track 67

THE CONDENSED SHORT DOUBLE-CUT ROLL

The difference between a condensed short roll and a condensed short double-cut roll are shown in Figure 15-14.

Figure 15-14. Comparison of the condensed short roll and the condensed short double-cut roll.

As before, most elements of the condensed short roll are preserved in the condensed short double-cut roll. The only difference between the two is that, while the first sixteenth-note beat of the condensed short roll is one cut sixteenth note, the first sixteenth-note beat of the condensed short double-cut roll is comprised of two cut thirty-second-notes.

I indicate a condensed short double-cut roll by adding two small cut symbols just to the right of the symbol for the condensed short roll. Remember that the symbol for the condensed short roll is the same as that of the short roll; it appears however above an eighth note instead of a quarter note. The symbol for the condensed short double-cut roll is shown in Figure 15-15.

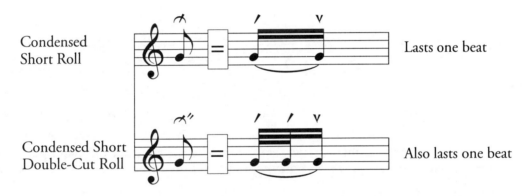

Figure 15-15. A new symbol for the condensed short double-cut roll.

TRY SOME CONDENSED SHORT DOUBLE-CUT ROLLS

Let's play the condensed short double-cut roll on low G that is shown in 15-14 and 15-15.

As usual, set your metronome at a comfortable tempo somewhere around 60 beats per minute. You are going to play along with the metronome in a cycle (or meter) of two beats, each beat representing an eighth note. Count out the two beat pattern until you are comfortable with it. Then, on beat one, cut a low G with T2 at the same moment that you tongue or throat it. (Remember: your cutting finger should be in the air at the moment you tongue or throat. If you cut slightly after you tongue or throat you will hear the cut an instant late.) Still playing, and without interrupting the air flow, cut the G again at the point exactly *one-fourth* of the way between beats one and two with T1. Then, *halfway between beats one and two* strike the G with B1. On beat two, stop and take a breath if you wish. Try this a few more times.

225

Experiment with this as you wish and once you are ready, start again and keep the pattern going, as shown below in Exercise 15-13.

Exercise 15-13. Practicing condensed short double-cut rolls on G, shown in exploded view.

Track 68

Remember that what you are now playing can also be written as shown below in Figure 15-16.

Figure 15-16. Condensed short double-cut rolls on G, shown in normal view.

Try playing these rolls in the high register too.

The F-sharp condensed short double-cut roll is the next easiest one. Set up the metronome as before and play these exercises in the same manner you played exercise 15-13. Play the first cut with T3, the second one with T2, and then strike with B2. Leave B1 in place.

Exercise 15-14. Practicing condensed short double-cut rolls on F-sharp, shown in exploded view.

Next work with the E condensed short double-cut roll. Don't forget to lift your bottom-hand pinky when it's time to strike the E. Play the first cut with B1, the second one with T3, and then strike with B3. Leave B2 in place.

Exercise 15-15. Practicing condensed short double-cut rolls on E, shown in exploded view.

Try the A condensed short double-cut roll next. Play the first cut with T1, the second one with T2, and then strike with T3.

Exercise 15-16. Practicing condensed short double-cut rolls on A, shown in exploded view.

On whistle and unkeyed flutes, you cannot do a condensed short double-cut roll on B because there is only one finger with which you can cut a B. However, on certain keyed flutes you can use the long C key to play one of the two cuts required.

USING CONDENSED SHORT DOUBLE-CUT ROLLS IN *THE SKYLARK*

The following setting of *The Skylark* makes use of the four condensed short double-cut rolls we have just been practicing. I use condensed short double-cut rolls very rarely, but include several of them here for purposes of practice. Curiously, they seem to me somewhat more useful than condensed long double-cut rolls.

*Figure 15-17. A setting of the reel **The Skylark** using condensed short double-cut rolls on A, G, F-sharp and E.*

Track 69

227

In the following figure, you may view and compare all four settings of *The Skylark* that are given in this chapter.

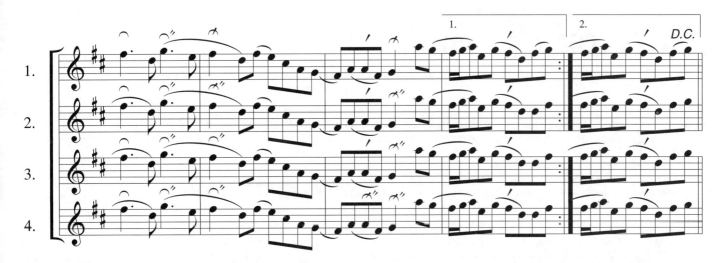

*Figure 15-18. Four settings of the reel **The Skylark**, given in Chapter 15 as Figures 15-4, 15-9, 15-13, and 15-17. These examples serve to illustrate some possible uses of the four double-cut rolls, other rolls, cuts, slides, phrasing, and general variation. I have put them in score form so that you can easily compare them. Long double-cut rolls are introduced in #1 (on E, F-sharp, G, and A); short double-cut rolls in #2 (on E, F-sharp, G, and A); condensed long double-cut rolls in #3 (on E and F-sharp); and condensed short double-cut rolls in #4 (on E, F-sharp, G, and A).*

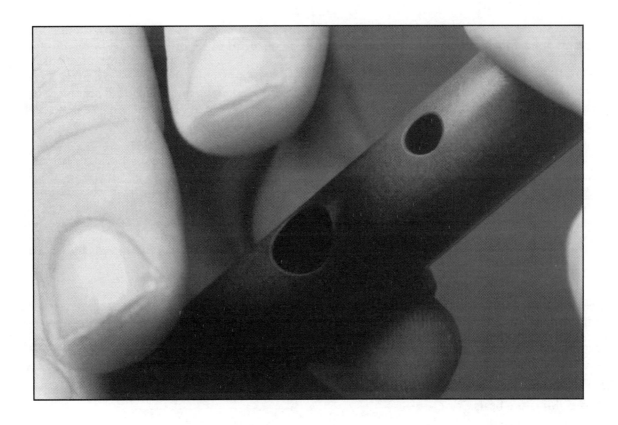

[i] L. E. McCullough, *The Complete Tin Whistle Tutor* (New York: Oak Publications, 1987), p. 28.

chapter 16: cranns

In all of the preceding discussions on rolls I have told you that you cannot do a roll on D because there is no way to strike a D. Yet D is such a critically important note in this music. How can we use ornamentation to draw attention to it?

Enter the **crann**. The crann is an ornament that came to us from the uilleann piping tradition. It makes use only of cut notes, no strikes.

Cranns are traditionally played not only on D but on E as well, especially by pipers. They can be played on other notes too, but we rarely hear that with traditional flute and whistle players who seem to prefer rolls over cranns where rolls are possible. One reason for this preference may be that double-cut rolls sound very similar to cranns and are generally easier to play than cranns.

One notable example of cranning on notes other than D and E comes from the great tin whistle player Donncha Ó Briain (Denis O'Brien) (1960–1990). He played cranns on F-natural in his rendition of *The Flogging Reel*[i] (see my transcription of this performance on pp. 409-410 in Section 8). This is a very effective, creative, and challenging use of the cranning technique, considering that the F-natural itself is played by half-uncovering the B2 hole. But, precisely because of this half-holing, it is virtually impossible to do a strike (and therefore a roll) on F-natural on the whistle. Donncha Ó Briain could have chosen a number of easier options at this point in the tune. He was truly a master of the tin whistle and deserves more recognition than he has received. Others whom I have heard use cranns on notes other than D and E include Co. Limerick flute player Paddy Taylor and Co. Galway flutists Mike Rafferty and Jack Coen.

It seems that cranns became widely used among flute and whistle players only since the 1970s, though they have been in use by pipers for a much longer time. One can hear different forms of D and E cranns in recordings of uilleann piper Patsy Touhey that were made between 1900 and 1919. Since it has been very common for uilleann pipers to also play tin whistle and/or flute, it is only natural that various piping techniques such as cranning have made their way into traditional flute and whistle playing. However, most flute and whistle players find cranns to be quite challenging. There are quite a few flute and whistle players who don't use them at all, especially the players of older generations.

In the 1970s and 1980s, Matt Molloy's brilliant use of cranns inspired many flute and whistle players to regard cranning as an essential element of their styles. But his were not the first Irish flute or tin whistle recordings in which cranns were used. The earliest recordings I have found of cranning by Irish flute or whistle players are John McKenna's 1925 recording of the reel *The Five Mile Chase*[ii] and Tom Morrison's 1927 recording of the schottische *Sweet Flowers of Milltown*, the second of which you will find transcribed in Section 8 (on pp. 368-371). These were surprising discoveries, since I had shared the commonly held supposition that flute and whistle players did not begin to use the crann until the 1970s. Hopefully further research will shed more light upon the early use of cranning by flute and whistle players.

As far as I have been able to ascertain, subsequent recordings of cranning by flute and whistle players don't seem to show up until the late 1960s. Finbar Furey, a noted uilleann piper, used cranns on the tin whistle in his 1968 and 1969 recordings on the Nonesuch label.[iii] You can hear Paddy Taylor using cranns on his 1970 recording, *Boy in the Gap*.[iv] Paddy Carty used them in his 1974 recording of the reel *Cottage Groves*.[v]

There are long cranns and short cranns. As with rolls, long cranns take up three eighth-note beats while short cranns take up two eighth-note beats.

Although cranning techniques can differ quite a bit from player to player, there seem to be certain characteristics of the crann that are held in common by all. For example, since the crann is made up of cut notes, the lowest covered hole almost always remains covered (i.e. B3 in the case of D and B2 in the case of E).

Note that the crann is not the only ornamental gesture you can apply to a D. We will discuss others later.

The **long crann** is comprised of four slurred notes: an eighth note, two sixteenth notes, and another eighth note. The second, third, and fourth notes are cut. See Figure 16-1 below.

Figure 16-1. A long crann on D, shown in exploded view.

A NEW SYMBOL

I indicate a long crann as shown below.

Figure 16-2. The symbol for a long crann on D, and what it means.

You can think of the symbol as the letter C (for crann) or as the long roll symbol turned on its side.

FINGERING THE THREE CONSECUTIVE CUTS OF THE CRANN

As with double-cut rolls, consecutive cuts in cranns are not performed with the same finger. Of course here we have three cuts in a row instead of two.

In uilleann piping these three cuts are usually played by three different fingers. Many flute and whistle players have directly adopted such piping fingerings to their instruments. Cutting D with a finger as high as T3 works very well on the pipes. But the responsiveness of this fingering on the flute or whistle is not as good, and it is particularly weak in the second octave, especially on the flute.

I find that cranns on the flute and whistle sound tighter and more well defined if you follow the same principle I laid out in the last chapter on double-cut rolls, and take it one step further.

Play the first cut with your normal cutting finger. Play the second cut with the next finger up (toward the mouth-piece or embouchure). For the third cut, go *back* to your normal cutting finger. To see how this works on a low D long crann see Figure 16-3 (below).

Cut with: B2   B1   B2

Figure 16-3. The fingers to use for the cuts in a long crann on D.

231

This fingering pattern allows you to change fingers for each cut of the crann and still use the most responsive cuts possible. Beginning and ending with the normal cutting finger enables you to use the most responsive cut fingering twice, for the two cuts that fall on the most important subdivisions of the beat.

TRY THE LONG CRANN ON LOW D

Once again, set your metronome for a comfortable tempo around 60 beats per minute. You are going to play along with the metronome in a cycle (or meter) of four beats, each beat representing an eighth note. Count out the four-beat pattern until you are comfortable with it.

Then, on beat one, start playing a low D. Still playing, and without interrupting the air flow, cut the D on beat two with B2. Next, cut the D again, *exactly* halfway between beats two and three, with B1. Then, cut D for the third time right on beat three, using B2 again. On beat four, stop and take a breath if you wish. Try this a few more times.

Experiment as you wish and once you are ready, start again, and keep the pattern going, as shown below in Exercise 16-1.

Exercise 16-1. Practicing long cranns on D, shown in exploded view.

Track 70

Remember that what you are now playing can also be written as shown below in Figure 16-4.

Figure 16-4. Long cranns on D, shown in normal view.

VENTING FOR THE HIGH D CRANN

When you play the D crann in the high register you have an interesting fingering choice. You can finger exactly the same as you do with the low D crann, or you can "vent" the high D, that is, lift T1 as you play the crann. Venting the high D can make that note respond faster and sound more clear, especially on the flute. But it also gives you a very different sounding crann because when venting, the cuts produce articulations that are *lower* in pitch than the parent note. I usually use this vented high D crann on the flute because it seems to speak more responsively. But there are times when I prefer the sound of the non-vented crann. Experiment and see for yourself.

TRY THE LONG CRANN ON LOW E

Now try a long crann on low E. Set your metronome as before. On beat one, start playing a low E. Still playing, and without interrupting the air flow, cut the E on beat two with B1. Next, cut the E again, *exactly* halfway between beats two and three, with T3. Then, cut the E for the third time right on beat three, using B1 again. On beat four, stop and take a breath if you wish. Try this a few more times.

The crann on high E is fingered the same way as the crann on low E. You cannot vent the high E.

Experiment as you wish and once you are ready, start again, and keep the pattern going, as shown below in Exercise 16-2.

Exercise 16-2. Practicing long cranns on E, shown in exploded view.

Remember that what you are now playing can also be written as shown below in Figure 16-5.

Figure 16-5. Long cranns on E, shown in normal view.

The following setting of the reel *The Trip to Durrow* makes use of long cranns on low D and low E.

*Figure 16-6. A setting of the reel **The Trip to Durrow** which makes use of long cranns on D and E.*

Track 71

The **short crann** is comprised of three notes: two sixteenth notes and an eighth note. All three notes are cut. Note that when you remove the first note of a long crann a short crann remains.

Figure 16-7. A short crann on D, shown in exploded view.

The short crann is quite tricky to play in context, just like the short roll, because there is no preparation note before the first cut. It shares all the challenges of the short roll, described in Chapter 11. The long crann on the other hand, like the long roll, does starts with a preparation note, making its first cut the easiest kind, the cut between notes of the same pitch.

Sometimes you will hear players leave out the first cut of the short crann. This results in a simpler, softer crann with less attack. I encourage you to learn to play the short crann with all three cuts. You may then choose to omit the first cut as a matter of musical expression, not one of technical limitation. You will find that it is sometimes easier to execute the full three-cut short crann when you articulate it with tonguing or throating.

A NEW SYMBOL

I notate a short crann as shown below.

Figure 16-8. The symbol for a short crann on D, and what it means.

The symbol is that of the long crann with a slash through it. This shows that the short crann is a shortened or truncated form of the long crann. The slash, being the symbol for the cut, also draws attention to the fact that a cut note initiates the short crann. Note well that the symbol appears above a quarter note. The short crann is only two eighth-note beats in duration, the same duration as a quarter note.

TRY SHORT CRANNS ON D AND E

As usual, set your metronome for a comfortable tempo around 60 beats per minute. You are going to play along with the metronome in a cycle (or meter) of three beats, each beat representing an eighth note. Count out the three-beat pattern until you are comfortable with it. Then, on beat one, cut a low D with B2 at the same moment that you tongue or throat it. (Remember, your cutting finger should be in the air at the moment you tongue or throat. If you cut slightly after you tongue or throat you will hear the cut an instant late.) Still playing, without interrupting the air flow, cut the D again with B1 *exactly* halfway between beats one and two. Then, right on beat two cut the D again with B2. On beat three, stop and take a breath if you wish. Try this short crann a few more times.

Experiment as you wish and once you are ready, start again, and keep the pattern going, as shown below in Exercise 16-3.

Exercise 16-3. Practicing short cranns on low D, shown in exploded view.

Track 72

Remember that what you are now playing can also be written as shown below in Figure 16-9.

Figure 16-9. Short cranns on D, shown in normal view.

With the short D crann you have the same venting option in the second octave as you have with the long D crann.

Now try a short crann on low E. Set your metronome as before. On beat one, cut a low E with B1 at the same moment that you tongue or throat it. Still playing, without interrupting the air flow, cut the E again with T3 *exactly* halfway between beats one and two. Then, right on beat two cut the E again with B1. On beat three, stop and take a breath if you wish. Try this short crann a few more times.

Experiment as you wish and once you are ready, start again, and keep the pattern going, as shown below in Exercise 16-4.

Exercise 16-4. Practicing short cranns on E, shown in exploded view.

Remember that what you are now playing can also be written as shown below in Figure 16-10.

Figure 16-10. Short cranns on E, shown in normal view.

The short high E crann uses the same fingering as the low E crann.

TRY SOME SHORT CRANNS IN THE JIG *GARRETT BARRY*

The following setting of the jig *Garrett Barry* makes use of short and long cranns on D.

*Figure 16-11. A setting of the jig **Garrett Barry**, with short and long cranns on D.*

Track 73

HOW LONG CRANNS RELATE TO THE PULSE

In Irish tunes, the first note of a long crann quite frequently falls upon a primary pulse. In such cases it is only natural to give some emphasis to that first note of the crann with the breath (but don't overdo it). Here are two examples. For the first, let's look again at the beginning of *The Trip to Durrow*, shown below in Figures 16-12 and 16-13.

*Figure 16-12. The first two measures of the reel **The Trip to Durrow**
with a long crann on D, shown in normal view.*

237

*Figure 16-13. The first two measures of the reel **The Trip to Durrow**
with a long crann on D, shown in exploded view.*

Track 74

The second example is the beginning of the jig *The Humours of Ballyloughlin*, a tune that Matt Molloy plays brilliantly on his first album,[vi] shown below in Figures 16-14 and 16-15.

*Figure 16-14. The first two measures of the jig **The Humours of Ballyloughlin** with a
long crann on D, shown in normal view. (For a complete version of the tune see p. 339.)*

Track 75

*Figure 16-15. The first two measures of the jig **The Humours of Ballyloughlin**
with a long crann on D, shown in exploded view.*

Long cranns, however, do not always begin on a pulse, primary or secondary. For an example see the beginning of the third part of the reel *The Boys of Ballisodare*, shown below in Figures 16-16 and 16-17.

*Figure 16-16. The first two measures of the third part of the reel **The Boys of Ballisodare**
with a long crann on D, shown in normal view. (For a complete version of the tune see p. 348.)*

Track 76

*Figure 16-17. The first two measures of the third part of the reel
The Boys of Ballisodare with a long crann on D, shown in exploded view.*

In Figure 16-17 you can clearly see that the second note of the crann, its first cut note, falls upon a secondary pulse (the third eighth-note beat). The first and third beats of the crann fall on weaker non-pulse beats (two and four). Therefore you may choose to give the second note of the crann some rhythmic emphasis with your breath. In fact you may even find yourself doing so unconsciously, since it is natural to do so.

The second note of a long crann can fall on a reel's primary pulse as well. In Figures 16-18 and 16-19 you see the beginning of a variation on the reel *The Lady on the Island*. At the end of the first measure and crossing the barline into the second measure is a long crann on D. Notice that the second note falls on the primary pulse at the beginning of the second measure.

Figure 16-18. A variant on the first two measures of the reel **The Lady on the Island** with a long crann on D, shown in normal view. (For a complete version of the tune see p. 353.)

Track 77

Figure 16-19. A variant on the first two measures of the reel
The Lady on the Island with a long crann on D, shown in exploded view.

In jigs, long cranns in which the second note falls on a pulse are rather unusual, but they do occur. (Remember that jigs have no secondary pulse.) Figures 16-20 and 16-21 show the beginning of the third part of the jig *The Battering Ram* that yields just such a situation.

Figure 16-20. The first two measures of the third part of the jig **The Battering Ram** with a long crann on D, shown in normal view. (For a complete version of the tune see p. 335.)

Track 78

Figure 16-21. The first two measures of the third part of the jig
The Battering Ram with a long crann on D, shown in exploded view.

In a reel, it can happen that the fourth note of a long crann falls on either a primary or secondary pulse. In fact, in Figures 16-12 and 16-13 the fourth note of the D long crann fall on a secondary pulse. We hardly notice this, though, because the first note of this crann falls on the stronger primary pulse. This is a very common occurrence in reels.

How Short Cranns Relate to the Pulse

Whereas long cranns can be placed in a number of different ways relative to the pulse, short cranns seem to be appropriate in a more limited range of rhythmic placements, as is the case with short rolls. In reels you never seem to hear short cranns beginning on a beat that is not either a primary or secondary pulse. You could use them in this way, but when you do they seem to draw too much attention to non-pulse beats, in my opinion.

In jigs, short cranns can be used starting on pulse or non-pulse beats, though it is uncommon to hear them starting on non-pulse beats. Here is an example of a short crann starting on a pulse in the second part of *Old Joe's Jig*.

*Figure 16-22. The first two measures of the second part of **Old Joe's Jig** with a short crann on D, shown in normal view. (For a complete version of the tune see p. 342.)*

Track 79

*Figure 16-23. The first two measures of the second part of **Old Joe's Jig** with a short crann on D, shown in exploded view.*

Mary Bergin plays this tune brilliantly on her first album[vii] but she does not use a crann on this D. She ornaments the D in a different way, using something that I call a *shake*. We'll look more closely at this in Chapter 18.

"EXTENDED CRANNS"? GOOD QUESTION

An interesting situation can occur when a long crann is followed by another note of the same pitch. An example of this is the figure that occurs at the end of the first, third, and fourth parts of the jig *The Humours of Ballyloughlin*, shown below.

*Figure 16-24. The ending of the first, third, and fourth parts of the jig **The Humours of Ballyloughlin** with an "extended crann," shown in normal view.*

Track 80

*Figure 16-25. The ending of the first, third and fourth parts of the jig **The Humours of Ballyloughlin** with an "extended crann," shown in exploded view.*

In this example, the long low D crann is followed by another D note that is cut, so you actually have four cut Ds in a row. Is this an "extended crann"? If pressed, I would say that it is a simply a long crann followed by a cut D. We don't have to have a name for every way that ornaments can combine together. Notice that a similar thing happens at the start of this example, i.e. a long roll on A followed by a cut A note. Is this an extended roll?

Do condensed cranns exist? Yes, they do, but we don't often hear them.

A **condensed long crann** contains all the elements of the long crann but lasts only two eighth-note beats instead of three. It looks like this:

Figure 16-26. A condensed long crann on D.

The symbol for the condensed long crann is the same as that of the long crann but it appears over a quarter note instead of a dotted quarter note.

Figure 16-27. The symbol for a condensed long crann on D, and what it means.

A **condensed short crann** contains all the elements of the short crann but lasts only one eighth-note beat instead of two. It looks like this:

Figure 16-28. A condensed short crann on D.

It is the same as a condensed long crann without its first note.

The symbol for the condensed short crann is the same as that of the short crann but it appears over an eighth note instead of a quarter note.

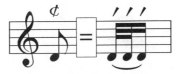

Figure 16-29. The symbol for a condensed short crann on D, and what it means.

An example of condensed long cranns appears in a variant on the beginning of the hornpipe *The Home Ruler* in Figures 16-30 and 16-31 (below).

*Figure 16-30. A variant on the first two measures of **The Home Ruler** with condensed long cranns on D, shown in normal view. (For a complete version of the tune see p. 355.)*

Track 81

*Figure 16-31. A variant on the first two measures of **The Home Ruler** with condensed long cranns on D, shown in exploded view.*

An example of a condensed short crann appears in a variant on the beginning of the jig *The Blarney Pilgrim* in Figures 16-32 and 16-33 (below).

*Figure 16-32. A variant on the first two measures of the jig **The Blarney Pilgrim** with a condensed short crann on D, shown in normal view. (For a complete version of the tune see p. 336.)*

① *Track 82*

*Figure 16-33. A variant on the first two measures of the jig **The Blarney Pilgrim** with a condensed short crann on D, shown in exploded view.*

Since this condensed short crann is preceded by a D eighth note, is it really a condensed long crann beginning on the third note of the measure?

Figure 16-34. The music of Figure 16-32 with the crann notated this time as a condensed long crann, shown in normal view.

Figure 16-35. The music of Figure 16-32 with the crann notated this time as a condensed long crann, shown in exploded view.

Well, what does it really matter? Call it what you like.

i Donncha Ó Briain, *Donncha Ó Briain*. Gael-Linn, 1979. CEF 083.

ii John McKenna and Michael Gaffney, on *Fluters of Old Erin, Flute, Piccolo and Whistle Recordings of the 1920s and 30s* (Dublin: Viva Voce 002, 1990).

iii Eddie & Finbar Furey, *Hornpipes, Airs & Reels: Irish Pipe Music*. Nonesuch, 1968. 72059. Also, Finbar Furey, *The Irish Pipes of Finbar Furey*. Nonesuch, 1969. 72048.

iv Paddy Taylor, *Boy in the Gap*. Claddagh, 1970. 4CC8.

v Paddy Carty, *Traditional Music of Ireland*. Daniel Michael Collins Master Collector Series, No. 1, 1974.

vi Matt Molloy, *Matt Molloy*. Mulligan Music Limited, 1976. LUN 004.

vii Mary Bergin, *Feadóga Stáin: Traditional Irish Music on the Tin Whistle*. Shanachie Records 79006, 1979.

chapter 17: charts of the rolls and cranns and their symbols

Now that we have covered all of the rolls and cranns in depth, here are two charts summarizing the symbols for these ornaments and what they mean.

The first chart is organized by "class," i.e. the long rolls, the short rolls, the long cranns, and the short cranns. *Pay close attention to the varying durations of the notes that appear under the symbols.*

The second chart is organized by duration of ornament in eighth-note beats, i.e. the three-beat ornaments, the two-beat ornaments, the one-beat ornaments. Note that:

  • The symbols for the three-beat ornaments all appear over dotted quarter notes.

  • The symbols for the two-beat ornaments all appear over regular quarter notes.

  • The symbols for the one-beat ornaments all appear over eighth notes.

Rolls and Cranns
Organized by Class
Pay close attention to the varying durations
of the notes that appear under the symbols.

THE LONG ROLLS

Long Roll

Long Double-Cut Roll

Condensed Long Roll

Condensed Long Double-Cut Roll

Double-Condensed Long Roll

THE SHORT ROLLS

Short Roll

Short Double-Cut Roll

Condensed Short Roll

Condensed Short Double-Cut Roll

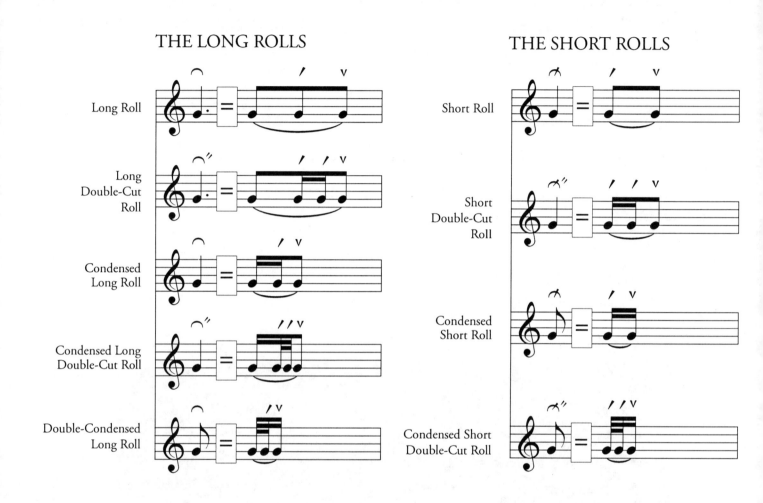

THE LONG CRANNS

Long Crann

Condensed Long Crann

THE SHORT CRANNS

Short Crann

Condensed Short Crann

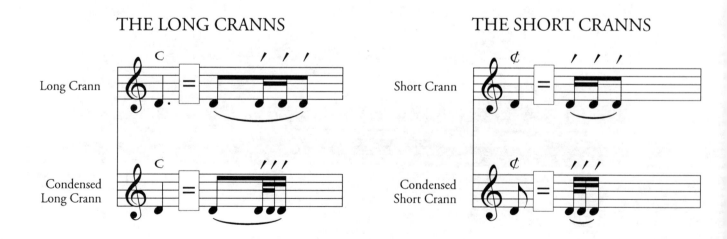

Rolls and Cranns
Organized by Duration
- *The symbols for the three-beat ornaments all appear over dotted quarter notes.*
- *The symbols for the two-beat ornaments all appear over regular quarter notes.*
- *The symbols for the one-beat ornaments all appear over eighth notes.*

THE THREE-BEAT ORNAMENTS

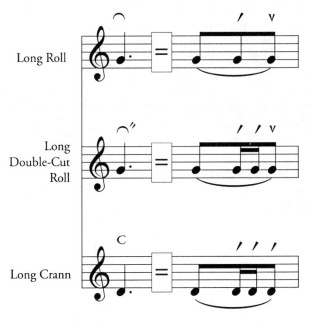

Long Roll

Long Double-Cut Roll

Long Crann

THE TWO-BEAT ORNAMENTS

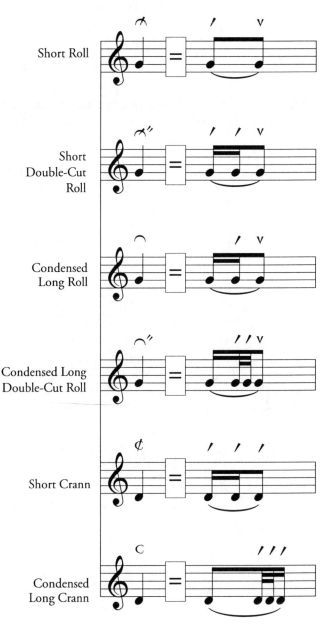

Short Roll

Short Double-Cut Roll

Condensed Long Roll

Condensed Long Double-Cut Roll

Short Crann

Condensed Long Crann

THE ONE-BEAT ORNAMENTS

Condensed Short Roll

Condensed Short Double-Cut Roll

Condensed Short Crann

Double-Condensed Long Roll

chapter 18: other multi-note ornaments

In the preceding chapters we have covered all the main body of ornamentation techniques used in Irish flute and whistle music: cuts, strikes, slides, and all of the varieties of rolls and cranns. All of the multi-note ornaments we have looked at so far, i.e. the rolls and cranns, are built upon the use of cuts and strikes.

There are a few more ornamental techniques that you should know about which do not make use of cuts or strikes. We will explore them in this chapter.

Vibrato

Vibrato is a slight and repeating fluctuation of the pitch, tone color, and/or loudness of a sustained note. One uses it to draw attention to a note and to intensify its emotional qualities.

Today's classical musicians have by and large adopted an aesthetic in which vibrato is used as an integral aspect of normal tone production. In such playing, the absence of vibrato becomes a potent expressive technique that draws attention to a particular note or notes. Varying the qualities of the vibrato also serves to shape phrases and draw the listener's attention where the classical musician wishes to direct it.

Traditional Irish musicians hold an opposing aesthetic. They use vibrato *only as an ornamental technique*. Overall, the music is played without vibrato. This is very much the same attitude that was held by art music flutists of the baroque and classical eras. John Solum writes, in *The Early Flute*,[i]

> Although there was undoubtedly a great deal of variation in the amount and use of vibrato by different players on the traverso in the baroque and classical ages, the taste of the time obliged performers to regard vibrato as an ornament. It was generally used only on longer notes as an expressive device, certainly not continuously.

Irish musicians mainly employ vibrato in slow airs and other slow or moderately paced tunes. But it is occasionally used in fast tunes as well. For example, you might occasionally use it in a place where you would otherwise play a long roll.

There are two very different means of producing vibrato on the flute and whistle: *finger vibrato* and *breath vibrato*. We'll explore finger vibrato first.

Finger Vibrato

It seems certain that the **finger vibrato** techniques we flute and whistle players use came to us, once again, from the piping tradition. Since a piper must supply a steady, unwavering stream of air to the reeds of the instrument she cannot create a vibrato with the air supply but only with her fingers. Baroque wind players also made use of finger vibrato for ornamental purposes, but I think it is unlikely, though possible, that the technique found its way into traditional Irish music from that source. Who knows, maybe it came to baroque flute players from their bagpiping colleagues.

The effect of finger vibrato can range from extremely subtle to very heavy, depending upon the finger or fingers used and whether or not the fingers cover their holes entirely. The gradations of color you can create with finger vibrato are nearly endless, and styles of using finger vibrato are varied and highly personal.

Note that in using finger vibrato you are always varying the pitch of the note only in a downward, or flattening direction. French baroque flutists called it *flattement* for that reason. Sometimes the amount of pitch change is so slight that we perceive a subtle oscillation in tone color more than pitch. In fact, finger vibrato does alter the tone color of the note as well as its pitch.

TOTAL-HOLE FINGER VIBRATO

First we'll look at the approach to finger vibrato in which you use an additional finger or fingers to completely cover a hole or holes that are ordinarily left open. We'll call this **total-hole finger vibrato**.

With total-hole finger vibrato, for any given note you must avoid covering the first open hole. For instance, with B you must not cover T2, for A you must not cover T3, and so on. Doing so would turn your finger vibrato into a trill. (We will get to trills later in the chapter.)

Any combination of the remaining open holes can then be completely covered and uncovered in a fairly quick repetitive manner. However many open holes you choose to cover and uncover, you will usually want to act upon them together as a group, though interesting and subtle effects can be obtained by the independent use of such fingers as well.

The intensity of the vibrato increases with two factors:

1. the number of fingers used, and

2. how close those fingers are to the headjoint or mouthpiece.

For example, with the note A, the possible finger combinations that you could use for total-hole finger vibrato, in order of greatest to least vibrato intensity, are:

B1, B2, and B3

B1 and B2

B1, or the pair B2 and B3 (this varies from instrument to instrument)

B2

B3

Try these various fingering combinations for yourself and see how your instrument responds.

In the course of applying total-hole finger vibrato to a sustained note you can vary the speed of the vibrato and also the combination of fingers which you are using. In this way you can beautifully shape the note as it develops, much as a singer does. This can sometimes produce the illusion that you are shaping the loudness, or dynamics of the note, a musical element that we have little actual control over on the whistle.

The speed of the vibrato does not necessarily have to bear any relation to the rhythm of the music, though it can.

PARTIAL-HOLE FINGER VIBRATO

Another approach to finger vibrato is **partial-hole finger vibrato**. As you have probably guessed, in this approach you use an additional finger or fingers to partially cover a hole or holes that are ordinarily left open. I like to call this partial covering *shading* the hole. This technique is not possible on the Boehm-system flute.

Partial-hole finger vibrato produces a continuously varying pitch, an effect which is quite different from the "on and off" nature of total hole finger vibrato. The effects of these two types of finger vibrato are illustrated below.

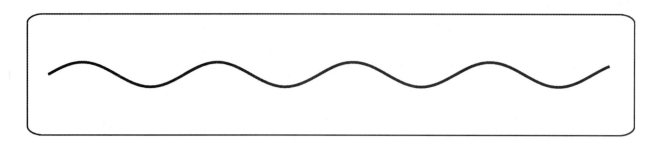

Figure 18-1: The pitch shape of partial-hole finger vibrato.

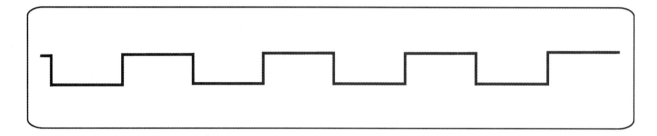

Figure 18-2: The pitch shape of total-hole finger vibrato.

To use partial-hole finger vibrato, I straighten the finger or fingers used, such that their movements affect only the near edge of their tone holes, leaving most of the hole untouched, as shown in Figure 18-3 (below).

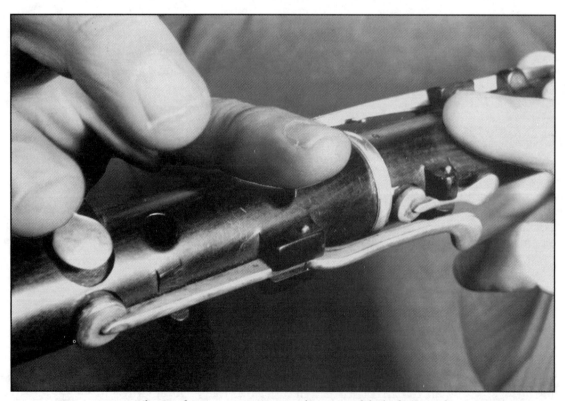

Figure 18-3. The B1 finger in position to play partial-hole finger vibrato on G.

Varying the angle of the finger or fingers varies the degree to which the pitch is flattened, which in turn translates into a varying degree of intensity in the vibrato. It can be very pleasing to begin with a very slight amount of shading, increasing it through the middle of the note and trailing it off again as the note ends. With the flute, you can use your embouchure to match this note shaping with changes in the loudness of the note.

With partial-hole finger vibrato, you don't need to avoid using the first open hole, but take great care in using it. The slightest shading of this hole is easily discernible and, if you're not careful, your vibrato will sound too deep.

The factors cited above which control the intensity of total-hole finger vibrato apply equally to partial-hole finger vibrato: the number of fingers used (one or two is usually enough) and the proximity of those fingers to the head-joint or mouthpiece.

Just as with total-hole finger vibrato, you can vary the speed of the vibrato and the fingers which you are using to shape the envelope of the note. But now you can also vary the *angle* of the fingers, i.e. the degree to which you shade the tone holes.

As you explore these techniques you will find that you can begin a note with partial-hole finger vibrato and gradually shift to total-hole finger vibrato, and back again if you wish. Add to all this the ability, on the flute, to shape the dynamics of the note with embouchure, and you see how vast are your powers of expression with finger vibrato.

You can also see why most of the subtleties of this technique are lost to the Boehm-system flute.

BREATH VIBRATO

Breath vibrato is completely different in character from both types of finger vibrato.

Both *volume and pitch* are varied in breath vibrato. The variance of the pitch in breath vibrato normally goes both above and below the pitch of the principal note, while the variance of pitch in finger vibrato occurs only as a flattening. In finger vibrato the volume of the principal note is not varied, though it may seem to be.

Some claim that breath vibrato is produced solely by the diaphragm, but I feel that the muscles of the abdomen and often the throat are also involved. You can experiment with breath vibrato by playing a long note and very gently pulsing the air, as if saying "ha-ha-ha-ha . . ." As with finger vibrato the gradations of intensity, attack, and speed are endless.

Sometimes you will hear a musician who comes from a classical background play Irish music with the nearly constant breath vibrato of the modern classical aesthetic. It can be very tough for a classical player to free themselves from this habit. Sometimes they are not even aware that they are in its grip. But free themselves they must if they want to be taken seriously by Irish musicians.

Some purists frown upon any use of any breath vibrato in Irish flute and whistle playing. I feel that they are overreacting to players who use it inappropriately. If you listen attentively to the first recordings of traditional Irish flute and whistle players from the early 20th century, as well as the acknowledged contemporary masters of Irish flute and whistle such as Matt Molloy and Mary Bergin, you will most definitely hear the use of breath vibrato, and not only in slow airs.

Breath vibrato can be used tastefully and beautifully in traditional Irish music. But it must be used sparingly, and only ornamentally. Often in playing a slow air, I will use breath and finger vibrato at different points in the same melody. Occasionally I use both at the same time, or begin with one and move to the other. I find that a very gentle breath vibrato is best.

TRILLS

Trills are not common in Irish flute and whistle music, but they are used from time to time, usually in slow airs or other slow or moderately paced tunes, but also in fast tunes. They are more often used by fiddlers and pipers than by other instrumentalists, it seems.

A trill is an ornament consisting of a rapid alternation between the principal note and the note above it in the scale or mode. In Irish music it seems that the trill may begin on either the principal note or the higher ornamental note. The trill begins right on the beat and can vary greatly in length from extremely brief to several beats long, though some consider long trills to be too showy or too much of an allusion to classical music. Certainly if you are pursuing a traditional style, trills should be used very sparingly and judiciously indeed. Such players as Matt Molloy have made beautiful use of trills.

When you hear an Irish flute or whistle player use a trill it is difficult not to be reminded of baroque music. No one seems to know for sure how trills entered into the Irish tradition, but I would not be surprised if it occurred through traditional musicians being exposed to baroque music. There certainly was significant interplay between traditional musicians and "art" musicians in Ireland during the Baroque period.

Interestingly, if you follow my recommendations for cut and strike fingerings, the trill is the only type of ornament in which we move the finger that is covering the lowest hole for any given note, for example the T3 finger with the note G. (The only other exception to this is in the playing rolls on B, when one must cut with T1.)

The favorite note for trilling among Irish flute and whistle players seems to be F-sharp. I'm not sure why this is, unless it is just because there is something physically pleasing about trilling with the B1 finger, the most agile finger for most people. You will hear trills done on other notes as well, but there remains something special about F-sharp.

THE TRILL SYMBOL

Since the trill is a well established ornament in baroque and classical music of later periods, it makes sense to use a symbol already widely recognized.

Figure 18-4. A widely used symbol for a trill.

THE SINGLE TRILL

There is one special case of the trill which deserves a closer look. I hear Irish flute and whistle players use it more than any other manifestation of the trill, yet it is so brief that it barely sounds like what we consider to be a conventional trill. I call it a *single trill*.

A SYMBOL FOR THE SINGLE TRILL

I use the following symbol for the single trill.

Figure 18-5. A new symbol for a single trill.

Some 17th- and 18th-century composers and players used this symbol to indicate a trill in general,[ii] but the symbol shown in Figure 18-4 is more commonly used today for that purpose.

Most often, you would use a single trill when descending in a melody by one step of the scale, though it can be used in other melodic contexts. Let's say we are descending from F-sharp to E and playing a single trill on the E. In this example you would arrive at the E, then play only one very quick F-sharp and return immediately to the E to continue the tune. Note that the first E comes right on the beat, not in anticipation of it.

The sounds produced by the actions of the B2 finger here are very quick and crisp, somewhat percussive like that of the strike. In fact, as with the strike, with single trills I like to raise my finger high enough in preparation that I can come down with a high velocity at the proper moment.

It is this percussive aspect of the single trill that distinguishes it from similar very brief trills that a baroque or classical player might employ, such as the ornament called a *schneller* or an *inverted mordent.*[iii]

Note that B2 comes down, then up, then down. The first down movement is the "percussive" one, the one requiring the preparation. Then B2 comes up just a tiny bit to produce the ornamental F-sharp. This is *not* like the rebound of the strike. The finger barely comes up at all before it must come down again to return to E. These movements happen in very rapid succession.

I consider both the first E and the F-sharp to be ornamental notes in this case, the second E being the actual melody note. The entire aggregate can then be thought of as a three-note ornament. Figures 18-6 and 18-7 show an excerpt from the second part of the hornpipe *Bantry Bay* in which a single trill can be used moving from an F-sharp to an E, as described above.

*Figure 18-6. An excerpt from the second part of the hornpipe **Bantry Bay** with a single trill on E, shown in normal view. (For a complete version of the tune see p. 149 or p. 152 in Chapter 8.)*

Track 83

*Figure 18-7. An excerpt from the second part of the hornpipe **Bantry Bay** with a single trill on E, shown in exploded view.*

Here I have notated the first two notes of the single trill as thirty-second notes, but they do not have to have exactly that duration. They should just be extremely quick.

Note that a cut or a strike could be used on this E just as well as a single trill. Cuts and strikes work very well in the same places where single trills work.

But the single trill is fundamentally different from the cut and strike. Whereas the cut and strike are articulations, the single trill is a three-note ornament in which each note is heard as distinct from the others, though when played extremely quickly, the single trill's effect begins to approach the crispness of the cut and strike.

Here is an example of the use of a single trill when descending by an interval larger than a second, in this case a fourth. Figures 18-8, 18-9, and 18-10 show the first two bars of the slip jig *The Whinny Hills of Leitrim*. Notice the single trill in the first bar.

*Figure 18-8. The first two bars of the slip jig **The Whinny Hills of Leitrim** with a single trill on F-sharp, shown in normal view. (For a complete version of the tune see p. 346.)*

Track 84

This single trill can be executed in two different ways. Figure 18-9 shows the normal way of playing the single trill.

*Figure 18-9. The first two bars of the slip jig **The Whinny Hills of Leitrim** with the normal way of playing the single trill on F-sharp, shown in exploded view.*

Figure 18-10 shows how the single trill can start on the G instead of the F-sharp. This adds an extra note and necessitates faster execution of the ornament. You must be precise with the timing of your fingerings here. You place T2 and T3 down at the same moment as B1 begins the single trill.

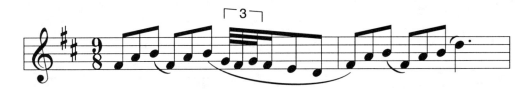

*Figure 18-10. The first two bars of the slip jig **The Whinny Hills of Leitrim** with a more elaborate way of playing the single trill on F-sharp, shown in exploded view.*

 Track 85

Take care not to overuse the single trill. Treat it only as an occasional extra spice. The cut is by far the dominant ornament to use in such situations.

THE SHAKE

There is a lovely ornament that I have heard in the playing of three great tin whistle players: Mary Bergin (see the transcription of her recording of *Father Dollard's Hornpipe* on pp. 407-408 in Section 8), Donncha Ó Briain, in *The Girl that Broke My Heart* (on his 1979 release *Donncha Ó Briain*, Gael-Linn CEF 083), and Breda Smyth (see the transcription of her recording of the reel *O'Mahony's* on pp. 413-415 in Section 8). I call it a **shake**. It is an alternative to the crann on the second D.

To play a shake you use a special fingering for C-sharp by covering the B1, B2, and B3 holes. To get from there to the second D you simply add the T2 and T3 fingers. These two fingers are in motion as a unit when playing a shake.

The shake is a four-note ornament consisting of three very rapid ornamental notes: C-sharp, D, C-sharp again, and then the principal note of D. Like all the other ornaments we have looked at, it begins right on the beat. My symbol for the shake appears below.

Figure 18-11. A symbol for a shake.

This symbol graphically mimics the sound of the shake. It has four "points" that progress rapidly from low to high to low to high, just like the pitches of the notes of the shake. It does look similar to the classical symbol for the *schneller* or *inverted mordent*, but don't be confused. It is not the same.

The shake is related to the trill, in that it is an alternation of an ornamental note with the principal note, but the baroque ornament called a *mordent* comes the closest to resembling the shake. A mordent is the same as the second, third, and fourth notes of the shake. It begins on the principal note, not the note below it. A mordent preceded by an *appogiatura* could be seen as the same thing as a shake.

Mary Bergin uses the shake quite a bit in the second part of the *Old Joe's Jig*. Below is an excerpt from the second part of that tune as she plays it on her first album.[iv]

Figure 18-12. An excerpt from the second part of Mary Bergin's recorded version of Old Joe's Jig with an example of a shake, shown in normal view. (For a complete version of the tune see p. 342.)

Track 86

Figure 18-13. An excerpt from the second part of Mary Bergin's recorded version of Old Joe's Jig with an example of a shake, shown in exploded view.

As with the single trill, I have notated the quick notes of the shake as thirty-second notes but they do not have to have exactly that duration. They should just be extremely quick.

Note the *ascending roll* that begins this example. (See the discussion of *ascending rolls* in Chapter 11, p. 192.)

TRIPLE TONGUING OR TRIPLE THROATING

Another ornamental technique that can be used as an alternative to cranning is triple tonguing. This is a very particular application within the larger area of multiple tonguing, which I address in depth in Chapter 20, *Tonguing, Multiple Tonguing, and Throating*. On the whole, tonguing is employed for phrasing, but in this instance it is used to create an ornamental technique.

As shown in Figure 18-14 below, a hard and very rapid "t-k-t" tonguing pattern can produce the rhythm and approximate effect of the short crann. (For a detailed discussion on the nature and use of such consonants in tonguing see Chapter 20.)

Figure 18-14. Comparison of a short crann and a triple tonguing.

Some players, such as Catherine McEvoy, are able to produce a similar effect with throating.

In an interview with Brad Hurley,[v] she describes her use of this technique in her recording of *O'Donnell's Hornpipe*[vi] as

> . . . a sound made from the throat. The only way I can think of describing it is maybe the way a bird warbles. Josie McDermott used it on the flute and it was from him that I got the hornpipe *O'Donnell's*. You can hear a similar technique used on a hornpipe on *Fluters of Old Erin* (flute, piccolo and whistle recordings of the 1920s and 30s).[vii] There is a hornpipe called *Dwyer's* played by a William Cummins (1894-1966) who came from Roscrea, Co. Tipperary. He uses the same technique and it is a great piece of flute playing.

You can see my transcription of William Cummins' recording of *Dwyer's Hornpipe* on pp. 372-374 of Section 8.

I don't think there is anything in throating analogous to the back and forth ability of the tongue, so I think that triple throating is done with a rapid *single throating*. It seems to me that there is much more agility and nuance offered by triple tonguing. I discuss throating in more depth in Chapter 20.

Getting back to triple tonguing, you will find that it is easier than cranning, so you must beware of laziness. Don't shirk from the labor of learning to crann. The crann is a beautiful and unique sound, one that is really more special than triple tonguing. Overuse of triple tonguing will take you outside the realm of traditional playing, which you will know if you are doing a lot of listening to traditional players.

Despite the above warning, there is another use of ornamental triple tonguing that I think can be very good to employ, even though I have not heard very many traditional players use it.

TRIPLE TONGUING TO MATCH BOW TREBLES OR TRIPLETS

If you listen to good fiddlers you will notice that they often make use of a very quick ornamental triple bowing technique that they call *bow trebles* or *bow triplets*. Technically these are not true triplets at all (see *The Fallacy of the "Triplet"* below), but nevertheless the name is in common use.

When playing in tight unison with a fiddler I will sometime use triple tonguing to match their bow trebles. This sounds wonderful and is exhilarating when done well. You can match the quality of their bow trebles by carefully crafting the emphasis and shortness of the individual "strokes" within your triple tonguing.

Note that fiddlers often (but not exclusively) use bow trebles on open strings, in part because they cannot play normal rolls on open strings. Thus, for example, in a tune where you might often use long rolls on your low A, which is an open string on the fiddle, a fiddler might use bow trebles instead. If so, you might want to try to match their bow trebles, or some of them, with triple tonguing. Note also that fiddlers sometimes employ a technique much like cranning on their open strings, which combines well with our cranns and rolls.

Triple tonguing might also prove useful in tight unison playing with other instruments such as accordions or plectrum instruments, but beware not to overuse the technique. Since plectrum instruments can't readily play fluid rolls, you won't want to abandon too many of yours.

THE FALLACY OF THE "TRIPLET"

The word *triplet* is used extensively, almost universally in fact, by Irish players to describe the rhythm of two sixteenth notes followed by an eighth note, as commonly used in reels, jigs, etc. The word *treble* is sometimes used instead of triplet.

You should be aware that this is not a true triplet in the sense that the word is used in most other musical traditions. A triplet is a group of three notes, all of *equal* duration, that are played in the space of time in which two such notes are normally played. They are notated as a group of three equal notes with a number 3 over the group, sometimes grouped with a bracket or slur, as shown below in Figure 18-15.

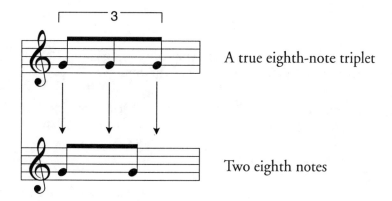

A true eighth-note triplet

Two eighth notes

Figure 18-15. A true eighth-note triplet is played in the same amount of time as two normal eighth notes, but fundamentally alters the subdivision of the beat.

A true triplet, as shown in Figure 18-15 above, changes the subdivision of the beat from duple to triple, something that, if used in most Irish tunes, would completely disrupt the rhythmic flow of the tune. Figure 18-16 on the previous page shows what Irish musicians mistakenly call a triplet.

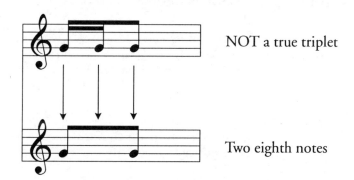

NOT a true triplet

Two eighth notes

Figure 18-16. An Irish "triplet," shown on the top staff above, is not a true triplet but simply two sixteenth notes followed by an eighth note. This ornament preserves the normal subdivision of the beat.

Many players think of the rhythm shown in Figure 18-16 as simply three fast notes, not noticing that the third note is twice as long as either of the first two.

One can see how the misnomer came about. It was simply convenient to borrow the term *triplet* from classical music without regard to its precise meaning. To someone from outside of the Irish music world or new to it, who uses the word "triplet" as most musicians do, the Irish musician's use of the term can be very confusing and lead to wrong playing.

Sadly, every Irish flute or whistle book I have thusfar seen reinforces and prolongs this confusion. Some of them, clearly written by people who have a solid background in classical music, specifically use the triplet notation to notate rhythms that are clearly not triplets. One has to wonder why they do so.

The term *triplet* is so widely used by Irish musicians that it is probably impossible to turn the tide. Nevertheless, I would suggest using the alternate name of *treble*, or adopting the word *triple* in the place of *triplet*.

With regard to triplets we need to take a special look again at hornpipes, mazurkas, schottisches, and other tunes that are commonly played with an overt, intentional unevenness of rhythm.

In Chapter 14, I explained my reasons for advocating the even-note style of notation for these unevenly played tunes. With that kind of notation I feel that the use of triplet notation is appropriate. When such tunes are played with a true triple subdivision, that is one in which the on-beat notes are played twice as long as the off-beat notes, triplet notation accurately conveys what is happening.

Experienced players more often feel the lilt of such tunes to be somewhere in between the two extremes of a one to one ratio (even notes, as notated in Figure 14-1 on p. 210) and a two to one ratio (triple subdivision, as notated in Figure 14-2 on p. 211). In those cases the notated triplets are played according to the underlying "feel" of the subdivision, not as true triplets, but the triplet notation is still appropriate.

TIGHT TRIPLETS

There is a lovely ornamental technique that some players call a **tight triplet**. As you might guess, its rhythm is not that of a true triplet. Instead it uses the rhythm shown in the upper staff of Figure 18-16.

The tight triplet makes use of a phenomenon called *crossing notes* or *crossing noises*. Though I do not believe it is an ornament or technique used in uilleann piping, its "bubbly" or "poppy" sound is suggestive of the tight or staccato fingering technique that is often used in uilleann piping, and also of some of the ornamental techniques of Scottish highland piping.

Pat Mitchell uses the term *tight triplets* in his book *The Dance Music of Willie Clancy*[viii] to describe a quick staccato three-note pattern. In playing this, pipers use *tight* fingerings in which only one or two holes are open for each note of the triplet. In between these notes, no sound is produced because the finger holes are all momentarily closed, as is the end of the chanter.

Crossing notes often occur accidentally as a result of sloppy fingering. For example, let's say you are playing a low-octave B and then move up a step to a C-natural. To play the B, only T1 covers its hole. To move to C, you simultaneously lift T1 and put down T2 and T3. If, however, you are late in lifting T1 you will get a momentary crossing note. A brief G will be heard in the moment that all three fingers, T1, T2, and T3, are covering their holes; while you are "crossing" from one note to the other.

Tight triplets make intentional use of these crossing notes. In all tight triplets, slur all the notes together and make the crossing notes as brief as possible so that they sound like "pops" or "burbles." The slurring together of these notes makes this sound quite different from the tight triplet of uilleann piping with its separated, or staccato notes.

The tight triplet seems to be most commonly applied to the sequence low B–C-natural–D, as shown in Figure 18-17 (below).

Figure 18-17. The most common notes for a tight triplet.

Track 87

The tight triplet can be applied in two ways in this note sequence. In the first application, a crossing note is placed only between the B and the C. To play this, use this fingering sequence.

1. Finger B by putting down T1 *and* T3.

2. Add T2 to get the crossing note of G, and

3. *immediately* lift T1 to play C. Then,

4. add B1, B2, and B3 to get to the high register D.

Note that T3 stays down for the entire sequence.

The same is true for the second application, in which an additional crossing note is placed between the C and the D. Finger this as follows:

1. Finger B by putting down T1 *and* T3.

2. Add T2 to get the crossing note of G, and

3. *immediately* lift T1 to play C.

4. Add T1 to get the crossing note of G, and then

5. *immediately* add B1, B2, and B3 to get to the high-register D.

Note that you end this sequence fingering the high-register D without venting it with T1. This may require you to use a slightly faster airstream to make the D speak well.

You can use the tight triplet technique with other note sequences as well, for example when playing the low octave notes A–B–C-natural.

Figure 18-18. Another note sequence
that can be played as a tight triplet.

Track 88

Again, this can be played with either one or two crossing notes. Let's look at the fingering sequence for the latter.

1. Finger A as usual by putting down T1 and T2.

2. Add T3 to get the crossing note of G, and

3. *immediately* lift T2 to play B. T3 remains down.

4. Add T2 to get the crossing note of G, and

5. *immediately* lift T1 to play C-natural.

Tight triplets can be played on a number of other stepwise rising and falling note sequences. Sometime the added fingers that are needed to create the crossing notes cause certain notes to sound too flat. This varies from instrument to instrument and between the two registers. Some tight triplets are more successful on the whistle than on the flute. You'll have to experiment to find what works on your instrument.

The imitation of uilleann piping is found again in flute and whistle players' occasional use of quadruplet figures in jigs. In these quadruplets, four notes of roughly equal duration are played in the time usually occupied by three eighth notes.

In uilleann piping these quadruplets are typically played with the tight fingering referred to above, which yields separated or *staccato* notes. In flute and whistle playing they are often slurred together, but are sometimes made staccato with the use of double or triple tonguing, a technique which is described in depth in Chapter 20.

For an example of a quadruplet, see the version of the first part of the jig *Garrett Barry* that is given below. Note the quadruplet in the fourth measure.

*Figure 18-19. A setting of the first part of the jig **Garrett Barry** with a quadruplet in measure four. (For a complete version of the tune see p. 237 in Chapter 16.)*

Track 89

In this case the first three notes of the quadruplet are made staccato with the use of triple tonguing. The figure could be slurred instead.

Compare the above setting with the two other settings of this jig that are shown in Figures 16-11 and 19-10. In those settings you will see a more usual three-note pattern in place of the quadruplet.

Another example of quadruplets in jigs can be heard in Seán Ryan's recording of the jig *The Frost is All Over*, a transcription of which appears in Section 8 on pp. 416-419.

i John Solum, *The Early Flute*. Oxford: Oxford University Press, 1992, pp. 138-139.

ii Betty Bang Mather, *Interpretation of French Music From 1675 to 1775, For Woodwind and Other Performers*. New York: McGinnis & Marx, 1973, p. 88.

iii Willi Apel, *Harvard Dictionary of Music*, (1944; 20th printing). Cambridge, MA: Harvard Univ. Press, 1968, p. 665-666.

iv Mary Bergin, *Feadóga Stáin: Traditional Irish Music on the Tin Whistle*. Shanachie Records 79006, 1979.

v Brad Hurley, Interview with Catherine McEvoy, "The Flute Interviews," <http://www.firescribble.net/flute/mcevoy.html> (4 September, 1998).

vi Catherine McEvoy, *Traditional Flute Music in the Sligo/Roscommon Style*, Clo Iar-Chonnachta CICD 117, 1996.

vii Various Artists, *Fluters of Old Erin*, Viva Voce 002, 1990.

viii Pat Mitchell, *The Dance Music of Willie Clancy*, 2nd ed. Cork, Ireland: Mercier Press, 1977, pp. 13-14.

chapter 19: ornamentation through melodic variation

As I wrote in the Introduction to Ornamentation, when I speak of ornamentation I am referring to ways of altering or embellishing small pieces or *cells* of a melody that are between one and three eighth-note beats long. Melodic variation often occurs over much longer spans than this. But in this chapter I will address only short duration melodic variations that can be thought of and can function as ornaments.

STEPWISE NOTES FROM BELOW

Often a traditional player will alter a melodic cell by introducing a stepwise note from below. There are many ways of using this technique, but a couple of examples should suffice to make my meaning clear and to spur your imagination. Once you understand this technique you will hear it cropping up all over the place.

In Figures 19-1 and 19-2 below, the opening bars of *The Glen Allen Reel*, the melodic cells in question are G quarter notes.

*Figure 19-1. A typical way of playing the first two bars of **The Glen Allen Reel**.*
(For a complete version of the tune see p. 350.)

Track 90

*Figure 19-2. Another way to play the first two bars of **The Glen Allen Reel**
using the melodic variation of stepwise notes from below.*

Track 91

The G quarter note in the first bar of Figure 19-1 is changed in Figure 19-2 to an F-sharp eighth note followed by a G eighth note. The same is true in the second bar of the example.

Note that, in this second case, the melodic ornament replaces the short roll on G shown in Figure 19-1. Melodic ornaments can often take the place of rolls and cranns, as you will see in other examples in this chapter.

Note also that, in Figure 19-2, you could cut the F-sharp or the G in either instance of this melodic variation. This way of beginning the tune can be added to the variants that are shown in Figure 12-4, which appears again here as Figure 19-3.

1. Played with a quarter note.

2. Played with a mid-note cut on a quarter note.

3. Played with a short roll.

Exploded view of above.

4. Played with a condensed long roll.

Exploded view of above.

*Figure 19-3. Four different ways to play the beginning of **The Glen Allen Reel**.*

Another example of this technique has already been discussed on p. 192 in connection with the *ascending roll*. The excerpt from Mary Bergin's version of *Old Joe's Jig* that is shown in Figures 11-19 through 11-22 (see pp. 191-192) illustrates this.

You can see that the gesture of sliding up into a note from below can be looked upon as a more subtle version of this same melodic variant.

By the way, this melodic variation would be called an *appogiatura* by baroque musicians.

OTHER MELODIC ALTERNATIVES TO ROLLS AND CRANNS

A roll or crann can be used where there is a melodic cell, centering on a single pitch, that lasts for two or three eighth-note beats. Traditional players often make use of small melodic variations in these same situations. (For the moment let's ignore one beat rolls and cranns.)

One of the most common and specific examples of this is the melodic alternative to a long crann on low D that is illustrated in Figure 19-5 below.

Figure 19-4. A long crann on D.

Figure 19-5. A melodic alternative to a long crann on D.

 Track 92

This is one of those ornaments that is usually, and mistakenly, called a triplet.

An example of how this can be used in a tune is shown at the start of the jig *Scotsman Over the Border* in Figure 19-6 below.

Figure 19-6. The first two bars of the jig Scotsman Over the Border.
(For a complete version of the tune see p. 343.)

 Track 93

A long crann could be played in the same place as the first four notes of this example. Though this example occurs in a jig, this variant can be used in reels, hornpipes, etc.

A similar variant can be used in place of a short crann.

Figure 19-7. A short crann on D.

Figure 19-8. A melodic alternative to a short crann on low D.

 Track 94

This same variant can be used, played an octave higher, to take the place of a short crann on high D.

Another variant on high D short crann is shown on the following page.

261

Figure 19-9. A melodic alternative to a short crann on high D.

Track 95

Of course others are possible as well.

An example of how all of these variants can be used to take the place of short and long cranns is shown in the following setting of the jig *Garrett Barry* in Figure 19-10 below. Compare this setting carefully with that given as Figure 16-11 on p. [000].

Figure 19-10. A setting of the jig **Garrett Barry** showing how the
melodic variants shown above can be used to replace short and long cranns.

Track 96

Now let's look at some melodic variations that can take the place of rolls. Figure 19-11 shows four variants on the long G roll in the first bar of the reel *The Shaskeen.*

Figure 19-11. Four melodic variants on the long G roll found in the first bar of the reel **The Shaskeen.** *(For a complete version of the tune see p. 354.)*

Track 97

The first variant begins on G, moves to a *neighbor tone* and then returns to G. A neighbor tone is a note in the mode of the tune that is either one step above or one step below the principal note. This is a very commonly used melodic ornament.

The second variant is similar to the first in that it starts and ends on the principal note of G. It moves to and from B instead, a note that is more distant from G, but one that, along with the G, belongs to a chord that could be played along with the melody at this point, namely a G-major chord. This is another very common type of melodic variation, one which implies a plausible underlying harmony.

The third variant again begins and ends on G but introduces more rhythmic interest. It could be seen as an elaboration on the first variant.

The fourth variant is more adventurous, changing the nature of the original melody a bit more. Here we are starting to go beyond the realm of melodic ornamentation and into an interpretive recasting of the melody.

There are numerous other melodic variants that would be stylistically acceptable, and all of them could be further enhanced with cuts and various approaches to tonguing and slurring.

WHAT TO DO WITH C-NATURAL AND C-SHARP

A sensible time to use such melodic ornaments is when a roll or crann is difficult or impractical.

263

As you know, the notes C and C-sharp are problematic ones for rolls. One can simulate rolls on these notes but many players, myself included, often find it more interesting and musical to do other things with these notes. Most traditional players make very little use, if any, of these simulated C and C-sharp roll techniques. There are some additional C and C-sharp ornaments that are possible only on the Boehm-system flute. For more information on this, see Appendix B.

A good opportunity to try out some of these melodic ornaments is in the fourth part of the reel *The Gravel Walk*.

Even though this part of the tune seems to be in C Ionian, the tune as a whole is in A Dorian, hence the mode signature of one sharp. If one were to use an F as part of a variation in this part of the tune it would probably be an F-sharp, in keeping with the overall mode of the tune.

*Figure 19-12. A simplified version of the first four bars of the fourth part of the reel **The Gravel Walk**. (For a complete version of the tune see p. 351.)*

There seems to be a perfect opportunity for a long roll on C starting on the last note of the first bar. You can certainly play one, using the simulated C roll fingerings given in the Chapter 10. Two-beat cells centering on C also appear, at the start of the first and third bars. Some alternative ways to ornament all of these cells of C are shown below in Figure 19-13. Compare them carefully to Figure 19-12.

*Figure 19-13. Three melodic variants of the beginning of fourth part of the reel **The Gravel Walk** showing various ways to ornament melodic cells centered on C-natural.*

① *Track 98—Includes Figure 19-13 and Figure 19-15*

Perhaps the most widespread and simple of all melodic ornaments is the filling in of melodic intervals, especially of thirds.

Figure 19-14 shows a basic form of the first part of the slip jig *A Fig for a Kiss*.

Figure 19-14. A basic version of the first part of the slip jig **A Fig for a Kiss**.
(For a complete version of the tune see p. 345.)

Notice that with the first three notes of the fourth bar the filling in of a third is part of the basic melody itself. The "unfilling" of that third would be considered a variation to the tune.

Figure 19-15 shows a variety of melodic ornaments of this type, as well as some others, in the first part of this tune. Compare these variants carefully with Figure 19-14.

Figure 19-15. Three melodic variants on the first part of the slip jig
A Fig for a Kiss *showing a variety of melodic ornaments.*

①Track 98—*Includes Figure 19-13 and Figure 19-15*

Take a look at the rhythms where the filling in of intervals occurs. You'll notice that:

- Quarter-note to eighth-note patterns become three eighth notes, and

- Eighth-note to eighth-note patterns become two sixteenth notes and an eighth note, the rhythm often erroneously called a triplet.

A different type of filling in is shown below in Figures 19-16 and 19-17, the beginning of the hornpipe *The Rights of Man*. (This tune is somewhat unusual because it is in the Aeolian mode.)

Figure 19-16. The beginning of a basic version of the first part of the hornpipe
***The Rights of Man.** (For a complete version of the tune see p. 356.)*

② Track 1 **(Figures 19-16 and 19-17)**

*Figure 19-17. The beginning of the first part of the hornpipe **The Rights of Man** with melodic ornaments.*

CREATING MELODIC ORNAMENTS USING CHORD TONES

If you have a knowledge or intuitive sense of plausible underlying chordal harmonies while playing tunes, you can often use chord tones in making melodic ornaments. Be careful not to overdo it though.

For some examples see the first part of *Jimmy Ward's Jig* in Figures 19-18 and 19-19 below. Figure 19-18 shows a normal way of playing this.

*Figure 19-18. A basic version of the first part of **Jimmy Ward's Jig**. (For a complete version of the tune see p. 340.)*

Figure 19-19 shows how the three long G rolls can be replaced by melodic ornaments that make use of notes that are (mostly) in a G major chord. In this example I'm on the verge of taking this technique too far, but I do so in the interest of demonstration. Compare this carefully with Figure 19-18.

266

Figure 19-19. The first part of **Jimmy Ward's Jig**, *with tasteful melodic ornaments that make use of chord tones.*

 Track 2

Don't use this technique arbitrarily but bear well in mind how your variants combine with the rest of the melody. They can enhance the shapes that are already inherent in the tune, as in the example above, or they can interfere with or obscure them, as demonstrated below in Figure 19-20.

Figure 19-20. The first part of **Jimmy Ward's Jig**, *with melodic ornaments that interfere with the natural contours of the melody.*

 Track 3

CHANGING REGISTERS

Since the fingering for a given note in the low register of the flute or whistle is generally the same as it is in the high register, it is quite easy to change the register of a note or group of notes at will. This is not necessarily true for other instruments, such as the fiddle or tenor banjo. Easy register changing is a special capability of the flute and whistle, one that they share with the uilleann pipes. Using this technique is perhaps more a means of variation than of ornamentation.

Traditional players use this technique for several reasons. The first is in response to the problem of encountering notes that are below the range of the instrument.

THE PROBLEM OF NOTES THAT ARE TOO LOW

Many tunes have notes that are lower than low D, the bottom note on the tin whistle and many simple-system flutes. Traditional players usually respond to this by simply playing the note or notes in question an octave higher. The resultant changes in the melody are usually fairly minor and may even go unnoticed when playing along with an instrument that does play the low notes in their original register, such as a fiddle or accordion.

Sometimes, however, the resultant changes in melodic contour are unexpectedly beautiful and a new version of the tune is born which others make a point to learn.

267

A fine example of this is Paddy Carty's version of the reel *The Jug of Punch*. His rendition of this tune, as recorded on his album *Traditional Music of Ireland* [i] is shown in its entirety in Section 8, pp. 384-385.

Even though Paddy Carty's Radcliff-system flute had keys that would allow him to play as low as C, he raised by an octave all the notes that fall below low D. Perhaps he had previously worked out this tune on a simple-system flute that didn't go below D, or on a whistle, or perhaps his low C-sharp and C keys did not function well. On the other hand, he clearly enjoyed playing with the ambiguity of F-sharps and F-naturals, which he freely changes throughout his rendition of the tune, something that would be difficult to do on a whistle or an unkeyed simple-system flute. Most musicians play only F-naturals throughout this tune.

Here are the notes he plays in the first statement of the A part:

*Figure 19-21. The notes of the first A part of the reel **The Jug of Punch** as played by Paddy Carty.*

Below is shown how this same A part would be played on a fiddle or other instrument that can play below low D. The notes that Paddy Carty raised by an octave are indicated by an asterisk.

*Figure 19-22. The notes of the A part of the reel **The Jug of Punch** as they would normally be played on a fiddle or other instrument capable of the notes that go below low D. The notes that Paddy Carty raised by an octave are indicated by an asterisk.*

Flute and whistle players also play with register changing for the pure joy of it. Many players, such as Tom Morrison and Seamus Egan, use this technique as a major tool of variation. For illustrations of this, see the transcriptions of performances by these two players, which appear on pp. 368-371 and 433-435 in Section 8.

When changing register for purposes of variation players sometimes play normally high passages in the low register, as well as the other way around.

Sometimes traditional players change registers unintentionally. This is often due to a lack of embouchure control or uncontained exuberance.

i Paddy Carty, *Traditional Music of Ireland,* Daniel Michael Collins Master Collector Series, No. 1, 1974.

section 4

———

phrasing,
articulation,
and
use of the breath

chapter 20: tonguing, multiple tonguing, and throating

TONGUING AND SLURRING DEFINED

To **tongue**, in the musical terminology of wind instruments, means to use an action of the tongue to articulate or separate notes. You can use the tongue to stop and to start the flow of air.

To **slur** means to connect two or more notes such that only the first note of the group is articulated. A slurred group of notes is played using an uninterrupted, continuous stream of air.

All the air that we blow through our flutes and whistles must pass over our tongues. The tongue is an exquisitely agile and sensitive muscle. We have already trained it to an extremely high degree through our mastery of everyday speech. We use a vast spectrum of nuance when we speak or sing.

Every time we use the consonants c, d, g, j, k, l, n, q, s, t, and z we are overtly tonguing, and we use our tongues in more subtle ways to help shape most of the other sounds of speech. Our tongues are probably more highly trained, eloquent, and sensitive than any of the other muscles we use in playing the flute or tin whistle, with the possible exception of the finger musculature.

THE PHYSICAL ACTION OF TONGUING

The physical action of tonguing is the same in flute and tin whistle playing. To get a feel for proper flute and whistle tonguing, try the following.

Whisper the syllable "too" and notice where and how your tongue contacts the roof of your mouth. It should touch the hard palate just slightly behind your upper teeth, but not touching the teeth. Now take a deep breath and place your tongue back on that spot. Again, whispering "too," pull your tongue away from the roof of your mouth, but not very far, just a fraction of an inch. This releases your reservoir of air to travel through your lips.

The way that you place and release your tongue determines the consonant of the sound (*t*, *d*, *l*, etc.) and the shape of your mouth cavity (which is also determined in large part by your tongue) determines the vowel of the sound (*oo, oh, ah, eh*, etc.). Of course, when playing Irish music you don't give voice to such vowel sounds. We use them simply to help us recognize the shaping that we can give to the mouth cavity. This shaping has a significant impact on the tonal quality of the music we make. (Actually some players of older generations did occasionally voice vowel sounds while playing. Willie Clancy and Séamus Ennis were among them. For more on this see the notes to my transcriptions of their recorded performances in Section 8.)

When your tongue is in contact with the roof of your mouth it seals it off and prevents the flow of air. When you pull it away, air suddenly is allowed to flow. You have a great deal of subtle control over how you place, shape, and release your tongue.

AVOID SLAP TONGUING

Walfrid Kujala, in *The Flutist's Progress*,[i] warns against *slap tonguing*, a term he uses to describe ". . . the ugly, percussive noise produced inside the mouth when the tongue is allowed to return to the palate contact position too quickly and violently (like pronouncing 'tooT')." Habitual slap tonguing has no place in Irish music.

Your tongue has a *resting position*, just as your playing fingers do. When you pull your tongue back from the roof of your mouth let it hang suspended and relaxed fairly close to it. Don't let your tongue rest against your lower teeth and don't pull it back into your throat. The principles of relaxation and economy of motion apply here as in every aspect of playing.

When you tongue in flute or whistle playing your embouchure must be prepared beforehand and it must remain stable. The areas of articulation (tongue) and air stream shaping and direction (lips and facial muscles) are separate and distinct. Your jaw should not move at all when you tongue.

THROATING

You can also start and stop the flow of air with your glottis, which is the opening between your vocal cords. I call this use of the glottis *throating*. I don't use this technique a great deal but many players find that they are naturally inclined to it.

If you are unfamiliar with your glottis, you can feel it closing just before you cough or clear your throat. During speech and singing your glottis is opening and closing rapidly and repeatedly, like your lips do when you make them "flutter," as they do when you imitate a horse's "lip trill" sound. When you whisper, your glottis opens somewhat further than during speech but it is still not completely open.

S. C. Hamilton, in *The Irish Flute Players Handbook*,[ii] writes that throating is very widely used among traditional flute players. He doesn't use the term *throating*, nor does he identify the glottis specifically as the source of its articulation, but I am confident that we are talking about the same thing. His discussion of throating is brief, but it is the most complete I have seen thus far. He writes that it

> . . . is brought about by a movement of the throat, which is probably best described as an underdeveloped cough! . . . Now cough into the flute while maintaining your embouchure—the result will be a shriek, as the airstream expelled by a cough is much too fast to produce a normal note. Repeat the experiment, but this time make the coughing movement much more gentle, almost as if it hurts to cough. This should produce the correct sound.

I hope that players who are expert at using throating will do more writing on the subject. Though I don't use throating very much, it is my opinion that a far greater degree of nuance and agility is possible with tonguing.

GRADATIONS OF TONGUING: SEPARATE VS. CONNECTED, HARD VS. SOFT

There are many subtle aspects of tonguing. Let's look first at how we use tonguing to interrupt and reinitiate the air stream.

When first learning to tongue, the natural inclination is to produce very separate, distinct notes. In doing so, you first whisper the letter "t" to give a clear attack to the start of the flow of air. In this action, you pull your tongue down away from the hard palate. Second, you replace your tongue to stop the air. After a brief pause you repeat the two-step process.

This way of playing, all with well-separated notes, is called **staccato** by classical musicians. *The Harvard Dictionary of Music* defines staccato more specifically as ". . . a manner of performance, indicated by a dot... placed over the note, calling for a reduction of its written duration . . . for half or more of its value."[iii] In other words, a staccato eighth note, for example, would be sustained for at most the length of a normal sixteenth note, half or less of its nominal duration.

After some experience with tonguing one discovers that it is possible to reduce the separateness of tongued notes to almost zero, to make them very smoothly connected. To do this you use a different sort of tonguing action. Instead of using a two-step process, as described above, in which the air stream is alternately and distinctly started and stopped, you use a one-step process in which the air flow is barely interrupted at all.

Instead of using a hard consonant sound like "t," try using a softer one like "d." When saying "d" in the softest possible way, the tongue action is a gentle "flicking" of the roof of the mouth. This consonant sound comes to resemble the gentle "r" sound of Spanish. Try whispering "doo, doo, doo . . ." in this smooth and gentle way. You'll notice that the tip of your tongue moves back in the direction of your throat with each "d," just barely brushing the hard palate as it goes by.

Playing in this manner produces notes that are softly articulated, very connected, and smooth. This manner of playing is what classical musicians call **legato** playing. *The Harvard Dictionary of Music* defines legato as a manner of performance ". . . without any perceptible interruption between the notes."[iv] For a wind player, the most legato playing possible is, of course, manifested in the slurring together of notes.

Think of how a fiddler changes the direction of her bowstrokes. An experienced player can do this in an exceedingly smooth fashion, yet theoretically there is by necessity a very brief, nearly imperceptible interruption in the flow when the bow changes direction. The same potential for smooth articulation exists for tonguing, especially when using multiple tonguing, which we will get to soon.

In tonguing, there are wide areas of gradation between the extremes of staccato and legato, hard and soft. All of these qualities have a place in Irish music. But to understand their proper places, you must first understand the following.

THE PASTORAL BAGPIPES, THE *PÍOB MÓR*, AND THE AESTHETIC OF LEGATO PLAYING

As has been discussed in Chapter 1, Irish flute and whistle stylings owe a great deal to the legacy of the uilleann pipes, which in turn developed out of the pastoral bagpipe and *píob mór* traditions. These older bagpipes could only play in a legato, slurred fashion, with a continuous, unbroken stream of air. Articulations were created solely by the fingers (cuts and strikes) and they did not interrupt the air flow. Flute, whistle, and uilleann pipe players didn't use these same finger articulations out of necessity, as the pastoral pipers did, but because they were are incorporating an established traditional mode of musical expression that had already evolved in the older piping traditions.

The uilleann pipes developed into an instrument with a capability very different from those of the pastoral bagpipe and *píob mór:* the ability to stop the flow of air through the chanter by covering all the finger holes and stopping the end of the chanter on the knee. This made staccato playing possible.

In fact, some uilleann pipers play in a predominantly staccato fashion. This is called *tight* or *close* piping and is exemplified by such players as Tommy Reck.[v] Even pipers who play in the more common *open* or *loose*, predominantly legato style make fairly frequent use of staccato figures such as the tight triplets and quadruplets referred to at the end of Chapter 18.

Uilleann pipers, Irish flute players, and tin whistle players *all* inherited a fundamental and deeply held legato aesthetic from these ancestral bagpipe traditions and combined it with their own staccato playing capabilities to create a new synthesis: **The music, in all its variety, springs forth from an underlying foundation of legato playing. The appropriate use of staccato playing exists in relation to that foundation, and takes on its meaning in contrast to it.**

Within this broad synthesis exist many different styles of playing, some of which make extensive use of the air-interrupting articulations of tonguing and/or throating. Nonetheless, they all hearken back to this common root.

As a matter of fact, all of the contemporary melodic instruments of traditional Irish music, including the fiddle, accordion, banjo, etc., derive their styles of playing ultimately from this same legacy of the ancestral bagpipes.

CONTRAST THIS WITH THE CLASSICAL WIND PLAYER'S ORIENTATION

This legato aesthetic is fundamentally different from that of modern classical music. The classical wind player is taught that all notes are to be tongued unless there is an indication in the notated music, such as a slur, to do otherwise. Most Irish players use tonguing intuitively as a phrasing device *against a general backdrop of slurring*. Classically trained musicians who wish to learn to play traditional Irish music must come to understand this critical distinction. Tonguing is used extensively in both traditions, but in each it is thought of in a completely different way.

A Greater Variety of Articulation

It seems to me that the traditional Irish musician has a much greater variety of articulation available to her than the modern classical wind player has. In classical wind playing, notes are *either* articulated *or* slurred. In Irish traditional music, notes can be articulated *and* slurred, because of its fingered articulations, the cut and strike. Classical wind players do not have a common practice of fingered articulations.

The Subtle Use of Tonguing

Much of the tonguing and throating used in Irish flute and tin whistle playing goes unnoticed because it does not take the music away from its fundamentally legato nature. This assertion will become more clear shortly, when we look at some musical examples.

Single Tonguing Defined

The tonguing techniques we have looked at so far fall into the category of **single tonguing**. In single tonguing, one repeatedly uses only one tongue action, represented by a single consonant sound such as "t" or "d". Though we can be quite agile with single tonguing, it is ultimately limited, especially at fast tempos.

Though this is an imperfect analogy, it is instructive to compare the movement of the tongue with the movement of a plectrum by players of the tenor banjo, guitar, or other plucked string instruments. If a tenor banjo player could only use the downward stroke of her pick, and never the upstroke, she would soon tire from the repetitive and excessive movement that is required. Using both downstrokes and upstrokes is physically much more efficient and relaxing and it allows for more agility and fluidity, especially in rapid passages.

We have a similar situation with repetitive single tonguing. Though it may not be as physically tiring as using only downstrokes on the plectrum banjo, there is a uniformity of sound that comes from using only one tongue action over and over. Double or triple tonguing yields a variety of articulations that give the music a much more interesting sound.

Multiple Tonguing Defined

Multiple tonguing is a pattern of tonguing that makes use of a sequence of differing tongue articulations. Let's look first at double tonguing.

Double Tonguing

Double tonguing is a pattern of tonguing that makes use of two alternating tongue articulations.

To experience double tonguing, try whispering, "doo-goo, doo-goo, doo-goo . . .". Then try "too-koo, too-koo, too-koo". When you apply these patterns to playing the flute or whistle, the latter gives you hard articulations while the former is softer.

Notice that you form "d" and "t" with the tip of the tongue. You form "g" and "k" further back on the tongue. So the two double tonguing patterns given above make use of an alternation between the tip of the tongue and a place further back.

There are other ways to double tongue. By using a sound like "did-dle, did-dle . . ." you can double tongue using a back and forth motion of just the tip of your tongue. This pattern fits the plectrum banjo analogy a little better than the others do. I find that I prefer to use the "doo-goo" or "too-koo" patterns most of the time, but this is a personal choice. Experimentation will yield still more variations on these double tonguing patterns.

Play a series of notes on one pitch, say low G, and use double tonguing to articulate them. Try out all three of the patterns given above, and experiment with others as you wish.

TRIPLE TONGUING

Triple tonguing is a pattern of tonguing that makes use of three tongue articulations in sequence.

An example of this would be "too-koo-too, too-koo-too, too-koo-too . . .." When this triple tonguing pattern is repeated, "too" is used at the end of one pattern and again at the start of the next. This amount of repetition of the "t" sound seems to pose no problem, even at fast tempos, as long as the middle sound of the triple tonguing pattern is different from "t".

One can use triple tonguing patterns which result in no repetition of tongue actions. Two examples are "too-koo-doo, too-koo-doo . . ." and "too-dle-doo, too-dle-doo, too-dle-doo . . .." The latter makes use only of the tip of the tongue.

DIFFERING AESTHETICS IN MULTIPLE TONGUING

Multiple tonguing is used widely in classical music, and certain baroque flutists were well known for their writings and opinions on the subject. For a fascinating look at this, see especially Johann Joachim Quantz's 1752 treatise *On Playing the Flute*,[vi] and Johann George Tromlitz's 1791 tutor *The Virtuoso Flute Player*.[vii]

The classical school of thought has been to work very hard to make the notes produced by multiple tonguing sound identical in their quality of articulation. This makes sense when one understands how multiple tonguing is used in classical and baroque music.

The use of multiple tonguing in Irish flute and whistle playing is fairly widespread, I believe, though it has rarely been acknowledged or spoken of. Among the traditional players who use it, it seems to arise naturally and for the most part unconsciously, for the same reasons that few of us think of and analyze the movements of our tongues while we speak. After all, the actions that produce these articulations are invisible to us, unlike the actions of the fiddler's bow or the banjo's plectrum. For those players who use it, multiple tonguing is simply a natural and automatic part of music making.

The various consonants of multiple tonguing naturally produce a series of subtly differing articulations. A "t" naturally gives a sharper attack than a "d," and a "k" naturally gives a sharper attack than a "g." Multiple tonguing patterns, such as "d-g, d-g, d-g . . ." as a matter of course produce an alternation of attacks that have slightly different qualities and character. It is just these natural differences that classical players work hard to overcome.

In Irish flute and whistle playing, these natural distinctions are an *asset* to the music, just as they are in everyday speech and in singing. There is no reason to make them uniform, because their natural beauty fits the music and because, unlike in classical music, these tonguing patterns are wedded to the subdivision of the pulse in Irish music. They enhance the inherent rhythms and phrasing of a dance tune. I give two examples of this below.

By the way, double tonguing is most useful in tunes that have a duple, or *simple* subdivision of the beat, such as reels, polkas, and hornpipes. Triple tonguing is most useful in tunes that have a triple, or *compound* subdivision of the beat, i.e. the various jigs and slip jigs.

DOUBLE TONGUING IN REELS

Let's take a close look at a sample rendition of the first two parts of the reel *The Gravel Walk* to see how single and double tonguing might be used in context. Bear in mind that this setting is in my own playing style, and represents only one of many ways that I might spontaneously choose to phrase the tune. A myriad of other interpretations of the tune are possible. (For example, listen to Matt Molloy's rendition of this tune on his album *Stony Steps*.)[viii]

277

The letters that appear beneath all of the tongued notes show the consonants I use to articulate them.

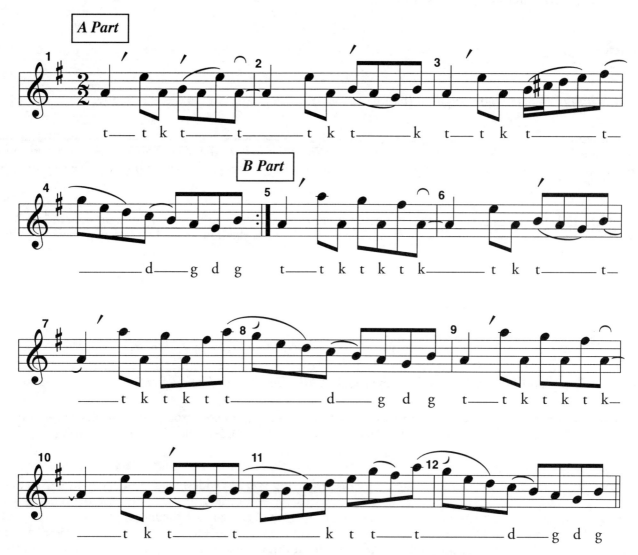

*Figure 20-1. The first two parts of the reel **The Gravel Walk**, showing possible single and double tonguing patterns. (For a complete version of the tune, see p. 351.)*

 Track 4

Listen to this example on CD #2 and you will discover that none of the notes are played staccato, even though most of them are tongued. The overall sound is legato, but rhythmically strong, active, and agile.

TONGUING HELPS MANAGE REGISTER-BREAK CHALLENGES

This particular reel calls for more tonguing than most because of the frequent large interval leaps that cross the register break. The third, fifth, and seventh notes of measures 5 and 9 and the third and fifth notes of measure 7 (all low As that follow upper register notes) are very difficult to play well without tonguing. If you try to play them without tonguing or throating, that is by only decreasing the air speed, they will tend to speak sluggishly or late. It is very difficult to decrease air speed so quickly and accurately. Throating can work fairly well here, but not as well as tonguing in my opinion.

It is also difficult to make the second note of measures 5, 7, and 9 speak well without tonguing. Moving from low A to high A quickly and nimbly requires articulation. However, you could slur note 3 to 4 and 5 to 6 in that measure, as shown below.

278

Figure 20-2. Slurs are feasible on some intervals that ascend across the register break.

Track 5

The adding of fingers seems to makes it feasible to execute these slurs. There is no need for double tonguing when using slurs like this.

TONGUING TO ENHANCE INHERENT RHYTHMS, PHRASING AND PERSONAL INTERPRETATION

Notice in Figure 20-1 that all of the tongued notes that fall on primary or secondary pulses are articulated with a "t," or the slightly softer "d." These are tip of the tongue sounds. Most of the tongued notes that do *not* fall on pulses are articulated with the softer, back of the tongue sounds "k" or "g." This serves to give subtle emphasis to the on-pulse notes. To further enhance this, and to give impulse and forward motion to the tune, I "lean into" the on-pulse notes slightly with my breath and "back off" the others.

Not all the tonguing in this reel is double tonguing. Where you see two or more "t"s in a row, this is single tonguing and is the result of choosing to give some emphasis to some off-pulse notes.

For example, I emphasize the last note of measure 1, which is the first note of a syncopated long roll that crosses into the next measure. In similar situations, the last notes of measure 5 and of measure 9, I don't choose to emphasize these rolls in this way. The last note of measure 3 is slurred to the first note of the next measure, so I choose to give it a strong tongue articulation. This also happens with the last notes of measures 6, 7, 10, and 11. These are all subtle but important touches.

There are many double-tongued *couplets*, groups of two notes that form a double-tongued unit. Examples are the second and third notes of measures 1, 2, and 3. This tonguing technique heightens what is already inherent in the melody. The E is stronger than the low A because of its high register and because it falls on a pulse. The low A is an off-pulse note.

Then there are some groups of notes that could be considered to function as *stretched couplets*. For example, the last note of measure 10 is slurred together with the first three notes of measure 11 and this slurred group is followed by a tongued note. Those five notes form a unit comprised of a slurred group plus a single note. The first note of the slurred group leads into an on-pulse note, so I give it a strong "t" articulation. The last, tongued note of the unit is an off-pulse note that I don't choose to emphasize so I give it a softer articulation. Thus you have a "t-k" double tongue pattern happening over the space of five notes. Similar situations occurs in measures 4 and 12, in these instances over a space of three notes.

Finally, notice how I use the "d-g" pattern to slightly soften the attacks of the notes in measures 4 and 12.

PURISTS WHO OPPOSE TONGUING NEED TO DO MORE LISTENING

Some purists feel that there is no place in Irish flute and tin whistle playing for tonguing. This attitude is an extreme one that reveals a certain lack of understanding. Perhaps it is an overreaction to the misuse of tonguing that is often heard among players from outside the tradition who do not yet understand the aesthetic of traditional Irish music.

There is no question that both throating and tonguing are widely used among traditional flute and whistle players. In comparison to flute players, whistle players tend to use throating much less and tonguing more. This was confirmed to me in a conversation with the master Irish whistle player Mary Bergin. She told me that she uses tonguing and no throating on the whistle, whereas she does add the use of throating when she plays the flute. With throating, I find that it is harder to control the whistle's tone and register than is the case with the flute, with it's greater embouchure control capabilities.

Throating and tonguing are rarely discussed by traditional Irish flute and whistle players. Most players seem to come to their accustomed practices of air articulation rather unconsciously and may never have thought much about them. As stated above, perhaps this is because the actions that produce these articulations are invisible to us, unlike the actions of the fiddler's bow or the banjo's plectrum. Flute and whistle *fingering* techniques on the other hand are highly visible and therefore are the subject of far more attention.

Unless you are well attuned to the sounds of throating and tonguing, and even when you are, it can sometimes be very hard to hear the differences between them. In addition, soft, legato tonguing can be very subtle indeed. It is often completely missed by listeners who are not familiar with such techniques from first-hand experience.

Just as in the case of breath vibrato (another taboo according to some underinformed purists), if you listen attentively to the first recordings of traditional Irish flute and whistle players from the early 20th century, as well as the acknowledged contemporary masters of Irish flute and whistle, you will most definitely hear the use of quite a bit of tonguing and throating. In fact, it is quite surprising to hear how extensively some of the early 20th-century players used very pronounced tonguings.

TRIPLE TONGUING IN JIGS

Now let's take a close look at a rendition of the jig *The Sporting Pitchfork* to see an example of how single, double, and triple tonguing can be used in a jig. This is the same setting of the tune that is presented as Figure 11-6 in Chapter 11. Bear in mind again that this setting is in my playing style, and represents only one of many ways that I might spontaneously choose to phrase the tune. A myriad of other interpretations of the tune are possible. (For example, listen to Paddy Glackin and Paddy Keenan's version on their album *Doublin'*.)[ix]

The letters that appear beneath all of the tongued notes show the consonants I use to articulate them.

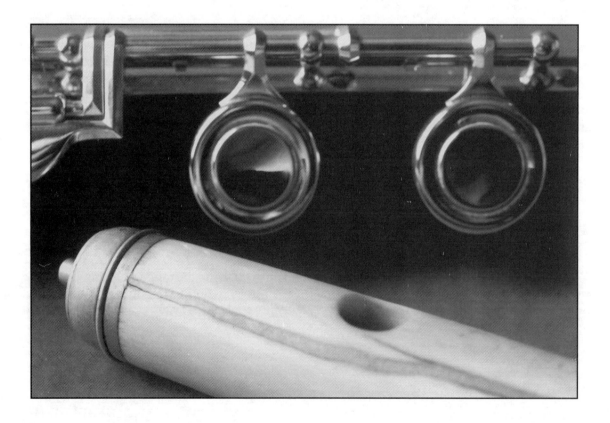

*Figure 20-3. A rendition of the jig **The Sporting Pitchfork** showing possible single, double and triple tonguing patterns.*

 Track 6

INSTANCES OF SIMPLE TRIPLE TONGUING

In the above example, let's look first at some instances of straightforward triple tonguing with groups of three eighth notes. In the second half of both measure 3 and 15 I use a "t-k-t" pattern that is slurred into the downbeat of the next measure.

281

The Typical Shaping of Three Eighth-note Groups in Jigs

Typically, the second note of such three eighth-note groupings in jigs is inherently less important than the first and third notes of the group. Such notes are not unimportant, of course, but if you had to leave out one of the three notes for the purpose of breathing, you would most often choose to omit the second. This is definitely true in these two cases. (For more discussion of this topic see the next chapter.)

The back of the tongue "k" sound is naturally less emphatic in its attack than the tip of the tongue "t" sound. Therefore using the "t-k-t" pattern helps bring out the inherent shape of these three note groups by "locating" the second note more back in the throat. In playing jigs, most players also employ some degree of lilt that delays this second note of the three note group, making the first note the longest, the second note the shortest, and the third note of intermediate length. This hierarchy of duration also reflects the relative importance of these notes. To further reinforce this, the second "t" is made to be not as strong as the first "t." Add to these devices (i.e. lilt and triple tonguing) the emphasis with the breath of the first note of the group, and ornamentation, and you can see how all of these elements unite to bring forth the inherent structure and beauty of the tune, according to the player's interpretation.

Creating Depth: Juxtaposing Soft and Hard Tonguings

In the second half of measure 14 I use the "d-g-d" pattern to give these three notes softer attacks than the surrounding notes. This helps them to recede into the background just a bit and make the following notes stand out a bit more. Such choices lend a three-dimensional quality to the music. These are very subtle touches.

An even subtler illustration of this can be seen in measure 13. Here I use a "t-k-d-t" pattern. This could be considered a quadruple tonguing pattern. The second, third, and fourth notes of the measure are all Ds, but the third one is a pivotally important note, the apex of the four measure phrase that it ends. In order to help bring out its proper prominence, I tongue the preceding Ds with the somewhat softer "k" and "d" articulations.

Some Stretched Triplets

When looking at *The Gravel Walk* (Figure 20-1 on p. 278) we saw that there were some groups of notes that functioned as *stretched couplets*. Similarly, in this jig there are some stretched triplets.

For example, look at measure 2. The three notes of the long roll are slurred into the following note to form a four note slurred group, which is followed by two tongued notes. Taken together, the whole measure functions as a stretched triplet that uses a "t-g-d" tonguing pattern. Or, you could say that this measure plus the three-note slurred group that follows it function as a stretched quadruplet that uses a "t-g-d-t" quadruple tonguing pattern.

Stretched triplets also appear in measures 4 to 5, 6, 7 to 8, 11, and 16 to 17.

In looking at *The Gravel Walk* we saw that it was a common occurrence for the first note of a slurred group to lead straight to an on-pulse note. Giving that first note of the slurred group a sharp attack, even though it is an off-pulse note, helps to emphasize the on-pulse note that follows.

This occurs in jigs as well. You can see examples of it at the end of measure 6 leading to the first note of measure 7 and at the end of measure 15 leading to the first note of measure 16.

Triple-Tonguing Elision

Something else interesting happens in both of these cases. The last articulation of one triple-tonguing pattern also functions as the first articulation of the next triple-tonguing pattern.

Single and Double Tonguings Are Also Used

You can see that single and double tonguings are also used in this rendition of the jig. Single tonguing can be seen in measures 1, 3, 5, 8, 10, 12, 13, 14, 15, and 17. True double tonguing occurs in measure 9 and 18 with a "t-k" pattern being applied to an on-pulse quarter note followed by an off-pulse eighth note.

Multiple Tonguing Brings the Texture of Speech and Song into Music

This use of multiple tonguing, with its wide variety of subtle articulation qualities, brings to the music a sense of the texture of speech or singing. It helps to create groupings of notes that function like syllables of longer words instead of monosyllabic words unto themselves. This is a lovely and important facet of playing the music that helps make it articulate and eloquent. To explore this analogy further, see Chapters 2 and 23.

It is intriguing to speculate that one's native speech patterns might have some effect on how one employs multiple tonguing. Could it be that a native Irish speaker might articulate the music somewhat differently than a native English speaker? Perhaps so, but I'll leave that question to someone else's research.

Triple Tonguing for Ornamentation

This subject has already been discussed in Chapter 18, *Other Multi-Note Ornaments*, on pp. 253-254.

Enhancing Natural Melodic Contours with Tonguing

The simple use of single tonguing can do wonders to clarify phrasing and bring forth what you understand as the natural contours of a tune. In this sense, the use of the tongue is like a well-placed comma in a sentence that helps you understand the sense of the phrases.

To see what I mean, look at the following two excerpts from the second part of the jig *The Banks of Lough Gowna*.

The first setting is one which seems to ignore the fundamental shapes of the melody, imposing what seem like arbitrary phrasing that is at odds with the tune. There is not much tonguing, so it is uniformly single, and its use gives emphasis to certain notes that really should not be emphasized, such as the fifth note of measure 2, the fourth note of measure 4, and the third note of measure 5.

In the second setting, the use of tonguing and slurring clarify and amplify the beautiful contours and phrases that are inherent in this melody. For example, the second note of measure 3 begins a six-note upward sweep. That note is highlighted by tonguing, as is the apex of the sweep, the first note of measure 4. Using the language analogy, tonguing the second note of measure 3 has the effect of putting a comma after the D that precedes it, clearly setting off the next phrase and giving it space to breathe. The multiple tonguing adds texture and depth.

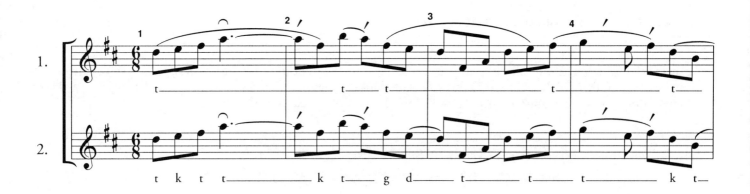

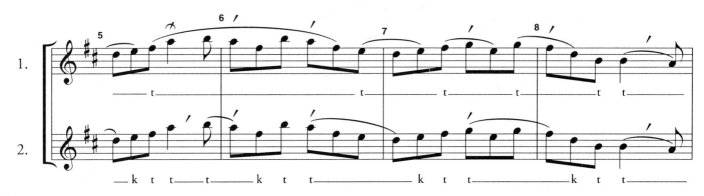

*Figure 20-4. Two settings of the second part of the jig **The Banks of Lough Gowna**.*
(For a complete version of the tune, see p. 288 in Chapter 21.)

 Track 7

ACHIEVING BALANCE

Within the fundamental legato aesthetic of Irish music, there is room for a wide variety of approaches to the question of playing notes in a connected or separated fashion. One should avoid rigid or arbitrary adherence to any concept of how you think you should be playing. If you play all legato or all staccato, the music will be restricted, unable to breathe. You may experience this physically as a sense of constriction.

Instead, let your choices be dictated by the music and how you feel about it, how it speaks to you, how you feel moved to express it in the moment. These choices should arise from within you, not be imposed upon the music from the outside. If you approach the music in this natural way, you will find a balance of staccato and legato, connected and separated playing, that will be your own. The music will be set free and it will breathe. You may experience this physically as a sense of expansion.

i Walfrid Kujala, *The Flutist's Progress.* (Evanston, Illinois: Progress Press, 1970), p. 18.

ii S. C. Hamilton, *The Irish Flute Players Handbook.* (Ireland: Breac Publications, 1990).

iii Willi Apel, *Harvard Dictionary of Music,* 20th printing. (Cambridge, Massachusetts: Harvard University Press, 1968), p. 708.

iv Willi Apel, p. 396.

v Tommy Reck, *A Stone in the Field.* (Danbury, Connecticut: Green Linnet Records, SIF 1008, 1977). Reck also appears on the uilleann pipe anthology *The Drones and the Chanters* (Dublin: Claddagh Records, CC11, 1971). He recorded two 78 sides for the Irish Recording Company (Dublin) in the 1950s. One of these was reissued on *From Galway to Dublin* (Cambridge, Massachusetts: Rounder Records, CD 1087, 1993). He also recorded two 78 sides for Gael-Linn, ca. 1959, but those have not been reissued as of this writing.

vi Johann Joachim Quantz, *Versuch einer Anweisung die Flöte traversiere zu spielen.* (Berlin: Johann Friedrich Voss, 1752); trans. Edward R. Reilly as *On Playing the Flute.* (London: Faber & Faber, 1966).

vii Johann Georg Tromlitz, *Ausführlicher und gründlicher Unterricht die Flöte zu spielen.* (Leipzig: Adam Friedrich Böhme, 1791); trans. and ed. Ardal Powell as *The Virtuoso Flute Player,* (Cambridge: Cambridge University Press, 1991).

viii Matt Molloy, *Stony Steps.* (Danbury, Connecticut: Green Linnet Records, GLCD 3041, 1987).

ix Paddy Glackin & Paddy Keenan, *Doublin',* Tara Records TARA 2007, 1978.

chapter 21: musical breathing

The flute and tin whistle are the only instruments of traditional Irish music that are not suited to nonstop playing.

One could see this as a disadvantage. But one could also look at it another way. Since we must create occasional small spaces in the tunes in order to breathe, we flute and tin whistle players are never allowed to forget that music itself needs a chance to breathe once in a while. We must breathe, so why not use the breathing spaces we create to enhance our phrasing and our definition of clear musical shapes?

Fine players of other instruments use space in this way too, even though most of them don't have to. Of course singers, the ones who many consider to be the most expressive musicians of all, must leave breathing spaces in their music, just as flute and whistle players must do. Insightful instrumentalists know how important it is to make their instruments "sing." A major aspect of achieving this is the creation of space.

One could overcome this apparent limitation by using circular breathing. Later in the chapter, I'll elaborate a bit on why I don't recommend this.

THE LANGUAGE ANALOGY RESURFACES

When we speak, we leave occasional spaces, sometimes in order to breathe, sometimes to make meaning more clear, sometimes for both reasons. So it is in playing the flute or whistle. In speaking, if we want the sense of a statement to sink in, we often create a bit of space before moving on: a comma, a period. All musicians can apply this kind of subtle shaping, or punctuation, to their music. Unfortunately, many don't. For flute and whistle players, it is built into the very act of playing, so we must learn how to use breathing articulately, in ways that clarify our interpretation of the music.

ARTICULATE AND INARTICULATE BREATHING

Articulate breathing has the effect of illuminating the phrasing and natural contours of a tune. Inarticulate breathing disrupts the music and draws attention to itself.

Often after concerts, listeners come to me and say something like, "It's amazing, you never breathe when you play!" I take this as a high compliment because, though I take frequent, deep breaths, I do so quickly, quietly, and as an integral part of my musical expression. When this is done well, a listener's attention is never drawn to the breathing but only to musical phrasing. Breathing has become my servant, not my master.

NOTE OMISSION AND NOTE SHORTENING

We flute and whistle players must become artistic music editors. We must learn to *omit notes* and *shorten longer notes* in a musically sensitive way. One can almost never sneak a breath between the regular notes of an Irish dance tune without detracting from the music. This can only be done successfully on occasion in slow airs and other slow or moderate tunes.

It is revealing to discover that not every note of a tune is indispensable. You can leave certain notes out without compromising the tune. On the other hand, there are many notes that you must not omit, and you must learn to discern the difference.

It is very important that you omit as few notes as possible and take very quick, deep breaths.

Note omission and note-shortening choices are fluid; they change all the time, depending upon numerous factors such as varying tempos, how loud you want to play in a particular setting, whether you are sitting or standing, how well rested or tired you are (which affects how deeply you breathe), whether or not you just ate a big meal, how well focused your embouchure is on a given day, even the altitude of the locale.

Classical musicians often choose and stick with consistent breathing places in each piece of music they play. Many composers who write for wind instruments wisely incorporate rests to accommodate breathing. Leaving out any of a composer's carefully chosen notes is generally frowned upon in classical music.

Such strategies do not work with traditional Irish music. This is not flute or whistle music *per se*. Each tune is part of a vast repertoire that is shared by *all* the melodic instruments of the tradition. Each player adapts the music in certain ways to her instrument. The flute or whistle player creates breathing spots spontaneously, according to the requirements and moods of the moment. This is, after all, an improvisational music, though extemporization exists within fairly conservative limits in comparison to musical genres such as jazz.

Note omission and note shortening contribute in important ways to melodic variation. Soon I will illustrate this with some examples.

What Is a Tune Anyway?

These realizations bring up such questions as: Just what is a tune? What are the "real" notes of a tune?

There is no simple answer, but an Irish tune is certainly not an established, unchanging, and unbroken sequence of notes, as you might presume by looking in the numerous printed collections that are available. It is something much more fluid and multidimensional, something large and living that music notation cannot contain. When we leave notes out, shorten notes, and change the melody in small ways that are appropriate within the language of Irish music, we are staying true to the tune and keeping it alive.

Each tune has a true essence that makes it immediately recognizable, beautiful, and whole, and it carries rich personal associations for the player. With maturity and experience one comes to intuitively grasp the spirit of a tune and shape it in one's own way.

Breathe Before You Have To

To breathe articulately, you must first attend to the physical requirements of deep breathing and the efficient use of your air supply. These topics are covered in depth in Chapters 5 and 6. Plentiful air, and your economic use of it, give you many breathing options.

You may have noticed that when you are about to run out of air your musical energy suffers. If you don't breathe well in the first place, or you use your air inefficiently, then you may *not* have noticed this, because you may almost always be short of air. When air becomes plentiful for you, you can play with strong, vibrant energy and breath support. It then becomes much easier to breath musically, instead of habitually breathing out of need.

Note Omission and Note Shortening Become Second Nature

Like so many other technical aspects of playing this music, note omission and note shortening need to become second nature. As you establish the habit of always tuning in to your body (see *A Physical Relationship, and Much More* in Chapter 5), you will continually be aware of your air supply status. This awareness will be relegated to some subsurface level of your mind which will keep track of your air while you are occupied with having fun playing music. When you are approaching low air supply, you will feel it in your body, and you will improvise a tasteful way to musically leave out or shorten a note, take a quick, deep breath, and continue on your merry way with a plentiful stock of air. When you do leave out a note in order to breathe, you can still hear that note in your mind's ear. If leaving out notes sometimes derails you or throws you off the tune, remember to hear the omitted notes in your mind.

These abilities will steadily improve as you become more adept at controlling your breathing and embouchure, and as your knowledge and command of the musical language deepen.

NEVER OMIT A NOTE THAT FALLS ON A PULSE

It is crucial that you never omit a note that falls on a primary or secondary pulse. Omitting an on-pulse note is definately not consistent with the language of traditional Irish music and represents the epitome of inarticulate breathing. If you omit such a note, knowledgeable players, listeners and dancers will feel that you are punching a gaping hole into the flow of the tune. If you choose to do so anyway, for dramatic effect, know that you are tinkering with one of the fundamental underpinnings of the music and that many people may see this as an indication of inexperience. However, you can shorten a long note by omitting the last eighth-note segment of it, whether or not that segment falls on a pulse.

DEVELOP AN ABSOLUTELY DEPENDABLE SENSE OF THE PULSE

It is one thing to understand that you shouldn't omit an on-pulse note. It is quite another to know by second nature which notes those are. You must develop an absolutely reliable sense of the pulse in the tunes you play. *This is the cornerstone of choosing good breathing spots.* A rock-solid sense of the pulse makes breathing choices far easier. Never omitting on-pulse notes narrows the field of candidates for note omission by as much as one-third (in jigs and slip jigs) or one-half (in reels).

If it is difficult for you to sense the pulse of a tune when you play, this means that you need to work on internalizing the music and feeling its rhythms in your body. Learning to dance to the music is a great way to do this. Tapping your foot on the pulse helps many players. Some cannot play without tapping their foot. When tapping however, be sensitive to those around you. If you tap loudly you may be annoying others. If your loud tapping is not rhythmically accurate, there is no doubt that you are annoying others, whether or not they have the nerve to tell you.

BREATHING SPOTS IN *THE BANKS OF LOUGH GOWNA*

Below, you will find three settings of the jig *The Banks of Lough Gowna.* The first setting, shown on the top staff, is notated in typical fashion, with no breathing spots indicated. The second and third settings show examples of appropriate breathing places with the kinds of musical adjustments a flute or whistle player might make to incorporate these spaces tastefully into the tune. The location of these breathing spots are indicated with rests, and with the comma symbol (above the rests) that is often used to indicate a breath.

Don't forget to also take note of the variations in ornamentation and phrasing and the small melodic changes that I have incorporated into the second and third settings of the tune.

*Figure 21-1. Three settings of the jig **The Banks of Lough Gowna**. The top staff shows the tune without breathing spaces. Examples of appropriate breathing spaces are shown in the second and third staves. The comma symbol above the staff indicates a breath. The indication "f. v." in measure 5 of the second setting indicates the use of finger vibrato on the dotted quarter-note B.*

Track 8   Track 9

These breathing places demonstrate three different breathing strategies. Let's take a close look at them.

BREATHING STRATEGY #1: SHORTENING A LONG NOTE

In most dance tunes, the eighth note is the basic, prevailing subdivision of the pulse. In some tunes, you will find notes longer than an eighth note. You can often shorten such notes by an eighth note, taking a breath during the resulting rest, without disrupting the flow of the tune. An example of this strategy is seen in measure 4 of the second setting. Here I shorten a D quarter note to a D eighth note followed by an eighth-note rest.

BREATHING STRATEGY #2: BREAKING A LONG OR SHORT ROLL

This strategy works *only* when the long or short roll begins on a primary or secondary pulse (see *It's Alive—It Has a Pulse* on pp. 173-174 in Chapter 10). When the long or short roll starts on a pulse, the second note of the roll necessarily falls on a weak, nonpulse beat and can be omitted to create a breathing opportunity without disrupting the flow of the tune. Of course, when you do this you no longer have a roll, so you can use whatever articulations you like for the note or notes that remain with the breaking of the roll.

Straightforward examples of this occur in measure 9 of the second setting and measure 3 of the third setting. (Note that you can also use this technique with long and short cranns. When you do, you omit the two sixteenth notes that together form the second beat of the long or short crann.)

The example in measure 12 of the third setting is a bit different. When simply breaking the long roll that is played in measure 12 of the first setting, the result would normally be a G eighth note, followed by an eighth-note rest, followed by another G eighth note. However, the new phrase sounds better if you change that last G eighth note to an E. The insight to automatically make such changes comes with a deepening knowledge of the language of Irish music, and this can only come from extensive listening and playing.

If you try this technique on a long or short roll that begins on a nonpulse beat, you will very quickly hear why it doesn't work. For example, take a look at the first two measures of the reel *The Drunken Landlady*.

*Figure 21-2. The first two measures of the reel **The Drunken Landlady**.*
(A complete version of the tune appears on p. 349.)

 Track 10

These long rolls on E begin on weak, nonpulse beats. If you leave out the middle note of either roll, as shown below, then *nothing happens* on the strong secondary pulse and you get a nonidiomatic "hiccuping" effect. A better example of inarticulate breathing in traditional Irish music could hardly be found.

*Figure 21-3. The first two measures of the reel **The Drunken Landlady** showing an example of inarticulate breathing produced by breaking a long roll that begins on a nonpulse beat.*

 Track 11

BREATHING STRATEGY #3: OMITTING A "NON-ESSENTIAL" NOTE

Most notes are essential to the spirit and shape of a tune but some are not. Such "non-essential" notes can often be omitted without any ill effect. Their omission can in fact become a refreshing variation in itself, which is why people often don't notice that a breath is occurring in such instances. They are enjoying the well-shaped phrases of music that are caressing their ears or urging on their dancing feet and they feel no disruption to the flow of the music. (Or could it be the compelling conversation they're having with someone across the table?)

These nonessential notes almost never occur on primary or secondary pulses. (In fact I can't think of any examples where they do.) What does that leave? Only off-pulse notes. An example can be seen in measure 6 of the third setting of *The Banks of Lough Gowna*, above. The F-sharp in question is a note that links two phrases together, just as the word "and" is used in the second to last sentence of the preceding paragraph (the one that begins, "They are enjoying . . ."—go back and take a look). When the note is omitted, the two musical phrases remain perfectly intact, but their relationship is changed in an interesting way. Applying this idea to that sentence in the last paragraph, it is as if you had removed the "and" and put in a semicolon. The sense is the same, but the rhythm, phrasing, and some shadings of meaning have changed.

BREATHING AT THE END OF A PART

The A part or B part of a tune will often end in a way that presents an ideal breathing spot, using one of the above strategies. *The Banks of Lough Gowna*, however, is not such a tune. The end of one part continues beautifully into the next and it would be a pity to break the connection. For an example of a tune that does offer such opportunities, see the various settings of the jig *The Sporting Pitchfork* in Figure 13-11 on pp. 208-209.

You will come across many more tunes that offer this breathing option. Even with such tunes, it is nice to sometimes not breath in those obvious places and carry the energy right into the next part of the tune.

DON'T LET BREATHING INTERFERE WITH NATURAL MUSICAL CONTOURS OR FORWARD MOTION

There are plenty of breathing places that may seem to fall beautifully into one of these three strategies, but breathing there may nevertheless be disruptive to the tune. This is because such notes are needed to define the natural contours of the melody or to help maintain its forward motion.

To see what I mean, let's look at the first two measures of the reel *The Trip to Durrow*.

*Figure 21-4. The first two measures of the reel **The Trip to Durrow**.
(A complete version of the tune appears on p. 234 in Chapter 16.)*

Below you will see an example of inarticulate breathing in this tune excerpt. I have omitted the last note of the first measure, an off-pulse note that might at first seem to serve simply as a connecting note.

*Figure 21-5. The first two measures of the reel **The Trip to Durrow** with an example of inarticulate breathing.*

Track 12

In fact, this note is an essential note, even though it might at first seem to fit the description of strategy #3, above. In fact, its omission is very disruptive of the upward sweep and forward motion of the melody.

If you want to breath somewhere in these measures, you would do better to choose one of the two options shown below in Figures 21-6 and 21-7.

*Figure 21-6. An example of an articulate breathing spot in the first two measures of the reel **The Trip to Durrow**, which is created by breaking a long crann.*

Track 13

*Figure 21-7. Another example of an articulate breathing spot in the first two measures of the reel **The Trip to Durrow**. This one is created by breaking a long roll.*

Track 14

CIRCULAR BREATHING

If you could use circular breathing you could play tunes without ever having to break the constant flow of notes. Wouldn't that be great? Well, I'm not so sure. Circular breathing is quite difficult on the flute and whistle because these instruments offer so little air resistance or "back pressure." The very few times I have heard it attempted with Irish flute or whistle the result has sounded anemic, not to mention monotonous.

It's true that the method of air supply for bagpipes is basically a mechanical equivalent of circular breathing. If you mastered circular breathing on the flute or whistle, perhaps you could sound more like a piper. It would be very challenging, though probably not impossible, to manage the mechanics of circular breathing, produce a strong and supple tone and still be completely free to use tonguing, throating, and note omission in a fully musical way.

I am not an uilleann piper, but I would think that it would be very easy for them to fall into a pattern of playing in an overly verbose, unpunctuated fashion. The use of tight or closed fingerings to produce staccato notes provides one way for them to avoid this hazard.

Traditional music very often takes a natural characteristic of an instrument, even when it seems to be a limitation, and turns it into an essential and beautiful element of the art. The implications of noncircular breathing have had a huge impact on the evolution of traditional Irish flute and tin whistle styles over many, many decades. This is a rich legacy that we have the privilege of partaking in. If you wish to explore the possibilities of circular breathing, go right ahead, but be careful not to injure the music. And remember that taking a breath is a pleasant thing in life. Just think how sorry you'd be if some particularly wordy people you know were to learn the technique of circular breathing.

SUBTLE BREATH PULSE OR WEIGHT

The flow of air that you blow is much like the hair of the fiddler's bow as it travels across the string. Just as a fiddler can change the pressure and speed of her bowstrokes to emphasize certain notes and to impart rhythmic stress, weight, or impulse, you can give such life to your music with changes in the qualities of your breath. Just as a fiddler can "lean into" the bow, you can "lean into" the breath. I elaborate upon this in Chapter 10, in the sections *Rhythmic Emphasis Within the Long Roll* and *It's Alive—It Has a Pulse*, which appear on pp. 173-174.

HEAVY BREATH PULSING

This is a technique that I have not incorporated into my own playing, but it is one that I admire nonetheless. You will hear it in the recordings of such flute players as Tom Morrison, John McKenna, Tom Byrne, Eddie Cahill, Conal Ó Gráda, Kevin Henry, Catherine McEvoy, and Lawrence Nugent.

You rarely hear whistle players using heavy breath pulsing because the technique makes it difficult to control the whistle's pitch and register. The flute, on the other hand, offers the player ways to manage the strong bursts of air that result. The heavy pulses seem to be produced by the glottis and diaphragm and seem to be closely tied to the preference for throating over tonguing among many flute players.

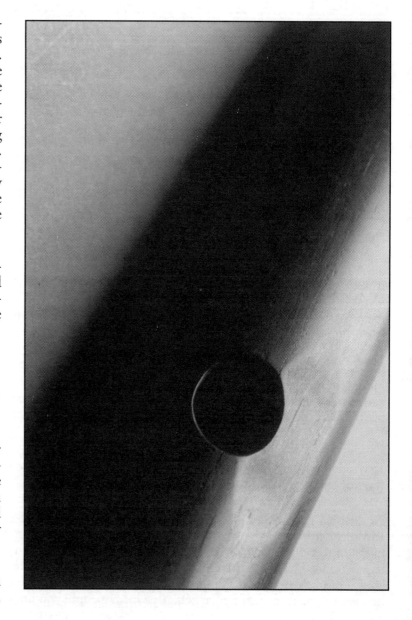

Heavy breath pulsing appears to come from a relatively old style of loud playing that emphasizes forceful and driving rhythm over smooth lyricism. It is a style that is great for dancing, and makes one think of the days before amplification when flute players had to work hard to be heard alongside fiddles, accordions, pipes, banjos, drums, and other louder instruments. S. C. Hamilton, in describing Conal Ó Gráda's flute sound, writes that it has ". . . an earthy, raucous tone reminiscent of the saxophone . . .",[i] an instrument that did find its way into some céilí bands. It's interesting to speculate whether this hard-driving, "huffy-puffy" flute style existed before such bands began to appear.

In its extreme, the breath pulses have a strong pronounced attack. Players such as Eddie Cahill and Kevin Henry, who use breath pulses almost continuously and rarely slur notes together, make little use of fingered articulations and ornaments.

TUNE COLLECTIONS WITH MY BREATHING SUGGESTIONS

My books *Celtic Encyclopedia for Flute* and *Celtic Encyclopedia for Tin Whistle* are Irish tune collections tailored to the needs of flute and tin whistle players. One of the ways I address their needs in these books is by showing the locations of good breathing options for each tune. There are very often more of them than you might suspect.

More tunes, in transcription and audio form, with breathing suggestions, are available at my website, <www.greylarsen.com>.

[i] S. C. (Hammy) Hamilton, in the liner notes to Conal Ó Gráda's recording *The Top of Croom*, Claddagh Records CCF27CD, 1990

section 5

———

final matters

chapter 22: on playing slow airs

I feel that the masterful playing of slow airs demands a higher level of experience and maturity from the flute or whistle player than does any other aspect of this art.

SLOW AIRS AND *SEAN NÓS* SINGING

A slow air is an instrumental interpretation of a *sean nós*, or "old style" song. *Sean nós* singing is a highly personalized mode of unaccompanied solo singing traditionally done in the Irish language. Its tradition is very old and the streams which branch off from it run deep throughout the soul of Irish music.

Sean nós songs are sung in a free, loosely measured rhythm that is determined by the natural flow of the poetry, which changes from verse to verse, and its unity with the melodic line. The style is highly ornamented, yet restrained and entirely undramatized. The persona of the singer nearly vanishes as the import and depth of the lyrics is laid out as fully as possible. The *sean nós* singing tradition is strongest in the remaining Irish speaking areas of Ireland, but it has also been applied to songs sung in English by singers throughout Ireland.

Interpreting a *sean nós* song to create a slow air requires insight into the art of *sean nós* singing as well as considerable mastery of one's instrument and fluency in the larger language of Irish music, to the extent that one can improvise eloquently within it. Fluency in the verbal Irish language itself is a great plus, too, though many musicians who are not Irish speakers seem to do a very good job of playing slow airs. If you do not speak Irish, it is probably best to make slow airs from *sean nós* style songs that are sung in English. That way you can bring to bear the phrasing and subtle rhythms of the words as well as all the shades of meaning and emotion that they convey to you from verse to verse.

Improvisation plays a much broader part in the making and playing of slow airs that it does in any other form of instrumental Irish music. It takes a great deal of time, devotion, and care to create an instrumental interpretation of a *sean nós* song and internalize it so that it becomes a vehicle for one's own deep musical expression.

EXPRESSIVE TECHNIQUES

In playing slow airs, the instrumentalist both emulates the *sean nós* vocal style, in its delivery and ornamentation, and exploits the unique qualities and abilities of her instrument. It is enigmatic that although vibrato is almost never used by a *sean nós* singer, both finger and breath vibrato are often used liberally by the player of the flute, whistle, and uilleann pipes in playing slow airs.

Techniques of sliding are also widely used, as are cuts and strikes. Rolls and cranns are sometimes used, but this varies greatly from player to player. Some use very little ornamentation of any sort, while others play slow airs in quite a florid way. Slow air playing is by far the most individualized vehicle of expression for the traditional Irish instrumentalist. In playing slow airs, your instrument becomes your voice.

"LEARNING" A SLOW AIR

To "learn" a slow air really means to create an interpretation of the song on your instrument. It is widely agreed that the best way to do this is through learning the *sean nós* song from a particular singer. It is not necessary that you learn to actually sing it yourself, but it is important to understand it as a song. A thorough knowledge and understanding of the lyrics is key to creating a meaningful interpretation that is true to the original. Personal or specific knowledge of the singer and her interpretation is very helpful as well.

When making a slow air from a singer's rendition of a *sean nós* song, one sometimes has more than one choice of where to place the melody in the range of the flute or whistle. Remember that a singer places the melody in a range that is comfortable for her voice. There is no need for you to play it at the pitch level that the singer has chosen.

If you have a keyed flute you may have more choices in this regard than you would with an unkeyed flute or whistle. Explore all of the possibilities. Usually one pitch placement will clearly emerge that best fits your "voice" as you explore the air. The different tonal centers and registers carry very different qualities, and each one brings out a unique set of sounds, tonal characteristics, and ornamentation possibilities in an instrument.

There are a small number of slow airs that seem to exist only as instrumental pieces, and some others that are more well known as instrumental pieces. It could be that these "instrumental" airs did originate as songs, but that for some reason they have ceased to be sung and the lyrics have been lost.

As Always, Extensive Listening is Crucial

You may not want to attempt to learn a slow air until you have reached a fairly high level in your knowledge of traditional Irish music. However, it is never too early to seek out and listen to *sean nós* singing and the playing of slow airs by great instrumentalists. *Sean nós* singing is such an important part of traditional Irish music that every player should make a point to seek it out. Tomás Ó Canainn, in his *Traditional Music in Ireland*, states that ". . . no aspect of Irish music can be fully understood without a deep appreciation of *sean nós* (old style) singing. It is the key which opens every lock."[i] Ó Canainn's book gives a very complete and detailed picture of the *sean nós* singing tradition and repertoire.[ii]

I am not going to attempt to notate any of the many fine renditions of slow airs that exist on recordings. The compromises of representing Irish dance music on paper are already substantial enough. Far more severe compromises would be necessary in notating slow airs. You simply must learn them in the traditional aural manner.

The great uilleann piper and singer Séamus Ennis, on his recording *The Return From Fingal,* gives both sung versions and uilleann pipe slow air versions of several *sean nós* songs. It is very instructive to hear his interpretations of these airs as both a singer and a piper.

Recorded examples of slow airs are very numerous. For flute, whistle, and uilleann pipes, I recommend listening to the recordings of Matt Molloy, Mary Bergin, Pat Mitchell, Cathal McConnell, Paddy Keenan, Seamus Cooley, and Josie McDermott among others. Also be sure to listen to slow airs played on the fiddle and other instruments.

[i] Tomás Ó Canainn, *Traditional Music in Ireland.* London: Routledge & Kegan Paul Ltd., 1978, p. 49.
[ii] Tomás Ó Canainn, pp. 3, 49–80.

chapter 23: the language analogy revisited

Now that we have thoroughly explored ornamentation, variation, blowing, phrasing, articulation, the use of the breath, and the playing of slow airs, you can see that the depth of Irish flute and tin whistle playing is comparable to the richness of your own native language. The possibilities for expression are truly endless.

We have seen how spoken language and flute and whistle playing exhibit many parallels in the areas of breath, articulation, phrasing, punctuation, intonation, and inflection; how both embody variation, improvisation, embellishment, and the interpretation of large, complex structures.

REACHING FLUENCY

If you have not grown up immersed in traditional Irish music, then you can also see that learning it is something akin to learning a foreign language. In the early stages you have to give most of your attention to the details and mechanics of the language and the techniques of producing the proper sounds. As your mastery grows, these small scale characteristics become more and more second nature and you are able to continually shift your focus to the larger aspects of the language, eventually achieving fluency: the ability to express yourself readily and effortlessly, to think and "speak" in the new language without internal, mental translation. As you progress in this way, your view of the new world that this language makes possible becomes ever wider and wiser.

As you have worked your way through this book, you have been progressing toward fluency in the language of Irish music. Continued playing, listening, and practice will take you ever further down that road. If you are not there yet, you can look forward to a time when you will no longer need to think about the individual elements of rolls and cranns, about where and how to ornament, about where and how to breath, about when or how to slide into or out of a note. You will no longer have to think about whether or how to use vibrato, single or multiple tonguing, staccato notes, dynamics. All of these tools and techniques will simply be at your fingertips, ready to be called upon by your intuition.

With fluency you can stay in the intuitive, emotional, playful, and interactive part of your mind and spirit. You no longer have to be analytical, though you may choose to be. As your technical prowess and confidence grow, you will continue to relegate technique to *muscle memory*, freeing the conscious layers of your mind to be more creative, expressive, and interactive. We'll look more at muscle memory in the next chapter.

FROM MONOLOGUE TO CONVERSATION TO COMMUNION

With fluency comes the ability to communicate with others on the highest levels.

Unlike spoken conversation, in music we "converse" by playing all at the same time. This is not workable in speech. The closest thing to it I can imagine would be a group of people reciting or chanting a poem together, each interpreting it and improvising on it harmoniously while keeping to the meter—or a group of singers improvising together on a song, but then we have left speech and entered back into music.

With instrumental music, becoming fully "conversational" means that you are able to listen so expansively that you are completely aware of what and how you are playing, and, at the same time, you are listening beautifully to the other musicians around you. (Just as you can play beautifully, you can listen with a quality of beauty.) Each musician hears and understands the expressions of the others and all simultaneously tailor their playing such that they bring forth a musical entity that is greater than the sum of its parts. This is the ideal music session, the transcendent experience that Irish musicians live for.

The same kind of expansive interaction can extend outward from a group of musicians to include dancers and listeners.

Music, Like Language, Becomes a Mirror and a Projector

As you become fluent and eloquent in Irish music, it becomes a mirror and a projector of your soul. The way you speak reveals and expresses a great deal about who you are and how you see the world. The same is true of playing music, but the "light" that music reflects back to you and projects out to others is of a wholly different spectrum than that of spoken, symbolic language. How does one describe it? Here words truly do fail. But when you listen to the playing of a master musician, you "know" something of their soul, immediately and intimately, and you can feel your own beautiful potential in the unique mirror that their music holds before you.

With growing mastery, the musical waters become clear. The spiritual nature of the music is revealed and becomes apparent to anyone who is receptive to it. In the playing/listening experience the illusion of separateness begins to dissolve. All master musicians experience the insight that their music does not originate in them but instead flows through them. They become an instrument of something greater. Perhaps the non-symbolic language of music provides a more direct route to this insight than verbal language can.

Looking Up into a Tree

Being fully musical, like being fully alive, calls for us to learn to be widely perceptive and functional on a variety of planes simultaneously. Here's an illustration, in an experience that we can all have.

One beautiful day, while talking with my young daughter in my backyard, I lay down under a poplar tree. I lay on my back, with the top of my head touching the trunk, and gazed upward. It was a warm, sunny spring day and a very gentle breeze moved through the leaves. I saw the single trunk, the major limbs, the many smaller branches, and the myriad of twigs, which gave rise to tens of thousands of green stems and leaves. The leaves drank in the sunlight and moved in a thousand-fold unison dance to the constantly shifting air. I could see, feel and take it in *all at once*: the trunk, which continued deep below my back into the soil of the earth and gave unity and structure to the whole tree; the large limbs that divided themselves into smaller branches; all the way out to the tips of the leaves which drank in the sunlight and the atmosphere.

I realized that this way of experiencing the tree, something we can all do if we create a few moments of quiet, is just like the ideal of being fully musical. Imagine that the tree is a tune. From such a vantage point one can listen and play on every level at once and understand how all the levels are interrelated: the details of individual notes, note groupings, motifs and phrases, the larger structures, how those are united into A, B, C, parts, etc.; how they form one piece of music, how that piece of music is rooted in a body of music and the soil of a tradition where it is related to every other tree in the forest.

If one were to hover above the tree and gaze down at the dense canopy of leaves, or sit upon a branch closely examining a single leaf, one could not see the beautiful whole and feel its rootedness. When playing music, choose to plant yourself at the base of the trunk, looking up.

chapter 24: on practice and "muscle memory"

PRACTICE STYLES

The word *practice* has appeared many times throughout this book. Clearly practice is essential. What you mean by practice depends upon your reasons for playing this music and your goals. Some people enjoy a very relaxed approach and are content with slow or sporadic progress, others are driven to learn voraciously and progress quickly. Most of us find ourselves somewhere in between.

Whatever your learning style and your drive, no doubt you hope to continually improve your skills and deepen your insights. Since you have reached this point in the book, it's clear that Irish music has touched you deeply. I hope that your respect for its traditions inspires humility and the desire to join the tradition in the best ways that you can. That means "doing your homework," attentively listening to the older players as well as the new, and honing your own skills so you can play in a conscious and ever-improving way. It also means venturing out of your practice space to play with other people so that you can partake of the entire experience of community music making, which is an essential part of the "practice" of Irish music.

For now let's turn our thoughts to private, at-home practice.

ABOVE ALL, LISTEN

Though it may appear that practicing is a process of repeating the physical movements involved in playing, in fact *effective* practice is at least 90% attention, mental focus, and listening. It may sound obvious, but listening, *truly attentive, inquisitive listening*, is the cornerstone of effective practice. Physical repetition will not do you much good if you are not listening well and paying attention to yourself. In fact, it may serve to reinforce bad habits instead.

Throughout this book, I've been hammering away at how important it is to immerse yourself in listening to the fine players of the past and present. Being in their physical presence is the best of all and you should seek out such opportunities as you are able.

Even if you cannot play very well yet, you *can* be a virtuoso listener. Soak up the sounds of great flute and whistle players. With the help of this book you can now understand what they are doing. Store their sounds in your mind's ear: Mary Bergin's short rolls, her use of tonguing, her lean, agile style; Matt Molloy's cranns and condensed rolls and his florid style full of dramatic tone color and dynamic changes; John McKenna's heavy breath pulsing; Paddy Carty's even, silky sound.

You can memorize the sounds of the well-played cut, strike, long roll, etc., and store these sounds in a memory bank of ideal sounds. Then, as you work on training your body to learn the needed skills, continually compare the sounds you are making to the ideal sounds in your memory and imagination. Hear yourself playing with the eloquence of Cathal McConnell or Josie McDermott. Without self-criticism or judgement, notice well the differences between the reality and the ideal. Those differences are like gold; they show you where you need to direct your efforts. With patience and self-compassion, keep striving to come closer to your ideals. Little by little you will get there.

SLOW PRACTICE WILL GET YOU THERE SOONER

We all want to be able to play fast, but it is more important to play well and beautifully. What is the point of playing poorly at a fast pace? Having reached this point in the book you know extremely well that Irish music is vastly more than a simple succession of notes. What you see in tune books are simply frozen skeletons of snapshots of settings of tunes, some a bit more fleshed out than others. Why race along flinging frozen skeletons to and fro when you could be sipping and savoring nectar at the banquet table?

W. A. Mathieu writes beautifully about this in *The Listening Book*.[i] He says,

> . . . you cannot achieve speed by speedy practice. The only way to get fast is to be deep, wide awake, and slow. When you habitually zip through your music, your ears are crystallizing in sloppiness. It is OK to check your progress with an occasional sprint. But it is better to let speed simply come on as a result of methodical nurturing, as with a lovingly built racing car.

> Yet almost everyone practices too fast . . . We want to be the person who is brilliant. This desire is compelling, and it can become what our music is about . . .

> Pray for the patience of a stonecutter. Pray to understand that speed is one of those things you have to give up - like love - before it comes flying to you through the back window.

When you play slowly you can much more easily notice and pay attention to the sounds you are making and the physical movements and positions that you are using to make them. How can you change and improve if you are not aware of these things?

To the extent that you can, you should practice playing well instead of playing poorly. This sounds ridiculously obvious. But the repetition of playing well is what builds the desired skills. Repetition of poor playing reinforces itself.

SOME WORDS OF WISDOM FROM MARTIN HAYES

Martin Hayes is one of the finest musicians, and he is deeply insightful and highly articulate about his art. In an interview in *Fiddler Magazine* he was asked how he chooses the pace for a particular tune. This was his response.

> . . . I tend to *not* start out a maximum speed and maximum volume, but somewhere at a medium to slow speed and volume. When I want to heighten the expression into excitement or vigor, I can do that. I can strive upwards and outwards . . . I think it's foolish to start out at full speed and at full volume. You're eliminating all sorts of possibilities . . . Playing a tune at full speed would be like driving through a country road at full speed. You may get the excitement of driving fast through a country road, but there's a lot of little gaps and avenues and trees and houses and such that you miss along the way. And it's like that with a tune. There's all these little dips and hollows in the tune that are self-explanatory, but time should be taken to go through them slowly. They explain themselves, they interpret themselves. They almost show what should be done.[ii]

THE METRONOME: A GREAT TOOL

A metronome can be a great aid to slow, conscious practice. By keeping a steady beat for you, it frees up part of your mind which you can devote to deeper listening.

Let's say you are sitting down to practice long rolls, or a phrase of a tune. Use the metronome to help you find a comfortable speed at which you can play your best. Stay and play at that tempo for a while, listening to and reinforcing your best playing. When you are ready, increase the tempo just a notch or two and see how that feels. If the new tempo is too challenging, return to the slower tempo. If you can do fairly well at the new tempo, if it stretches you but doesn't break you, stick with it until it feels quite comfortable. Then stay there for a while before moving on to try a faster tempo. And so on.

When doing metronome practice and gradually increasing your speed, try this approach, too. Adjust the metronome faster by three notches and play there for a while if you can. Then adjust the metronome slower by two notches. Play there for a while and notice the differences in your playing and sound. Then increase by three notches, decrease by two, increase by three, decrease by two, and so on.

Don't be in a rush. It seems that our muscles learn more slowly than our minds, but muscle memory is very long lasting and dependable. There are intriguing physiological reasons for this, which I will discuss a bit later in the chapter.

A metronome provides a rigid time reference which can be extremely revealing. For example, you want to gain control over your cuts so you can place them wherever you want them. It is easy to fool yourself into thinking that you have gained such control when perhaps you really haven't. Try placing cuts where the metronome tells you to place them, right on a steady beat. When you *externalize* the definition of the beat to a machine, you come to see how your own internal sense of the beat can tend to speed up or fluctuate. It's hard for us to maintain a steady beat at an unusually slow speed. We want to speed up, even when we are not ready to. Of course we don't want to play like machines, but machines can help us gain insight into how to play better as a human.

PAY ATTENTION TO YOUR ENERGY

A short period of conscious practice is much more beneficial than a long period of practice when your attention is flagging. It does you little good to practice if you are not focusing well. If you find that your mind is spinning its wheels, take a break and come back later refreshed.

It seems that some part of our mind keeps on practicing, even while we are away from our instruments. Many people have had the experience of working very hard on a particular challenge, not making much headway, and then, coming back after hours, or even days, finding that, in the meantime, they have suddenly, somehow, progressed to a higher level.

FIND A PLEASANT PRACTICE SPACE

Since you want to make practicing an experience that you will look forward to, do what you can to find the best practice space. Ideally you should find a room that is quiet and private, a place free of distractions and away from others if they make you feel self-conscious. It should be well lit and ventilated and not too cramped. The acoustics are very important. If the room is too dead it may be unflattering and discouraging. If it is too reverberant it may hide your true sound from you, though stairwells and the like can be a lot of fun to play in now and then.

A MIRROR CAN HELP IN SEVERAL WAYS

One of the hazards of practicing flute or whistle is that we tend to stare out into space while we play. Since we don't have our instrument clearly in our view, like for example fiddlers do, it is easy for us to become distracted. Closing your eyes can help a great deal.

Or, taking the opposite approach, playing in front of a mirror can help. Not only does the reflection engage you visually, like the metronome, it externalizes an aspect of the experience, allowing you to see what your body is actually doing, not just what it feels like it is doing. Comparing your body's sensation of itself with an objective visual reflection of it can be very enlightening.

The mirror not only reflects your image, it reflects your sound back to you, making it easier to hear the details of what you are doing. When a wind player plays walking around in a room you will often notice that she unconsciously gravitates towards a wall. The wall reflects her sound back and she can hear the details of her playing more clearly.

ISOLATE CHALLENGING AREAS

One sign of flagging attention is when you find yourself playing through a tune, repeatedly glossing over places that you don't really play very well. When you catch yourself doing this, stop. Take a break if you need to. When you resume, listen for a problem spot and stop when you come to it.

Take a close listen, examine the challenging area and try to isolate the note, notes, or technique that is catching you. Work on a very small group of notes, maybe just two or three, that contains the problem area. Use a metronome to stay at a slow enough tempo to do good work. Perhaps a mirror will help you see what is going on. When you have begun to make some good progress with the challenge, slightly expand the passage you are working on by adding a note or two before, then a note or two after. See how the problem manifests in this slightly larger context. When you are comfortable, expand the passage some more and see what that is like.

301

Listen to Your Body

Watch out for physical pain. This is a signal telling you to take a break, check for undue muscle tension, poor posture, etc. Get up and move around, shake out your arms, hands, legs. Stretch. Maybe it's time to stop practicing for the day. There are a lot of information resources available today that can help musicians prevent or deal with stress-related injuries and problems. Hopefully you can prevent them from occurring.

Another Useful Tool: an Audio Recorder

Audio recorders of various types are in the possession of most traditional musicians these days. They are certainly very handy for capturing music that you wish to learn later. Beware, however, of becoming over-dependent on them. It's all too easy to record a tune and not really listen to it, since you know you can listen to your recording later. In your archiving zeal, don't forget to live in the present. If you have the opportunity to attend a regular session, try learning tunes by simply soaking them in through repeated exposure. One day you will realize that you have already learned the tune in your head. Then it is simply a matter of translating it from your mind's voice onto your instrument. Even if you do not have contact with other Irish musicians, you can learn this way by listening repeatedly to favorite recordings, letting the music wash over you until you have absorbed it.

Once on a trip to Ireland, I left my cassette recorder back in the states because I wanted to work on training myself to listen more deeply, like musicians must have done in older times. I did learn some tunes that way and learned them very well, but I'm afraid many escaped me entirely. It was great ear training, but it was also a rash decision, considering I was not able to visit musicians repeatedly during my fairly brief stay. So, moderation in all things is a wise policy.

It can be very revealing to record yourself. Listening back you will no doubt hear things that you didn't notice while you were playing.

Some recorders are equipped with a variable speed control. It can be very instructive to slow down the playback of a great player. For the computerized, there are also ways to capture music and manipulate it with software, some of it free or very inexpensive.

Give Yourself Positive Messages

A musician always has more to learn, no matter how many years she has been practicing her art. Everyone is a beginner in some sense.

Even if your playing skills are rudimentary, your listening abilities are not. If you didn't have wide-open ears you wouldn't be drawn to embark on the serious work of learning a musical language and how to play a musical instrument.

Be encouraging to yourself. One can always find fault if one wants to, but one can also find progress, commitment, and devotion. Give yourself positive messages.

The Physiology of "Muscle Memory"

Many people find it frustrating that it seems to take so long for them learn to perform physical actions that they can quickly understand conceptually. The cut, for instance, is not hard to grasp, especially once you have heard it played well. Yet it takes a very long time to gain the needed fine muscle skills. Why should it be that our muscles take longer to learn things than our minds do?

Research in biology, anatomy, and neurology has begun to address this question. It is intriguing and reassuring to know that during that long learning period you are literally building new nerve pathways that are very persistent and reliable. What follows is a somewhat technical explanation, courtesy of my friend Lawrence Washington, a musician and molecular biologist.

As we first start learning a new group of movements, such as the fingering motions used to execute a G long roll, we have to think consciously about each component of the group and command the muscles to move. The part of the brain responsible for conscious thought (the cerebral cortex) sends impulses through the muscle-control part of the brain (the cerebellum) and onward to the finger muscles. Since there are so many different, very precise muscle movements in a roll, its execution is at first slow and tedious, requiring great concentration. The thought process may go something like this: "Do a G roll: (1) place T1, T2, T3 on their holes, (2) blow, (3) lift T2, (4) replace quickly, (5) raise B1 high, (6) bring B1 down sharply . . ." and so on, all the while keeping the proper timing, embouchure, breathing, and a raft of other elements in mind. There is so much to think about that it is no wonder we can feel overwhelmed and frustrated.

But there is comfort to be found in the biology of learning. When we repeat a complex set of muscle motions, specific patterns of nerve pathways are assigned to repeat them. This is a physical process, an actual structural change at the microscopic level of our neurons. Gradually the muscle commands, which originate from the thinking part of the brain, the cerebral cortex, are taken over directly by the muscle-control centers of the cerebellum, which previously had only mediated them. All that remains at the conscious level is the initiating command: "Do a G roll." With that, the cerebellum takes over and commands all the individual movements, which we had to think about one by one when we were first learning. It is as though we have gradually built a very specific machine and now only have to flip a switch for that machine to do its job.

Naturally, once we no longer have to think about each movement of the long roll it becomes possible to perform it quickly and with fluidity. It literally becomes "second nature." In fact, it may be that the movement of a proper cut, for example, is so very quick that most people cannot do it until it becomes established in the cerebellum and we no longer have to "think" about it.

The more times the pattern of movements is repeated, the more strongly the neuronal pattern is established. With the right microscope you would be able to see an increase in the density of the synapses and dendrite branches. The nerve connections become physically stronger, as a path through the woods becomes better defined the more times a family of deer walks along it.

One implication of this fact is that we should take care to practice and repeat only what we want our muscles to learn. If we are early with the timing of a strike as we practice it, and remain inattentive to that fact, our muscles will become expert at playing strikes early.

Of course, in the early stages of learning the cut, for instance, we cannot do them quickly enough. By necessity we practice them "too slow," making them as crisp as we can at that time. But if we remember the sound of the ideal cut, and constantly strive for it in our playing, we continually and gradually revise the pattern of nerve pathways that controls how we execute the cut. Once we finally learn to perform cuts well, the new, improved nerve pathways are well established.

When we keep our ideal sounds well in mind, we establish a feedback loop that continually compares the sensations with the ideal. For instance, when the cerebral cortex tells the cerebellum to execute a roll, you listen carefully to how it sounds, "think" about it, compare it to the ideal roll, and instruct the cerebellum how to modify the roll toward the ideal. You see how very important it is to listen well to ourselves, and to our models.

Fortunately for the beginner it does not matter that we execute movement patterns slowly as we learn them. After the neuronal pathways have established their circuits, we can go as fast as our muscles can move. The family of deer walking many times the same way through the woods clears a nice trace. Later they can run as fast as they like down the smooth trail, gracefully as a perfectly timed roll. And the established neural pathway is amazingly persistent. Once made, the additional synapses and increased density of nerve branches stay. We may easily forget how to describe the details of a roll, but the nerves in our brain and fingers have made very strong connections that can be executed anytime we "flip the switch."

i W. A. Mathieu, *The Listening Book*. Boston: Shambhala Publications, 1991, p. 101.
ii Mary Larsen, "Martin Hayes, A Lilt All His Own," *Fiddler Magazine*, Spring 1994: p. 50.

section 6

—

forty-nine studies
for
ornamentation practice

section 6: forty-nine studies for ornamentation practice

This collection of studies addresses the fundamentals of ornamentation technique, but it is not exhaustive. It addresses cuts, strikes, slides, long rolls, and short rolls but not condensed rolls, double-cut rolls, cranns, or other ornamentation techniques. However, if you work through the studies diligently you will gain mastery that will serve you very well in learning those more advanced techniques.

Studies 1 - 17:	Cuts	╱
Studies 18 - 22:	Strikes	V
Studies 23 - 32:	Slides	⌣ ⌐
Studies 33 - 41:	Long Rolls	⌢
Studies 42 - 49:	Short Rolls	⋏

Most of these studies are notated only in the low register, but you can adapt them to the upper register if you wish. Since the objective of these studies is to work on fingering techniques, I feel it is sufficient, and perhaps more relaxing, to work on them in the low register. In almost all cases, the fingering techniques are the same in both registers.

The studies are written in jig or reel time, that is 6/8 or 2/2, but you can use these techniques in all the tune types.

I have deliberately made no provision for breathing places. Create your own, as you would in any tune. See Chapter 21 for help with this.

Practice slowly. Remember you can work on just one small part of a study before trying to work through the whole thing. When you find a passage difficult, reduce it to a manageable size, zeroing in on the problem spot. Find a speed at which you can play reasonably well, even if it seems extremely slow. Playing slowly is a very good thing. As you improve, increase your speed gradually, never playing beyond your ability. This is the most efficient and effective kind of practice. Using a metronome can help a great deal with this approach. For more guidance on practice, refer to Chapter 24.

Some of the studies are based on traditional tunes. But please don't construe them as tasteful tune settings. They aren't. They are intended only as vehicles for practicing ornamentation. Being based on real tunes, hopefully they will make practicing a little more enjoyable.

For the time being, do not tongue the cuts, strikes, and slides in these studies. This is the best way to monitor the coordination of your fingering, and it will clearly reveal, if you pay attention, whether or not you are placing articulations accurately in time. Later you can tongue the cuts, strikes, and slides if you wish. Just be aware that when you do so, because of the small gap of silence that tonguing introduces into the stream of sound, some of the consequences of sloppy fingering (that which occurs during the silences) will be hidden from you.

STUDIES 1–4: CUTS ON REPEATED NOTES

This first group of studies addresses cuts on repeated notes. In each instance, the finger to use for the indicated cut is shown below the notehead. These four studies are derived from the melody of the A part of jig *The Sporting Pitchfork*. For several settings of the complete jig, see Figure 13-11 on pp. 208-209.

Study 1. Cuts in a jig on repeated notes that fall on the first and second subdivisions of the pulse.

Study 2. Cuts in a jig on repeated notes that fall mostly on the third subdivision of the pulse.

Study 3. Cuts in a jig on repeated notes that fall on the first and second subdivisions of the pulse.

Track 18

Study 4. A variety of cuts on repeated notes in a jig. In measure 15, there are three As in a row. Tongue the second one, as indicated.

STUDIES 5–9: CUTS ON ASCENDING NOTES

Studies 5 through 9 address cuts on ascending notes.

Studies 5 and 6 are derived from the A part of the reel *John Stenson's*. For a complete setting of the tune see p. 352 in Section 7.

Track 19

Study 5. Cuts in a reel on ascending notes that fall on the secondary pulse.

Study 6. Cuts in a reel on ascending notes that fall on the primary and secondary pulse.

Studies 7 through 9 feature cuts only on notes that ascend by intervals larger than a second (i.e. leapwise). More cuts are added as you progress through Studies 7 through 9.

 Track 21

Study 7. Cuts in a jig on leapwise ascending notes.

Study 8. Adding a few more cuts on leapwise ascending notes.

Study 9. Adding still more cuts on leapwise ascending notes. This study includes cuts on consecutive notes. This is not often done in the tradition, but it makes for good practice.

STUDIES 10–13: CUTS ON DESCENDING NOTES

Studies 10 through 13 feature cuts on descending notes. In Studies 10 through 12 the notes in question descend stepwise only (i.e. by only one step of the mode or scale) and therefore employ normal cut fingerings. Study 13 features cuts on notes that descend leapwise. These cuts require special fingerings. For a discussion of this, see *Cuts on Notes that Descend by an Interval Larger than a Second* in Chapter 7, pp. 130-133. As in the earlier studies, fingerings for all cuts are shown below the notes.

Note that the cut on B in measure 7 (Studies 10 through 12) is more easily sounded when tongued.

Study 10. Cuts in a reel on stepwise descending notes that fall on the secondary pulse.

Track 25

Study 11. Cuts in a reel on stepwise descending notes that fall on the primary and secondary pulse.

Track 26

Study 12. A few more cuts on stepwise descending notes that fall on the primary and secondary pulse.

312

Study 13. Cuts in a jig on leapwise descending notes. Pay special attention to the indicated cut fingerings in this study. They are not the normal ones. Instead, they are determined by the fingering of the note that precedes the cut. In this study, and in Studies 14–17, the fingerings for leapwise descending cuts are shown in bold type. (Fingerings for *stepwise* descending cuts are shown in normal type.)

313

Studies 14 and 15 are based on the reel *The Mountain Road.* For a complete setting see p. 353 in Section 7.

In these two studies, be sure to tongue the second A in measure 7. I suggest tonguing the Bs in measures 13 and 15 if you vent the Ds that precede them. By "venting" I mean playing D with T1 raised off its hole.

 Track 28

Study 14. A variety of cuts in a reel, including mid-note cuts.

314

Track 29

Study 15. A larger variety of cuts in a reel.

Studies 16 and 17 are based on the C part of *The Monaghan Jig*. For a complete setting see p. [000] in Section 7.

 Track 30

Study 16. A variety of cuts in a jig, including mid-note cuts.

 Track 31

Study 17. A larger variety of cuts in a jig.

STUDY 18: STRIKES ON REPEATED NOTES

In the studies on strikes, strike fingerings are indicated below the noteheads.

Track 32

Study 18. Strikes on repeated notes in a jig.

317

Track 33

Study 19. Strikes in a reel on stepwise descending notes.

Track 34

Study 20. More strikes in a reel on stepwise descending notes.

Track 35

Study 21. Strikes on leapwise descending notes in a jig.

Track 36

Study 22. Strikes in a jig on ascending notes that cross the register break. The only strikes possible on ascending notes occur with certain combinations of notes which cross the register break. For a summation of them see Figure 8-14 on p. 146. Note that these strikes, if they were confined to one register, would in fact be descending strikes. This study incorporates all of them.

Study 23 features stepwise simple slides.

The slide up to C-natural ascends to the half-hole fingering for that note. Once you have done the slide up to the half-hole C, it is easy to slide back down to B. The descending simple slide from C-natural to B, and G to F-sharp, are the only descending simple slides in these studies. Opportunities to use them abound in the repertoire. Other descending simple slides are possible but are more difficult. Feel free to work on them if you like.

 Track 37

Study 23. Stepwise simple slides.

 Track 38

Study 24. Simple slides that ascend by a third.

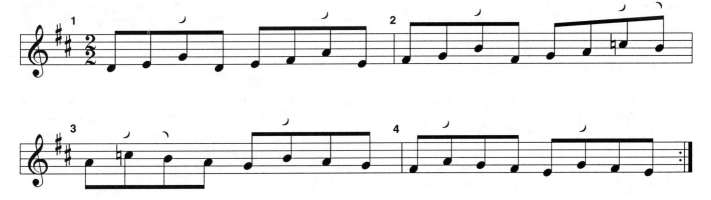

321

Track 39

Study 25. Simple slides that ascend by a fourth.

Track 40

Study 26. Simple slides that ascend by a fifth.

STUDIES 27–30: ADDED-FINGER SLIDES

Added-finger slides are easily done when a melody is descending. You approach the note in question melodically from above and slide up into it from below. It is possible to invert this—to approach a note melodically from below and slide down into it from above—but it is difficult and is rarely done in the tradition. These studies address only the former.

The additional finger to use for each slide is indicated below the notehead.

Track 41

Study 27. Stepwise added-finger slides.

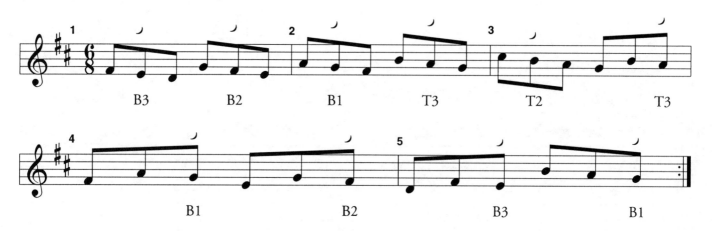

Track 42

Study 28. Added-finger slides on notes that descend by a third.

Track 43

Study 29. Added-finger slides on notes that descend by a fourth.

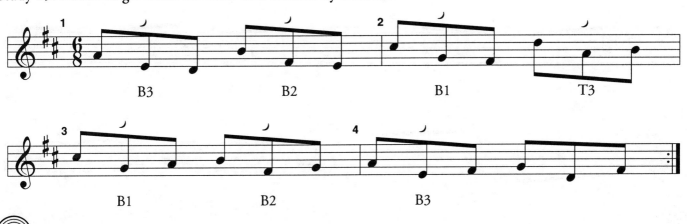

Track 44

Study 30. Added-finger slides on notes that descend by a fifth.

Study 31 contains both simple and added-finger slides—quite a few, for the sake of practice. More are added in Study 32. Both studies are based on the A part of *The Monaghan Jig*. (For a complete setting of the tune see p. 341 in Section 7.) There are fingering indications under the noteheads of the *added-finger slides* only.

Note especially the ascending and descending simple slides on G and F-sharp in measures 1, 3, and 5 of both of these studies. These slides can be very subtle, as they require only tiny movements of B1.

②*Track 45*

Study 31. Simple and added-finger slides in a jig.

②*Track 46*

Study 32. More simple and added-finger slides in a jig.

Studies 33–41 feature long rolls that begin in differing places in relation to the pulse. In each study, make sure you know which note of the roll falls on the pulse: either the first note, the cut note, or the struck note. Give that note some emphasis. In studies 34, 35, 37, and 39, it is especially important that you play the rolls in an even rhythm.

Track 47

Study 33. In a jig, long rolls that begin on the pulse.

Track 48

Study 34. In a jig, long rolls that begin on the second subdivision of the pulse.

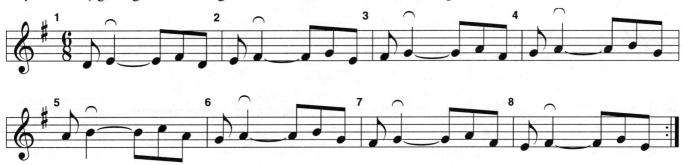

Track 49

Study 35. In a jig, long rolls that begin on the third subdivision of the pulse.

Study 36. In a reel, long rolls that begin on the primary pulse.

Study 37. In a reel, long rolls that begin on the second subdivision of the primary pulse.

Study 38. In a reel, long rolls that begin on the third subdivision of the primary pulse (or, looking at it another way, that begin on the secondary pulse).

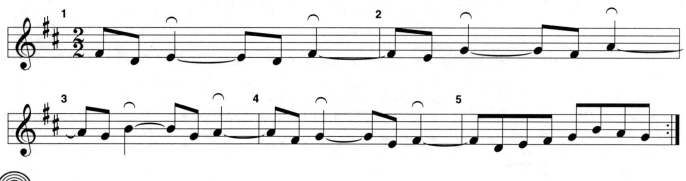

Study 39. In a reel, long rolls that begin on the fourth subdivision of the primary pulse.

Track 54

Study 40. A jig containing long rolls that begin on each of the three subdivisions of the pulse. This study is based on the A part of *Willie Coleman's Jig*. (For a complete setting see p. 344 in Section 7.) It contains long rolls, on E, G, A, and B, that begin on each of the three subdivisions of the pulse.

Track 55

Study 41. A reel containing long rolls that begin on each of the four subdivisions of the primary pulse. This study is based on the A part of the reel *The Mountain Road*. (For a complete setting of the reel see p. 353 in Section 7.) It contains long rolls, on E, F-sharp, G, A, and B, that begin on each of the four subdivisions of the primary pulse.

STUDIES 42–49: SHORT ROLLS

Studies 42–49 features short rolls in jigs and reels. Since short rolls begin with a cut note, your practice on ascending and descending cuts will pay high dividends when it comes to playing short rolls. Consequently, in the following group of short-roll studies I do not go through all ascending and descending cut scenarios that I explore in Studies 5–13. Also, short rolls rarely begin on nonpulse notes, so I don't address such situations in these studies.

Track 56

Study 42. Stepwise ascending short rolls in a jig.

Track 57

Study 43. Stepwise descending short rolls in a jig.

Some of the following studies feature leapwise descending short rolls. Since these short rolls begin with leapwise descending cuts, special fingerings for those cuts are needed. When those fingerings are called for, they are shown in bold type.

In studies 44 and 47, the short rolls on A in measure 4 and 6 need to be tongued. The short roll on B in measure 5 is more easily played tongued if the D before it is vented.

Track 58

Study 44. Leapwise descending short rolls in a jig.

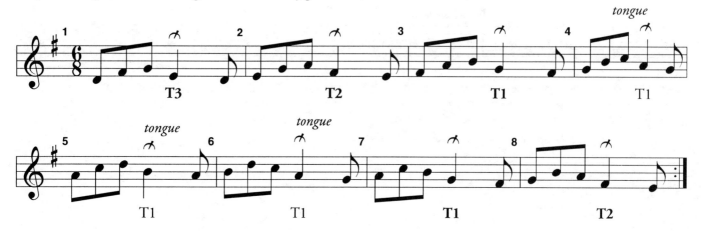

Track 59

Study 45. Stepwise ascending short rolls in a reel.

Track 60

Study 46. Stepwise descending short rolls in a reel.

Track 61

Study 47. Leapwise descending short rolls in a reel.

Study 48. A jig containing a variety of short rolls. This study is based on the A part of the jig *The Rose in the Heather*. (For a complete setting see p. 342 in Section 7.)

Study 49. A reel containing a variety of short rolls. This study is based on the A part of *The Glen Allen Reel*. (For a complete setting see p. 350 in Section 7.)

⁘ section 7 ⁘

—

complete versions
of
excerpted tunes

section 7: complete versions of excerpted tunes

I have shown excerpts from a number of tunes for purposes of illustration in Chapters 1 through 21. Complete versions of these tunes can be found in this section.

The following settings are fairly basic, playable ones, however they are not meant to be "standard" or "generic" versions. Instead they contain some ornamentation and variation that are idiomatic to the flute and tin whistle. They are not meant to illustrate any style in particular, but they do inevitably reflect my own playing style to some degree. For the most part, I have included fairly spare ornamentation, and I have not indicated phrasing or breathing places. The ornaments shown may not work as well with your style of playing as they do with mine, so feel free to alter them, build upon them, ignore them, or substitute your own ornamentation.

When a tune goes below low D, as played by most players of instruments that are capable of this, I have taken the liberty of changing the register of such notes. In these cases, the notes that are normally played below low D are shown with diamond noteheads.

On CD #2, I play these tunes as notated here, with my own phrasing and accommodations for breathing, i.e. note omissions, note shortenings, and variations that result or follow from these. I often play the repeats of parts somewhat differently than their first statements, and when you compare carefully what is notated with what I actually play, you will find many small differences. This is an improvisational music and I do find it difficult to adhere exactly to what is printed on the page.

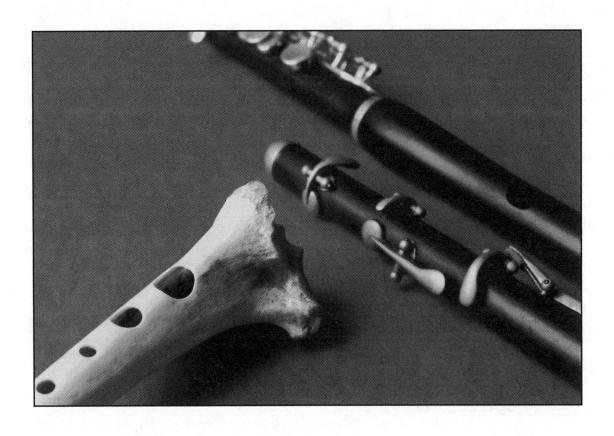

1. The Battering Ram

Double Jig

Track 65

2. The Blarney Pilgrim

Double Jig

3. The Cliffs of Moher

Double Jig

Note that I have written out both B parts. There are many ways to approach the melodic cell that is contained in the first, second, fifth, and sixth bars of the first B part, and the first, second, and fifth bars of the second B part, some of which I have shown in this transcription.

4. Tom Billy's Jig

Double Jig

This jig is in the Dorian Pentatonic mode with the tonal center of A. In other words there are no thirds (C-naturals) or sixths (F-sharps) in the melody, thought these may be added as passing tones or variations.

5. The Frost Is All Over

Double Jig

338

Track 69

6. The Humours of Ballyloughlin

Double Jig

Note the "cuts" on C-natural in the B part. These are played with a strike fingering that is shown in Figure 8-8 on p. 140. Note also the slide into a half-hole C-natural in the third bar of the C part, followed by a regular fingered C-natural in the next bar.

7. Jimmy Ward's Jig

Double Jig

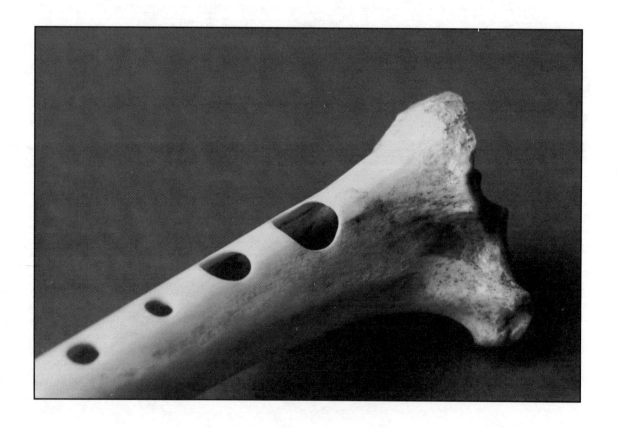

8. The Monaghan Jig

Double Jig

There are many ways to play the first, third, and fifth measures of the A part. Three are shown here.

341

Track 72

9. Old Joe's Jig

Double Jig

 Track 73

10. The Rose in the Heather

Double Jig

11. Scotsman Over the Border

Double Jig

12. Tripping Up the Stairs

Double Jig

Track 76
13. Whelan's Jig

Double Jig

Track 77
14. Willy Coleman's Jig

Double Jig

15. The Star Above the Garter

Single Jig or Slide

You may wish to try struck slides on the Gs at the beginning of the third and seventh bars of the B part.

16. A Fig for a Kiss

Slip Jig

The strikes on E can be played as struck slides. This setting is from flute player Tom Byrne.

Track 80
17. Hardiman the Fiddler

Slip Jig

Track 81
18. The Whinny Hills of Leitrim

Slip Jig

19. Christmas Eve

Reel

The first part of this reel is in the Ionian Pentatonic mode on G. In other words, it lacks notes on the 4th and 7th degree of the Ionian scale: C-natural and F-sharp. The second and third parts of the tune fall almost completely within that five-note scale as well.

Track 83

20. The Banshee

Reel

 Track 84

21. The Boys of Ballisodare

Reel

Track 85

22. Roaring Mary

Reel

Track 86

23. The Drunken Landlady

Reel

24. The Glen Allen Reel

Reel

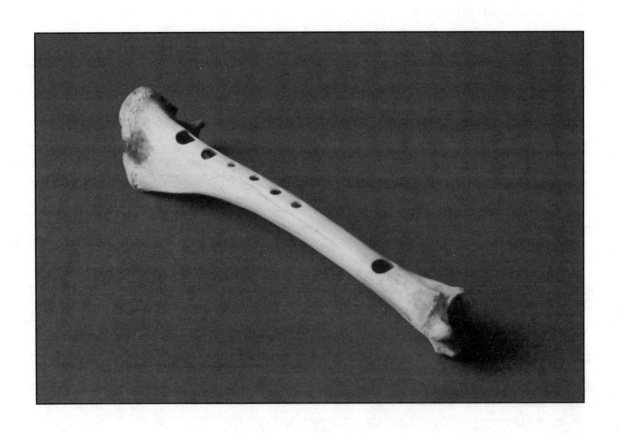

350

Track 88

25. The Gravel Walk

Reel

There are many ways to play the D part of this tune. The D part as written here is just one of them. See Figure 19-13 on p. 264 for some other ideas. The second ending to the D part shown here is not widely played, but I prefer it.

26. John Stenson's Reel

Reel

27. Lad O'Beirne's Reel

Reel

Track 91

28. Lady on the Island

Reel

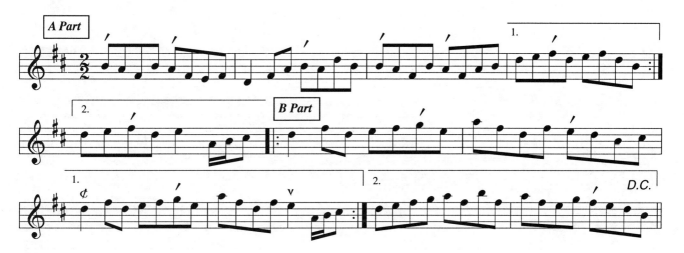

Track 92

29. The Mountain Road

Reel

Track 93

30. The Shaskeen

Reel

Track 94

31. Tuttle's Reel (in E Dorian)

Reel

This reel is in D Dorian, which is a problematic mode for flute and whistle because of its F-naturals. If you play it on a C whistle and use the fingerings shown below, it will sound one whole step lower than it is written here. Thus it will *sound* in the correct mode of D Dorian, shown below as tune number 32.

32. Tuttle's Reel (in D Dorian)

Reel

Here is how the above-notated version of *Tuttle's Reel* will sound when played on a C whistle.

Track 95

33. The Home Ruler

Hornpipe

Note that there are three kinds of cranns in this rendition of the tune: a condensed long crann in m. 5, a long crann in m. 10 and a short crann (followed by a cut D) in m. 14. These may be challenging for many players. Of course the cranns are not required at all. You can play these passages in many ways.

34. The Rights of Man

Hornpipe

35. Maids of Ardagh

Polka

Note that the A part of this tune is in D Ionian and the B part is in A Ionian.

36. Lord Mayo

March

Composed by the harper Dáithí Ó Murchadha (17th century).

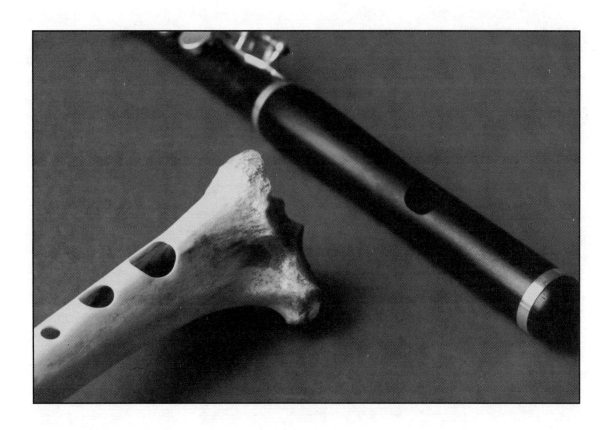

37. Tabhair dom do Lámh (Give Me Your Hand)

Harp Piece

Composed by Rory "Dall" Ó Catháin (ca. 1550–ca. 1640).

The strike and slide symbols over the last note indicate a "struck slide" (see p. 160 in Chapter 9). The articulation of the note is a strike, but B1 does not rebound from the instrument as with a normal strike. Instead, it eases off of the tone hole, resulting in a rising slide. To hear this, listen to the tune on CD #2.

❖ section 8 ❖

———

great performances transcribed

section 8: great performances transcribed

transcriptions of commercial recordings from important flute and tin whistle players, 1925—2001.

In this section, I present my transcriptions of 27 flute and tin whistle performances of traditional Irish tunes which have been released on commercial recordings dating from 1925 to 2001. Twenty-two players are included here, representing a wide variety of playing styles. Using my notation innovations, these very detailed transcriptions give us a new way to look deeply into such performances. While transcribing, I have used digital technology to slow the recordings down so that I could more easily discern the details of the music.

The transcriptions are presented in chronological order according to the year of recording. I have departed from this scheme in order to group pairs of transcriptions together when they are by the same player, and in one case to present side by side two different players' versions of the same tune.

This collection is not meant to be an exhaustive survey, but instead a representative sampling of a wide variety of flute and whistle players and their music. There are so many fine players to choose from that, by necessity, many of them are not represented here. Some are not included because it was not possible to obtain the necessary permissions. It has been difficult to narrow the choice of players down to a number that is manageable for this book. I hope to issue more such collections in the future. (You may refer to my website, <www.greylarsen.com>, for information on such future projects.)

Introducing each transcription, I give some brief biographical information and make some comments and observations on the player's style as shown in that particular performance.

Remember that there are many important aspects of performance that are not possible to notate, such as the various elements that make up *swing* or *lilt* (for more on this see Chapter 1). There are other aspects of playing that I have chosen not to notate, such as multiple tonguing and tonguing vs. throating (some players use one, some use both). In a few cases, I will indicate the use of finger vibrato and breath vibrato. Since transcriptions can never show everything. Listening to the recordings of these performances while referring to the transcriptions will give you the fullest possible understanding. It is my hope that in the future I can facilitate the issuing of a CD compilation of the recordings transcribed here. As of this writing, however, it is proving very difficult to obtain the necessary permissions. (Check my website for updates.) For now, I strongly encourage you to seek out each artist's recording of these performances. (You will find the needed information in the Discography.)

It is important to realize that I use slurs in a very specific way in these transcriptions. A slurred group of notes is played using an uninterrupted, continuous stream of air. Only the first note of a slurred group is articulated by the use of tonguing or throating. All notes that are *not* within a slur *are* articulated with tonguing or throating.

Some flute players, such as Josie McDermott, use a relatively gentle breath pulsing technique to play repeated notes on one pitch which are nevertheless connected in one continuous breath. In such cases, these repeated notes appear under a slur to show that the notes are separate but that the airstream is not interrupted. (For an example of this, see the transcription of Josie McDermott's rendition of *The Pigeon on the Gate* on pp. 390-391.) One could also describe this technique as a type of very rhythmic, distinct, breath vibrato. When listening to recordings, it is sometimes difficult or impossible to tell whether a player is using this kind of breath pulsing or a subtle kind of throating.

In addition to the ornamentation symbols explained in earlier chapters, I use the commonly used sign for staccato, or very short notes (a dot above a notehead), and the breath sign (a comma) above rests to show where the player takes a breath.

A number of the players in this section make occasional use of a C note that in pitch is in between the equal-tempered C and C-sharp. This is often called a "neutral C," or a "piping C" as Breandán Breathnach refers to it in his book, *Folk Music & Dances of Ireland*.[i] The pitch may be altered with embouchure and/or by fingering, for example by covering only the T2 hole. In these transcriptions the use of the "piping C" is indicated with an asterisk. For more on this see "Outside the Modal Boundaries" on p. 27 of Chapter 1.

In these transcriptions, the various repetitions of the tune are presented as separate staves in a score format. The first time through the tune is shown on the top staff, the second time through on the staff below that, etc. This allows for easy comparisons of any given passage for each time the tune is played.

I hope these transcriptions will provide valuable insight into the music of many of the important players whose performances have been preserved since the dawn of the recording age. While it can be very instructive to play through these renditions, I do not encourage you to do so with the goal of "taking on" the style of any of these players. First of all, this is not really possible, and second of all, it is best to develop your own style that reflects who you are.

For detailed information on the recordings transcribed here, see the Discography.

The transcriptions are:

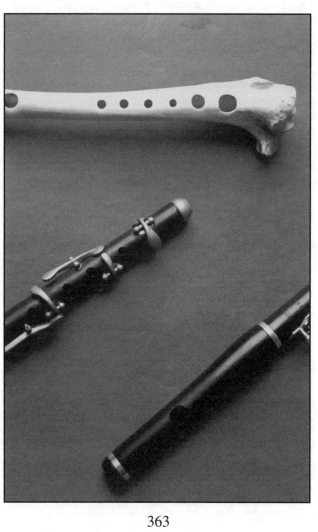

363

1. **John McKenna** (flute)—Reel: *The Corry Boys*. This is transcribed from John McKenna's 78-rpm release, which was issued in America in 1925 on the O'Byrne DeWitt Label, and reissued by the John McKenna Traditional Society on their compilation cassette *John McKenna, His Original Recordings*. This tune is the second in a medley of two reels, the first one being *The Sailor on the Rock*. Mode: G Ionian (major).

John McKenna was one of the most influential flute players of the 20th century. He was born in 1880 near the village of Tarmon in Co. Leitrim and died in 1947 in New York.[ii] After working for some years in the Arigna coal mines, in 1911 he emigrated to New York City and worked at first as a fireman. His first records, recorded in 1921, list him in fact as "Fire Patrolman McKenna." Through the thirty 78-rpm recordings that he made between 1921 and 1936, McKenna had a great deal to do with establishing the flute as a prominent instrument in Irish music. These recordings also brought a number of Leitrim tunes into the common repertoire. His duet recordings with fiddler James Morrison are especially cherished by traditional musicians.

This Leitrim single reel is fascinating in itself because of its irregular phrase length in the A part, which I have notated using measures in 3/2 time. Such "crooked" tunes are rarely heard in Irish music today, though I think this way of playing must have been much more common in older times. Another crooked tune can be seen in the transcription of my whistle performance of Michael J. Kennedy's setting of the hornpipe, "The Cuckoo's Nest" (see transcription #27 later in this section). Perhaps the crooked phrasing of some of these older Irish tunes has been preserved and integrated into local musical traditions in places such as Québec and America.

In this tune, McKenna seems to use no tonguing and very little in the way of throating articulation. Some exceptions can be found, but only on repeated notes, as seen in m. 1, fourth time; m. 5, first, second, third, and fifth times; and m. 9, fourth time. However, he does make frequent use of breath pulsing to add to the rhythmic drive to the music.

McKenna's ornamentation is fairly spare. In other recordings he can be heard using a wider variety of ornaments, such as condensed rolls. As mentioned in Chapter 16, his recording of *The Five Mile Chase* is the earliest recording I have found of cranning on the flute or whistle.

Even though he plays this tune six times through, you can see that he introduces very little in the way of variation. As Jackie Small writes in the liner notes to *John McKenna, His Original Recordings*,[iii] McKenna's music was ". . . primarily for dancing, hearty music with a fine 'lift' imparted by his rhythmic, breathy style." But the variations he does employ are very interesting. Perhaps the most adventurous one comes in the very first measure of the first time through the tune. Another similar melodic variation occurs in m. 6 of the first time through. The alternative to the long G roll that he uses in m. 1, fourth time, and m. 5, first, second, and third times, is reminiscent of the bow treble of the fiddle, or the staccato "triplet" of the pipes, though McKenna does not play them staccato. The use of the single trill in m. 5, fifth time, is a slight variation on this. This particular kind of ornamentation is rarely heard in the music of more modern flute and whistle players.

John McKenna and John Gaffney

The Corry Boys

traditional Irish reel
as played by John McKenna, Irish flute,
on his 1925 recording on the O'Byrne DeWitt Label,
reissued by the John McKenna Traditional Society
on *John McKenna, His Original Recordings.*

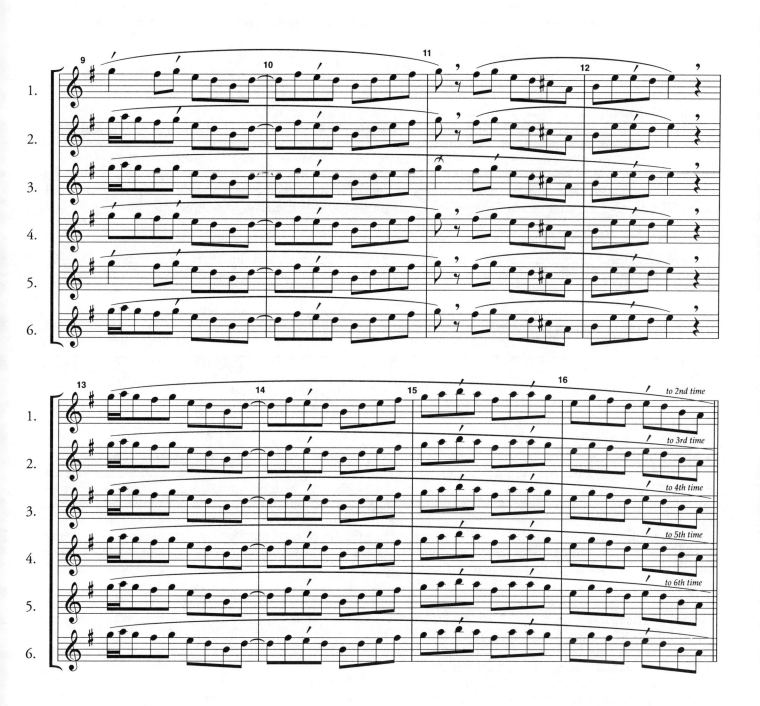

2. **Tom Morrison** (flute)—Schottische: *Sweet Flowers of Milltown*. This is a transcription from Tom Morrison's 1927 New York recording for the Columbia label, reissued on *Fluters of Old Erin*, Viva Voce 002. *Sweet Flowers of Milltown* is the first in a medley of two schottisches, the second one being *The Boys from Knock*. On this recording, Morrison was accompanied by tambourine and bodhrán player John Reynolds from Drumsna, Co. Leitrim. Mode: G Ionian (major).

According to Harry Bradshaw,

> Tom Morrison (1889-1958) was ... born in Whitepark, near Glenamaddy, Co. Galway. As a young man, Tom worked in the north of England and began playing music on the whistle, later taking up the flute and accordion. In 1909 Tom left for New York and settled on Carlton Avenue in Brooklyn, an area renowned for its immigrant musicians. His recording career began in 1924 when he teamed up with accordion player P. J. Conlon to record for the Gennett Company. On his records, Morrison's flute playing has echoes of old fifing style about it with great drive and a compelling rhythm. Tom Morrison (no relation to James Morrison) recorded 27 sides by 1929 and became a respected figure on the New York music scene, and an uilleann piper later in life.[IV]

Since older styles of playing such as Morrison's are rarely heard these days, and since they are so important to the evolution of this music, I will go into some depth in analyzing and describing his playing of this tune.

Here, Tom Morrison shows himself to be a brilliant improviser. In playful and highly imaginative fashion he varies his articulations, phrasing, ornamentation, and the octave register of the music. But perhaps the most remarkable of his variations comes from his overt manipulation of the lilt or swing of the music. His predominant lilt is one typical of schottische playing, a highly uneven subdivision of the pulse in which the on-pulse or odd-numbered eighth notes (i.e. the first, third, fifth, and so on) get greater weight and duration than the off-pulse or even-numbered eighth notes. (For more on this subject see Chapter 1, the section called "Lilt, or Swing" on pp. 40-42 and the sections that follow it, as well as Chapter 14.) This heavy lilt allows for true triplets, as are commonly heard in hornpipes. (See "The Fallacy of the 'Triplet'" on pp. 254-255 in Chapter 18.)

In numerous phrases, which are enclosed in the following transcription by dotted line brackets, Morrison dramatically evens out the notes, playing them with *equal* duration and weight, that is with little or no lilt at all. When he does so, he also plays most, and sometimes all, of the notes staccato, with uniform, choppy single-tongue or throat articulations. Sometimes he easily, quickly, and subtly moves in and out of this pointed, even style, as in the second time through the tune, m. 1–2. At other times he uses this change to make a bold statement, as in the second time through, m. 4–6. One needs to listen to this recording to truly appreciate Morrison's masterful use of this technique. When you do, you will hear that the tambourine player tends to play quite evenly throughout, so when Morrison adopts the even style of playing, he suddenly comes into sync with the tambourine on every note, not just the on-pulse notes.

As for his articulations, from careful listening to the recording at reduced speed, I am nearly certain that he uses single and multiple tonguing as well as throating. Sometimes it is impossible to tell whether he is throating or tonguing, but at other times it does seem clear. The beginning pickup measure, which established the beat, tempo, and lilt for his accompanist (and would do the same for dancers when they were present), consists of seven eighth notes that I am fairly sure are played with a rhythmically definite and clear, yet smoothly connected double tonguing pattern. In m. 4 of the second time through, the first four notes are double tongued whereas the notes of m. 5 and 6 are played with choppy, uniform, single tonguing. In many other places he is clearly using throat articulation, such as on the repeated Gs at the ends of every A part. (Note that these Gs are slurred and not tied.)

Morrison's use of two opposite patterns of alternating between staccato and legato eighth notes further illuminates the fascinating subtlety of his articulation variations. In the first time through, in m. 1 and m. 19–20, he alternates between playing legato on-pulse eighth notes and staccato off-pulse eighth notes. Then he uses just the opposite pattern, i.e. staccato on the pulse and legato off the pulse, in the third time through, m. 3, 11, and 27–28.

Another important aspect of Morrison's bold style of improvisation is his free-form approach to frequent changes of octave register. He varies the speed and force of his airstream often, taking notes that would ordinarily be played in the low register up high. (It is interesting to note that, in this tune at least, he never does the opposite, i.e. bringing high notes down into the low register.) To see an example, look at m. 2. In the second time through, he plays in a normal fashion, whereas in the first time through he takes five notes up into the high octave. As you look and listen, you find many more instances of this register jumping, a natural result of this loud and punchy style of dance playing from the days before amplification.

Sometimes the change in the airstream is gradual enough, especially in a fast tune like this, that certain notes actually sound in both registers at once, something that is possible on the flute, whistle, fife, and piccolo but not, I believe, on any other of the instruments of traditional Irish music. For example, in the first time through, m. 32, there are three G eighth notes in succession. When you listen to the recording, you will hear that the first G is firmly planted in the low register and the third in the high register. But the second, though it is notated here in the low register, is actually in both registers at once. In this recording, there are numerous other notes like this that are not totally in one register or the other.

Tom Morrison, like most of the players of this period, uses ornamentation fairly sparingly. While many of his cuts fall right on the beat, many others do not, coming instead somewhat after the attack of the note. This delaying of cuts appears to be a common trait of this period. There are mid-note cuts too, such as the cut on B in m. 31, first time through. Sometimes a cut comes so late and is so elongated that it sounds like a note unto itself, as is the case in the second time through, m. 10. Here I notate the first three notes of the measure as a sixteenth-note triplet, three notes, instead of two Gs with the second one cut. The boundaries blur in such cases. You can make up your own mind about this and other cuts that I have notated here. The music is what it is and ultimately it doesn't matter how we analyze it and identify its tiny parts.

Rolls appear only in three places: first time through, m. 17 and 25 and third time through, m. 29. It is interesting that in m. 21, all three times through, Morrison does not use a roll to ornament the three eighth-note beats of A in the second half of the measure. Instead he plays three staccato A notes that sound like they are single tongued. This is similar to older styles of ornamentation among players of other instruments such as the melodeon and concertina.

In m. 10, second time through, Morrison plays a crann on middle D. He plays this with the T1 hole uncovered so that the cuts sound lower than the parent note of D. It is quite hard to hear this crann unless you slow down the recording. So far, this is the second earliest recorded example I have come across of cranning on the flute, the first being in John McKenna's 1925 recording of the reel *The Five Mile Chase*.[v]

Morrison also makes numerous lovely small melodic variations, such as those found in m. 19, the second time through, in which he changes an E to a B, and the falling chain of cuts found the second time through in m. 28. The high C-sharp he plays the third time through in m. 11 was probably not intentional. Notice also the rhythm reminiscent of Scottish music (a sixteenth note followed by a dotted eighth note) in the first time through, m. 13 and 29.

Tom Morrison

369

Sweet Flowers of Milltown

traditional Irish schottische
as played by Tom Morrison, Irish flute,
on his 1927 recording on the Columbia label,
reissued on *Fluters of Old Erin,* Viva Voce 002

𝅗𝅥 = approx. 100

370

3. **William Cummins** (flute)—Hornpipe: *Dwyer's Hornpipe*. This is from his 1930 Dublin recording on the Parlophone label, reissued on *Fluters of Old Erin*, Viva Voce 002. Mode: G Ionian (major).

According to Harry Bradshaw's liner notes to *Fluters of Old Erin*,

> William (Billy) Cummins (1894-1966) came from Roscrea, Co. Tipperary, where he learned music in the local flute band. In later years he also played fiddle and accordion in his own band which regularly broadcast on Radio Éireann.

> Although Billy was playing the flute to within three years of his death, this Parlophone record of 1930 was his only commercial disc. The master disc intended for the other side of the record seems to have been damaged and a song by the soprano Molly Shillman appeared in its place.[vi]

Though he is a little-known player, I am glad to be able to include the playing of William Cummins in this collection because it gives a rare glimpse into an older virtuoso style of playing which is very rarely heard today. Cummins' playing helps us realize how very diverse traditional Irish flute styles have actually been.

He plays this rollicking four-part hornpipe at a very fast clip indeed. One can only imagine that this was one of Billy Cummins' favorite show pieces. On the recording, he plays the tune twice through in its full form (AABBCCDD) and then plays the first two parts again (AABB) to close. Here I am presenting only the first time through his performance of the tune, in part to save space but also because, in his second and third rounds, he plays the tune almost identically to the first. His rendition of this tune has very little in the way of variation, so it would be of little use to show more than this.

For ornamentation, he makes no use of rolls, using only cuts and a remarkable, very rapid multiple-throating technique that calls to mind bow trebles on the fiddle or the plectrum work of a fine tenor-banjo player. Some modern players, such as Catherine McEvoy, have taken notice of this remarkable technique and have incorporated it into their own styles. No doubt Cummins' early experience playing in a local flute band, with its staccato style of fluting and fifing, made a deep impression on him. It sounds to me like he used no tonguing at all in this tune. And apart from his amazing rapid, staccato, throated triplets, he plays with a completely legato approach throughout, only articulating the first note after taking a breath. I have placed breath marks over every rest but, in fact, due to the low fidelity of the original recording, it is impossible to tell whether or not he actually took a breath in all of these places. Notice that many of his cuts are mid-note cuts.

Like many other players of his time, he liked to kick lower register notes up into the high register. In this tune, he does this only with his throated triplets and within the four-note groups formed by such triplets and the notes that follow them. In these cases, the four-note group begins in the low register but ends up high. The register change often takes place over the space of the four notes so that, on many occasions, the second and/or third notes are actually in both octaves at once. When this occurs, I have notated the first three notes low and the fourth note high, such as in m. 6, 8, etc. This same kind of register shifting effect can be seen in the preceding transcription, Tom Morrison's recording of the schottische *Sweet Flowers of Milltown*, though Morrison, being a bold improviser, used it in a much more adventuresome way.

The label from William Cummins' rare 78-rpm recording of Dwyer's Hornpipe. Courtesy of the Irish Traditional Music Archive. (There are no photographs of William Cummins in print at the time of this writing.)

Dwyer's Hornpipe

$\downarrow$ = approx. 116

traditional Irish hornpipe
as played by William Cummins, Irish flute,
on his 1930 Dublin recording on the Parlophone label,
reissued on *Fluters of Old Erin,* Viva Voce 002

373

374

4. **Séamus Ennis** (tin whistle)—Jig: ***The Thrush in the Straw.*** This is from his 1959 recording, *The Bonny Bunch of Roses*, originally on Tradition Records, TLP 1013, reissued as Ossian OSS 59. He plays this jig on its own, not as part of a medley. Mode: G Ionian (major).

Séamus Ennis (1919–1982) was born in Jamestown, Finglas, Co. Dublin. He is revered as one of the finest pipers of the 20th century; also a great tin whistle player, a singer in Irish and English, and a storyteller. His immense influence on the world of piping and Irish traditional music in general is due not only to his musicianship but also his tireless work as a collector of traditional music and as a radio and television host of programs on traditional music. He learned piping first from his father James Ennis from Naul "who was considered to be the last of the pipers in the idiom or dialect of the old piping tradition."[vii] The family home was filled with the music-making of the elder Ennis and a wide variety of visiting players. Séamus Ennis began playing on a Brogan set of pipes at age 13 and was an expert player by his early twenties.[viii]

This is the most legato of all the performances transcribed in this collection. There is very little tonguing, and no multiple tonguing. He plays very long phrases in long, unbroken breaths: five, six, seven, even eight measures long (for example m. 17–24, first time, the entire first B part). When he takes a breath, he sometimes uses the duration of two eighth notes to do so, instead of the usual one, which it seems would give him time to take in a great deal of air and play those very long phrases. Even when he plays three As in succession he does so tonguing only once. You can see and hear this in m. 4 and 12, both times. He slurs into the first A, tongues the next, and then, slurring into the third A, cuts it. This gives each A a different quality of articulation which is a lovely and subtle gesture.

The long roll in the pickup measure is more of an introductory flourish of notes that are not in a particular rhythm. This, and the final staccato high D, show a contained sense of showmanship and awareness of presentation. But in the tune itself his playing is humble and subtle.

His ornamentation is straightforward for the most part. Some cuts are mid-note cuts, as in m. 1, 9, 13, and 31. The cut on C-natural in m. 28, first time, and m. 10, second time, is produced by fingering the middle D, leaving the T1 hole open, and then quickly removing B1, B2, and B3.

He uses slides beautifully. The slide on C-natural in m. 2 and 6, first time, is played by fingering C in the common manner of closing T2 and T3. He then raises the pitch up a bit by removing either T2 or T3. The three consecutive slides in m. 30–31, first time, are lovely, creating a shape that could suggest a swooping bird. He does a similar thing in m. 26–27, the second time through. Here you can see how his variations tend to be subtractive: that is, he often takes away notes to create a new melodic shape. In a similar spirit, in m. 7, second time, he refrains from playing a roll where one normally would and instead plays a reposeful, unadorned dotted quarter note.

Séamus Ennis

In m. 13, second time, he hums along with the first three notes, an octave lower than he plays them on the whistle, so that you momentarily hear those notes in parallel octaves! A wavy line over the music shows where this occurs. This remarkable technique is very similar to the "throat buzzing" that Willie Clancy uses in *The Woman of the House*, the transcription that follows this one. It's interesting that, as far as I know, players of newer generations have not picked up this dramatic effect.

The Thrush in the Straw

traditional Irish jig
as played by Séamus Ennis on an E-flat tin whistle,
on his recording, *The Bonny Bunch of Roses*, Ossian OSS 59.
Transposed to G Ionian (recording is in A-flat Ionian).

376

5. **Willie Clancy** (tin whistle)—Reel: ***Woman of the House***. This is from a 1967 field recording, originally issued in 1969 on Topic Records, later reissued on *The Breeze from Erin*, Ossian OSS-26. This is the second reel in a medley of two reels, the first being "The Morning Dew." Mode: G Ionian (major).

Willie Clancy (1918–1973), the renowned and beloved uilleann piper, was born just outside of Milltown Malbay in west Co. Clare. Both his parents were singers and concertina players and his father was a fine flutist who had learned a great deal from the blind piper Garret Barry (d. 1900). Willie took up the whistle at age five, and, not long after, the flute, which he played until he lost his teeth. He also played fiddle, was a step dancer, and was a great *sean nós* singer. It was not until he was 18 that he first saw and heard the uilleann pipes, in the hands of Johnny Doran. At the age of 20 he managed to procure a set and within ten years he had established himself as one of the greatest pipers of his time.[ix]

Clancy was a carpenter by trade. Following work, he moved to Dublin in 1951 and to London in 1953 where he renewed an acquaintance with Séamus Ennis. Upon the death of his father in 1957 he returned to and remained in Milltown Malbay. He had planned to become a maker of uilleann pipes and had acquired the necessary tools and equipment just at the time of his death.

Pat Mitchell writes that "although Willie's approach to acquiring music and the background to it was very serious, his performance of that music was always gay and lively..."[x] This fact comes through loud and clear in this rendition of the well-known reel "The Woman of the House." Here Clancy shows his deep knowledge and inventive genius, tossing off a brilliant, playful, and constantly changing set of variations on this tune.

The piper and whistler Bill Ochs pointed out to me two elements in the tin whistle music of Willie Clancy, and other players of his time and before, that seem to have disappeared from modern tin whistle playing. The first is breath pulsing. Clear examples of this occur with the first note of m. 26, first time, a repeated D which is articulated only with a breath pulse, and in m. 13, second time, where the second roll is begun with a breath pulse (note that this roll is under a slur).

The second was a technique previously unknown to me in the Irish tradition, one which I was astonished to hear in this recording, a "buzzing throat" or humming technique that creates a kind of growling effect. I have indicated such buzzing in this transcription with a wavy line over the music in m. 1, 6, 9, and 30. This is truly remarkable and must be heard to be appreciated. Séamus Ennis' use of this same technique is shown in the preceding transcription.

Clancy's ornamentation repertoire is very broad. Some of the more unusual ornaments, in addition to the buzzing throat, are true trills and a crann on E, both of which are used more by pipers than whistle and flute players. These trills, in m. 2 and 6, are full, five note trills. He also uses the more common single trill technique in m. 20 and 31. The crann on E appears in m. 14.

Long and short rolls abound. His combinations or chains of rolls are particularly nice in m. 1, second time, m. 5, both times, and m. 13 both times. In m. 9, both times, where one would normally play a long roll on B, Clancy instead plays the note sequence B–C–B, sliding up to a half-hole fingering for the C-natural, then sliding back down again to B. He uses the same kind of sliding and half-holing technique in m. 28, both times, sliding down from A to G-sharp and back up again to A.

His melodic variations are plentiful, rich, and inventive. The most unusual ones are some of those involving the addition of sixteenth-notes as seen in m. 6, second time, m. 14, first time and m. 27, first time, and his use of high C-sharp in m. 27, both times. These and other melodic variations abound, streaming out in a free flow of improvisation.

Like others of the earlier high-energy players, such as Tom Morrison, (see the transcription of Morrison's "Sweet Flowers of Milltown"), Clancy is fond of using register jumping to spice up the music. He does this especially at phrase endings, such as in m. 3, 7, 14, and 15, but also at the start or within a phrase, such as in m. 7, 15, and 31–32. The first E in m. 8 begins in the low register but ends in the high, though it is notated only as a high E.

In this tune, Clancy shows a mastery of multiple tonguing. By listening closely, especially at half-speed, you can clearly hear that most, if not all, of his successively tongued notes have the differing qualities of articulation that multiple tonguing provides. These notes could hardly be tongued so nimbly at this fast tempo by using single tonguing. Examples occur in m. 6–7, 12, 15, 27, 32, and others.

Willy Clancy

Woman of the House

traditional Irish reel
as played by Willie Clancy, tin whistle,
on the recording, *The Breeze from Erin*, Ossian OSS-26.

𝅗𝅥 = approx. 120

6. **Paddy Taylor** (Radcliff-system flute)—Reel: ***The Boy in the Gap***. This is from Paddy Taylor's 1970 release *The Boy in the Gap,* Claddagh 4CC8. Mode: D Ionian (major).

Paddy Taylor, (1914–1976), was born at Loughill, Co. Limerick.[xi] His father was a singer, his mother played concertina, and her brothers were flute players. His maternal grandfather, flute player Patrick Hanley, was his most important early musical influence. When he was 18 years old, Taylor's father died and the family moved to Hammersmith, London where Paddy found work as a television and film lighting engineer. He rose to become a central figure in the London Irish music scene into the 1940s where he played with the Garryowen band as well as with Joe O'Dowd and Martin Wynne. In 1939, he made a recording with uilleann piper Leo Rowesome, but unfortunately it was never released and the master recording was lost during the war. He was a highly emotive and lyrical player who had a deep influence on the London Irish music scene during his lifetime.

In my view, Taylor was one of the most inventive flute players of recent times. He made use of a very wide palette of ornamental techniques and applied them in very original ways. His melodic variations reveal quite an active musical imagination. Notice the variations in the first A part of the second time through the tune.

Like Paddy Carty (see the following transcription), Paddy Taylor started out on simple-system flute but switched over to the Radcliff-system. I suspect that some of his unusual ornamental techniques are idiomatic to the particular fingering characteristics of that system.

His was a smooth style overall. He made only occasional use of tonguing, using breath pulsing more, but in a fairly subdued way. He was noted for his very fine slow air playing in which he used both breath and finger vibrato, sometimes both at once. His ornamentation tended to be very dense and he is one of the few players who used a variety of double-cut rolls, cranns on notes other than D, and condensed cranns.

Since his ornamentation approach is so unusual, I would like to look into it in some detail. I really am not entirely sure what he is doing in some cases, not being a Radcliff-system player.

Where you see consecutive notes of the same pitch under a slur, with no cut or strike on the repeated notes, he articulates these notes very softly with subtle breath pulsing. This is almost a rhythmic vibrato in effect and it does not interrupt the flow of air. In m. 13, the first time through the tune, he plays three Ds in a row this way. You can see that he uses this technique in m. 12, 18, and in a number of other places.

In m. 8, the second time, he articulates four notes in a row with a breath pulsing that is somewhat more pronounced, while also cutting two of them. The flow of air is interrupted more here, so these notes do not appear under a slur.

I am fairly certain that he tongues certain notes. In m. 22, first time, I believe he tongues the G after the breath, and perhaps also the cut E after that. In m. 11, the second time, he plays a tongued staccato note on last note of the measure, and in m. 36, the second time, he tongues the cut F-sharp.

As already stated, Paddy Taylor uses double-cut rolls. You can hear them in m. 14, 21, and 29. You can hear condensed long double-cut rolls in m. 14, second time (on A), and in m. 23, second time (on E). In m. 36, first time, he uses a quick double cut as an ornament in itself. These double cuts are definitely not played with a single finger.

When I listened to this tune very closely, with the recording slowed down, I could discern, in two instances, that what sound like double-cut rolls seem to be something a little different, i.e. rolls with two *strikes* instead of two cuts. (I nevertheless notate these as double-cut rolls.) I do not know how he is fingering these ornaments on his Radcliff-system flute. These occur with the long "double-cut" roll on F-sharp in m. 17, first time, and with the short "double-cut" roll on E in m. 23, first time.

In m. 6, you can hear a condensed long crann on A followed by a long crann on G. These are quite unusual. The short cranns on A in m. 32 do not start with cuts, i.e. they have only two cuts, not three. The trill that is indicated in m. 24, second time, is brief and unusual. It almost sounds like a crann. I suspect that there is some nonstandard trill fingering going on here, perhaps something unique to the Radcliff-system. The ornamental notes sound a lot like cuts.

Mid-note cuts occur in m. 28, first time, m. 38, both times, and m. 44, both times. Delayed cuts (not mid-note) occur in m. 32, both times on G. A delayed strike appears in m. 28, second time.

The pickups to m. 5 are very quick and sound like the result of some kind of nonnormal, cut-type fingerings. In m. 14, it sounds like he missed the strike in an intended long roll on C-natural. In m. 43, it sounds like he missed the strike on the long double cut roll.

Paddy Taylor playing a Radcliff-system flute.

381

The Boy in the Gap

traditional Irish reel
as played by Paddy Taylor, Radcliff-system flute,
on his recording, *The Boy in the Gap*, Claddagh, 4CC8.

♩ = approx. 112

382

7. **Paddy Carty** (Radcliff-system flute)—Reel: ***The Jug of Punch***. This tune is transcribed from Paddy Carty's 1974 release *Traditional Irish Music*, Shanachie 34017. It is the first in a medley of two reels, the second being *The Cottage Groves*. Mode: D Dorian, with occasional sharp thirds (F-sharp) suggesting D Mixolydian.

Paddy Carty (1929–1985) was born at Rafford, Loughrea, Co. Galway.[xii] Though he learned his music on tin whistle and simple-system flute, he made the switch to Boehm-system metal flute and eventually, as did Paddy Taylor (see the preceding transcription), to a wooden Radcliff-system flute. This is a closed-hole keyed flute, physically similar to a Boehm flute, but with certain fingering differences that made its playing more similar to the simple-system. Carty won several All-Ireland titles in the early 1960s and continued to play regularly in and around his home area, especially at Moylan's Pub, until the time of his death. He was a highly creative player and his beautifully lyrical music continues to influence and inspire musicians today.

Paddy Carty with Radcliff-system flute.

Many tunes, including this one, have notes that are lower than low D, the bottom note on the tin whistle, uilleann pipes, and most simple-system flutes. Traditional flute, whistle, and uilleann pipe players usually respond to this situation by simply playing the note or notes in question an octave higher. The resultant changes in the melody are usually fairly minor and may even go unnoticed, especially when they play along with an instrument that does play the low notes in their original register, such as a fiddle or accordion.

Sometimes, however, the resultant changes in melodic contour are unexpectedly beautiful and a new version of the tune is born which others make a point to learn. Such is the case here. Even though Paddy Carty's Radcliff-system flute had keys that would allow him to play as low as C, he raised by an octave all the notes that fall below low D. Perhaps he had previously worked out this tune on a simple-system flute that didn't go below D, or on a whistle, or perhaps his low C-sharp and C keys did not function well. (The unaltered notes of the A part of *The Jug of Punch* appear in Figure 19-22 on p. 268.) On the other hand, he clearly enjoyed playing with the ambiguity of F-sharps and F-naturals, which he freely changes throughout his rendition of the tune, something that would be difficult to do on a whistle or an unkeyed simple-system flute. Many musicians play only F-naturals throughout this tune, and flute players do not often play it.

Paddy Carty provides a prime example of the moderate-paced, smooth and even, dark and subdued, Galway style of flute playing. This is more listening music than dancing music. He does not use tonguing at all and only occasionally articulates a note by throating. His sixteenth-note pickup notes are particularly unusual (see the pickups to m. 9, 17, and the pickup to the beginning of the second time through the tune) as is the descending sixteenth-note device seen in m. 5 and 13. His cuts on F-natural and rolls on C-natural are also unusual in Irish flute playing. The keywork and fingering system of the Radcliff flute presumably made these easily accessible to him.

The Jug of Punch

traditional Irish reel
as played by Paddy Carty on a Radcliff-system flute,
on his recording, *Traditional Irish Music*, Shanachie 34017.

385

8. **Grey Larsen** (flute)—Reel: ***The Jug of Punch***. This is from the 1987 release of the group, Metamora, which is entitled *The Great Road*, Sugar Hill SH/PS-CD-1134. The tune is played on its own, not as part of a medley. Mode: D Dorian, with occasional sharp thirds (F-sharp) suggesting D Mixolydian.

For biographical information see "About the Author" on p. 478.

I based my version on the Paddy Carty version that precedes this transcription. I kept many of the things that I love about his setting: the use of certain F-sharps in the A part, the unusual melodic contours that result from lifting the low notes of the original fiddle version up an octave, the silky, smooth, dark Galway approach.

I also changed many things, mostly in an unconscious way, in making the tune my own. First, I slowed it down considerably and took a softer approach. I made significant use of vibrato as an ornament, both finger vibrato and breath vibrato. Though I don't normally do so, in this transcription I have notated the use of vibrato, since it is such an important element of the setting and since it may interest others to see how it can be used. You'll see finger vibrato indicated as "fv" and breath vibrato as "bv", above the notes that are affected. All other notes are played without vibrato.

In comparing my setting of this tune with Paddy Carty's, you will see that I have taken away some of the melody notes and played longer notes in their place, especially in the A parts the third time through. It's good to remember how effective it can be to vary a melody by making it less dense. This requires that you first develop a good understanding of the larger shapes of the melody.

Dynamics are also an essential part of this setting. I have not notated them except in one place. In m. 13 and 14, the third time through, I play an F-natural for three quarter-note beats. I get softer during the note (which is shown with a decrescendo indication below the note) and let the pitch naturally drift somewhat flat as it approaches the E in measure 14. This creates a *breath-only* (i.e. unfingered) falling pitch slide which is tied to the dynamic and tonal shape of the note. I have suggested the beginning, ending, length, and shape of the pitch slide by placing and stretching out the symbol for the falling slide (which makes it look somewhat like a slur). This is meant to demonstrate how specific and detailed one could be in preparing transcriptions, should one want to be.

In measures 6 and 14, I play what sounds and functions like a cut on C-natural, following a low D. This is actually a "crossing note" that is produced by a particular fingering pattern. To understand this, try the following: Finger and play low D. Then, lift T1 while blowing a bit faster to get a D in the second octave. Then, just an *instant* later, lift B1. This produces a quick D before the C and leaves you playing C-natural with a special cross-fingering in which T2, T3, B2, and B3 cover their holes.

When you listen to the recording you will hear that Pete Sutherland's beautiful guitar accompaniment is an inseparable part of the fabric of the arrangement. We are playing together intimately and continually affecting each other's improvisation. His constantly shifting chord progressions, which cast each melodic passage in different shades of light upon each repetition, inspired me to vary the melody in differing ways.

Grey Larsen

386

The Jug of Punch

traditional Irish reel
as played by Grey Larsen, Irish flute,
on the recording by his group, Metamora,
The Great Road, Sugar Hill SH/PS-CD-1134.
Based on the tune as played by Paddy Carty.

9. **Josie McDermott** (flute)—Reel: ***The Pigeon on the Gate***. This is from his 1976 release, *Darby's Farewell*, Ossian CD 20, first issued as Topic Records 12TS325. It is the second in a medley of two reels, the first one being *The Kerry Man*. Mode: E Dorian.

Josie McDermott (1925–1992) is revered as a great traditional flute player, whistle player, and singer. He spent his life in the musically rich area where Counties Sligo, Roscommon, and Leitrim meet, living just outside of the Roscommon town of Ballyfarnan. While traditional Irish music was the first music he heard and played, his musical interests were very wide-ranging. He played the trumpet, as well as the alto and tenor saxophones, in a wide variety of local bands, and is quoted as saying, "If you put a good ceili band, a good traditional jazz band, a good country and western band, and a small orchestra in four halls, I'd find it very hard to know which of them I'd go to hear. I'd want to hear all four of them!"[xiii] I had the very good fortune of visiting Josie McDermott in his home in 1979.

McDermott was playing tin whistle and trump (Jew's harp) by the age of six.[xiv] His mother sang and played the concertina. The home of his neighbors, the Butler's, was a ceili house and he spent a great deal of time there immersed in traditional music and dance. At age fourteen, he was singing in a local jazz dance band. He remained very active in both traditional music and more modern forms, the onset of blindness from eczema in 1962 hardly slowing him down at all.

McDermott made virtually no use of tonguing on the flute but used it with great virtuosity on the whistle. (This is shown in the transcription of his tin whistle performance of *The Keadue Polka* which follows this transcription.) Through his use of throating and breath pulsing, he makes his flute music very rhythmic, yet beautifully lyrical at the same time. He often uses a gentle kind of breath pulsing in such a way that it sounds like he is both slurring and articulating notes. You can hear this particularly clearly when he plays repeated notes without interrupting the flow of air. For example, see m. 17, first time, where he plays four E notes in a row without breaking the airstream. One could describe this technique as a kind of very rhythmic, distinct breath vibrato. Another instance of this can be heard in m. 31–32, first time. Here the slurred notes are played in one continuous breath but they almost sound articulated. Sometimes it is very hard to tell whether he is using this kind of breath pulsing or a subtle kind of throating. When he plays slow airs, he uses breath and finger vibrato, as well as a wide variety of tone colors and dynamics.

His use of ornamentation is fairly spare and economical, which lends clean, clear, and agile qualities to his playing. He seems to prefer short rolls over condensed long rolls, though he does use the latter in m. 13, third time. In m. 28, first time, he plays a kind of short crann on A, one without a cut on the first note. Note the mid-note cut on the B eighth note in m. 2, second time.

Another beautiful and fascinating aspect of his music is his use of the "piping C". I have indicated his use of this note with asterisks.

McDermott's melodic variations reflect a fresh and highly creative mind. The most dramatic variation occurs in m. 30 of the second time through and m. 2 of the third time. In other instances small changes send out large ripples, such as in m. 26, second time, where he leaves out the B sixteenth-note and turns what is usually a passing C-sharp into a principal melody note. He returns to this variation in m. 18 and 22 of the third time through. He uses register changing in very effective ways in m. 7, third time; m. 8, second time; and m. 12, third time.

Josie McDermott posing by a portrait of Turlough O'Carolan, 1978.

The Pigeon on the Gate

traditional Irish reel
as played by Josie McDermott, Irish flute,
on his recording, *Darby's Farewell,* Ossian CD 20.

♩ = approx. 108

10. **Josie McDermott** (tin whistle in C)—Polka: ***The Keadue Polka***. This is from his 1976 recording, *Darby's Farewell*, Ossian OSS CD 20, first issued as Topic Records 12TS325. It is the second in a medley of two polkas, the first being *Murphy's Polka*. This tune is also known as *John Ryan's Polka*. Many modern players know it from the 1974 recording of the Irish band Planxty, *Cold Blow and the Rainy Night*.[xv] Mode: C Ionian (major), transposed here to D Ionian to reflect how this would be played on a D instrument.

Josie McDermott (1925–1992) was one of the greatest flute and whistle players of the 20th century. For some background on his life see the introduction to the preceding transcription, *The Pigeon on the Gate*.

In this dazzling and highly inventive rendition of *The Keadue Polka*, McDermott demonstrates a stunning command of very rapid double and triple tonguing. As is true of many traditional players who play both flute and whistle, McDermott seems on the whole to reserve the use of tonguing for whistle playing. (See the preceding transcription of his flute rendition of *The Pigeon on the Gate*.) In this rhythmic tour de force McDermott tosses off some amazingly complex and effective flourishes that can only be analytically understood by slowing down the recording, most notably those at the start of m. 25, all three times.

McDermott uses a great deal of both legato and staccato tonguing, but it is the staccato triple tonguing that really stands out. Instances of this can be heard throughout the tune. A few prime examples occur in m. 2, 3, 5, 9, 10, 11, etc. When the pitches change within these extremely rapid triple-tongued note groups, such as in m. 10, 11, 17, etc., a truly masterful coordination and synchronization of tongue and finger movements is required.

In two instances, in the third time through the tune, m. 2 and 5, McDermott articulates the third note of rapid repeated note groups with a breath pulse instead of the tongue (note the slur connecting notes two and three in these cases).

He uses no rolls or strikes in this rendition, but plays many cuts as well as some unusual cranns on E in m. 4 and 12. There is a mid-note cut on an E sixteenth note, the last note of m. 26, first time. There are some articulations that function as cuts (and are notated as such) which are not truly cuts in the usual sense. In the second time through the tune, m. 18, 22, and 30, and the third time through in m. 30, there are "cuts" on E notes which are approached from above by F-sharps. These are produced by a tongue articulation which comes ever so slightly before the B2 finger is put down, resulting in a very brief F-sharp that functions as a cut on the E. In m. 11 of the third time through, the "cut" on B (which also is approached stepwise from above) is the same kind of articulation. In m. 14, second time, and m. 10, third time, McDermott uses a cut fingering to move rapidly from A up to the "piping C" and back to A again by lifting only T1 instead of both T1 and T2. This is a much simpler maneuver at this fast tempo.

The Keadue Polka

♩ = approx. 132

traditional Irish polka
as played by Josie McDermott on a C tin whistle
on his recording, *Darby's Farewell,* Ossian OSS CD 20.
Transposed to D Ionian (recording is in C Ionian).

393

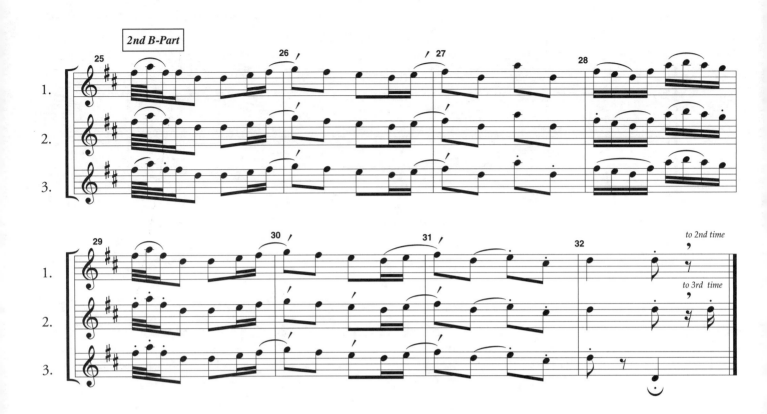

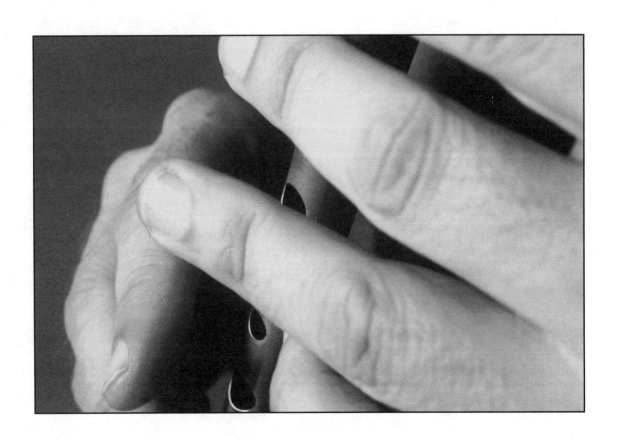

11. **Matt Molloy** (flute in E-flat)—Jig: *The Humours of Drinagh*. From his 1976 debut solo release, *Matt Molloy*, Mulligan LUN 004, Green Linnet GLCD 3008. It is the first in a medley of two jigs, the second one being *The Mist on the Mountain*. Mode: E-flat Ionian (major), transposed here to D Ionian to reflect how the tune would be played on a D instrument.

Many consider Matt Molloy to be the greatest Irish flute player of our time. There is no doubt that his genius has had a tremendous influence on nearly all players since the 1970s. His brilliant music is highly florid, energetic, and dynamic. He and whistle player Mary Bergin were my two biggest inspirations in my early years as a player. In grateful acknowledgement of their influence on my music, and that of many others, I am including two transcriptions of their playing in this section of the book.

Matt Molloy was born in 1947 in Ballaghaderreen, Co. Roscommon. His family is deeply rooted in the North Roscommon–South Sligo region, which is renowned for its flute and fiddle playing legacy. Molloy's father, uncle, and grandfather were all flute players and opportunities to learn from them, as well as neighbors and nearby musicians, such as the whistle player Jim Donoghue, abounded in his early years. His solo recordings and his work with the Bothy Band, Planxty, and the Chieftains, among other collaborations, have had a huge influence on Irish traditional musicians, much as Michael Coleman's recordings did decades earlier.

Molloy plays this jig on an E-flat flute. In a 1997 interview he talked about his use of that instrument:[xvi]

> It became quite the fashion ... for people to play in E-flat, but I think I was one of the first people to do that. I was playing around with Tommy Peoples, the fiddle player. He looked to crank up, he looked to play sharp. But it was quite by accident. A friend of mine introduced me to a friend of his who had had an accident with his hand. He used to play flute in a brass and reed band; they played in E flat. I didn't know anything about that, but he wanted to sell me the flute, which he did. There was great tone off it, great bang off it. So I was thrilled with this thing. But I had nowhere to go with it. All the sessions were in D. But Tommy heard me play this. He used to love to crank the strings up into E-flat and play, so that's how we got the whole thing started. And I made the first solo album with that flute.

In this tune, Molloy uses many condensed and highly condensed ornaments, including some that are rarely heard, such as the double-condensed long rolls in m. 9, 11, 22, and 30, the condensed short rolls in m. 1, 7, 15, 18, 23, 26, and 31, and the condensed short cranns in m. 2, 4, and 10. Also he creates sequences or strings of ornaments such as the long roll and condensed short roll combination in m. 7, 15, 23, and 31.

The mid-note "cut" on D in m. 12 is an unusual one. He is fingering D with T1 off of its hole and probably creates the cut, as one would in a crann, by quickly lifting and replacing B2 or B3. This produces a quick C below the parent note of D, not a note above the parent note as is usual with cuts.

Molloy makes beautiful use of rising slides leading into rolls in m. 19, 20, 23, 25, and 27. He also uses the more unusual falling slide in m. 21 and 29.

Though his approach to ornamentation here is very dense and dramatic, it is also judicious, perfectly complimenting his long, smooth phrasing and his intense forward motion. He seems to use no tonguing in this tune, using throating and gentle breath pulses instead, as most traditional flute players do. His occasional use of staccato notes, on the middle note in groups of three eighth notes, adds spark to the powerful glide of the music. Unlike most traditional flute players, Molloy makes bold use of dynamics in shaping his phrases, heightening the drama of the music and forging a very personal interpretation.

His variations in this tune are subtle but powerful. He does not stretch beyond the melody itself but remains within it, using ornamentation, phrasing, dynamics, and pacing to develop and heighten its intrinsic energy.

Matt Molloy

The Humours of Drinagh

traditional Irish jig
as played by Matt Molloy on an E-flat Irish flute,
on his recording, *Matt Molloy*, Mulligan, LUN 004.
Transposed to D Ionian (recording is in E-flat Ionian).

♩. = approx. 132

397

12. **Matt Molloy** (flute)—Reel: ***Griffin from the Bridge****.* From his 1987 solo release, *Stony Steps,* Claddagh 4CCF18, Green Linnet GLCD 3041. It is the third in a medley of reels, the first one being *Stony Steps* and the second *Michael Dwyer's Favorite.* Mode: G Ionian. This is a single, two-part reel, apparently, it seems to me, made up by a fiddler. The high B that comes between the low Ds in m. 3 and 7 are probably played as low Bs on the fiddle.

For biographical information on Matt Molloy see the introduction to the preceding transcription.

One of the reasons I chose to transcribe this particular performance is that Molloy elongates certain cuts on low E, producing, at this fast tempo, a beautiful and distinctive fluttering sound. You can hear these in m. 1, 3, 5 (second time), and 7. To my ear, these are not truly cuts but instead are heard as actual G notes unto themselves. That is to say, instead of hearing two E eighth notes with the second one articulated with a cut, we hear three notes: an E thirty-second note, a G thirty-second note, and then an E sixteenth note. I'm sure however that Molloy uses a cut fingering, not the usual G fingering, to produce these very quick G notes. (For more on elongated cuts see Chapter 7, p. 137.)

He also uses a very distinctive ornament combination, in this and other tunes, which can be heard in m. 4, 9, 11, and 16. In these places, he plays a cut high G eighth note followed by a single trill on the F-sharp eighth note below it. This produces a different kind of lovely, fluttering sound. In m. 9, second time, the cut in this gesture is delayed.

Molloy doesn't use as many condensed ornaments in this tune as he does in *The Humours of Drinagh* (see the preceding transcription). But he does use two: a condensed long roll in m. 11, second and third times, and a condensed short roll in m. 9, third time.

The three techniques addressed in the preceding paragraphs produce three different qualities of fluttering sounds. Molloy uses a fourth one as well, "tight triplets." (For an explanation of this, see "Tight Triplets" on pp. 256-257 of Chapter 18].) In this tune, wherever he plays the ascending note sequence B sixteenth note, C-natural sixteenth note and D eighth note, he does so using the tight triplet technique. You can hear these in m. 4, 10, and 16. Notice that, in m. 8, he instead plays this gesture in the more common way, using C-sharps.

As in *The Humours of Drinagh,* Molloy seems to use throating and no tonguing in this reel. The phrases are long and smooth for the most part, and the forward drive is unstoppable. Some of the throat articulations are so subtle that they go by almost unnoticed.

Molloy keeps the music fresh and constantly changing with a great many subtle variations. For example, see the three different ways he ornaments the third and fourth notes in m. 9. Some other variations are more outgoing, such as in m. 10–12, second and third time; and m. 2–3, third time, where he kicks up briefly into the high register to great effect. Overall this a stunning performance in which Molloy explores and interprets the tune in a highly personal way, yet stays close and true to the melody.

Griffin from the Bridge

traditional Irish reel
as played by Matt Molloy, Irish flute,
on his recording, *Stony Steps,* Green Linnet GLCD 3041.

13. **Cathal McConnell** (flute)–Reel: *Peter Flanagan's*. This is from his 1977 recording, *On Loch Erne's Shore*, Topic 12TS377. It is the third tune in a medley, the first being the slow air *The Wedding of Molly* and the second being the jig *The Three-Hand Jig*. Mode: A Dorian Pentatonic. Note that there is an F-sharp in the mode signature, even though there are no F-sharps in the melody. The Dorian Pentatonic mode on A does not include the 3rd or 6th degree, i.e. C or F-sharp. (For more on the pentatonic modes found in Irish music see "Pentatonic Modes" in Chapter 1, p. [000].)

McConnell (born 1944), from Ballinaleck in Co. Fermanagh in the north of Ireland, represents the fourth generation of flute players in his very musical family. He is also a great tin whistle player (see the next transcription, *The Long Slender Sally*) and an outstanding *sean nós* singer. His playing style is deeply rooted in the Fermanagh traditions of his family and the many great musicians who surrounded him in his youth. Among those musicians was his neighbor Peter Flanagan who played the whistle and fiddle and instructed McConnell on the former. McConnell learned this reel from Flanagan and names it for him, though it seems to be a version of the reel *Down the Broom*. While deeply rooted in Fermanagh music, McConnell is also a very broad-ranging musician, being a founding member of the pan-Celtic traditional band, The Boys of the Lough.[xvii] He is a left-handed player.

McConnell's Fermanagh style is quite unique among the players presented in this book and he is one of the few well-known exponents of this beautiful dialect of music. As in much of the music of northern Ireland, the influence of Scotland is clear. The lilt in McConnell's playing is quite special, and immediately recognizable as his own. Very often throughout this performance, the eighth notes which fall on the primary and secondary pulses of the reel's rhythmic pattern (i.e. the first, third, fifth, and seventh), are played with a *shorter* duration than the off-pulse eighth notes (the second, fourth, sixth, and eighth). This is just the opposite of what is normally heard among Irish players from most regions of the country. You can even hear this short-long lilt in the internal rhythms of the long rolls in m. 17–19, the first time through the tune. These rolls begin on weak, off-pulse notes. The second, cut note is the strongest. This and the third, struck notes of these rolls, are played with the short-long lilt.

When you exaggerate this short-long pattern beyond the subtleties of lilt, you finally arrive at the characteristic Scottish rhythm of a sixteenth note followed by a dotted eighth note. You will hear this rhythm quite a few times in McConnell's playing of this tune (see m. 1, 5, 9, 13, 27, and the ending of nearly every A and B part). But you also hear him at times slip effortlessly into the reverse, the more common long-short, long-short lilt, in certain phrases. His lilt is in fact completely fluid, changing and shifting as if the tune were a ballad and McConnell were singing it in his mind, allowing the natural rhythms of lyrics to dictate the rhythms of his playing. I have no doubt that his expertise as a *sean nós* singer informs the phrasing of his flute playing.

Another aspect of his playing which seems to set him apart from the other players presented in this book, except perhaps his fellow Ulsterman Desi Wilkinson (see the transcription of Wilkinson's playing on pp. 411-412), is his special use of strikes. Few players make extensive use of the strike outside of its common function as one of the articulations contained in the various rolls. But McConnell does, using the strike as a primary articulation in its own right. You can see and hear how he uses the strike to articulate the second note of the sixteenth-note–dotted-eight-note combination that ends nearly every A and B part of the tune. But he uses it elsewhere too, sometimes playing a very soft and subtle strike which is quite different in character from the decisive, more percussive one we are more used to. Listen to the strikes the second time through the tune in m. 5, 13, 14, 25, and 27. These are very soft strikes indeed. When you carry this softening of the strike still further you come to a motion that becomes a finger vibrato, as you can hear him do in m. 15, the second time (indicated in the transcription by the letters *fv*). So, in McConnell's playing we find a variety and refinement in the use of strikes that is rarely heard elsewhere, and that seems to evoke a musical gift that the Scots must have brought to Fermanagh.

The single trill is also in the strike family, and McConnell uses it in the A part of the tune in m. 3, 4, 7, 11, 12, and 15.

You can hear both throat and tongue articulations in McConnell's playing and some instances of double tonguing in the first time through the tune, m. 7, 8, 16, and 24. His playing is very legato throughout, so the occasional use of tongued staccato notes is very effective.

This is a fairly steady and even style of playing, not densely ornate, which is somehow related to the music of such players such as Paddy Carty and entirely different from the punchy music of the likes of Tom Morrison.

Cathal McConnell

Peter Flanagan's

traditional Irish reel
as played by Cathal McConnell, Irish flute,
on his recording, *On Lough Erne's Shore*, Topic 12TS377

402

14. **Cathal McConnell** (tin whistle)—Reel: ***The Long Slender Sally***. This is from his 1977 recording, *On Loch Erne's Shore,* Topic 12TS377. It is the last in a medley of three reels, the first being *Johnny Going to Ceilidh* and the second being *The Gossoon that Beat his Father.* Mode: A Mixolydian.

For biographical information on Cathal McConnell, see the introduction to the previous transcription, *Peter Flanagan's.*

In the liner notes to his recording, McConnell writes that he learned this tune from a whistler at the Kilnaleck Fleadh and that he plays it with an old fifing style, in the manner of whistle player Johnny Maguire of Co. Cavan, the father of fiddler Sean Maguire.[xviii] He doesn't elaborate on this particular whistle style, but the hard-blown high Ds at the end of each part, and in m. 20, must certainly be an aspect of it. This tune is played AAB, that is by repeating the A part but not the B part. Or one could think of the B part as being short, only four measures, and that it is repeated.

It is generally true that whistle players use more tonguing and less throating than flute players, throating not being as effective or controllable on the tin whistle as it is on the flute. When a single player plays both flute and whistle, this difference in articulation style generally holds true. This is certainly the case with Cathal McConnell, as you can see by comparing *Peter Flanagan's* and *The Long Slender Sally.* There are many throat articulations in the former but none at all it seems in the latter. *The Long Slender Sally* in fact calls for quite a bit of tonguing since there are so many rapid leaps across the register break.

McConnell uses the sixteenth-note–dotted-eighth-note combination and strikes in this tune as he does in *Peter Flanagan's* (see the introduction to that transcription). You can hear and see the former in m. 7, 15, 18, 19, 22, and 23. In m. 18 and 22, the second note of this rhythmic gesture is struck. In m. 9, 11, and 13, he plays short rolls with this rhythm.

This performance is full of double tonguing, which is especially useful with the passages, such as in m. 2, that repeatedly cross the register break, bouncing off of low A.

Unlike his performance of *Peter Flanagan's,* in this tune McConnell plays with a predominant long-short lilt (see the introductions to *Peter Flanagan's*). He departs from this when employing the sixteenth-note–dotted-eight-note combination referred to above, but in very few other places.

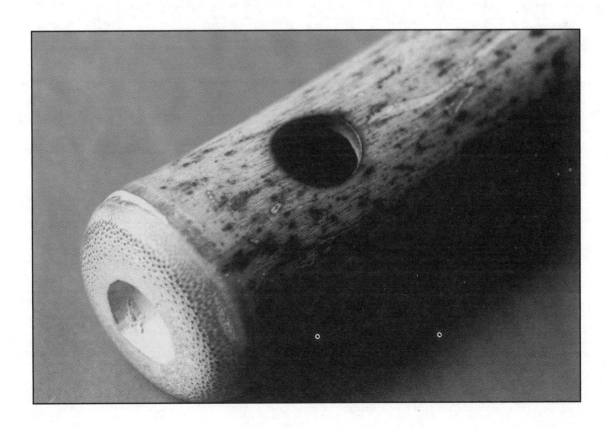

The Long Slender Sally

traditional Irish reel
as played by Cathal McConnell, tin whistle,
on his recording, *On Loch Erne's Shore*, Topic 12TS377

♩ = approx. 112

15. Mary Bergin (tin whistle)—Reel: ***Bean Uí Chroidheáin (Mrs. Crehan's Reel).*** From her 1979 debut release, *Feadóga Stáin.*, Gael-Linn CEFCD 071, Shanachie 79006. This is a single reel, the first in a medley that also includes *Gearóid Ó Comáin (Gerry Commane's)* and *An Lá Báistí (The Rainy Day)*. Mode: G Ionian (major).

Mary Bergin was born in 1949 in Shankill, which is now a suburb of Dublin but was in the countryside at that time.[xix] She and her sisters, among them the renowned traditional harper Antoinette McKenna, grew up in a musical household, their mother playing both classical violin and traditional fiddle and their father playing melodeon. Mary took up the whistle at age nine and plays the instrument left-handed. Many musicians would visit the house such as Paddy Hill, Elizabeth Crotty, and Kathleen Harrington. Bergin was also much influenced by the whistle playing of Willie Clancy (see transcription #5, of Clancy's recording of the reel *Woman of the House)* as well as many other older musicians such as flute player Packie Duignan. Bergin began to frequent nearby sessions and her exemplary playing soon made her a leader in the active Dublin music scene. She took part in Comhaltas tours of the United Kingdom and the United States with musicians such as Matt Molloy, Seamus Begley, and James Kelly. In the 1990s, she expanded the scope of her tin whistle playing by exploring baroque music with her group Dordán. At the time of this writing she lives in western Co. Galway. An active whistle teacher, she has been a role model for countless whistle players since the 1970s.

Bergin has a beautifully lean, pure, and economical style that allows her to play with great agility, drive, and speed, all with apparent ease. This is due in part to the fact that she makes little use of condensed ornaments or cranns, none in this tune. She plays short rolls where other players might use condensed long rolls. Precise, clean, short rolls are harder to play than condensed long rolls and their use is a key element of her elegant, streamlined style.

Bergin shows a mastery of smooth, conjunct, double tonguing in this reel, an approach to multiple-tongue articulation very different from the pointed, staccato style used by whistle player Josie McDermott in his rendition of *The Keadue Polka* (see transcription #10 on pp. 392-394). Her tonguing does not draw attention to itself but is a means for interpreting and bringing out the natural shapes in the melody and for accommodating quick leaps up and down across the register break. For examples see m. 1, 3, 5, 7, 12, and 15. Her judicious use of staccato notes is extremely effective, adding rhythmic spark to the otherwise smooth drive of her music. Many times she chooses to cut and tongue notes at the same time (see examples in m. 2, 6, 11, 12, 13, and 16), giving those notes a special quality and emphasis.

Mary Bergin

Bergin uses two different fingerings for C-natural in this reel. When approaching C from the B below, she chooses to half-hole the C, sometimes taking the opportunity to play a slide up to the C (see m. 4, 8, and 15). When approaching C from a note above, in m. 12 and 15, she uses the normal cross-fingering, presumably covering T2 and T3. These two ways of fingering C produce very different tonal and pitch qualities. In m. 9 and 10 you can hear the common practice of using C-sharp when playing a quick passing note between B and D.

Her variations here are subtle ones that arise from small changes in phrasing, breathing, ornamentation, and articulation.

Bean Uí Chroidheáin
(Mrs. Crehan's Reel)

traditional Irish reel
as played by Mary Bergin, tin whistle,
on her recording, *Feadóga Stáin*, Shanachie 79006.

406

16. **Mary Bergin** (tin whistle in E-flat)—Hornpipe: ***Father Dollard's Hornpipe.*** From her 1993 solo release, *Feadóga Stáin 2*, Shanachie 79083. This is the second in a medley of two hornpipes, the first one being *The Humours of Ballyconnell* (not to be confused with the well-known reel by the same name). Mode: E-flat Ionian (major), transposed here to D Ionian to reflect how the tune would be played on a D instrument.

For biographical information on Mary Bergin and observations on her playing style see the introduction to the preceding transcription.

Though Bergin makes no use of condensed ornaments in this tune, she does play some cranns in m. 1, 5, 9, and 13. I have notated these as short cranns. This is the most clear and convenient way to notate them, in accordance with how I have defined cranns in Chapter 16. However, there are other ways to hear and think of what she is doing here. In each case, these short cranns are preceded by a quarter-note D and followed by an eighth-note D that is articulated with a cut, all of these Ds being slurred together. Taken as a group, then, there are five D notes in this slurred sequence and all but the first one are articulated with cuts. One could look at the unit formed by the quarter-note D plus the short crann as a kind of *long* crann particular to hornpipes and other such tunes with uneven subdivision of the beat (see Chapter 14 for more on this subject). As stated in Chapter 16, cranns are rather personal ornaments that are played in a variety of ways by different players in differing contexts. The hornpipe setting is a somewhat unusual one for cranning and it is useful and instructive to hear how Bergin uses them here.

She uses shakes in m. 24 and 32, but these are a little different from normal shakes as defined in Chapter 18. Here the shakes are preceded by eighth-note C-sharps. The first of the four notes of a normal shake is C-sharp, so in this case Bergin naturally omits that first note and plays a three-note version of the ornament. This is the same as what classical musicians call a mordent.

In m. 24, the first time, she plays what sounds like a cut on C-sharp. The C-sharp is approached from above by a D. When tonguing the C-sharp, she is momentarily still fingering the D. Just an instant after tonguing she lifts B1, B2, and B3 to produce the C-sharp and we hear the very brief D as a "cut".

As in *Bean Uí Chroidheáin*, Bergin uses double tonguing with a subtle grace. Occasional staccato notes on weak beats serve to give emphasis to the following on-pulse note, for example in m. 20

Father Dollard's Hornpipe

traditional Irish hornpipe
as played by Mary Bergin on an E-flat tin whistle,
on her recording, *Feadóga Stáin 2*, Shanachie 79083.
Transposed to D Ionian (recording is in E-flat Ionian).

♩ = approx. 96

408

17. **Donncha Ó Briain** (tin whistle)—Reel: ***The Flogging Reel***. This is from his 1979 release, *Donncha Ó Briain*, Gael-Linn CEF 083. It is the second in a medley of two reels, the first one being *Kitty Gone a Milkin'*. Mode: G Ionian (major).

Donncha Ó Briain (1960–1990), more commonly known as Denis O'Brien, was, in my opinion, one of the very greatest of modern whistle players. It is a shame that he and his music are not more widely known. He was born into a family bursting with music in Artane, Co. Dublin, and lived a short life, confined to a wheel chair due to muscular distrophy, able to move only his fingers and head. He played left-handed. He was an avid teacher of tin whistle and compiled a book of tunes entitled *The Golden Eagle*.

Charlie Lennon wrote about him, in his book *Musical Memories*,[xx]

> I first came to know Denis O'Brien when he was in his early teens, quietly struggling to come to terms with the conflict of a very active mind contained within an unresponsive and very inactive body. As a result of this he had to achieve a level of discipline of mind over body about which even his closest companions were only vaguely aware. He conquered pain and smiled through it all. He had the ability to get the very best out of people in his company and at the same time make them very happy in the process. His love of music must have helped him enormously because it opened gateways for his wheelchair to all the best sessions, gave him a part to play in the proceedings, allowed him to banter everyone around and probably helped him to forget his earthly prison for even a little while.

His music is tremendously energetic, inventive, and eloquent, and his slow airs are just as spectacular as his dance music. His approach to ornamentation is very broad ranging, making use of nearly every type of ornament. Although he does not use condensed or double-cut ornaments in this tune, he does use them quite a bit in others.

One reason I chose to present this tune is to show how Ó Briain treats the F-naturals in the C part. Clearly he was not one to shy away from challenge. (There are a number of common ways to play this part of the tune that do not involve F-naturals.). He shows his half-holing technique to be of the highest order, even playing cranns on F-natural in m. 20, first and second time. These are long cranns but they contain only two cuts instead of three. They are like long rolls, with a second cut replacing the strike of the roll. The two cuts are played by T3 and T2, respectively, while half-holing with B2 to produce an F-natural.

He uses delayed cuts on the G in m. 23, second time, and on the very last note of the tune, which he also colors with finger vibrato.

He tongues a great deal and plays many staccato notes to make his phrasing clear and crisp. I can hear that he uses multiple tonguing as a matter of course in his playing, which makes possible a very fast, yet fluid and agile delivery, and gives a rich variety of articulation qualities. The passages in m. 19 and 20 are perfect examples of this.

Donncha Ó Briain (Denis O'Brien) ca. 1979.

The Flogging Reel

traditional Irish reel
as played by Donncha Ó Briain, tin whistle,
on his recording, *Donncha Ó Briain*,
Gael-Linn CEF 083.

18. **Desi Wilkinson** (flute)—Highland: ***Bidh Eoin (Eoin's Boat).*** This is from Desi Wilkinson's 1987 recording, *Three-Piece Flute,* Spring Records CSP 1009. *Bidh Eoin* is the first in a medley of two highlands, the second one being *Charlie O'Neill's.* Mode: B Dorian.

Flute player, multi-instrumentalist, and singer Desi Wilkinson was born in Belfast in 1954.[xxi] He first entered into traditional Irish music through many visits and kitchen sessions with his neighbor, the renowned Co. Fermanagh fiddler Tom Gunn. Mrs. Gunn ran a bed and breakfast where many musicians would stay and Wilkinson was a part of numerous musical gatherings there during the 1970s. Frequent visitors included the Co. Fermanagh flute and whistle player and singer Cathal McConnell (see the transcriptions of McConnell's playing, #13 and #14, earlier in this section). Wilkinson also names Donegal fiddler Charlie O'Neill as a major early influence on his music. As of this writing, he has performed with Dé Dannan, Donal Lunney, Liam O'Flynn, Máirtín O'Connor, and Andy Irvine as well as with Sean Corcoran and Ronan Browne in their group, Cran. He is a musician and scholar with wide musical interests and has a particular devotion to the music of Brittany. He lived in Brittany from 1992 to 1994 and considers it to be a home away from home. While the tune given here is a spare and terse one, Wilkinson is a player of wide-ranging technique and beautiful expressiveness.

The music of Scotland has had a special influence on the music of nearby Ulster. In fact, *Bidh Eoin* is a tune and song from the western isles of Scotland which Wilkinson adapted to the flute, putting it into the rhythm of an Irish highland.

There are striking parallels between Wilkinson's playing and that of his fellow Ulster musician, Cathal McConnell. In addition to cuts, both players make extensive use of strikes as articulations for individual notes that are *not* contained within rolls. From my observation, this seems to be a characteristic of Ulster flute and whistle playing, while players from outside of Ulster use strikes for this purpose far less. It would be interesting to see if deeper investigation would support this generalization.

This is a simple and rhythmically very pointed tune. Wilkinson keeps it simple and very lively with suitably spare ornamentation—no rolls or cranns, only cuts and strikes, used as described above, using cuts about twice as often as strikes. He uses throating and tonguing, and rhythmic breath pulsing to bolster the pulse of the music. The Scottish-influenced sixteenth-note–dotted-eighth-note rhythm is prominent in the tune, as seen in m. 1, 4, 5, 8, 9, 12, 13, and 16. Aside from these places, the overall lilt is one in which the odd-numbered, on-pulse notes are given more weight and duration while the off-pulse notes recede. Wilkinson keeps the variations subtle and minimal here, in keeping with the music, varying mainly his phrasing and note omission.

Desi Wilkinson

Bidh Eoin
(Eoin's Boat)

traditional Scottish song
adapted into traditional Irish highland rhythm by Desi Wilkinson
As played by Desi Wilkinson, Irish flute,
on his recording, *Three-Piece Flute* , Spring Records CSP 1009

412

19. **Breda Smyth** (tin whistle in E-flat)—Reel: *O'Mahony's.* This is from the 1989 recording of various Galway traditional musicians, *Ceol Tigh Neachtain (Music from Galway),* Gael-Linn CEF CD 145. I chose this tune in part because it is a fine example of the use of shakes. Smyth plays *O'Mahony's* only one time through on this recording. It is the first in a medley of two reels, the second one being *The Swallow's Tail.* Mode: E-flat Ionian (major), transposed here to D Ionian.

Breda Smyth, born in 1968 into a highly musical family, is a brilliant whistler and fiddler. She is originally from the village of Straide in Co. Mayo. Her father, who plays the fiddle, taught her the tin whistle, she says, "...although he never played a note on this instrument himself. He just knew what sounded right to him."[xxii] She was highly influenced by the playing of Mary Bergin (see the two transcriptions of Bergin's whistle playing, #15 and #16, earlier in this section), Tom McHale, and Deirdre Collis. As *O'Mahony's* illustrates, Smyth is not one to shy away from difficult music. "I remember as a child always challenging myself with tunes which weren't necessarily written for a wind instrument, be it in a difficult key or a difficult register. This allowed me a lot more dexterity in the session situation." Smyth has toured extensively on the festival and club circuit in Europe, Scandinavia, North America, and Japan and has presented music programs for the Irish National Television station R.T.E. and the B.B.C. She is also a medical doctor.

Smyth's style of playing is crisp, tight, and popping with energy. She is a master of multiple tonguing. Most of the notes in this reel are tongued but the overall sound is still very connected, although she makes beautiful use of staccato notes as well (see especially m. 41–48). Wherever there is more than one tongued note in succession, I am certain she uses double tonguing. Some of the more obvious double-tongued passages are in m. 7, 15, 43, and 47.

There are no condensed ornaments in this tune, except the shakes, which could be considered condensed. Having heard very few recordings of Smyth, I can't generalize about her style. But the lean, economical style of ornamentation seen in this tune, for instance her preference for short rolls over condensed long rolls, allows her music to fly like the wind. The tin whistle playing of Mary Bergin, who is also from Co. Galway, shares this same quality.

Shakes can be heard in m. 8, 16, and 24. In m. 40, the fifth, sixth, and seventh notes form a group that sound and function like a shake, but it begins a bit differently. The first D sounds like it is cut. There is an E preceding this D. When tonguing the D, the B3 finger is put down just an instant after tonguing so that there is an extremely brief E (the "cut") sounded before the D note arrives. The D–C-sharp–D sequence is fingered by playing D with T1 off of its hole, then lifting only T2 and T3 for the C-sharp, then putting them back again for D.

There are some other "cuts" of this type that are worth looking at and understanding. In m. 24 and 32 there are "cuts" on E. In moving from A down to E, Smyth puts down T3 and B1 an instant before B2, so there is an extremely brief F-sharp note produced which sounds and functions like a cut on the E. In m. 32, the "cut" D is really like the first part of a shake. Here the D is preceded by a C-sharp. Smyth fingers the C-sharp with B1, B2, and B3 down. When tonguing to articulate the D, she delays just for an instant putting down T2 and T3, so there is a resultant brief instant of C-sharp which sounds and functions like a cut. There is a mid-note cut on the B in m. 44.

What I call "ascending rolls" (see "*The Ascending Roll*" on p. 192 of Chapter 11) occur in m. 3 and 11. The ascending roll can be thought of as a variant of the long roll in which one plays the first note of a long roll one step lower than normal. It is therefore notated as an eighth note followed by a short roll a whole or half step higher than the eighth note.

Smyth is also a master of half-holing and slides. In m. 12, 36, and 44 her half-holing for D-sharp and G-sharp are so precise that one doesn't hear any sliding of pitch. In m. 17, 20, and 25 she uses sliding to great effect. Here she plays a note, slides down a half step by half-holing and slides back up to the beginning note. In m. 35 and 39, she does virtually the same thing, but by tonguing the third note she eliminates the rising slide.

When you listen to her recording, you will hear that Smyth begins the tune with an introductory measure at a very slow speed, then gradually and steadily increases the tempo until she has reached full speed at about m. 4. This is a style of starting a tune that many players employ.

413

Breda Smyth

O'Mahony's

♩ = approx. 116

traditional Irish reel
as played by Breda Smyth on an E flat tin whistle
on the recording *Ceol Tigh Neachtain (Music from Galway)*,
Gael-Linn CEF CD 145
Transposed to D Ionian (recording is in E flat Ionian)

415

20. Seán Ryan (tin whistle in E-flat)—Double Jig: *The Frost is All Over*. This is from his 1989 recording *Siúil Uait (Take the Air)*, Gael-Linn CEF CD 142. It is the second in a medley of two jigs, the first being *Coughlan's*. Mode: E-flat Ionian (major), transposed here to D Ionian.

Seán Ryan was born in Cashel, Co. Tipperary, in 1949. From the start, he was surrounded by traditional music. His father played the fiddle and mouth organ and his grandmother, who lived in nearby Ardmayle and often hosted house dances, played the concertina. Ryan took up the whistle at age four or five. In those very early years, he was taken with the whistle playing of an elderly neighbor, Timmy Ryan, a rudimentary player but inspiring to young Seán nonetheless. He listened a great deal to the 78-rpm recordings of flute player John McKenna and uilleann piper Patsy Tuohy, and the fiddler Sean McGuire was one of his musical heroes. As a youth, Ryan traveled with ceili bands such as the Doyle Brothers and Sam Dougherty's Ceili Band, in which he sang and played whistle and melodeon, and also spent time playing in the Irish pubs of London. Since that time, he has toured extensively in Europe and America with a wide variety of musicians and dancers.

Ryan has a brilliant tin whistle style that is truly unique. For that reason, it is essential that he be included in this collection. When listening to his recordings you hear some lovely fluttering and stuttering gestures that remind one of the bowing techniques of the great fiddler Tommy Peoples. You can tell that Ryan is using tonguing in a unique fashion to achieve these effects. In conversation, Ryan has told me that these elements of his playing style have evolved quite naturally and unconsciously over the years.

These special tonguing techniques are so mercurial, rapid, and subtle that I find it impossible to discern exactly what he is doing without slowing down the recording considerably. By doing so, I have been able to understand these articulations and have heard some that I hadn't noticed at all when listening to the tune at normal speed.

Ryan is a master of subtle single and multiple tonguing, lending to his music a rich palette of articulation while preserving a very smooth, legato delivery that is swift and agile. There is a tonguing pattern that he employs frequently: slurring the third note of a grouping of three eighth notes to the first note of the next grouping, tonguing the second note of the group, then again slurring the third note to the first note of the next group. You can hear this in many places throughout the tune, for example in m. 4–6, first time.

Ryan has two unique ways of playing long rolls. Normally the three notes of a long roll are slurred together. In this tune, he uses this standard kind of long roll only in m. 17, where they are indicated with the normal long-roll symbol. All the rest of his long rolls involve internal tonguing. I have notated them in exploded view, that is showing each of the roll's constituent notes, and have enclosed the notes of these rolls under dotted brackets. Micho Russell used internal tonguing in his rolls, using tongue articulations in the place of strikes. (See the transcription of his recording of *Cloichíní Beaga na Farraige (The Small Stones of the Sea)*, #22, later in this section.) Ryan incorporates *both* tonguing and striking in his long rolls.

These special long rolls fall into two types. The first type is the same as the normal long roll, except that the third, or struck, note is also tongued. These occur in m. 9, all three times; m. 13, second time; m. 16, first and third times; m. 20, all three times; m. 22, second and third time; m. 25 first and second time; m. 26, third time; and m. 28, all three times. The third notes of these rolls are usually slurred to the next melody note.

The second special type of long roll consists of four notes: an eighth, two sixteenths, and another eighth. In its rhythm and sound it is very similar to a long double-cut roll. But, instead of the third note being a cut note, as it is in a long double-cut roll, Ryan tongues this note. Such rolls occur in m. 8, first and second time; m. 13, second and third time; m. 16, second time; m. 17 and 18, all three times; m. 22, first time; and m. 25 and 26, first and second times. The softness or hardness of the internal tonguing varies considerably, some of them being so subtle that they are barely discernable. The only other player that I have heard using this type of roll is Josie McDermott. On his recording *Darby's Farewell*,[xxiii] he played a reel, *The Flowers of Ballymote*, on the tin whistle and uses this type of long roll several times, but this was a technique he apparently very rarely employed. Ryan knew McDermott quite well but had not heard him use this technique and did not pick it up from him. Apparently both men arrived at it independently. Ryan says that he was not even aware that he tongues within rolls until a student pointed it out to him.

In m. 1, second and third time, and m. 31–32, first time, there are note sequences which sound like an eighth note, two sixteenth notes, and an eighth note but, on very close examination, one finds that the rhythm is more complex due to remarkably fast tonguing of a repeated C-sharp. At full speed these passages have a fluttery, tumbling sound but it is impossible to tell exactly why. At half speed, one can hear the extra note. Slowed down even more, one can make out the tonguing pattern. Similar uses of tonguing can be heard in m.5, second and third time. The rhythms in these passages are not exactly as written here but are a bit more fluid.

In m. 5, the third time, we see true jig quadruplets, that is four notes of equal duration played in the time that three eighth notes are normally played, a melodic variation that is especially associated with uilleann pipers (see "Quadruplets in Jigs" on p. 258 of Chapter 18).

Many of Ryan's cuts are delayed, but not so delayed as to be mid-note cuts. The "cut" on F-sharp in m. 14, third time, is the result of putting down B2 an instant after the tongue articulation. The first note of m. 12, third time, is stressed with a breath pulse.

Seán Ryan

The Frost is All Over

traditional Irish jig
as played by Seán Ryan on an E flat tin whistle
on his recording , *Siúil Uait (Take the Air)*,
Gael-Linn CEF CD 142
Transposed to D Ionian (recording is in E flat Ionian).

♩. = approx. 140

418

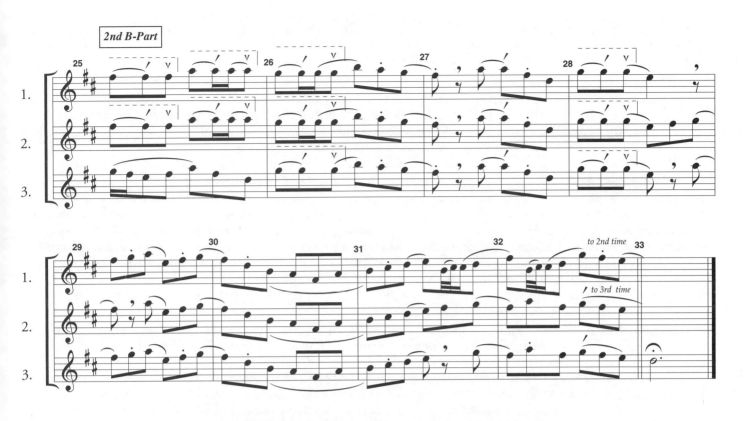

419

21. **Conal Ó Gráda** (fife, or flute in F)—Slip Jig: ***Ride a Mile.*** This is from his 1990 recording *The Top of Coom*, Claddagh CCF27CD. It is the first tune in a medley of two, the second being the jig *Haste to the Wedding*. Mode: B-flat Ionian, transposed here to G Ionian to reflect how this would be played on a D instrument.

Conal Ó Gráda was born in 1961 in Co. Cork.[xxiv] He was greatly influenced early on by hearing sessions with Jackie Daly, Séamus Creagh, and others in his family home. He first played the uilleann pipes and was active in the Cork Piper's Club in the early 1970s which was then led by Mícheál Ó Riabhaigh. Before long he changed over to the flute and became very active and well known in the traditional music scene around Cork. Séamus Mac Mathúna, the Co. Clare flute player then living in Cork, was also a great influence upon him, as were the 78-rpm recordings of Tom Morrison and John McKenna (see their transcriptions, #1 and #2, earlier in this section).

More than most other contemporary players, Ó Gráda has adopted much of the driving spirit and sound of the likes of Morrison and McKenna. He plays with an "earthy, raucous tone reminiscent of the saxophone,"[xxv] very loud, using heavy breath pulsing, throating articulations and making powerful use of the "hard D" sound (though not just on low D). Unlike Morrison and McKenna however, Ó Gráda uses ornamentation in a more dense style, similar in approach to his contemporaries such as Matt Molloy and Kevin Crawford (see their transcriptions, #11, #12, and #24).

Ó Gráda plays *Ride a Mile* on a flute in F by Boosey, which he calls a fife, an instrument pitched a minor third higher than the typical D flute. (Many fifes are pitched still higher, in B-flat.). He writes in his liner notes, "There can be little doubt that the former popularity of the fife in Ireland derived from the late 19th century vogue for marching bands."[xxvi] He learned this tune by listening to *Flute for the Feis,*[xxvii] the recording of the Newcastle-upon-Tyne piccolo player, John Doonan. It is a three part slip jig with a very unusual second C part. That part has only three measures instead of the expected four, although it can be thought of as having one bar in 9/8 time and then three bars in 6/8. I have transcribed the part as having three bars of 9/8, but the brackets appearing above its final two bars show how they can be heard as three bars of 6/8.

The most immediately remarkable aspects of Ó Gráda's playing are the things discussed above which I cannot convey in music notation: his remarkably powerful, pulsing drive, and his hard-edged, punchy, and raucous tone. You will need to listen to his recording to appreciate these. He seems to use throating to the total exclusion of tonguing, although the staccato sixteenth-notes heard in m. 4, 8, 21, and 23 could possibly be tongued. I cannot really tell from listening alone. Some repeated notes are articulated only by breath pulse, such as the repeated Bs in m. 10, 14, 18, 19, 21, and 22. Note that these notes fall under slurs.

Ó Gráda's playing here is very fast which makes his liberal use of ornamentation feel quite dense. Note his frequent use of condensed long rolls, which can be seen wherever a long roll symbol appears over an undotted quarter note: m. 3, 4, 7, etc. Normal long and short rolls abound as well, and he uses a single trill at the end of the second time through the tune. Notice the long rolls in m. 1, 3, 5, 7, 12, and 16 which begin on weak beats. Here the long roll symbol appears over an eighth note which is tied to a quarter note.

Ó Gráda employs an unusual "cut" on C-natural in m. 4, 8, 12, and 20. In all these instances the C is approached stepwise from below by a B. I believe he achieves this cut sound with the following fingering sequence. The B is played of course by closing the T1 hole. Next uncover that hole while simultaneously placing the other five fingers down. Then instantly lift off B1, B2, and B3, leaving T2 and T3 down to sound the C-natural. A very brief D is produced this way to provide a "cut" on C. The finger movement is not that of a cut, but the sound is. The very rapid putting down and picking up of B1, B2, and B3 can be almost percussive, similar to the movement of a strike.

Also notice Ó Gráda's use of the "tight triplet" technique in m. 2 and 6. Normally such quick passing Cs between B and D are played as C-sharps, but by using the tight triplet technique the C comes out as a C-natural.

Conal Ó Gráda

Ride a Mile

$\bullet$. = approx. 142

traditional Irish slip jig
as played by Conal Ó Gráda on a fife (F flute)
on his recording, *The Top of Coom*, Claddagh CCF27CD.
Transposed to G Ionian (recording is in B-flat Ionian).

422

22. **Micho Russell**—(tin whistle in C) Reel: *Cloichíní Beaga na Farraige* (**The Small Stones of the Sea**). This is from a 1993 recording included in his 1995 release, *Ireland's Whistling Ambassador*, The Pennywhistler's Press PWCD 80001. Mode: C Ionian (major), transposed here to D Ionian.

According to Bill Ochs' liner notes, the title of this tune refers to a jetty or breakwater. This setting, which Micho learned from Pat Shannon, a flute-playing neighbor, is an old two-part version of the well-known reel *The Spike Island Lasses*. On the recording he plays on a C whistle, though it plays a bit sharp of concert C.

Micho Russell (1915–1994) was born in the townland of Doonagore, part of what is now Doolin, Co. Clare. He was well-known and well-loved as a singer as well as a whistle and flute player. Bill Ochs writes,

> Micho's approach to playing the tin whistle was highly unconventional by modern standards, rooted in an old-fashioned style of concertina playing he had heard in his youth. His repertoire abounded with rare and unusual pieces acquired from old North Clare musicians in the days before radios and gramophones were common. And he had a knack for transforming whatever music he touched, imbuing it with little twists that were unmistakably his own. ... The simplicity and honesty of his approach, his warmth and humility, and the pure joy of his music won Micho a loyal and enthusiastic following in many quarters.[xxviii]

Russell began to teach himself to play whistle at age eleven.[xxix] His home was remote, apart from the world of such modern conveniences as gramophone records, and his repertoire was specific to his locale. At age fourteen, he left school to farm and he received a wooden flute from his uncle. He and his brothers, Gussie and Packie, began playing for house dances. As the years progressed Micho began to play in pubs locally and then in Dublin. The musical revival of the 1960s brought him great attention and before long he became an international traveling performer, as much at home before a festival audience of thousands in Germany as when playing for a handful of neighbors at home.

> ...the freshness of Micho's style [was] both startling and captivating. His melodies were neither cluttered with ornament nor driven by beat. Instead he had a rudimentary tune-line—deceptively simple but rhythmically complex. A thoroughly individual player—subtlety was his hallmark—he was influenced by the "push and pull" concertina style and kept double time with both his feet.[xxx]

Russell's approach to ornamentation is spare and unique. He rarely used the kind of rolls that are commonly heard today, but instead, as shown in this tune, he played a special kind of long roll. Instead of articulating the third note of the roll with a strike, he articulated it with a smooth, connected, tongue articulation. This kind of roll can easily be mistaken for the more common type, but on close listening you will hear the difference. Since, like the crann, this kind of roll does not involve a strike, Russell can and does use it on D, as you can hear in m. 1, 3, 5, and 15. According to Bill Ochs, it appears that only a few other players use this technique, among them the East Galway flute player Jack Coen and Micho's brother Gussie. But neither of them used this type of roll as extensively as Micho did.

I have transcribed these special rolls in exploded view, showing each of the constituent notes and articulations, and not using the long roll symbol. Dotted brackets (above the top staff only) encloses the notes of these rolls, which Russell plays in exactly the same places all three times through the tune. In addition to the rolls on D just mentioned, such rolls appear twice in m. 9 on F-sharp and once in m. 10 on A.

Like Josie McDermott in *The Pigeon on the Gate*, Micho Russell employs C-sharps, C-naturals, and, in m. 8, the "piping C". I have indicated this note with an asterisk. He fingered this note by covering a hole only with T2.

He occasionally uses a gentle breath pulse to separate repeated notes. This can be heard in m. 5 where he separates the last of four consecutive Ds from the third one. The two Ds in question are here joined with a slur to show that the breath is not interrupted. This same situation is seen in m. 15.

Russell's variations in this tune are very small, involving only subtle changes in tonguing and slurring. All the notes, rhythms, ornamentation, and breathing places remain consistent.

Micho Russell

Cloichíní Beaga na Farraige
(The Small Stones of the Sea)

traditional Irish reel
as played by Micho Russell on a tin whistle in the key of C,
on his recording, *Ireland's Whistling Ambassador*, Pennywhistler's
Press, PWCD 80001.
Transposed to D Ionian (recording is in C Ionian).

23. **Joanie Madden** (Boehm-system flute)—Reel: ***Dogs Among the Bushes***. This is from her 1994 recording, *A Whistle on the Wind*, Green Linnet GLCD 1142. This reel is the third tune in a medley, the first being the slow air *A Whistle on the Wind* and the second being the reel *The Jug of Punch*. Mode: F Mixolydian, however the B part has mainly raised sevenths (E-naturals instead of E-flats) which makes this part sound mainly in F Ionian.

Joanie Madden was born in the Bronx, New York in 1965.[xxxi] Her mother came from West Clare and her father, button accordion player Joe Madden, was born in Tipperary but grew up in East Galway. Joanie thus grew up in a home steeped in traditional Irish music and culture. At age nine, she took up the tin whistle and began lessons with her neighbor, the great East Galway flute player Jack Coen. Soon after she added the flute, and prefers the modern Boehm-system flute for its versatility, because she can "play tunes in odd keys such as F, G minor, D minor, and C a little easier than on the wooden flute,"[xxxii] for its extended low range, and because repairs on the modern instrument tend to be easier to obtain. She is perhaps the best known of a small number of musicians who have adapted Irish music beautifully to the Boehm-system flute and have taken it to its full heights of virtuosity and expression. She is able to do this so brilliantly because she knows the language of traditional Irish music inside-out and has modeled her flute-playing style on the great traditional simple-system Irish flute players. (For specific information on adapting Irish music to the Boehm-system flute, including comments from Joanie Madden, see Appendix B.) Madden is a founding member of the all-female Irish American band Cherish the Ladies and is also one of the finest tin whistle players of our time.

She plays this reel soulfully at a relaxed, moderate pace. Showing one of the advantages of the Boehm-system flute, she has taken the tune from its usual tonal center of G down to F, which gives it a richer, darker sound. Rolls on F, which abound in her performance, are quite easy on the Boehm-system flute but would be difficult even on a keyed simple-system flute. Still she uses the "hard D" sound on the low note of the tune, which in this case has become a C. Madden once related to me that the East Galway flute player Mike Rafferty, who used to play the Boehm-system flute, recommended that she turn the embouchure hole dramatically inward, at about a 45 degree angle to the line formed by the centers of the tone holes. Learning to play this way forced her to play very hard, giving her the hard D (or C in this case) as well as a deep, rich tone. Madden grew up playing with her accordion-playing father, so she had to learn to play hard to balance with the louder instrument.

Her ornamentation style in this tune, in keeping with her East Galway-style interpretation, is spare and economical. Her cranns on E-flat, m. 20 and 28, are beautiful. Her slides, in m. 8, 16, 31, and 33, are very effective even though they are not continuous pitch slides but discreet half-step movements.

Madden defines certain repeated notes only with breath pulses: the repeated Fs in m. 2, 22, and 30 and the repeated E-flats in m. 12. The only two repeated notes that she tongues are the two Cs in m. 14, the second time. A free approach to register jumping, a hallmark of many traditional players, can be heard in her playing as well. In m. 12, the first time, she lifts the repeated E-flat just referred to up into the second octave in anticipation of the next phrase which starts on the same note. In m. 14, the second time, the third and fourth notes sail up into the high register.

Joanie Madden with Boehm-system flute.

Dogs Among the Bushes

𝅗𝅥 = approx. 88

traditional Irish reel
as played by Joanie Madden, Boehm system flute,
on her recording, *A Whistle on the Wind*, Green Linnet GLCD 1142.

24. **Kevin Crawford** (flute)—Reel: *Maids in the Meadow*. From his 1995 release, *'d' flute album*, Green Linnet GLCD 1162. This is the second reel in a medley of three, the first being *Dillon's Fancy* and the third being *Toss the Feathers*. Mode: D Ionian (major) with a number of flat sevenths (C-natural) suggesting D Mixolydian.

Kevin Crawford was born in Birmingham, England in 1967. His parents were from West Clare and he spent his school summer holidays there, listening to and playing with many of the "local legends such as Junior Crehan, P. J. Crotty, Eamonn McGivney, and Bobby Casey."[xxxiii] In 1989 Crawford settled in Ennis, Co. Clare and began playing music professionally. At the time of this writing he plays regularly with the fiddler Tommy Peoples and performs with two bands, *Moving Cloud* and *Lúnasa*. The traditional flute players whom he feels have most influenced him are Matt Molloy, P. J. Crotty, Patsy Moloney, Paul Roche, and Marcus Hernon. Crawford learned *Maids in the Meadow* from the East Galway fiddler Conor Tully.

He plays this reel in a very fast, highly energized, and intense fashion, sparked by crisp, dense, and tight ornamentation but contained by very consistent and steady legato phrasing. His variations are subtle ones of note choice, ornamentation, and phrasing and in this tune his breathing spots are absolutely consistent.

Crawford uses single trills extensively and he plays them in a very crisp, percussive way, with the downward finger movements being like strikes in their effect. Some special fingerings can help in getting this kind of precise quick response out of the instrument. For example, let's look at the single trills on E that occur in m. 4 and 8. If, after playing the long roll on E, you keep B2 covering its hole while playing the C-natural and G that follow, then when you get to the next E you can perform the single trill by moving only B1 and not have to move B1 and B2 together. Depending upon the instrument, leaving B2 down in this way may produce some flatness in the C and G, but you can compensate for this with embouchure.

An unusual ornament occurs in m. 6, 9, 11, and 13, two sixteenth note C-sharps with a strike on the second one. This strike can be played by T2, T3, or both and the effectiveness of these different fingerings will vary from instrument to instrument. In m. 9, 11, and 13, the ornament is preceded and followed by Ds. In this case B1, B2, and B3 can all be left covering their holes throughout the fingering sequence. In the case of m. 6, B1, B2, and B3 can be put down as soon as you are finished playing the G at the end of m. 5.

Other notable ornaments include the cranns in m. 9, 11, and 13, the condensed short rolls in m. 12, and the dramatic slide from F-natural into an F-sharp roll in m. 14–15. He also plays a "tight triplet" on the note sequence A–C–D the third time through the tune in m. 2. To play such a tight triplet, when moving from A to C leave T1 down for just an instant after putting down T3, producing a very brief "crossing noise." The cuts on C-natural that occur in m. 4 and 8 of the third time through are unusual as well. These can be played by lifting and putting back down quickly either or both T2 and T3. Again, the effectiveness of these fingerings will vary from instrument to instrument.

He uses the "piping C" in m. 1, the first time through, and in m. 3, all three times. These Cs are indicated with an asterisk.

Wherever repeated Ds occur in the tune Crawford defines the second one with a strong breath pulse. The sound does not actually stop between the two Ds, so each time they appear under a slur.

Kevin Crawford

Maids in the Meadow

traditional Irish reel
as played by Kevin Crawford, Irish flute,
on his recording, 'd' flute album
Green Linnet GLCD 1162.

25. **Catherine McEvoy** (flute)—Fling: *Mrs. Galvin's Fling.* This is from Catherine McEvoy's 1996 release, *Traditional Flute Music in the Sligo-Roscommon Style*, Cló-Iar Chonnachta CICD 117. Mode: D Ionian (major).

Catherine McEvoy was born in 1956 in Birmingham, England. Her parents, both traditional musicians from Co. Roscommon, came to settle there in the 1940s. Through her parents and the musicians of the Birmingham Ceili Band, McEvoy was from the start steeped in the musical traditions of Sligo and Roscommon. As a teen she took up the accordion, piano, and flute and became a member of the band. One of her most cherished mentors was the flute and whistle player, composer, and singer from Ballyfarnan, Co. Roscommon, Josie McDermott. Transcriptions of McDermott's flute and whistle playing can be found earlier in this section of the book. Though McEvoy's playing of dance music is of the highest order, her slow air playing is particularly captivating and is not to be missed. She plays the flute left-handed.

Nóirín Ní Ghrádaigh writes, in the liner notes to McEvoy's album,[xxxiv]

> Catherine...is universally accepted as one of the finest exponents of the Sligo-Roscommon style of flute playing. Through her exemplary musicianship she skillfully combines thoughtfulness with exuberance; sensitivity with drive; she brings new vigor and a freshness to the world of flute playing, all the while cherishing the rich and distinct local style of Ireland's most renowned flute region.

McEvoy writes about this tune,[xxxv]

> I learned this fling from John Kelly Junior. John Kelly Senior had learnt the tune from Mrs. Galvin who was a very well respected fiddle player from between Kilkee and Kilrush. John...describes her playing as "very sweet, using double stopping and a full bow." ... John also describes her as having "a great pair of arms."

McEvoy's playing here is full of drive and at the same time it is focused and poetic. She does a great job of emulating Mrs. Galvin's "great pair of arms" with the vigorous energy she puts into this fling.

Her use of long trills, which are not frequently employed in traditional Irish flute playing, is especially notable. She uses these trills at the cadence of every A and B part. McEvoy also uses cuts liberally, giving great lift to the tune.

Her variations illustrate the improvisational use of long rolls and a free approach to phrasing. She exemplifies how a fine player will use the necessity of creating breathing places as a vehicle for melodic variation. You can observe this particularly in m. 6 and 14–15 where she varies the phrasing by breaking long rolls and by leaving out off-pulse passing notes.

Catherine McEvoy and her husband Tom McGorman in Miltown Malbay, Co. Clare.

Mrs. Galvin's Fling

♩ = approx. 92

traditional Irish fling
as played by Catherine McEvoy, Irish flute,
on her recording, *Catherine McEvoy: Traditional Flute Music
in the Sligo-Roscommon Style*, Cló Iar-Chonnachta CICD 117.

431

26. **Seamus Egan** (flute)—Reel: *The Yellow Tinker.* From Solas' 1996 debut release, *Solas*, Shanachie 78002. This is the first in a medley of three reels. The second and third ones are *Cranking Out* and *Master Crowley's #2.* Mode: G Ionian (major) with a number of flatted sevenths (F-naturals) suggesting G Mixolydian.

Seamus Egan was born in Hatboro, Pennsylvania in 1969 and moved to Ireland with his family at the age of three. Egan's father was from Co. Mayo and his mother's parents were from Co. Donegal. They lived in Foxford, Co. Mayo before returning to the United States to settle in Philadelphia in 1980. While in Ireland, Egan studied traditional music with Martin Donaghue and became deeply inspired by the flute playing of Matt Molloy. Egan later went on to win all-Ireland championships on four different instruments by the time he was fourteen, an unprecedented accomplishment in Irish music. His work has been best known through his associations with Mick Moloney and Eugene O'Donnell and with the groups Chanting House and Solas.[xxxvi]

Egan's playing in this tune is fast, agile, and highly energetic, yet very connected and smooth. His playing of occasional staccato notes helps define his rhythmic interpretation. His music is full of subtle dynamic changes and his expansive variations often venture outside of the traditional melody line.

Egan's style of ornamentation is very dense, calling to mind the playing of others such as Matt Molloy and Kevin Crawford (see transcriptions of their playing, #11, #12, and #24, earlier in this section). Interestingly though, in this tune he never uses condensed long rolls, opting for short rolls instead. He does play condensed short rolls in m. 10 and short cranns in m. 2 and 4.

His use of single trills is truly a hallmark of his style (see m. 14, 15, and 16). The sequence of two single trills in a row in m. 16 produces a wonderful fluttering sound. He plays the first one before the beat. The second is closer to being on the beat.

In m. 20 and 23, Egan plays long rolls on F-natural. I believe he is playing F using the long F key while fingering the cut and strike of the roll as one would for a roll on E.

Whenever Egan plays the quick ascending note group B–C–D, which occurs in m. 2, 6, 9, 11, 13, 17, 18, 21, and 22, he plays this as a "tight triplet."

In this reel, you can hear Egan's free and improvisational approach to changing octave register. For examples, see m. 2, 3, 5, and 17–18.

Seamus Egan

The Yellow Tinker

traditional Irish reel
as played by Seamus Egan, Irish flute,
on the Solas recording, *Solas,* Shanachie 78002.

♩ = approx. 104

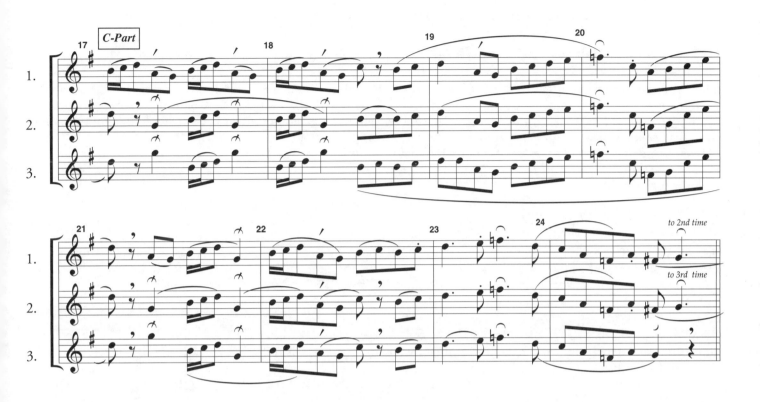

435

27. **Grey Larsen** (whistle in B-flat)—Hornpipe: ***The Cuckoo's Nest***. From his 2001 release with Paddy League, *The Green House*, Sleepy Creek Music SCM 102. This is the first in a medley of three tunes. The second tune is *Fitzgerald's Hornpipe* and the third is the reel *The Indian on the Rock*, more commonly known as *The Hunter's Purse*. Mode: E-flat Ionian (major), transposed here to G Ionian to reflect how the tune would be played on a D instrument.

For biographical information see "About the Author" on p. 462.

This unusual setting of *The Cuckoo's Nest* is from the unique melodeon repertoire of Michael J. Kennedy (1900–1978). Michael Kennedy was born and raised on a farm near the village of Flaskagh, three miles northeast of Dunmore in Northeast Co. Galway. Until emigrating to the U.S., he had never traveled further than about ten miles from his home. At age 11, greatly inspired by the melodeon playing of two village girls, Maggie McGee and Winnie Dowd, Kennedy went to Dunmore and bought a melodeon for the equivalent of $1.50. All his life he played a one-row, ten-button melodeon in the key of G. Michael often used to say, "There was never anybody as crazy for a melodeon as I was."

In 1923, fed up with the hard labor of farming, he emigrated to Cincinnati, Ohio, my hometown, working for 42 years for the Louisville & Nashville Railroad. He lived out the rest of his years there, and just across the Ohio River in Covington, Kentucky. Kennedy's repertoire was unchanged by his years in America, being entirely composed of tunes and settings he had learned in his native locality. I met and befriended him in 1973, fell in love with his music, and played with him at every opportunity until his death five years later. You can hear him play *The Cuckoo's Nest* on the melodeon and talk about his life in three bonus tracks on the above-mentioned CD.

Kennedy's version of *The Cuckoo's Nest* seems to be unrelated to other tunes by the same title. It is a "crooked" tune and its unusual departures from regular hornpipe meter suggest that it is rooted in an early era that is seldom represented in Irish music as it is played today. Kennedy had many crooked tunes in his repertoire and their irregular structure remained consistent nearly every time he played them. In my rendition, however, I interchange the straight and crooked version of the phrase in question in an improvisational manner, using the crooked phrase more than Michael did. The crooked phrase is most easily notated in 5/4. You can see that in the second time through the tune I play the music crooked in places where I played it straight the first time, i.e. m. 5, 13, and 21.

In keeping with Kennedy's melodeon style, I have kept my ornamentation simple and straightforward, using only cuts and long rolls. There are mid-note cuts in the pickup bar and in m. 2, 6, 8, 10, 14, 19, 20, 22, and 30. I have substituted long A notes for groups of shorter notes in m. 4, 12, 20, and 28, sometimes using finger vibrato and slides to heighten their effect. In m. 12, the second time through, there is a cut on a passing sixteenth note. In m. 20, the second time through, I play what could be heard as an A half note with a cut on its fourth eighth-note subdivision, a different kind of mid-note cut.

Most of the variation is on a subtle level and is accomplished with phrasing improvisation and note omission. I play a number of staccato notes, again inspired by Kennedy's melodeon style. Note the use of the piping C in m. 8 and 32. The note preceding and following these Cs are As. By lifting and replacing only T1 (the finger also used to cut A) the fingering is made easy and the piping C results.

I use double tonguing throughout except for triple tonguing for the triplets in m. 4, 8, and 32.

*Michael J. Kennedy with melodeon and the author with anglo concertina
outside Kennedy's home in Covington, Kentucky in 1975.*

The Cuckoo's Nest

♩ = approx. 196

traditional Irish hornpipe
as played by Grey Larsen on B-flat tin whistle
on his recording, *The Green House*, Sleepy Creek Music SCM 102.
Transposed to G Ionian (recording is in E-flat Ionian).

438

i Breandán Breathnach, *Folk Music & Dances of Ireland*, (Dublin: The Talbot Press, 1971), p. 14.

ii The biographical information in this paragraph comes from *The Companion to Irish Traditional Music*, Fintan Vallely, ed. (New York: New York Universtiy Press, 1999), p. 237.

iii Jackie Small, from the liner notes to *John McKenna, His Original Recordings*, the John McKenna Traditional Society, Drumkeerin, Co. Leitrim, Ireland, ca. 1982.

iv Harry Bradshaw, from the liner notes to *Fluters of Old Erin: Flute, Piccolo and Whistle Recordings of the 1920's and 30's*, Viva Voce, Dublin, 002, 1990.

v John McKenna and Michael Gaffney, on *Fluters of Old Erin, Flute, Piccolo and Whistle Recordings of the 1920s and 30s*, Viva Voce, Dublin, 002, 1990.

vi Harry Bradshaw, from the liner notes to *Fluters of Old Erin: Flute, Piccolo and Whistle Recordings of the 1920's and 30's*, Viva Voce, Dublin, 002, 1990.

vii Liam O'Flynn, from the liner notes of *Seamus Ennis: The Best of Irish Piping*, Tara Music Company, Ltd., Dublin, TARA CD 1002, 1973.

viii Vallely, ed., *The Companion to Irish Traditional Music*, p. 118.

ix This biographical information comes from Pat Mitchell's introduction to his book, *The Dance Music of Willie Clancy* (Dublin: The Mercier Press, 1976), pp. 9–11, and from *The Companion to Irish Traditional Music*, Vallely, ed., pp. 71–72.

x Pat Mitchell, *The Dance Music of Willie Clancy* (Dublin: The Mercier Press, 1976), p. 10.

xi The biographical information in this paragraph comes from *The Companion to Irish Traditional Music*, Vallely, ed., p. 392.

xii The biographical information in this paragraph comes from *The Companion to Irish Traditional Music*, Vallely, ed., p. 58.

xiii Morton, Robin, from the liner notes to Josie McDermott's release, *Darby's Farewell, Traditional Music on Flute and Whistle and Songs from Sligo*, Ossian, Cork, CD 20, 1976.

xiv The biographical information in this paragraph comes from *The Companion to Irish Traditional Music*, Vallely, ed., p. 233.

xv Planxty, *Cold Blow and the Rainy Night*, Polydor 2383 301, 1974.

xvi This is from an interview with Matt Molloy by Sean McCutcheon, a flute player from Montréal, that took place on September 26, 1997. I found it on Brad Hurley's website, "A Guide to the Irish Flute," <http://www.firescribble.net/flute/molloy.html>.

xvii Most of the information in this paragraph comes from Robin Morton's and Cathal McConnell's liner notes to the album, *On Loch Erne's Shore*, Flying Fish Records, Chicago, FF-058, 1978.

xviii Cathal McConnell, liner notes to the album, *On Loch Erne's Shore*, Flying Fish Records, Chicago, FF-058, 1978.

xix Some of this biographical information comes from the article by Mic Moroney, "Whistling up a Storm," *The Irish Times*, May 20, 1999.

xx Charlie Lennon, *Musical Memories*, (Dublin: Worldmusic, 1993), 1:70.

xxi This biographical information comes from my correspondence with Desi Wilkinson and from Brad Hurley's interview with him that appears on Hurley's website, "A Guide to the Irish Flute", <http://www.firescribble.net/flute/wilkinson.html>.

xxii These quotes are from my correspondence with Breda Smyth.

xxiii Josie McDermott, *Darby's Farewell*, Ossian Publications, Cork, OSS CD 20, 1989.

xxiv This biographical information comes from Hammy Hamilton's and Conal Ó Gráda's liner notes to Ó Gráda's recording, *The Top of Coom*, Claddagh Records, Dublin, CCF27CD, 1990.

xxv Hammy Hamilton, ibid.

xxvi Conal Ó Gráda, ibid.

xxvii John Doonan, *Flute for the Feis*, Ossian Publications, Cork, OSS 42, 1977.

xxviii Bill Ochs, from the liner notes to *Ireland's Whistling Ambassador*, The Pennywhistler's Press, New York, PWCD 80001, 1995.

xxix The biographical information in this paragraph comes from *The Companion to Irish Traditional Music*, Vallely, ed., pp. 324–5.

xxx *The Companion to Irish Traditional Music*, Vallely, ed., p. 324.

xxxi The material in this paragraph comes from my conversations with Joanie Madden and from Mick Maloney's liner notes to her recording *A Whistle on the Wind*, Green Linnet Records, Danbury, CT, GLCD 1142, 1994.

xxxii From the liner notes to Joanie Madden's recording *A Whistle on the Wind*, Green Linnet Records, Danbury, CT, GLCD 1142, 1994.

xxxiii This quote, and much of the information in this paragraph, comes from my personal correspondence with Kevin Crawford.

xxxiv From the liner notes to *Traditional Flute Music in the Sligo-Roscommon Style*, Cló-lar Chonnachta, Indreabhán, CICD 117, 1996

xxxv Ibid.

xxxvi Some of the information in this paragraph comes from an article by Steve Winick entitled, "Seamus Egan: Serendipity," *Dirty Linen*, June/July 1996: 64.

appendix a: contents of the companion cds

Both CDs contain computer software that you can access by placing the disc in your computer's CD-ROM drive. Here you will find important links to supplementary materials.

The first CD contains selected figures and exercises from Chapters 1 through 19.

The second CD resumes with selected figures and exercises from Chapters 19 through 21, continues with the 49 studies from Section 6, and concludes with the 37 tunes from Section 7.

In those exercises that feature a metronome click along with the flute or whistle, the click is heard only in the left channel and the flute or whistle only in the right channel. As a result, you can adjust the balance of the two (or eliminate either element altogether) by adjusting your left-right balance control.

All selections are played by the author on flute, tin whistle, or concertina. Flute performances are played on a six-key flute by Firth, Pond & Co. (ca. 1847–1863) with a replacement headjoint by Chris Abell. Whistle performances are played on a small Copeland D whistle, except CD #1 track 5 and CD #2 track 93 which are played on an Abell C whistle. Concertina performances are played on a 40-button Wheatstone anglo concertina in D and A, made in London in 1934.

All selections recorded, mixed, edited, and mastered by the author at Sleepy Creek Recording and Grey Larsen Mastering, Bloomington, Indiana, USA, June through September 2002.

CD # 1:

1. **Figure 1-1:** The seven so-called church modes. *Concertina.*
2. **Figure 1-2:** Comparisons between the Ionian and Mixolydian modes, and the Aeolian and Dorian modes. *Flute.*
3. **Figure 1-4:** Examples of the two pentatonic modes found in Irish music. *Flute.*
4. **Figure 1-5:** The first part of *Tuttle's Reel*, in D Dorian. *Concertina.*
5. **Figure 1-6:** The first part of *Tuttle's Reel*, transposed up to E Dorian. *Whistle in C.*
6. **Figure 1-7:** An example of the use of slur notation. *Whistle.*
7. **Figure 1-10:** The opening bars of the march **Lord Mayo**. *Whistle.*
8. **Exercise 7-1:** Practicing cuts on repeated Ds. *Whistle.*
9. **Exercise 7-7:** F-sharp to a cut G. *Flute.*
10. **Figure 7-15:** A version of *The Lonesome Jig*, which makes use of cuts only on repeated notes and stepwise ascending notes. (For comparison, a rendition of the tune without cuts follows.) *Flute.*
11. **Exercise 7-12.** D to a cut F-sharp. *Whistle.*
12. **Exercise 7-13.** D to a cut G. *Whistle.*
13. **Exercise 7-14.** D to a cut A. *Whistle.*
14. **Exercise 7-15.** D to a cut B. *Whistle.*
15. **Exercise 7-22.** G down to a cut F-sharp. *Flute.*
16. **Exercise 7-27.** F-sharp down to a cut D. *Flute.*
17. **Figure 7-16.** A version of the slip jig *The Boys of Ballisodare* that makes use of examples of every class of cuts. (For comparison, a rendition of the tune without cuts follows.) *Whistle.*
18. **Figure 7-17.** The first two bars of the slip jig *Hardiman the Fiddler* with a cut placed at the onset of the first note. *Whistle.*
19. **Figure 7-19.** The first two bars of the slip jig *Hardiman the Fiddler* with a cut placed at the midpoint of the first note. *Whistle.*
20. **Exercise 8-1.** Practicing repeated strikes on G. *Flute.*
21. **Exercise 8-8.** Practicing strikes on F-sharp when descending from G. *Flute.*
22. **Figure 8-15.** A version of the hornpipe **Bantry Bay** using cuts, and strikes only on repeated notes and descending

stepwise notes. *Flute.*

23. **Exercise 8-13.** Practicing strikes on E when descending from G. *Whistle.*

24. **Figure 8-16.** A version of the hornpipe *Bantry Bay* using cuts and a variety of strikes. *Whistle.*

25. **Figure 9-1.** Sliding up from E to F-sharp. *Flute.*

26. **Figure 9-6.** The opening bars of *The Blarney Pilgrim* with a simple slides from B up to C-natural and back down to B. *Flute.*

27. **Figure 9-8.** An excerpt from a variation on the beginning of the jig *The Cliffs of Moher. Flute.*

28. **Figure 9-9a.** The opening bars of *The Star Above the Garter* with an added-finger slide up to G followed by a simple slide up to C-natural. *Whistle.*

29. **Figure 9-9b.** Played again, this time using a struck slide as described in the text. *Whistle.*

30. **Figure 9-10.** The opening bars of *Willie Coleman's Jig. Flute.*

31. **Exercise 10-1.** Practicing long rolls on G. *Flute.*

32. **Figure 10-5.** The jig *The Sporting Pitchfork* with long rolls on G, F-sharp, and E. *Whistle.*

33. **Figure 10-6.** The jig *The Sporting Pitchfork* with long rolls on B, A, G, F-sharp, and E. *Whistle.*

34. **Figure 10-16.** The first two bars of the reel *The Banshee* with long rolls on G. *Flute.*

35. **Figure 10-18.** The first two bars of *Whelan's Jig* with a long roll on E. *Flute.*

36. **Figure 10-20.** The first two bars of the reel *The Drunken Landlady* with long rolls on E, which begin on the second eighth-note beat of the bar. *Flute.*

37. **Figure 10-22.** The first two bars of the reel *The Gravel Walk* with a long A roll beginning on the eighth eighth-note beat of the first bar. *Whistle.*

38. **Figure 10-24.** The first two bars of a variation on *The Monaghan Jig* with a long roll on E beginning on the third eighth-note beat of the bar. *Whistle.*

39. **Figure 10-26.** The first four bars of the B part of *The Rose in the Heather,* which includes a long roll on E beginning on the second eighth-note beat of the fourth bar. *Whistle.*

40. **Figure 10-30.** Sliding into long rolls at the start of the reel *Roaring Mary. Whistle.*

41. **Exercise 11-1.** Practicing short rolls on G. *Whistle.*

42. **Figure 11-6.** A setting of *The Sporting Pitchfork* using short rolls on G, F-sharp, and E. *Flute.*

43. **Figure 11-7.** A setting of *The Sporting Pitchfork* using short rolls on B, A, G, F-sharp, and E. *Flute.*

44. **Figure 11-8.** A variant on the start of *Lad O'Beirne's Reel* demonstrating an awkward-sounding short roll that begins on a non-pulse beat. *Whistle.*

45. **Figure 11-9:** A more musical variant on the start of *Lad O'Beirne's Reel. Whistle.*

46. **Figure 11-10.** A more common way to play the start of *Lad O'Beirne's Reel. Whistle.*

47. **Figure 11-11.** A short roll in the second bar of *The Lonesome Jig. Flute.*

48. **Figure 11-12.** Short rolls in the opening bar of the jig *Tripping Up the Stairs. Flute.*

49. **Figure 11-14.** A variant on the opening bars of the jig *The Frost is All Over. Flute.*

50. **Figure 11-15.** An example of a short roll preceded by an eighth note of the same pitch. *Whistle.*

51. **Figure 11-19.** The first part of the reel *The Drunken Landlady. Whistle.*

52. **Figure 11-20.** The opening bars of *Old Joe's Jig* beginning with a long roll. *Whistle.*

53. **Figure 11-21.** The opening bars of *Old Joe's Jig* beginning with an ascending roll. *Whistle.*

54. **Figure 12-4.** Four different ways to play the beginning of *The Glen Allen Reel. Whistle.*

55. **Exercise 12-1.** Practicing condensed long rolls on G. *Flute.*

56. **Figure 12-7.** A setting of *The Sporting Pitchfork* using condensed long rolls on G, F-sharp, and E. *Flute.*

57. **Figure 12-8.** A setting of *The Sporting Pitchfork* using condensed long rolls on B, A, G, F-sharp, and E. *Flute.*

58. **Figure 13-6.** A condensed short roll on F-sharp in the third bar of the polka *Maids of Ardagh. Whistle.*

59. **Exercise 13-1.** Practicing condensed short rolls on G. *Whistle.*

60. **Figure 13-9.** A setting of *The Sporting Pitchfork* using condensed short rolls on G, F-sharp, and E. *Whistle.*

61. **Figure 13-10.** A setting of *The Sporting Pitchfork* using condensed short rolls on B, A, G, F-sharp, and E. *Whistle.*

62. **Exercise 15-1.** Practicing long double-cut rolls on G. *Flute.*

63. **Figure 15-4.** A setting of the reel *The Skylark* using long double-cut rolls on A, G, F-sharp, and E. *Flute.*

64. **Exercise 15-5.** Practicing short double-cut rolls on G. *Whistle.*

65. **Figure 15-9.** A setting of the reel *The Skylark* using short double-cut rolls on A, G, F-sharp, and E. *Whistle.*

66. **Exercise 15-9.** Practicing condensed long double-cut rolls on G. *Flute.*

52. **Study 38.** In a reel, long rolls that begin on the third subdivision of the primary pulse. *Whistle.*

53. **Study 39.** In a reel, long rolls that begin on the fourth subdivision of the primary pulse. *Whistle.*

54. **Study 40.** A jig containing long rolls that begin on each of the three subdivisions of the pulse. *Flute.*

55. **Study 41.** A reel containing long rolls that begin on each of the four subdivisions of the primary pulse. *Whistle.*

56. **Study 42.** Stepwise ascending short rolls in a jig. *Flute.*

57. **Study 43.** Stepwise descending short rolls in a jig. *Flute.*

58. **Study 44.** Leapwise descending short rolls in a jig. *Flute.*

59. **Study 45.** Stepwise ascending short rolls in a reel. *Whistle.*

60. **Study 46.** Stepwise descending short rolls in a reel. *Whistle.*

61. **Study 47.** Leapwise descending short rolls in a reel. *Whistle.*

62. **Study 48.** A jig containing a variety of short rolls. *Flute.*

63. **Study 49.** A reel containing a variety of short rolls. *Whistle.*

64. *The Battering Ram. Whistle.*

65. *The Blarney Pilgrim. Whistle.*

66. *The Cliffs of Moher. Whistle.*

67. *Tom Billy's Jig. Flute.*

68. *The Frost Is All Over. Flute.*

69. *The Humours of Ballyloughlin. Flute.*

70. *Jimmy Ward's Jig. Whistle.*

71. *The Monaghan Jig. Whistle.*

72. *Old Joe's Jig. Whistle.*

73. *The Rose in the Heather. Flute.*

74. *Scotsman Over the Border. Flute.*

75. *Tripping Up the Stairs. Flute.*

76. *Whelan's Jig. Whistle.*

77. *Willie Coleman's Jig. Whistle.*

78. *The Star Above the Garter. Whistle.*

79. *A Fig for a Kiss. Flute.*

80. *Hardiman the Fiddler. Flute.*

81. *The Whinny Hills of Leitrim. Flute.*

82. *Christmas Eve. Whistle.*

83. *The Banshee. Whistle.*

84. *The Boys of Ballisodare. Whistle.*

85. *Roaring Mary. Flute.*

86. *The Drunken Landlady. Flute.*

87. *The Glen Allen Reel. Flute.*

88. *The Gravel Walk. Whistle.*

89. *John Stenson's Reel. Whistle.*

90. *Lad O'Beirne's Reel. Whistle.*

91. *Lady on the Island. Flute.*

92. *The Mountain Road. Flute.*

93. *The Shaskeen. Flute.*

94. *Tuttle's Reel*, notated in E Dorian, sounding in D Dorian. *Played on a whistle in C.*

95. *The Home Ruler. Whistle.*

96. *The Rights of Man. Whistle.*

97. *Maids of Ardagh. Flute.*

98. *Lord Mayo. Flute,* and *Give Me Your Hand. Flute.*

appendix 6: adaptations for the boehm-system flute

Though I am familiar with the Boehm-system flute, I do not play Irish music on it. I have gathered the following information by consulting with two accomplished players of Irish music on the Boehm flute: Joanie Madden, of the group *Cherish the Ladies*, and Noel Rice, of the Academy of Irish Music in Chicago and the group *Baal Tinne*. I have also consulted with Chris Abell, a fine flute player who is better known as a renowned builder of wooden Boehm-system flutes, wooden headjoints for all flutes, and wooden whistles. All three play the tin whistle and have played the simple-system flute in the past but prefer to play Irish music on the Boehm-system flute. As you would expect among any group of fine musicians, they use differing techniques and hold a range of opinions on issues related to playing Irish music on Boehm-system flutes.

If you have not yet read Chapter 3, you may want to do so now. It contains general and historical information on modern flutes, simple-system flutes, their places in traditional Irish music, and my own reasons for preferring the simple-system flute for Irish music.

ADVANTAGES OF THE BOEHM-SYSTEM OPEN-HOLE FLUTE

Joanie Madden and Noel Rice both favor the open-hole over the closed-hole or plateau Boehm-system flute. Joanie Madden feels that the tonal qualities of the open-hole flute are superior overall. However, the primary reason for their preference is the fact that it is nearly impossible to play slides with the fingers on the closed-hole flute. (For an in depth examination of slides see Chapter 9.)

Chris Abell chooses not to use finger slides in his playing and, for several reasons, which I will detail shortly, prefers the closed-hole flute.

SLIDES

Although sliding on the open-hole flute is not as direct and simple a thing as it is on the simple-system flute or tin whistle, with some practice it quickly becomes quite natural. One can play rising slides by first gradually easing one's finger off the open hole onto the rim of the key, and then allowing the key mechanism to rise. Slowly removing the finger from the open hole raises the pitch about a quarter-tone. Lifting the key then completes the rising half or whole step. As with the simple-system flute and tin whistle, it is important that you find a way to do this that leaves your hands in good playing position.

Although more difficult than rising slides, it is possible to play falling slides by reversing these movements, that is depressing first only the rim of the key and then gradually adding the finger to the open hole.

These fingering techniques alone will not produce a perfectly continuous pitch slide, but their effect comes close to it. The rising slide begins with a continuous rise in pitch followed by a discreet lift in pitch as the key is allowed to rise. The falling slide begins with a discreet drop in pitch as the key rim is depressed, followed by a continuous downward slide as the finger is eased onto the open hole.

One can also use embouchure techniques to create rising or falling slides, and these can be combined with the fingering techniques described above. To create a falling slide you can rotate the flute inward or dip your head, thereby increasing your lower lip's coverage of the embouchure hole and changing the angle of the airstream, while decreasing its speed. Reversing these maneuvers will produce a rising slide. However, it is difficult to apply these embouchure techniques in a quick and agile fashion.

Joanie Madden and Noel Rice use the embouchure approach rarely, only in slower tunes. However, Chris Abell prefers to use embouchure sliding techniques instead of finger sliding. He employs only very small pitch slides, of a

445

quarter tone or less, and finds falling slides to be somewhat more natural to play than rising ones.

When sliding up through a whole step, it can be effective to gently depress the key that would produce the intervening half-step note while gradually removing the finger from the open hole of the lower note. For example, in sliding from D to E (the interval of a whole step), while slowly removing B3 from its open hole, you can simultaneous and slowly depress the D-sharp key. With some practice you will be able to play a very smooth and nearly continuous slide from D to E. Working with the airspeed and embouchure at the same time, if there is enough time, can enhance the effect of such a slide.

If your open-hole flute is well padded, habitually sliding the fingers off the holes and onto the rims of the keys should not necessitate any periodic adjustment of your keywork, according to Chris Abell.

In fast music there is often just not enough time to perform the delicate finger or embouchure maneuvers that I have been describing. In such cases, one can effectively suggest the slides of the simple-system instruments by quickly easing into the principal note from the note a half step below, for a rising slide, or from above for a falling slide. For instance, when moving from G to A in a fast tune you can use the G-sharp key to suggest a slide into the A.

This technique was used a great deal and to fine effect by Paddy Carty, the great traditional player from Co. Galway who used a closed-hole Radcliff-system flute (see the section entitled *Modern Flutes Enter the Irish Tradition* on pp. 53-54 of Chapter 3, and the transcription of Paddy Carty's recording of *The Jug of Punch* on pp. 384-385 in Section 8). Noel Rice has recounted to me conversations with Paddy Carty in which Carty had expressed a wish that he could have had an open-hole flute.

On the simple-system flute and tin whistle, I often employ very subtle slides that begin on a pitch that is in between the half steps. I do this by "shading" the tone hole, just covering or affecting a portion of the hole with a somewhat straightened finger. This is quite easily done even in fast tunes and it contributes a great deal to a feeling of fluidity in the music. This is a very important element of my playing style, which I believe is impossible on a Boehm-system flute.

ADVANTAGES OF THE CLOSED-HOLE FLUTE

As I stated above, Chris Abell prefers to use a closed-hole flute for playing Irish music. His personal style of playing does not involve finger slides, so the closed-hole flute's disadvantages in that area are not an issue for him. He feels that the larger playing surfaces of the closed-hole flute's keys offer him a more comfortable way to finger the flute. Also, for reasons of ease and comfort, he prefers an offset G. In addition, Chris points out that the timbre of the notes throughout the closed-hole flute's range are more consistent, since all of its keys are closed. The open-hole flute has only five holes that are actually open, the majority being closed.

Very Small Hands

Children, and adults who have very small hands, may well find the closed-hole flute better suited to them than the open-hole flute.

Boehm-system flute players, being accustomed to relatively close finger spacing, sometimes complain of the added stretch when they try playing a simple-system flute. For most people, the finger spacing of the simple-system flute becomes quite comfortable after an initial period of adjustment, as long as they learn to hold the instrument properly.

FINGER VIBRATO

Partial-hole finger vibrato is not possible on the Boehm-system flute, but total-hole finger vibrato is. See Chapter 18 for explanations of these terms.

Joanie Madden does not use finger vibrato at all on the Boehm flute, feeling that it sounds too heavy and unnatural on the instrument. She uses breath vibrato instead. She does however use finger vibrato on the whistle.

Noel Rice does use finger vibrato on the flute, but, due to the workings of the Boehm key system, finds it suitable only on A, B, C, and C-sharp, using various combinations of B1, B2, and B3 to create the vibrato.

On A, you can use any combination of these three fingers, depending upon the depth of vibrato desired.

On B, you can use B2 and B3, but not B1. The B1 key closes the tone hole that is under the T2 finger and this causes a pitch fluctuation that is too extreme.

On C-natural and C-sharp you can use any combination of B1, B2, and B3. You can also use T2 and/or T3.

On notes below A, it seems that one cannot avoid an overly heavy finger vibrato. One exception to this is that on E a good finger vibrato can be played with the E-flat key.

The subtleties of total-hole and partial-hole finger vibrato that are possible on the simple-system flute and tin whistle are vast. This is an area where they are unquestionably superior to the Boehm-system flute.

THE F-SHARP QUESTION

There are two available fingerings for F-sharp. The one that classical musicians consider to be best is produced by depressing the T1, T2, T3, B3, and the E-flat keys. You can also play F-sharp by substituting B2 for B3. Classical players consider this second option to be an alternate fingering.

The two fingerings do not yield exactly the same sound. The venting is better with the B3 fingering, which makes the note a bit brighter, and it is slightly better in tune with the rest of the instrument, according to equal temperment. The B2 fingering is a few cents flatter and is just a bit darker in color. Interestingly, for these very reasons the B2 fingering comes closer to the sound of the wooden, simple-system flute, which has an F-sharp that tends to be a little on the flat side, again—according to equal temperament.

Joanie Madden and Noel Rice favor always using the alternate fingering for F-sharp, that is, using B2 instead of B3. Noel Rice feels that this is the only way to get "smooth transitions" when fingering and ornamenting the notes around F-sharp.

On the Boehm flute, F-sharp is struck with B1, not B2 as you might conclude from reading the description of simple-system strike fingerings in Chapter 8.

Chris Abell takes a different approach to fingering F-sharp. He makes use of both fingerings and chooses between them based on the melodic context of the F-sharp in question. Though he has no hard and fast rules on this, when an F-sharp is preceded or followed by an E he tends to use the B2 fingering. This way, B2 is common to both the F-sharp and the E fingering, and the result is less finger movement. When F-sharp is preceded or followed by a D he tends to use the B3 fingering. He feels it is more natural to move the adjacent fingers, B1 and B2, as a unit when moving to or from D than it is to move the separated fingers, B1 and B3. When an F-sharp is preceded or followed by notes other than D and E, neither F-sharp fingering offers any fingering advantage over the other.

Deciding how to use the F-sharp fingering options is, he feels, the most "squirrely" aspect of playing Irish music on the Boehm-system flute. Since one cannot always anticipate the context of an F-sharp, and since some F-sharps are flanked by a D on one side and an E on the other, the best fingering choice is not always obvious. If a particular tune presents challenges in this regard, Chris finds it best to take time to work out the optimal fingerings for that tune.

Perhaps the ideal would be for a player to be so adept at both fingerings that she could fluently use either one in any situation. You'll have to try different approaches and decide what is best for you.

A FINGERING CAVEAT

When moving quickly from the low end of the second octave down into the high end of the first octave, some players habitually leave the B1 key depressed. If you do this, you may be surprised to find that when you intend to play a B-natural you will get a B-flat instead.

CUTS

All three of these players use the same approach to choosing Boehm-system cut fingerings as they would take with a tin whistle or a simple-system flute, with a few exceptions resulting from the particular fingering differences of the Boehm flute. They feel that the goal is to make the Boehm flute sound as much as possible like the simple-system flute in this regard.

Joanie Madden cuts the notes from D up through G with T3. She cuts A with T2 and B with T1.

Noel Rice normally cuts with the fingerings that I recommend in Chapter 7.

Chris Abell cuts as Joanie Madden does, except that he cuts B with the thumb key.

All definitions and descriptions of cuts are not, however, created equal. *Mel Bay's Complete Irish Flute Book,*[i] by Mizzy McCaskill and Dona Gilliam, is a book on Irish flute playing that is intended primarily for Boehm-system flute players. In it, the authors define and notate cuts as grace notes with specific pitches. A reader could logically conclude, from the authors' description and notation of cuts, that cuts are meant to be heard as notes unto themselves, with discernible pitches. The authors go on to present exhaustive fingering charts showing every possible cut for each chromatic note throughout nearly three octaves of the Boehm flute's range. They give a brief description of cuts, and imply, through the presentation of voluminous fingering options, that one should consider choosing cut fingerings that will produce grace notes with pitches that fall within the mode signature of the tune at hand. I feel that this approach demonstrates a misunderstanding of the sound and function of cuts in traditional Irish music and injects a great deal of unnecessary complexity into the picture. Actually, the task of choosing optimal cut fingerings for the Boehm-system flute is quite simple. Proper understanding of cuts, which are explained in depth in Chapter 7, leads the Boehm-system flute player to nearly the same choices that simple-system flute and tin whistle players make. This fact is confirmed by today's leading players of Irish music on the Boehm flute, as we have just seen.

STRIKES

On the simple-system flute and tin whistle, the strike is a highly percussive movement in which the finger hits the tone hole at a high velocity and rebounds back from the body of the flute (see Chapter 8). Due to the Boehm-system flute's key mechanism, the strike is necessarily a bit different on this instrument. It is still percussive, but the finger hits the key, which in turn hits the tone hole. It is not hard to produce a good crisp strike as long as the keys are in good working order. You may want to experiment to see if you want to use the kind of finger position and movement described in Chapter 8, or whether you would prefer to hit the keys more with your fingertips. Closed-hole flutes offer more choice in this regard because the key should seal its tone hole completely regardless of how or where the finger contacts it.

There is an aspect of simple-system flute and tin whistle striking technique which is not possible on the Boehm-system flute. This is described in the section entitled *Varying the Strength of the Strike,* on pp. 175-177 of Chapter 10. It involves striking on just a portion of the tone hole.

You may notice a problem with the noise of key "clicks" when performing strikes. The better the instrument the less of a problem this is. Note that the key clicks are usually produced more by the return of the key to its normal position than by the pad hitting the edge of the tone hole. The cork on the tail of the key, if it is smooth or worn out, may hit noisily against the body of the flute as the key returns to its normal position. Keywork can also become noisy if the tubing is too big for the rod and there is too little oil inside. An "oil and adjust" is probably needed if this is the case.

Noel Rice suggests refining the movement of the strike so that the impact is light, not heavy or hard. He advises that the motion can still be large and fast, just light on impact.

Striking should not necessitate especially frequent adjustment of your keywork unless you have a poorly made flute. Over a long period of time, pads could become worn out from striking.

For the Irish musician, one of the unique features of the Boehm-system flute is that it offers some intriguing options for ornamenting C-natural and C-sharp.

Rolls and Cranns on C-natural

Striking C-natural with T2 does not produce an effective articulation. One can strike with the thumb key instead, although this feels a bit strange to many players. Still, one can play an effective roll on C by cutting with T1 and striking with the thumb.

Another option is to strike on the trill key that sits to the right of B1's key. This strike produces a D *above* the principal note of C, so it actually sounds more like a cut. But it is useful nonetheless in playing a kind of roll on C, in which you cut with T1 and strike with B1 on the trill key. Since the cut and the strike both produce pitches higher than the principal note, this roll has the quality of a crann to it. (Cranns are explained in Chapter 16.)

Striking the trill key that sits to the right of B2's key also produces an effective "cut" on C. Using combinations of these three "cuts", i.e. T1 and the two trill keys, one can construct a variety of different crann-like ornaments on C.

A Roll and Crann on C-sharp

There is a way to play a normal-sounding roll on C-sharp. You can perform a "cut" by striking the trill key that sits to the right of B1's key, producing a D above the C-sharp. Then strike with T1, which produces the C below the principal note of C-sharp.

As with C-natural, you can make a "crann" on C-sharp by striking with the two trills keys.

THE HARD D

Uilleann pipers sometimes give the bottom note of the chanter, the low D, a hard, loud, ringing sound by forcing more than the usual amount of air through the chanter. This *hard D* is a sound dear to the hearts of Irish flute players as well. On the flute, the hard D is played loud and sometimes has a harsh edge to it. It is produced by blowing a very fast stream of air through a very small aperture, leaning hard into the note with your breath. You can hear examples in the recordings of Matt Molloy, Conal Ó Grada, John McKenna, and many others. Some feel it is easiest to produce a fine, ringing, hard D on simple-system flutes that have D as their lowest note.

Noel Rice feels that the use of a low B footjoint tends to hamper somewhat the production of a good, ringing, hard D.

Joanie Madden does use a low B footjoint and certainly has no trouble playing a good hard D. She related to me that Mike Rafferty, who used to play the Boehm-system flute, recommended that she turn the embouchure hole dramatically inward, at about a 45-degree angle to the line formed by the centers of the tone holes. Learning to play this way forced her to play very hard, giving her the hard D as well as a deep, rich tone. Joanie grew up playing with her father, an accordion player, so she had to learn to play hard to balance with the louder instrument.

Chris Abell agrees that it is easier to get a good hard D with the shorter footjoint. In fact, he makes a special footjoint that only goes down to D for those who prefer this. Using this foot joint makes the flute more "chirpy and bright" overall, since it gives the flute a shorter but not a narrower bore.

However, he feels that other factors are more important than the footjoint for getting a good hard D. Most significant is having perfectly tight pads. Next is the cut of the headjoint. If the embouchure hole is too big, it will be difficult to get a good hard D. These two factors also apply to simple-system flutes.

It is important to point out that both Joanie Madden and Noel Rice make quite a bit of use of the low C-sharp, C-natural, and B that their B footjoints make possible. They place a high value on having these low notes at their disposal. Many simple-system flutes also include such extended low notes.

INSTRUMENT OPTIONS

There are a number of options available to Boehm flute players. There is the open-hole/closed-hole question that has been discussed above. Then there are choices in footjoint length, metal vs. wood instruments, metal vs. wood headjoints, and in-line vs. offset G. Of course, there are no right or wrong choices. But you would be wise to become aware of the implications of these options so you can make selections that reflect your preferences and style.

Chris Abell personally prefers the C or D footjoint. With the C footjoint, the bore-to-length ratio is more "correct," so the brightness of tone in the low octave is consistent. With the B footjoint the tube is effectively lengthened without being made proportionately wider. As a result, he feels that the flute is not as even sounding as it might otherwise be. The B footjoint does, however, give the flute a somewhat darker tone overall, which can be an asset if you would like to emulate the tone of a simple-system flute, as many Irish players do. Chris points out that a good headjoint can overcome these footjoint vagaries.

All wood instruments, like the original Boehm-system flutes, have a darker, "woodier" tone according to most players. These instruments have a larger outer diameter than metal flutes do. Therefore, the offset G will provide more fingering comfort for most wooden Boehm flute players.

A replacement wooden headjoint can do wonders for a metal flute. The wood imparts a lovely dark, rich tone to the instrument and an expertly cut embouchure hole will improve its responsiveness in numerous ways. I have two Abell headjoints for my simple-system flute which have enhanced my instrument a great deal. The headjoint of a flute is something like the bow of a violin. The right bow can make a violin come to life in surprising ways.

Chris Abell also recommends playing a flute pitched at A=442. His reasoning is that it is easier to adjust your pitch down slightly by pulling out the headjoint than "lipping it up" to the sharper pitch that one sometimes encounters in Irish music sessions.

THE ADVANTAGES OF A WIDE-SPREAD INSTRUMENT

All three players pointed out to me the advantages of playing an instrument that is very widespread. There are a great many makers of fine modern flutes as well as a plentiful supply of good used instruments. Repairs of metal instruments tend to be easier than those of wood, and there are more experienced technicians for the modern instrument.

WIDE-SPREAD, BUT HIGH MAINTENANCE

The Boehm-system flute has a great many moving parts and is therefore a fairly high-maintenance instrument. To play well, you must keep the instrument in good working order. Chris Abell recommends that if you are an active player you should have your instrument in the shop at least once a year for routine maintenance. Your pads will need to be replaced every two to five years, and other mechanisms regularly wear down.

[i] Mizzy McCaskill and Dona Gilliam, *Mel Bay's Complete Irish Flute Book* (Pacific, Missouri: Mel Bay Publications, 1997), p. 30-1, 32-6, 180-3.

appendix c: fingering charts

Two fingering charts are included here: one for the tin whistle in D and one for the eight-key simple-system flute in D. The first page of each chart is for the low register of the instrument, the second page for the high register. Explanations of the charts and their symbols are given in the captions on the first page of each chart.

fingering chart
for the tin whistle in d
low register

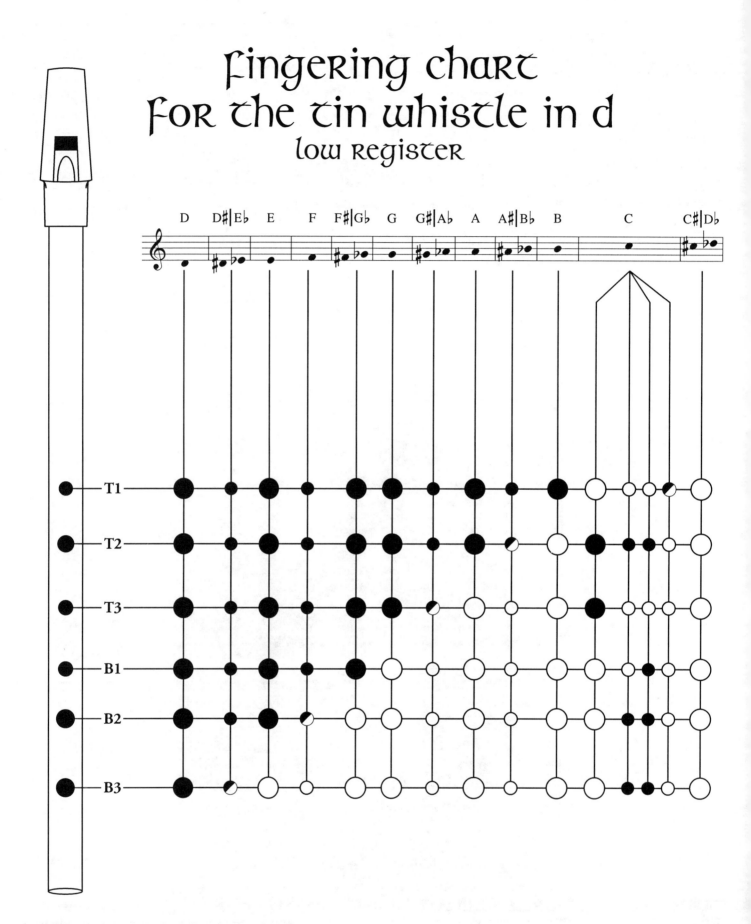

Fingering Chart for Tin Whistle in D. Filled circles indicate closed finger holes, open circles indicate open finger holes, half-filled circles indicate partially covered finger holes. Large circles show the primary, most used notes of the whistle, small circles the lesser-used notes or fingerings. Note that some notes have more than one fingering. Try differing fingerings on your whistle and find out what works best for you. You may also find workable fingerings for your whistle that do not appear in this chart. Note that pitches sound one octave higher than written.

fingering chart
for the tin whistle in d
high register

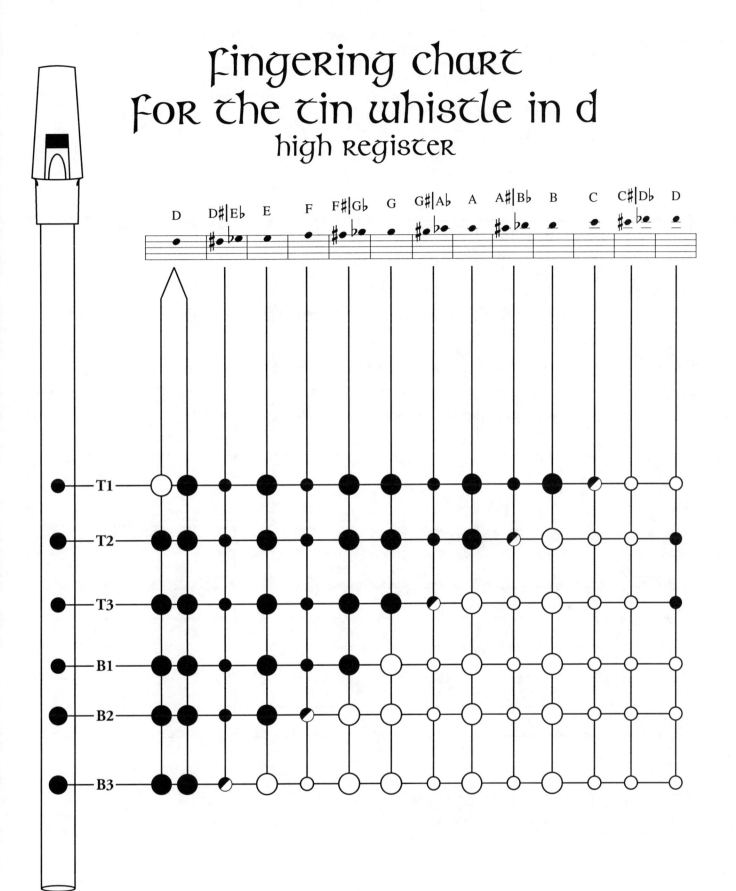

fingering chart for the 8-key simple-system flute
low register

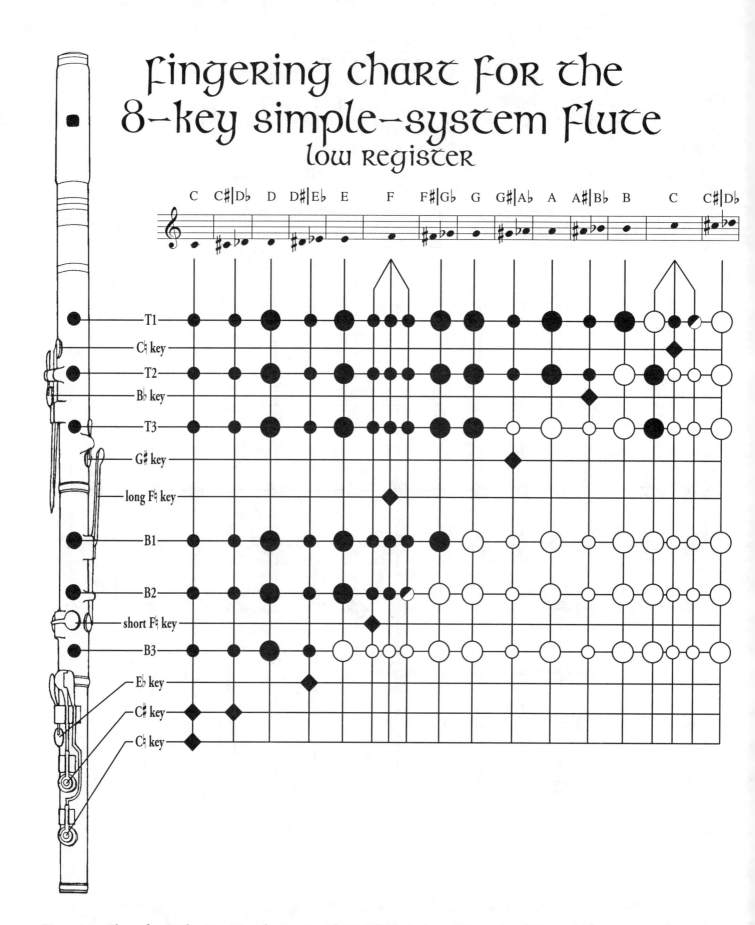

Fingering Chart for Eight-Key Simple-System Flute. Filled circles indicate closed finger holes, open circles indicate open finger holes, half-filled circles indicate partially covered finger holes and diamonds indicate the use of keys. Large circles show the primary, most-used notes of the flute, small circles the lesser-used notes or fingerings. Note that some notes have more than one fingering. Try differing fingerings on your flute and find out what works best for you. You may also find workable fingerings for your flute that do not appear in this chart.

fingering chart for the
8-key simple-system flute
high register

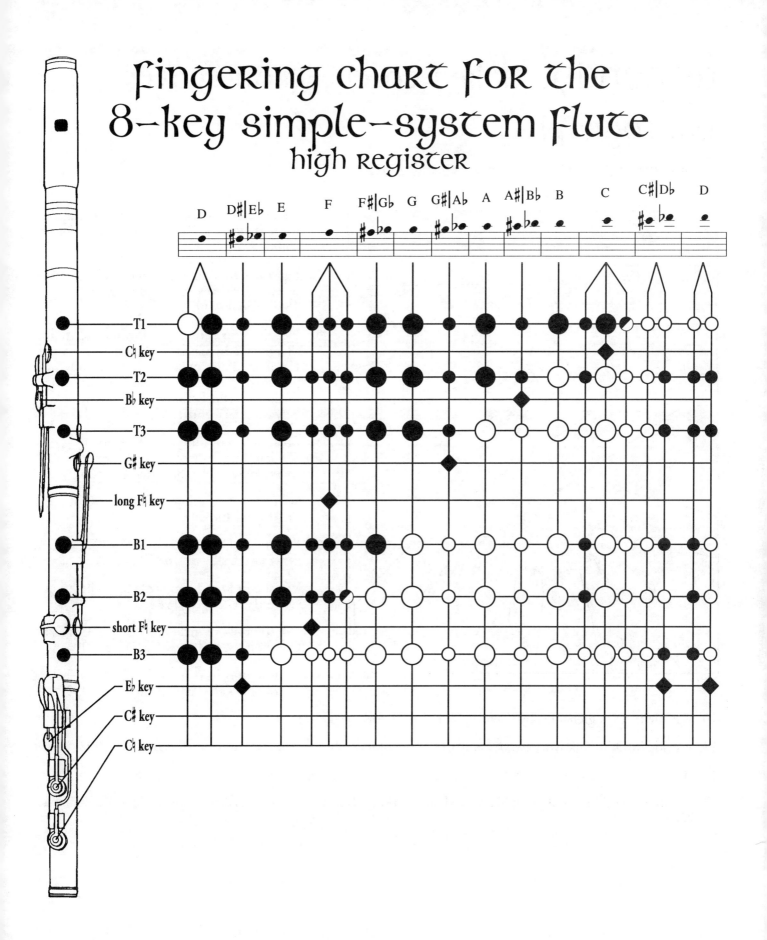

appendix d: key to the front cover photograph

The instruments pictured on the front cover are identified here.

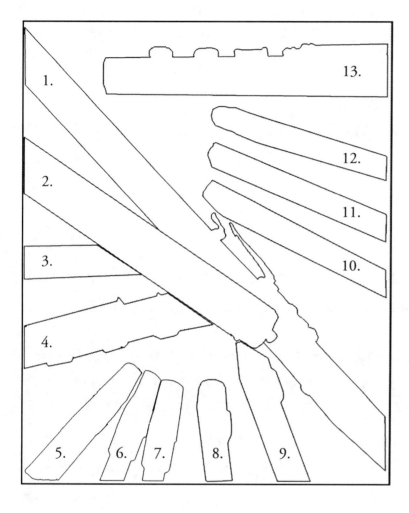

1. Six-key flute in cocuswood and sterling silver made by Patrick Olwell in Massies Mill, Virginia, 2000.

2. Eight-key flute in cocuswood and silver made by Rudall & Rose in London, England, 1844. Serial # 4973.

3. Headjoint in African blackwood and sterling silver made by Chris Abell, Asheville, North Carolina, 2001, on a six-key flute body (not pictured) in cocuswood and German silver made by Firth, Pond & Co., New York City, between 1847 and 1863.

4. Boehm-system flute in silver made by the William Haynes Company, Boston, Massachusetts, 1978. Serial # 44166.

5. Whistle in D in kingwood by Pat O'Riordan, Ft. Wayne, Indiana, 1994.

6. Whistle in D in nickel made by Generation, Oswestry, U.K., ca. 1988.

7. Whistle in D in brass made by Generation, Oswestry, U.K., ca. 1988.

8. Whistle in C in nickel by Michael Copeland, Conshohocken, Pennsylvania, ca. 1995.

9. Whistle in A in brass by Michael Copeland, Conshohocken, Pennsylvania, ca. 1995.

10. Whistle in D in grenadilla by Glenn A. Schultz, Oxford, Michigan, ca. 1995.

11. Whistle in D in pink ivory (wood) and 14K rose gold by Chris Abell, Asheville, North Carolina, 2002.

12. Whistle in D in cocuswood and 14K rose gold by Chris Abell, Asheville, North Carolina, 2002.

13. Boehm-system flute in African blackwood and sterling silver made by Chris Abell, Asheville, North Carolina, 2001.

bibliography

Apel, Willi, *Harvard Dictionary of Music*. Cambridge, MA: Harvard Univ. Press, 1968.

Boehm, Theobald, *Die Flöte und das Flötenspiel* (1871); trans. Dayton C. Miller as *The Flute and Flute-Playing*. New York: Dover Publications, 1964, Vol. 5: 1999.

Breathnach, Breandán, *Ceol Rince na hÉireann, Vol. I–5*. Dublin: An Gúm. Years of first publication: vol. 1: 1963, vol. 2: 1976, vol. 3: 1985, vol. 4: 1996, Vol. 5: 1999.

Breathnach, Breandán, *Folk Music and Dances of Ireland*. Dublin: The Talbot Press, 1971.

Cotter, Geraldine, *Geraldine Cotter's Traditional Irish Tin Whistle Tutor*, 2nd ed. Cork: Ossian Publications, 1989.

Jourdain, Robert, *Music, the Brain, and Ecstasy*. New York: Avon Books, 1997.

Hamilton, S. C., *The Irish Flute Players Handbook*. Coolea, Ireland: Breac Publications, 1990.

Hurley, Brad, Interviews with Catherine McEvoy, Matt Molloy, and Desi Wilkinson, "A Guide to the Irish Flute," 1998. <http://www.firescribble.net/flute>.

Kelly, John, "Following His Own Act," *The Irish Times*, 5 September 1998.

Kujala, Walfrid, *The Flutist's Progress*. Evanston, Illinois: Progress Press, 1970.

Larsen, Mary, "Martin Hayes, A Lilt All His Own." *Fiddler Magazine*, Spring 1994.

Lloyd, Valery and Carole L. Bigler, *Ornamentation, A Question & Answer Manual*. Van Nuys, California: Alfred Publishing Co., 1995.

Mac Aoidh, Caoimhin, *Between the Jigs and Reels—The Donegal Fiddle Tradition*. Nure, Ireland: Drumlin Publications, 1994.

Mather, Betty Bang, *Interpretation of French Music From 1675 to 1775, For Woodwind and Other Performers*. New York, McGinnis & Marx, 1973.

Mather, Betty Bang and David Lasocki, *Free Ornamentation in Woodwind Music, 1700-1775*. New York, McGinnis & Marx, 1976.

Mathieu, W. A., *The Listening Book*. Boston: Shambhala Publications, 1991.

McCandless, Brian E., "The Pastoral Bagpipe," *Iris na bPíobairí (The Pipers' Review)* #17 (Spring 1998), 2: p. 19–28.

McCullough, L. E., *The Complete Tin Whistle Tutor*. New York: Oak Publications, 1976.

Mitchell, Pat, *The Dance Music of Willie Clancy*, 2nd ed. Dublin: Mercier Press, 1977.

Neal, John & William, *A Collection of the Most Celebrated Irish Tunes, Proper for the violin, German flute or hautboy*, first published 1724, facsimile edition by Nicolas Carolan, Dublin: Folk Music Society of Ireland, 1986.

Ó Briain, Donncha (aka Denis O'Brien), *The Golden Eagle*. Cluain Tarbh: Comhaltas Ceoltóirí Éireann (CCE), 1993.

Ó Canainn, Tomás, *Traditional Music in Ireland*. London: Routledge & Kegan Paul Ltd., 1978.

O'Farrell (first name unknown), *O'Farrell's Collection of National Irish Music for the Union Pipes*. London: John Gow, 1804. Compiled, edited and reconstructed by Patrick Sky, Chapel Hill, North Carolina: Grassblade Music, 1995.

Ó hAllmhuráin, Gearóid, *A Pocket History of Traditional Irish Music*. Dublin: O'Brien Press, 1998.

O'Neill, Frances, *O'Neill's Music of Ireland*, arranged by James O'Neill. Originally published in Chicago: Lyon & Healy, 1903. Reissued in an edition edited by Daniel Michael Collins, Pacific, Missouri: Mel Bay Publications, 1996.

O'Neill, Frances, *1001 Gems, The Dance Music of Ireland*, arranged by James O'Neill. Chicago: Lyon & Healy, 1907.

Quantz, Johann Joachim, *Versuch einer Anweisung die Flöte traversiere zu spielen*. Berlin: Johann Friedrich Voss, 1752; trans. Edward R. Reilly as *On Playing the Flute*. London: Faber & Faber, 1966.

Rockstro, Richard Shepherd, *A Treatise on the Construction, the History, and the Practise of The Flute, Including a Sketch of the Elements of Acoustics and Critical Notices of Sixty Celebrated Flute Players*. Buren, the Netherlands: 1986, Frits Knuf. First published in 1889.

Solum, John, *The Early Flute*. Oxford: Oxford University Press, 1992.

Toff, Nancy, *The Flute Book*. Oxford: Oxford University Press, 1996.

Tromlitz, Johann Georg, *Ausführlicher und gründlicher Unterricht die Flöte zu spielen.* Leipzig: Adam Friedrich
     Böhme, 1791; trans. and ed. Ardal Powell as *The Virtuoso Flute Player.* Cambridge: Cambridge University
     Press, 1991.
Wye, Trevor, *A Trevor Wye Practice Book for Flute,* 6 vols. Kent: Novello & Co. Ltd., 1981.

discography

The following is a list of recordings referred to in this book.

Mary Bergin, *Feadóga Stáin: Traditional Irish Music on the Tin Whistle*. Shanachie Records 79006. 1979.

Mary Bergin, *Feadóga Stáin 2*. Shanachie 79083. 1993.

Paddy Carty, *Traditional Music of Ireland*. Daniel Michael Collins Master Collector Series, No. 1, 1974. Reissued as *Traditional Irish Music*, Shanachie 34017. Perhaps the title was changed to avoid confusion with Paddy Carty, Conor Tully: *Traditional Music of Ireland*, GTD Trad. H.C. 002. Recorded 1985, issued 1990.

Willie Clancy, *The Breeze from Erin*, Ossian OSS-26. 1967.

Kevin Crawford, *'d' flute album*, Green Linnet GLCD 1162. 1995.

William "Billy" Cummins, with various artists, *Fluters of Old Erin, Flute, Piccolo and Whistle Recordings of the 1920s and 30s*. Produced by Harry Bradshaw. Viva Voce 002. 1990.

John Doonan, *Flute for the Feis,* Ossian, OSS 42, 1977.

Seamus Egan, with Solas, *Solas,* Shanachie 78002. 1996.

Séamus Ennis, *The Return From Fingall*, RTE 199. 1997.

Eddie & Finbar Furey, *Hornpipes, Airs & Reels: Irish Pipe Music*. Nonesuch 72059. 1968.

Finbar Furey, *The Irish Pipes of Finbar Furey*. Nonesuch 72048. 1969.

Paddy Glackin & Paddy Keenan, *Doublin',* Tara TARA 2007. 1978.

Martin Hayes, *Martin Hayes*, Green Linnet GLCD 1127, 1993.

Grey Larsen, with Metamora, *The Great Road,* Sugar Hill SH/PS-CD-1134. 1987.

Grey Larsen, with Paddy League, *The Green House,* Sleepy Creek Music SCM102, 2001.

Joanie Madden, *A Whistle on the Wind*, Green Linnet GLCD 1142. 1994.

Cathal McConnell, *On Loch Erne's Shore*, Topic 12TS3775. 1977.

Catherine McEvoy, *Traditional Flute Music in the Sligo/Roscommon Style*, Clo Iar-Chonnachta CICD 117. 1996.

Josie McDermott, *Darby's Farewell*, Ossian OSS CD 20. 1976.

John McKenna, *John McKenna, His Original Recordings*, The John McKenna Traditional Society, Drumkeerin, Co. Leitrim, Ireland, ca. 1982.

John McKenna, with various artists, *Fluters of Old Erin, Flute, Piccolo and Whistle Recordings of the 1920s and 30s*. Produced by Harry Bradshaw. Viva Voce 002. 1990.

Matt Molloy, *Matt Molloy*, Green Linnet GLCD 3008. 1987.

Matt Molloy, *Stony Steps*, Green Linnet GLCD 3041. 1987.

Tom Morrison, with various artists, *Fluters of Old Erin, Flute, Piccolo and Whistle Recordings of the 1920s and 30s*. Produced by Harry Bradshaw. Viva Voce 002. 1990.

Donncha Ó Briain (Dennis O'Brien), *Donncha Ó Briain*, Gael-Linn CEF 083. 1979.

Conal Ó Gráda, *The Top of Coom*, Claddagh CCF27CD. 1990.

Tommy Reck, *A Stone in the Field*, Green Linnet SIF 1008. 1977.

Micho Russell, *Ireland's Whistling Ambassador*, Pennywhistler's Press PWCD 80001. 1993.

Seán Ryan, *Siúil Uait (Take the Air)*, Gael-Linn CEF CD 142. 1989.

Breda Smyth, with various artists, *Ceol Tigh Neachtain (Music from Galway)*, Gael-Linn CEF CD 145. 1989.

Paddy Taylor, *The Boy in the Gap,* Claddagh CC8. 1970.

Desi Wilkinson, *Three-Piece Flute*, Spring CSP 1009. 1987.

index of tune titles

Note: Page references in boldface refer to complete versions of tunes.

general index

A

A (note)
    cuts on, 120, 125, 127-128, 130
    double-cut rolls on, 216-217, 220-221
    long rolls on, 167, 179, 198-199, 223
    short rolls on, 186-187, 206-207, 227
    strikes on, 139, 144, 148, 152

A Aeolian mode, 25

Abell, Chris, 445-450

Abell flutes, 54, 55-56

Abell whistles, 61

added-finger slides, 155, 159-160, 322-324

A Dorian mode, 25

Aeolian (minor) mode, 22-25

A Ionian mode, 25

"All-Hallow Eve in Ireland" (Maclise), 57

A Mixolydian mode, 25

anchor points
    in flutes, 86-88, 91-92
    in whistles, 65-66, 72-73

A part, B part notation, 30

appogiatura, 253, 260

articulate breathing, 285-291

articulation. *See also* cuts; strikes; tonguing
    cuts as pitched, 113, 115-116
    in Irish bagpipes, 39-40
    in language analogy, 43, 45, 112
    terminology, 113

ascending rolls, 192

asthma, 94

audio recorders, use of, 302

B

B (note)
    on Boehm-system flutes, 447
    cuts on, 120, 125, 127-128, 133-134
    double-cut rolls on, 214
    long rolls on, 167, 198-199
    short rolls on, 186-187, 207
    slides from, 157-158
    strikes on, 139, 144, 148

B Aeolian mode, 25

bagpipes. *See* Irish bagpipes

Bane, Joe, 19

barn dances, 31

baroque flutes, 50, 53

B Dorian mode, 25

beats per minute (bpm), 32

Bergin, Mary
    in *Bean Uí Chroidheáin*, 405-406
    in *Father Dollard's Hornpipe*, 407-408
    use of ascending rolls, 192
    use of breath vibrato, 249
    use of melodic variations, 260
    use of shakes, 240, 252-253
    use of short rolls, 195
    use of tonguing and throating, 280

B-flat, cuts on, 121

biology of learning, 302-303

body-position memory, 92, 302-303

Boehm-system flutes, 445-450
    bottom-hand keywork on, 54
    clicking keys on, 448
    closed-hole, advantages of, 446
    C-natural on, 27, 449
    cuts on, 448

C

sliding into, 160-161

on stepwise ascending notes, 123-126, 309-310

on stepwise descending notes, 128-130, 311-312

strength of, in long rolls, 174

studies on, 307-316

tonguing or throating at the same time as, 134

whistle players, word of caution to, 121

C whistles, 27-29

D

D (note)

on Boehm-system flutes, 449

condensed cranns on, 241-242

cuts on, 119, 129-131

hard, 108, 449

long cranns on, 230-232, 237-239

melodic alternatives to cranns on, 261-262

shakes on, 252-253

short cranns on, 235-237, 240

dance music, 30-31, 40-42

D Dorian mode, 28-29, 52

diaphragm exercise, 94-95

D Ionian mode, 25, 78, 106

distance reduction kissing technique (DIREKT), 101-102

D Mixolydian mode, 25

Doonan, John, 56

Dorian mode, 22-25, 78, 106

Dorian Pentatonic mode, 26

double-condensed long rolls, 200-201, 244-245

double-cut rolls, 214-229

condensed long, 221-224, 244-245

condensed short, 225-227, 244-245

fingerings of, 214-217, 219-220

long, 214-218, 221-224, 244-245

notation of, 215, 218-219

short, 218-221, 244-245

double graces, 136

double jigs, 34, 36, 335-344

double tonguing, 276-278

double tunes, 30

drones, 20, 37-38

duple meter, 32-33, 173

dynamics, 105

E

E (note)

condensed long double-cut rolls on, 223-224

condensed long rolls on, 196-197

condensed short double-cut rolls on, 226

condensed short rolls on, 205

cranns on, 230, 232-233, 236

cuts on, 119, 125, 129, 132

double-cut rolls on, 216-217, 220-221

long rolls on, 165, 178, 179-180

short rolls on, 184-185

sliding from, 155-156, 157, 159

strikes on, 138, 143-144, 147, 149-150

E Aeolian mode, 24-25

E Dorian mode, 24-25, 78, 106

E-flat, cuts on, 121

Egan, Seamus, 136, 269, 433-435

electronic tuning machines, 77, 105

Ellard, Andrew, 59

embellishments. *See* ornamentation

embouchure

changes with notes, 100-101

changes with octave, 101

DIREKT maneuver, 101-102

dynamics and, 105

F

O

P

T

U

V

vibrato

breath, 246, 249, 280

finger, 246-249, 446-447

about the author

Grey Larsen was born in 1955 in New York City. His family moved to Cincinnati, Ohio, the following year. Beginning piano lessons at the age of four, he enjoyed a childhood and youth full of musical exploration, his inner world filled with the keyboard music of Bach and Mozart, the rock, R & B, and Motown sounds on the radio, the songs of contemporary folk music interpreters, and traditional Appalachian and Irish music.

From 1970 to 1972 he studied composition and early music at the Cincinnati College–Conservatory of Music before moving on, in 1973, to continue at the Oberlin Conservatory of Music in Oberlin, Ohio. While pursuing early and modern classical music on the one hand, he came ever more deeply under the spell of traditional music on the other, and for several years he followed both streams with equal energy and dedication. In these and later years, he spent a great deal of time learning traditional Irish music from elder musicians, especially immigrant Irishmen Michael J. Kennedy (1900–1978), Tom Byrne (1920–2001), and Tom McCaffrey (born 1916), in Cincinnati and Cleveland, Ohio.

Upon completing his Bachelor of Music degree at Oberlin in 1976, the streams forked. He bid a fond farewell to the academic side of music and set a course following his love of traditional music, exploring other waterways that would branch, cross, and rejoin over the decades. He leads a varied and rich musical life as a performer, teacher, author, recording artist, record producer, mastering engineer, and as the Music Editor of *Sing Out!* magazine. Since the early 1970s, he has also devoted himself to the traditional fiddle music of his native Midwest and Appalachia. But that's another story.

He has three children and lives in Bloomington, Indiana, USA.

also by grey larsen:

Books
The Essential Tin Whistle Toolbox
Celtic Encyclopedia for Flute
Celtic Encyclopedia for Tin Whistle
The Lotus Dickey Songbook

Selected Recordings
Dark of the Moon
The Green House
The Orange Tree
The Gathering
Morning Walk
The Great Road
Metamora
Thunderhead
The First of Autumn
Banish Misfortune

Online
Grey Larsen's Irish Tune Bank

Information at www.greylarsen.com and
www.melbay.com

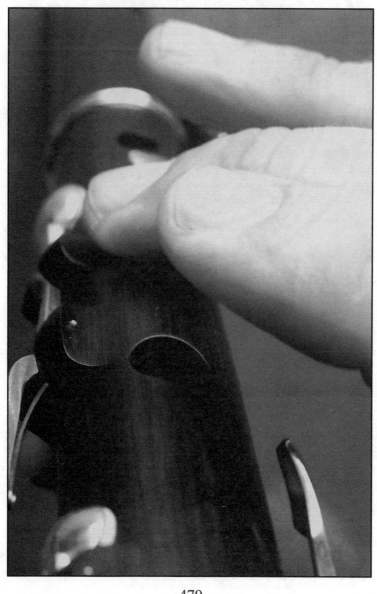

EXCELLENCE IN MUSIC

MEL BAY®

Since 1947